THE PSYCHIC SONIC YOUTH STORY ~~XXXXX X~~ CONFUSION

THE PSYCHIC SONIC YOUTH STORY ~~XXXXX X~~ CONFUSION

THE PSYCHIC SONIC YOUTH STORY XXXXX X CONFUSION

BY STEVIE CHICK

THE PSYCHIC SONIC YOUTH STORY XXXXX X CONFUSION

OMNIBUS PRESS

LONDON / NEW YORK / PARIS / SYDNEY / COPENHAGEN / BERLIN / MADRID / TOKYO

Picture research by Sarah Bacon

ISBN: 978.1.84449.931.1
Order No: OP50941

Exclusive Distributors
Music Sales Limited,
14/15 Berners Street,
London, W1T 3LJ.

Music Sales Corporation,
257 Park Avenue South,
New York, NY 10010, USA.

Macmillan Distribution Services,
53 Park West Drive,
Derrimut, Vic 3030,
Australia.

Typeset by Phoenix Photosetting, Chatham, Kent
Printed and bound by Gutenberg Press, Malta

A catalogue record for this book is available from the British Library.

Visit Omnibus Press on the web at www.omnibuspress.com

Contents

INTRODUCTION

NYC Ghosts & Flowers

The first time I met Sonic Youth, they didn't disappoint. Profiling the group for UK heavy rock weekly *Kerrang!* – a broad enough church to encompass avant eggheads like the Youth alongside the rockers and punks and cathedral-burners who typically flood the magazine – around the time of their *Murray Street* album in 2002, I interviewed them en masse backstage at London's Shepherd Bush Empire, where they were playing that night.

On the walls of the dressing room in this one-time music hall and BBC television studio were old playbills and posters for past events, including one for former Rolling Stones bassist Bill Wyman's all-star group The Rhythm Kings. By way of opening gambit, I contrasted the Stones – still coining filthy lucre touring songs they'd written as spry young men 40 years before – with Sonic Youth, two decades into their own career but eschewing easy nostalgia in favour of new material that was among the best they'd ever recorded. This admittedly "soft-ball" conversation-starter, I hoped, would prompt the Youth to discuss their longevity and their enduring creative focus.

"Jagger, yoooooooouuuu suuuuuuuuuuck!" yelled Thurston Moore, at the top of his lungs, in adenoidal Yank slur, as the interview swiftly devolved into a five-person symposium on the merits of The Rolling Stones, offering an insight into the personalities of the various members of the Youth.

There was Thurston, arguing that Mick Jagger was a roundly substandard rock lyricist, and that Bill Wyman didn't fit in and should quit the band, attacking his theme with the gusto of a lifelong record nerd. There was Lee Ranaldo, cool and bemused, indulgently informing his band-mate and friend that Wyman had in fact quit the group almost a decade before. There was Kim Gordon, wisely maintaining a mature detachment from the melee, and suggesting that Jagger's lyrics were perhaps undone by his faux-American accent. There was Jim O'Rourke, sitting cross-legged at Thurston's feet and expounding upon the more obscure corners of Bill Wyman's solo catalogue. And there was Steve Shelley, looking up to the sky and softly asking himself, "How did we end up talking about Bill Wyman?"

Though this hubbub didn't yield much material for my feature, for a young writer meeting his heroes for the first time, it was a pretty heady experience. Buying their *Bad Moon Rising* album on recommendation of a piece by Keith Cameron in *NME* tracing the origins of Nirvana, blew this 16-year-old Pearl Jam fan's mind, opening up a universe of subterranean, experimental and avant-garde thrills to explore (I know this experience is common for many of my generation). And here they were, behaving exactly like I'd always thought they might: irascible, funny and sharp pop-cultural obsessives. It was like meeting the actors from your favourite TV show, and discovering they behaved like their characters off-set.

"I'm listening to a lot of 'commune-rock' at the moment," announced Thurston, faux-loftily, seeming eerily identical to the Thurston I'd come to "know" from interviews I'd pored over, and his narratorial turns in Dave Markey's rockumentary *1991: The Year Punk Broke*. "It's music made in hippy communes during the Seventies. Free love, free music, free acid. Steve listens to a lot of ska and rock-steady. Lee listens to fuckin' Dylan and Springsteen, maaaan. And Jim… We knocked on his hotel door the other day, and he came out in a dressing gown, trailed by a cloud of Gauloise cigarette smoke, with this high-pitched whiny noise coming from his room. I asked him what he was doing. He said, 'Listening to music'."

A couple of years later, for *Loose Lips Sink Ships*, an underground magazine I edit with photographer Steve Gullick, I again interviewed Thurston and Kim, this time on a one-to-one basis, at the 2004 All Tomorrow's Parties festival, which they helped curate. In their chalet at Camber Sands Holiday Village, Thurston greeted a seemingly endless stream of visitors, proffering records and fanzines as gifts to the Noise-Rock Monarch. Later, Thurston railed at the Bush administration and the Iraq war, talked about obscure corners of Sonic Youth's career, and spoke glowingly of the groups who were playing the festival, artists who had seemingly sprung up in Sonic Youth's shadow. Kim, meanwhile, spoke of Mariah Carey and sexism in the pop-cultural mainstream, and of her own extra-curricular work in the visual arts, collaborating with figures like Mike Kelley and Tony Oursler. Both seemed possessed of minds in constant motion, forever fascinated and energised by their own creativity, and the creativity of all those around them. Again, inspirational.

The last time I met Sonic Youth was surreal, their presence somehow comforting. I was lodging with a gang of fellow writers and photographers from *Plan B* magazine at a youth hostel in Stockholm, Sweden in July 2005, covering that year's Accelerator festival. We woke on the morning of the 7th a little groggy from spending most of the preceding night drinking wine-and-coca-cola cocktails by the river, ordering breakfast at a nearby restaurant. As our meals arrived, our mobile phones began to buzz, carrying frantic text messages asking where we were, if we were safe. The television behind the bar was carrying footage of central London, of police vans gathered around Tube stations, injured bodies stretchered to waiting ambulances.

We were in shock, confused. None of us spoke Swedish, so the news bulletin was impossible to decipher; we ate quickly and moved on to a nearby hotel, where *Plan B* editor Everett True was staying (profiling Accelerator headliners Sonic Youth for a *Plan B* cover feature), to watch English-language news reports on his television. BBC Worldwide was playing on the lobby television when we got to the hotel; we settled on their sofas and tried to process the news of the 7/7 Tube bombings, calling home when we could get a signal, and sending emails and scouring news websites in the hotel's web-café.

Minds clouded with panic, it took a while for any of us to really notice the other tourists in the lobby. Similarly spread out across the sofas, tapping at laptops and watching the news solemnly, were the members of Sonic Youth, as concerned and as panicked and as horrified as we were. To be far from home at that moment, to feel so afraid for our loved ones back in London, so helpless, left us all sickened and unsteady. Somehow, the presence of these oddly familiar faces, who all of us had somehow looked up to from afar, like older brothers with cool music taste who only exist in a photograph on an album sleeve, was a brief but welcome comfort; to fall in amongst the warmth of the Sonic Youth family for a few moments, when we were so far from our own.

* * *

Like Walt Whitman in his *Leaves Of Grass*, Sonic Youth are large; they contain multitudes. They have chased inspiration in myriad directions, trawled the sonic subterranean and flirted with the mainstream (only for as long as it suited them). Check the music message-boards of the internet and you'll discover riotous debate over just exactly which of their many releases, their shifting phases, is best, a discourse that never reaches a consensus. Their music threatens and soothes, toys with recognisable rock'n'roll tropes or throws out all the clichés in favour of noise that's entirely new.

This book is a sincere attempt to make sense of all these contradictions, of all that the group has reached for and achieved, a chance to tell the story of a band that has traced an entirely wilful and idiosyncratic path through rock'n'roll. The book also explores the pop cultures that have influenced Sonic Youth and the noise they make, and examines the colossal impact they in turn have made upon modern rock music: their influence, how they wield it, and how this power sits with them. It's also a celebration of a series of records and videos and live performances of a group that has spent over 26 years engaged in furious, productive and enlightening self-expression, building a canon of noise subsequent generations hold as sacred.

Stevie Chick, June 2007.

CHAPTER ONE

Early American

Sonic Youth's is a New York story; indeed, it couldn't have happened anywhere else.

New York is surely America's most famed, most fabled city. The symbol for so much of what the country believes it believes in, the Statue Of Liberty stands in New York's harbour, upon a pedestal engraved with 'The New Colossus', poet Emma Lazarus' sonnet immortalizing the promise of A Better Life for all who seek refuge at America's shores: *"Give me your tired, your poor, your huddled masses yearning to breathe free..."*

It's a city where that American Dream is played out, at perilously high stakes; a city of legendary success, infamous failure. Wall Street, Manhattan's hub of financial activity, is synonymous with both 1929's calamitous stock market crash (and the grim depression that followed) and the surfeit of aspirational excess that marked the "yuppie" era of the Eighties.

It's a city of violent contrasts, great wealth and great poverty rubbing tense shoulders, the friction both productive and destructive. The sheer divergence of cultures and communities barely contained within its five boroughs is vital to the art created therein – art that has crucially shaped America's cultural self-image – and yet, like San Francisco and New Orleans, New York is conspicuous and somehow suspect for the very multitudes it contains, for its cosmopolitan racial and gender make-up and for its liberal outlook, in stark contrast to the relative (perhaps imagined) conformity of the "mainstream" heartlands of America.

The violence enacted upon the city on September 11th 2001 united the country in sympathy for the wound New York sustained, and was used as motivation for the subsequent military actions in Afghanistan and Iraq, haemorrhaging lives and money with no clear end in sight (actions that the majority of New York's citizens by no means support). Still, however, New York has a perceived exoticism, an otherness, which means it is often only reluctantly embraced by the rest of America. When the city was at its lowest financial ebb in the middle of the Seventies, on the cusp of bankruptcy, President Gerald Ford refused a federal bailout of New York's debts, in part to appease those on the right wing of the country who wished to see the Big Apple punished for its perceived "sins".

Woody Allen articulated this sensibility, this anxiety, in his 1977 Oscar-winning movie *Annie Hall*, subtitled "A Nervous Romance". In conversation with his WASP-ish, soon-to-depart-for-California friend Rob, Allen's character, comedian Alvy Singer, cites the failure of the country to come to New York's aid as "anti-semitism... The rest of the country looks upon New York like we're left-wing Communist, Jewish, homosexual, pornographers. I think of us that way, sometimes, and I live here."[1]

By no means threatening Hollywood's status as prime locus of America's movie industry, New York's film-makers have nevertheless played a crucial role in shaping the country's cinematic vocabulary, and defining its visual iconography. The camera has a seemingly unquenchable fascination for New York, and the camera *loves* the city: even in Martin Scorsese's unflinching meditation upon the squalor of Seventies New York, *Taxi Driver,* the lens scanning the teeming midnight streets for the grime and filth cited in Travis Bickle's acrid monologues can't help but deliver a dreamy montage of lurid neon, with even a seedy porn cinema radiating a harsh, ugly beauty, a corroded glamour. Allen's movies – his 1979 monochrome love letter to the city, *Manhattan*, in particular – posit New York as a cultural Mecca, his characters living out their neuroses against a backdrop of art galleries and cinemas and museums and night clubs, even, in *Hannah And Her Sisters*, a CBGBs-styled punk dive.

New York's geography is indeed studded with cultural landmarks of all stripes, sizes and importance, locations where art "happened", or still happens. Musicians arriving in the city can make pilgrimages to countless sites that resonate with historical importance. Bebop hatched from jam sessions between master musicians at Minton's Playhouse in Harlem. Jimi Hendrix made his American debut at Café Wha? in Greenwich Village, while Gerde's Folk City, in West Village, was the site of Bob Dylan's first New York performance, in 1961. The Roxy in Chelsea was location for the breakdancing scenes in early hip-hop flick *Beat Street.* Harlem's Apollo Theatre has been *the* proving ground for generations of black musicians, the body of James Brown, The Hardest Working Man In Showbiz, returning to the site of his greatest successes one last time before taking his final rest. The disco era played out on the dancefloors and in the bathrooms of Studio 54, Paradise Garage, and Mudd Club. Where the buildings themselves might no longer be standing, they still cast a shadow.

There's a synergistic relationship between New York and the music it produces. The city inspires both the words and the noise composed by its citizens. The realities of life in New York's impoverished housing projects shaped early social polemic in the form of Grandmaster Flash & The Furious Five's 'The Message', while the shrieking din of the urban jungle was echoed and emulated and bested by the Bomb Squad's productions for Public Enemy, turntables and samplers coaxing a dense squall of sirens, breakbeats and James Brown's trademark grunt, blended with a backwards-sample of Miles Davis' horn.

With great pride in their roots, rappers eulogise their neighbourhoods, composing elaborate rhymes celebrating allegiance to their particular corner of the city; not long after those epochal first block parties from whence hip-hop sprang, rappers were playing out verbally pugilistic territorial beefs across tracks like 'The Bridge' and 'South Bronx', as Queensbridge's Juice Crew and South Bronx's Boogie Down Productions sparred for credit as hip-hop's birthplace on their respective neighbourhoods' behalf. The Wu Tang Clan wreathed their borough of Staten Island in a mysticism derived from imported kung fu movies – an aesthetic that surfaced in Jim Jarmusch's urban samurai film *Ghost Dog*, scored by chief Wu gambino RZA – while Cannibal Ox painted life in the rotten core of the Big Apple as scenes from a violent, metaphysical comic book with their 2001 album *The Cold Vein*, their art transcending their environment but never escaping its mark.

Along with its native artists, the city attracts creatives the world over, drawn to the Big Apple's rich cache of myth and legend, to the cultural energy crackling beneath the very paving stones of New York, billowing out of those iconic Manhattan manholes. The winding paths traced by the Beat Generation of poets across America, yielding epochal work drawing upon those travels, intersected early on in New York, leading lights William Burroughs, Jack Kerouac and Allen Ginsberg meeting there shortly after the Second World War.

Attracted by the relatively cheap rents in the lofts and warehouses of areas that had or would soon become slums, visual artists and film-makers and writers and musicians settled together, sharing homes and workplaces. A spirit of creative liberation prevailed, as did multi-tasking; poets painted, film-makers made music, the dividing lines between disciplines dissolving. In 1965 Andy Warhol, the world's premier Pop Artist and a New York celebrity of considerable notoriety and visibility, extended his reach to pop music when he adopted a local rock'n'roll group as an attraction within his Exploding Plastic Inevitable performance art happenings, multimedia events that mixed light shows, screenings of Warhol's films, and performances from The Velvet Underground and other luminaries from within The Factory.

While The Factory's in-house movie director Paul Morrissey later said, "Andy didn't want to get into rock'n'roll, I wanted to get into rock'n'roll to make money"[2], Warhol recognized something of himself in the Velvets. "He told me that what we were doing with the music was the same thing he was doing with painting and movies and writing, i.e., not kidding around," recalled the Velvets' frontman, Lou Reed. "To my mind, nobody was doing what even approximated the real thing, with the exception of us."[3]

The group Warhol had selected were a singular bunch: Moe Tucker, a revolutionary, primitivist drummer who only played the toms and never the cymbals, because (as their fractious band-leader would hiss), "Cymbals eat guitars"; a quietly radical guitarist and bassist, Sterling Morrison; John Cale, a Welsh music scholar who had collaborated with experimental composers John Cage and La Monte Young, who contributed searing viola tones and a dry, macabre wit; and Lou Reed, the group's malevolent, simian-savant singer and guitarist, with a history of electroshock therapy and penning novelty songs for bargain-bin label Pickwick Records behind him. Warhol's most notable adulteration of the group's sound and dynamic was to introduce ice-blonde German chanteuse Nico to the line-up. Otherwise, The Velvet Underground were very much of their own creation.

In San Francisco, the psychedelic age was dawning. The Velvet Underground provided a very New York response; taking their name from a lurid Sixties sexploitation paperback, their music had a darker, harder edge; "the real thing" of which Reed spoke. While the rest of the country bathed in the warmth of the Summer Of Love, The Velvet Underground's narcotic vignettes were cast in harsh documentary focus: 'I'm Waiting For My Man' an urgent amphetamine strum doused in the anxiety and paranoia and desperate yearning of hooking up with your dealer, 'Heroin' a turbulent squall grimly and perversely celebrating the drug.

Their debut, 1967's *The Velvet Underground And Nico*, was nominally produced by Warhol, though his greatest contribution was doubtless the album's iconic sleeve, a yellow decal of a banana, which, when "peeled" by the purchaser, revealed suggestively pink fruit beneath. Peaking at number 171 in the *Billboard* charts, it would win the group their highest placing in their lifetime, prompting the oft-quoted truism, credited to Brian Eno, that while the Velvets only sold a few thousand albums in their lifetime, everyone who bought one would go on to form a band.

Parting ways with Warhol but retaining the radical, artistic glow he lent them, The Velvet Underground would record three further albums, each radically different to what came before: 1968's *White Light/White Heat*, their last with Cale, a gloriously, maliciously anarchic din that peaked and closed with 'Sister Ray', a dense, volume-saturated groove that burned away for a sulphurous, cuss-mouthed 17 and a half minutes, by which time the sheer sonic overload had driven the engineers from the studio; 1969's self-titled third, a suite of hazy murmured lullabies thick with nuance and melancholic poetry, inspired in part by the theft of their Vox amplifiers while on tour; and 1970's set of perfectly perverse, delicately off-centre pop, *Loaded*. The ears of the mainstream would elude them, but those who *were* listening, who were seduced by the very qualities that posited The Velvet Underground as misfits and outsiders at the increasingly avaricious, conformist and corporate rock'n'roll banquet, would explore and draw rich inspiration from the riot of nuance, complexity and experimentalism contained within those eight sides of vinyl.

Rock'n'roll had been subterranean, dangerous, derided by the mainstream. But as its brightest lights eclipsed the stars of Hollywood in glamour and celebrity (not to mention ego and insane ambition), it embarked upon an inexorable rise towards mainstream acceptance as an institutionalised, bountiful entertainment industry. With outrageous commercial success came a fast-encroaching conservatism. "One of the good things that happened during the Sixties was that at least some music of an unusual or experimental nature got recorded and released," wrote pop avant-gardist Frank Zappa. "Old cigar chomper guys listened to the tapes and said, 'I dunno. Who knows what the fuck it is? G'head, put it out! Who knows? I dunno.' We were better off with that attitude that we are now. The 'bright young men' are far more conservative and more dangerous than the old guys ever were."[4]

The Velvet Underground were at odds with rock'n'roll's growing orthodoxy, its aspirations to mainstream acceptance, at odds with the mainstream itself. Theirs was an aesthetic that didn't crave palatial rock mansions in Laurel Canyon, that recognised or conjured a damaged glamour and romance in the archetype of the starving artist, took a narcissistic pride in its own self-destruction. And it prized the music, the performance, as *art*, something to challenge and confront and unsettle and provoke the listener. Their dark, literate, dissonant pop peeled away the growing pomposity of rock'n'roll, replaced the saccharine buzz of psychedelia with a new, bitter, street-wise poetry that ignored the chimeric Age Of Aquarius in favour of the junkies and transvestites, the (sur)realities that surrounded them.

The Velvet Underground found champions in those similarly ambivalent, like rock critic Lester Bangs, who essayed Reed as a fascinating, contrarian, sadistic anti-hero, as much his nemesis as his muse. Introducing perhaps the most pugilistic of their infamous interview face-offs, Bangs wrote, "I wanted to emulate the most self-destructive bastard I could see, as long as he moved with some sense of style. Thus Lou Reed. Getting off vicariously on various forms of deviant experience compensated somehow for the emptiness of our own drearily 'normal' lives."[5]

These dissenting sounds weren't just coming from New York; in Michigan, The Stooges and The MC5 forged a separate but kindred aesthetic, built on confrontation, experimentation and outrage. The roots of Detroit's Motor City Five lay in their early days as an R&B party band, playing raw blues and soul covers at weddings, barbecues and school dances. The music they recorded as The MC5 retained that dancefloor urgency, that testifying passion, tempering the furious, earnest attempts of Wayne Kramer and Fred "Sonic" Smith to translate the frenzied free expression of jazz titans like John Coltrane, Albert Ayler and Sun Ra into ecstatic electric guitar din. Add frontman Rob Tyner's galvanising near-gospel holler, their affiliation with The White Panthers – a radical political group founded by their activist manager John Sinclair, espousing "rock'n'roll, dope, and fucking in the streets" – and what they themselves eloquently described as "liquid frenzy", and The MC5 were a proposition potentially seditious enough to earn the unwelcome attention of the FBI.

Their debut album, 1969's *Kick Out The Jams*, was recorded the year before, at one of the group's many performances at Detroit's Grande Ballroom. Perfectly capturing their electrifying chaos, the album was a wild, anarchic mess, the deafeningly loud guitars ringing out of tune, the tempo charging as the group played with careering abandon, feeding off the energy of the audibly charged audience. The bruised chords and droning siren feedback of 'Rocket Reducer No 62 (Rama Lama Fa Fa)' raised up a delirious, beautiful discord, and the group valiantly attempted to break Earth's orbit with a closing cover of 'Starship' by Saturnian jazz maverick Sun Ra. A band-funded advert in the press reading "Fuck Hudsons!", in response to the Detroit department store's refusal to stock the album on the grounds of Tyner's on-vinyl call to the masses to "Kick out the jams, motherfuckers!", saw the group ditched from Elektra Records (Atlantic released 1970's *Back In The USA* and 1971's *High Time*), but not before they'd helped get "little brother" band and fellow Grande house act The Stooges signed to the label.

The Stooges were based in Ann Arbor, a liberal college town in

Michigan. Beginning as a decidedly avant-garde performance-art outfit called The Psychedelic Stooges (frontman Iggy Pop, aka Jim Osterberg, wailing on lead vacuum cleaner and kitchen blender), the group dropped the "Psychedelic", wrote a handful of songs and recorded a debut album, produced by Velvet-in-exile John Cale, at the behest of Elektra representative Danny Fields, a former Factory scenester, who signed the group shortly after The MC5 (though for considerably less money). Curtailing their wild improvised freakouts, Cale finessed The Stooges' violent tunes into taut, malevolent pop, songs like '1969' and 'No Fun' thriving on guitarist "Rock Action"'s elegantly primal riffs and Iggy's vacant, dangerous snarl.

The Stooges' rabid menace was at odds with the era's hippy positivity, and with critics misinterpreting their brute eloquence as inartful clumsiness, sales were modest. The following year's *Fun House* saw producer Don Gallucci – a former member of The Kingsmen, who scored pop paydirt with their cover of foul-mouthed shanty and garage-rock standard 'Louie Louie' – faithfully capture the sonics of a live show that regularly saw Iggy sliced open by broken glass or smothered in peanut butter, with the aim of truly assaulting the audience's senses. The album's first side was a suite of seductive, sinful rock'n'rollers chasing a sleek, metallic groove, evoking the unhinged hedonism that was rapidly enveloping the group. Side two was the brutal comedown, '1970' and 'Fun House' priapic ruts where the primordial riffs rang on and on, a strung-out Iggy howling "I feel all right" so often you knew he was anything but, Steve Mackay's acid-spitting sax runs blurting an intense free-jazz skronk. The closing 'LA Blues' was apocalyptic rock'n'roll, five minutes of blurting, screeching and howling hewn from a near-unlistenable 20 minute "jam".

The group dissolved soon after, reforming briefly with new guitarist James Williamson to record 1973's adrenalised, steroidal *Raw Power*, before drug addiction and shows that broke down into pitch battles between the group and marauding Hell's Angels in the audience finally signalled their demise (*Metallic KO*, the historic bootleg of their final gig at Detroit's Michigan Palace, features Iggy singing 'Louie Louie' while dodging bottles and other missiles thrown from the crowd.)

"I invented punk. Everybody knows that," wrote Lester Bangs in 1981, long after the word had become firmly entrenched within rock's lexicon. "But I stole it from Greg Shaw, who also invented power pop. And he stole it from Dave Marsh, who actually saw Question Mark & The Mysterians live once. But he stole it from John Sinclair. Who stole it from Rob Tyner. Who stole it from Iggy. Who stole it from Lou Reed."[6] Bangs' list of artful thieves continues, defining an aesthetic cribbed from Hollywood stars, romantic poets, heroic politicos and finally sourced to Lady Godiva herself. But the Velvets, The MC5 and The Stooges form the canonical Holy Trinity clasped to the heart of the underground rock'n'roll movement that would become known as "punk" (along with a welter of garage bands across the country, high on cheap drugs and ragged electrified attempts at Troggs songs).

> "I grew up ten minutes from New York City. The legal drinking age in the Sixties and Seventies was 18, but in Manhattan they would sell liquor to anyone, and, as a teenager, my friends and I would hitch-hike into the city, buy a bottle of wine and explore the seedy Times Square area. I was 14 in 1969, and was way into the hippy/Yippie movement, and began exploring all things psychedelic. Around 1972, while I was in high school, I went to see The New York Dolls at Max's Kansas City, saw the Warhol retrospective at the Whitney Museum, and caught a screening of his movie *Trash*. It was also around this time that I heard the *Velvet Underground And Nico* album at my older brother's apartment. My perspective of everything changed quite drastically."[7]
>
> Bob Bert

"Punk" – a musical movement, an indefinite but potent political statement, a fanzine founded by John Holmstrom and Legs McNeil that chronicled the seething New York scene in arch prose and campy fumetti featuring these new stars – took its name from street/prison slang for a young, possibly homosexual outsider. Certainly this description fit The New York Dolls, five cross-dressing vandals teetering upon stack-heeled leather boots and cranking out a loose and raw R&B. Drugs in their veins and cherry-coloured wax smeared on their lips, they came on like a crude and debauched and deliriously witty take on early Rolling Stones. But where, by the early Seventies, the Stones were glamourous tax exiles, heads of the nascent rock aristocracy, the Dolls were a decidedly more low-rent proposition. Their take on Shadow Morton's 'Great Big Kiss', recorded by girl group The Shangri-Las, was hooligan doo-wop from a seamy street corner, while their 1973 eponymous debut, produced by power-pop godhead Todd Rundgren, conjured a most sordid glamour from its tales of drug-slaked mania, psychopathic love affairs and all-round hedonistic lasciviousness. "There was definitely nothing exciting and glittery and fun and sparkly and wild going on in rock'n'roll until the Dolls came along,"[8] recalled

Cyrinda Foxe, Warhol muse and later wife of Dolls frontman David Johansen.

They played the subterranean network that had hosted The Velvet Underground a couple of years before. Their first show was an impromptu set of covers for the residents and workers at the Endicott Hotel, a New York refuge for the homeless, on Christmas Eve 1971, the band later taking residency at the Mercer Arts Center in Greenwich Village and playing Max's Kansas City, location of an infamous Velvet Underground live recording by poet Jim Carroll. The Dolls' legend stems more from their lurid live performances than their recorded output, from the sheer glare of glitter and askew glamour, their scuffed, romantic riffage, and Johnny Thunders, their doomed guitarist, an iconic junkie romantic in the Keef Richards vein. They were a delicious mix of knowing leer and charismatic shimmy, a vital blast of energy just as "rock" was softening at the edges, but the title of their second album, 1974's Shadow Morton-produced *Too Much Too Soon*, proved prophetic; following a last-ditch rebranding as leather-clad communist rockers (under the aegis of Malcolm McLaren, soon to refine his concept with The Sex Pistols), the Dolls disintegrated in 1975.

By this time, however, focus had shifted to the noise emanating from a number of wretched downtown dives, including the infamous CBGBs; a swarming, incestuous scene of musicians who were also artists and poets, drawn inexorably to the Big Apple. Patti Smith was born in Chicago, raised in New Jersey and, following a short period in New York, spent some time in Paris with her sister Linda at the end of the Sixties, performing on the street. Returning to New York as the Seventies dawned, she reconnected with close friend, artist and photographer Robert Mapplethorpe, taking residence at the Chelsea Hotel, a famed residence for artists and writers then playing host to William Burroughs, Janis Joplin and many of Warhol's superstars – indeed, a chance meeting with Bob Dylan's "right-hand man" Bobby Neuwirth in the lobby of the Chelsea was the first of many important connections she would forge with the worlds of art, theatre, poetry and finally rock'n'roll.

Following success in the underground theatre scene with Sam Shepherd, Smith took the stage of St Mark's Church on the Lower East Side in 1971 during a weekly Poetry Project reading, opening for the co-founder of Andy Warhol's *Interview* magazine, Gerard Malanga. For three poems, Smith was backed by Lenny Kaye, a guitarist and writer soon to compile *Nuggets: Original Artyfacts From The First Psychedelic Era*, a 1972 anthology of American garage groups like The Strangeloves, The Leaves and The 13th Floor Elevators, a compendium of raw energy triumphing rudimentary skills, playing like a pre-echo of "punk". Two years later, Smith and Kaye performed together again at Le Jardin, a downtown dive name-checked by Lou Reed in 'Sally Can't Dance', for a "Rock'n'Rimbaud" festival. Soon, her Patti Smith Group began to take shape; a debut 7" surfaced in 1974 on Mer, a label funded by Mapplethorpe, a cover of The Leaves' 'Hey Joe' (preceded by 'Sixty Days', a monologue dedicated to kidnapped heiress Patty Hearst), backed with 'Piss Factory', a searing blues-poem that snarled of Smith's freedom flight from deadening assembly-line job to New York. Her John Cale-produced debut album, 1975's *Horses*, was one of punk's first full-lengths, even if much of what followed didn't often resemble this brazenly poetic, measured, sophisticated 'Babelogue'.

Playing lead guitar on 'Piss Factory' was Tom Verlaine, a musician, poet and, for a time, lover of Patti's who had changed his surname from Miller in tribute to romantic poet Paul Verlaine. Miller had attended a modest private boarding school in Delaware, where he met Richard Meyers, a trouble-maker from Kentucky who attended on scholarship. Following a week's suspension for misbehaving under the influence of "psychedelic" morning glory seeds, Meyers told Miller of his plan to escape the school once and for all and hitch-hike to Florida, with aims to live high off the land and become a writer. The duo made it as far as Alabama, where they were arrested after their illicit cornfield campfire swiftly got out of hand; Miller returned to Delaware with his parents, while Meyers stayed with his mother in Virginia, before dropping out of school at 16 and moving to New York. Swiftly familiarising himself with the city's cultural underground, he was soon printing his own books and magazines on a table-top offset printing press and having his poems published in national journals.

Verlaine followed Meyers to New York in 1969, and the two were again inseparable, often mistaken for brothers as they skulked in the darkness of nightclubs like Max's. They even published a tome of 17 poems by the fictional Theresa Stern, the jacket photo a composite of their faces. Verlaine invited a drummer friend from Delaware, Billy Ficca, up to New York, and the trio rehearsed and recorded a handful of songs as The Neon Boys, dense and nervy, Stones-y/Velvets-y shuffles characterised by the eloquent, chiming guitar of Verlaine and the Dionysian drawl of Meyers, now known as Richard Hell. The Neon Boys disbanded before they could play a show, but Terry Ork, manager of Cinemabilia, a film bookstore where Verlaine and Hell worked, introduced them to Richard Lloyd, a local guitarist.

Inspired by The New York Dolls' infamous residencies at the Mercer Arts Center, Verlaine and Hell scoped out a dive that would let their group, Television, play regularly: a club in the Bowery called CBGB (OMFUG) (an acronym for Country, Blue Grass and Blues and Other Music For Uplifting Gourmands). Opened by Hilly Kristal, a downtown legend who'd managed the Village Vanguard in the early Sixties alongside a career as a folk singer, the venue was planned as a showcase for the titular music forms; fibbing that they would play some Country, Blue Grass and Blues in their set, Television won three Sunday-night shows. Max's Kansas City having temporarily closed shortly before CBGB opened, New York's musical underground soon took the stage for themselves, finding a home within these grotty environs.

"It was quite literally a shit-hole, there was dog shit everywhere," remembers James Sclavunos, a Brooklyn-born musician and suave trouble-maker who regularly played audition night at CBGB with a band that was sometimes called Mimi & The Dreamboats, never quite winning a slot. "Hilly had these dogs, these ratty, skinny looking things, and he let them shit anywhere they wanted."[9] Word-of-mouth spread rapidly about Television; despite the stench, their early shows attracted the likes of Patti Smith and Danny Fields. Verlaine and Hell originally shared songwriting and frontman duties, until Hell – who took to the stage in torn clothes, spiky hair and shades, probably the first sighting of punk chic – departed the group, alienated by the other members' increasing musical proficiency, and alienating Verlaine by jumping flamboyantly during the guitarist's songs.

On their 1977 debut album, *Marquee Moon*, Verlaine and Lloyd traded solos like jazz luminaries, playing their brilliantly organised tangles of lyrical electric guitar with an erudite discipline in contrast to the more grandstanding approach of rock's reigning stadium guitar-heroes. *Marquee Moon*'s unabashed cerebral appeal translated into critical acclaim in the rock press, but the "punk" blueprint had been forged a year before, by four "brudders" from Forest Hills, in the borough of Queens. Clad in uniform black leather, torn blue jeans and thick black fringes, The Ramones played bubble-gum pop at bone-rattling velocity and volume, a head-banging ramalama of rapid, rocket-fuelled tunes interspersed with barked "1!-2!-3!-4!" countdowns to detonation.

The brutish rush of their noise hid the satiric attack of their lyrics, depicting with macabre B-movie relish their milieu of glue-sniffing, male prostitution and suburban insanity, set out like a *Mad Magazine* fold-in. Gleefully reflecting the psychosis of a post-Nixon, post-Vietnam America, and a New York in a state of rapid decay, The Ramones won a cultish herodom that sold millions of T-shirts emblazoned with artist friend Arturo Vega's Ramones logo and kept them on the road for over two decades, with modest financial returns. "It was an ugly life somehow,"[10] remarked bassist Dee Dee Ramone as the group was inducted into the Rock'n'Roll Hall Of

Fame in 2002, a belated nod of respect from an industry that had kept these scary droogs from Queens at arm's length during their lifetime. Two years later, three of the four "brudders" were dead.

Other CBGB groups, like Blondie and Talking Heads, enjoyed greater success, meeting the mainstream halfway and developing a music indelibly coloured by their arty, punk roots, but still able to "cross over" to the upper reaches of the pop charts. Chris Stein and Debbie Harry met and became lovers while playing in The Stilettos, a lovingly camp pastiche of the Sixties girl-group sound. Their next group, Blondie, translated high-trash kitsch, Brill Building songwriting and a certain New York "punk" edge into a most charming "pop". Under the guidance of Mike Chapman, who'd found success producing British glam-rock acts like Mud, The Sweet and Suzi Quatro, Blondie seduced the pop charts with songs that flirted with disco and reggae and, on their last great single 'Rapture', pioneering the fusion of rock with the burgeoning black street music, rap, while also saluting other pillars of hip-hop culture like graffiti and DJing.

Talking Heads moved to New York after forming at Rhode Island School of Art, their angular songs possessed of a nervous funk sketched by Tina Weymouth's instinctive bass playing, frontman David Byrne possessed of a faintly geek-ish otherness, perfectly inhabiting songs like 'Psycho Killer'. Their early records infected with the urgent anxiety of modern urban life, they took an inspired left turn with 1980's bravura *Remain In Light*, its elliptical riddles building upon Byrne's extra-curricular excursions into world music with producer Brian Eno. That the album also yielded breakthrough chart success with 'Once In A Lifetime' was further proof of Talking Heads' idiosyncratic pop gift, which thrived through the following decade.

The trajectory of most "punk" groups was more modest and earthbound, however. Following his exit from Television, Richard Hell hooked up with newly unemployed Dolls Johnny Thunders and Jerry Nolan and formed The Heartbreakers, winning the attention of Malcolm McLaren, who would later fashion the look of the "punk" clothing he'd sell at his London boutique, Sex, after Hell's torn shirts, held together with conspicuous safety pins. Hell abandoned The Heartbreakers within a year, before they could make it to a studio, forming The Voidoids with guitarist Robert Quine, who'd spent his youth bootlegging The Velvet Underground and practising guitar until he perfected the fractured, lucid spasms of sound that embellished The Voidoids' debut, *Blank Generation*. Hell's lyrics essayed a bleak, romantic nihilism, declaring life a "perpetual jive", the title track an existential blues that doubled as something of an anti-anthem. They scored a tour of the UK with The Clash at the height of Britain's punk era, but it proved a dispiriting experience, the Voidoids flecked with gobbed spittle from audiences who expected thrills at Ramones velocity, not the complex disquiet Hell was offering.

The Voidoids ultimately unravelled, Hell releasing the posthumous compilation *R.I.P.* on underground cassette label ROIR and exiting rock to concentrate on his literary work, publishing his harrowing, brilliantly lucid junkie road story *Go Now* in 1996. Patti Smith suffered serious injuries after a fall from a stage in 1978, releasing two more albums before marrying MC5 guitarist Fred "Sonic" Smith and retiring from music for a domestic life. Unable to trump *Marquee Moon* with the expert songcraft of 1978's *Adventure*, Television signed off with a three-night residency at The Bottom Line in Greenwich Village that summer. Verlaine closed the final show on Saturday July 29, leading the group through an enervated take on the Stones' 'Satisfaction', a setlist-staple that perhaps doubled that night as a comment on the frustrations that had finished the band.

"Few shows at CBGBs were ever sold out," says Sclavunos. "There was plenty of room when The Ramones played. I didn't have any trouble getting a seat; I sat there with my laughing gas, and enjoyed the show."[11] Indeed, soon after the initial buzz of interest around "punk" calmed, the Record Industry, the "bright young men" Zappa warned of, were marketing their new, "edgy" signings as New Wave, a manufactured genre that evaded the aggressive taint of punk and was flexible enough to embrace Talking Heads and Blondie, along with the new synthesizer-driven pop coming over from England. New Wave would prove the defining soundtrack of the rising MTV network.

The next noise to leak from New York's underground would, by design and by contrast, have no desire – nor any possibility – of crossing over. New Wave, meet No Wave.

> "What attracted me to New York was magazines like *Rock Scene* and *Circus*, The New York Dolls... It wasn't very far away. I knew I was going to do music, or something. So I just went."[12]
>
> Lydia Lunch

Born and raised in Rochester, upstate New York, Lydia Koch ran away briefly to Manhattan when she was 14, to check the place out. Two years later, she made the leap for good, settling in a loft in the Chelsea district, taking a room recently vacated by Lenny Bruce's daughter Kitty in a communal house populated by musicians, actors and artists. Soon, she would take the name Lydia Lunch.

"Chelsea was very close to where Max's Kansas City was. It was pretty desolate; because it was right below the garment district, there were a lot of big, ugly, dirty lofts. There were a couple of 'discos' there, like Le Jardin. These were very different from places like Studio 54; they were quite dark, frightening and degenerate. It wasn't really a *music* club, it was really just where drug-taking degenerates of all walks of life gathered. The music was happening at places like Max's and, later, CBGBs.

"I lived under one of these discos in Chelsea. It was the worst of all worlds: loud music every weekend, degenerate dopers on the doorstep. Dingy, poor, beautiful New York. The music was dance music, the beginnings of 'disco' – but it was more about the 'scene' than the music, at least to the people who were visiting these dank places at two or three in the morning. I was attracted to those places when I came to New York the first time, because I wanted to experience any kind of 'scene'. It's amazing to think that, at 14, I could just walk into one of these 24-hour discos.

"What people don't understand when they try to romanticise the 'punk' period, is how incredibly poor, dark, dirty, uninhabited and *destroyed* New York was. From the Bronx to the Lower East Side to Brooklyn, there had been a systematic ghettoisation of these areas. The Lower East Side of that time was a burned-out shell."

Arriving in 1975, Lunch soon familiarised herself with the music scene that had drawn her there. She wasn't much impressed with what she found. "I saw The Ramones, but I thought they were pretty silly. Television were boring, Patti Smith was too traditional, it was *all* too traditional, whether it was The Ramones sounding like The Rolling Stones, or Television sounding like The Grateful Dead."

Lunch felt more kinship with Suicide, a disturbing local duo comprising singer Alan Vega and synthesiser/drum-machine operator Martin Rev, who she soon befriended. As the Seventies dawned, Vega, an arts and physics graduate of Brooklyn College, was involved with a number of radical arts groups, living, working and experimenting with electronic music at the Project of Living Artists, a workshop and performance space funded by the New York State Council of the Arts. It was here that he formed Suicide with Rev, electric pianist in a local jazz group called Reverend B. Dressed in quasi-futuristic street garb and replacing the guitar-bass-drums orthodoxy with cold-blooded drum machines, thrift-store Farfisa organ squall and Vega's unsettling mutant-Elvis holler, their confrontational noise was the very *essence* of "punk", a shocking (d)evolution of rock'n'roll. They performed only very occasionally at art galleries and the Mercer throughout the first half of the decade, provoking audiences instantly, Vega brandishing a motorcycle chain to ward off attacking audience members. "There were riots," he remembered. "It was a nightly occurrence. We started getting booed as soon as we came onstage. Just from the way we looked they started giving us hell already."[13]

Lunch was soon a regular at Max's and CBGB. "I'd go down there and read my poetry. People were *terrified* of me – I was only 17, but David Byrne would literally run from me when he saw me. One person that didn't walk away was Lenny Kaye – he would stand there and listen; I was like a carnival barker, telling anyone who would listen about my horrendous poetry. Lenny Kaye was always very tolerant of me."

Lydia had also made friends with a number of musicians and artists who had relocated to New York en masse from the arts college of University of South Florida in St Petersburg, including members of Mars and DNA, two groups who would make a crucial impression upon her.

DNA was the brainchild of guitarist Arto Lindsay, who attacked the strings of his guitar with a violence bordering upon genius, while his fellow musicians stirred up a murky, disorientating squall of rhythm and noise. DNA also numbered Ikue Mori on drums, a visiting Japanese artist who had never played drums before and spoke very little English, and Tim Wright, a former member of Rocket From The Tombs (a legendary Cleveland, Ohio garage band of Stoogian intensity who were torn apart by violent musical differences before they could enter the studio, going on to spawn iconoclastic art-rockers Pere Ubu and nihilistic, self-destructive punks The Dead Boys), on bass, this trio recording some of the most compelling, enduring music of this era. An earlier incarnation of the group featured Mirielle Cervenka (sister of Exene, later singer with Los Angeles punks X) on drums and her husband, Gordon Stevenson, on bass, though the duo quit before the band inched outside of their rehearsal room.

"Mars remain one of the most outrageous bands of that period," Lunch recalls. "Their sound was so unique. It was insanity personified. Literally, the lead singer was insane – he was certifiably, beautifully, brilliantly insane." Sumner Crane formed the band in 1975 with guitarist Lucy Hamilton (playing as China Burg), bassist Mark Cunningham and drummer Nancy Arlen. A startling, chaotic tangle of abused guitar, primal drumming and caterwauling vocals Mars swiftly won attention with their early shows at CBGB. Their noise was, by turns, grisly, anarchic and inspired, the work of musicians of grand and uncompromising ambition – after the group split, the members would collaborate on *John Gavanti*, a radical, avant-punk interpretation of Mozart's *Don Giovanni* recorded with members of DNA.

"After seeing Mars I realised, OK, I need to get started, this has to happen," says Lunch. She had recently collided with James Chance, a saxophonist transplanted from Milwaukee, Wisconsin, playing skronk at improv nights at jazz clubs across New York. "We were both at Max's and CBGB all the time," remembers Lunch. "It was inevitable I was gonna meet the other cranky motherfucker in the room." Having worn out her welcome at the loft in Chelsea, she moved in with Chance, with whom she formed her first group, Teenage Jesus and The Jerks, soon after.

"James and I were both dirt poor, begging, borrowing and stealing any money we could. I realised I wanted to get the words out, and the best way was with music. Somebody gave me a guitar with four or five strings. It was almost like a bass, hideously un-useful, but I began to write with it. I had absolutely no training; the priority for me was to make it sound absolutely like nothing else."

Assembling a rhythm section (drummer Bradley Field, and a bassist visiting from Japan known only as Reck) in late 1976, Teenage Jesus rehearsed endlessly ("The band had to be tight," explains Lunch. "If they weren't, they'd get the wire coat hanger"), and were soon auditioning at CBGB. Their performances were intense, unforgettable, brief, Field and Reck wreaking near-industrial rhythms with clattering cymbal and snare and hulking bass, Lunch howling with abandon and throttling the neck of her busted guitar with a piece of broken glass she used as a slide.

"We played 10-minute sets, because I just didn't think it needed to go on any longer," continues Lunch. "It's like a knockout punch, you don't wanna go 13 rounds. I was so angry at the time, so desperate to just vomit out my hatred, it makes sense that it sounded like it did. I didn't conceive Teenage Jesus as poetry set to music, I assure you; it was more like *primal screams* set to music."

Chance didn't stay with Teenage Jesus for long, departing to form his own group, The Contortions. "James was about mingling with the audience," observes Lunch, "where Teenage Jesus was about building a wall between the stage and the audience – only those equally damaged could climb over it to get to the other side. If somebody would've dared get near the stage they would've gotten a guitar over the head." Singing and blowing murderous saxophone, Chance brought this brutality to the audience, leaping offstage to attack them while his Contortions played their serrated, frenetic music, an acid punk-funk that fused the squawking free groove of James Brown and Albert Ayler with the discord and dissonance of the punk avant-garde.

Teenage Jesus continued to play shows, Patti Smith Band drummer Jay Dee Daugherty handling their live sound until Patti herself intervened, following an incident at CBGB where Field screamed "Dirty stinking hippy!"

at her. Reck left for Japan, where he would form his own quasi-No Wave group, Friction; he was replaced by early DNA bassist Gordon Stevenson.

James Sclavunos, then a member of The Gynaecologists with Rhys Chatham and Nina Canal, had interviewed Lunch for his fanzine, *No*, which he regularly used to scam free entry to CBGB. "All the other guys from the magazine were scared of her. She wanted to fuck me, and I was a virgin, so I had even more reason to be afraid of her, but I wasn't going to let her know it. She finally cornered me one night and made her intentions very clear; she would have done it on the spot, I think, only I was too shy, and the bathrooms were too busy that night. It was at a loft in Tribeca where all these downtown art bands – DNA, Mars, Teenage Jesus, Theoretical Girls, and The Gynaecologists – played. I guess it was a defining moment for No Wave, because Eno came down, and that night inspired him to assemble *No New York*."

Anya Philips, Chance's lover and The Contortions' ever enterprising manager, had met Brian Eno, then visiting New York, and helped introduce the obscure strategist to Mars, DNA, Teenage Jesus and the other groups in this new underground scene. Inspired by their fearless, fearsome invention, he began to plan a compilation of the best groups; soon, however, the project changed from a snapshot of 10 of these underground bands to a showcase for four of them – The Contortions, DNA, Mars and Teenage Jesus – contributing four tracks each.

"It's been said that I had some influence over keeping the project's perspective narrowed to the most extreme bands of that period," says Lunch. "Compilations with just one song from each band are lame, they tell you *nothing*. All of these groups, if you heard one song you heard 'em all, but you might as well get a fat dose. But I wasn't the dictator on the project, I suggested the title, and that was it."

No New York, as the album would be titled, remains the essential document of the No Wave scene – even though it has officially been out of print for years, existing as a Japanese bootleg CD sold in the "import" bins – though Lunch wasn't happy with the sound of Teenage Jesus on the album. "Eno did absolutely nothing. I was much happier with the singles we recorded with Robert Quine. I ran up to Robert at CBGB and fell to my knees, praising him as *the* guitar god. He wasn't afraid of me – he kept a screwdriver in his pocket."

"I got involved with Teenage Jesus pretty much right after Lydia deflowered me," remembers Sclavunos, who replaced Stevenson after the No New York sessions. "I had a saxophone, which at the time qualified me as a saxophone player, but Lydia wanted me to play bass. I think the most important thing was the attitude; she always wanted the music to sound like rough sex, like a hate-fuck. I could relate to that, having recently been deflowered by Lydia."

James Chance aside, the bands on *No New York* didn't expand their discographies much further: Mars, who split in December 1978, recorded about another half-hour's worth of material, while DNA's 1980 debut, *A Taste Of DNA*, lasted 10 or so minutes, the group disbanding two years later. Teenage Jesus And The Jerks split in 1979, and Lydia left New York soon after for Los Angeles, and then Europe. Before she left, however, she made a wordless connection with a tall, young, blond-haired stranger on the Second Avenue subway.

"I have a very fond memory of one particular stare-off, when something sorta clicked," remembers Lydia. "Though I didn't meet actually him until I returned to New York."

"I lived on 13th Street, between A & B," wrote Thurston Moore, years later. "The only person I was aware of living on that street was Lydia Lunch… I saw Lydia standing on the corner of 13th and A and she had a nose ring. Nobody had nose rings in those days. I thought she was exquisite. Later I saw her on the platform of the L train at 1st Avenue. I came barrelling down the stairs through the turnstile and nearly ran her over. She stared at me very wide-eyed and I continued on. I became good friends with Lydia many years later and she told me she was obsessed with tall, skinny white guys at the time, and we were both of an age and demeanor where something wild could've definitely developed. Who knows what would've happened if I had become Lydia's lover at 18?"[14]

NOTES

1 *Annie Hall*, 1977
2 *Please Kill Me*, pg. 5
3 Ibid, pg. 7
4 *The Real Frank Zappa Book*, pg. 203
5 *Psychotic Reactions and Carburettor Dung*, pg. 172
6 Ibid, pg. 337
7 Author's interview, March 2007
8 *Please Kill Me*, pg 116
9 Author's interview, March 2007
10 *End Of The Century: The Story Of The Ramones*, 2003
11 Author's interview, March 2007
12 Author's Interview, February 2007
13 Ink19 interview, http://www.ink19.com/issues/january2003/interviews/alanVegaPartI.html
14 *Alabama Wildman*, pg 5

CHAPTER TWO

So You Wanna Be A Rock'n'Roll Star

> "I moved to New York early '77. I had planned it for the last couple of years; I fantasised about it constantly. My fantasies were fueled by the progressive development of punk. It was David Johansen to Patti Smith to John Cale to The Ramones to The Dictators to *Punk Magazine* to *New York Rocker* to *Rock Scene* to St. Mark's Place to Bleeker Bob's to Manic Panic to Gem Spa to Max's to CBGB."
>
> Thurston Moore[1]

For Thurston Moore, relocating to New York was the consummation of a love affair he'd been nurturing throughout his adolescence. Precociously rock-literate, he'd pored over the lurid pages of rock magazines like *Creem* and *Rock Scene* from an early age, scanning for photographs of favourites David Bowie and Alice Cooper, the two very separate figureheads of the early Seventies glam scene; an iconic shot of Iggy Pop spray-painted silver made a particularly deep impression.

The youngest of three children, Thurston had foraged on vinyl hand-me-downs from his older brother, so schooled in classic rock that the first record he purchased was Iron Butterfly's proto-metal epic 'In-A-Gadda-Da-Vida', later buying The Rolling Stones' *Their Satanic Majesties Request* simply because his older brother Gene said he should. He would later note that many of his musician contemporaries had experienced a similar formative indoctrination into the delights of Classic Rock from their elder siblings.

Thurston lived in Bethel, a town in south-western Connecticut. Born in Coral Gables, Florida, on July 25, 1958, his family moved to upstate

Tennessee and then finally Bethel, his father George E. Moore taking a post at Western Connecticut State College. A professor in music and philosophy who also played piano and composed classical works, George passed his abundant love of music on to his son.

As the rock press turned its attention to New York, so did Thurston, falling first for The New York Dolls, then Patti Smith; his first "punk" show would be a Patti Smith Group gig in nearby Westport. When Thurston was 17, The Ramones released their debut album, which he bought in a local department store. "I was at the perfect age to discover The Ramones," he'd later remember. "I was a 6′6 geek who was looked upon as a freaky dude, so it was great to discover a band that basically said, 'We're geeky, and we're gonna thrash.' Plus, there was an intellectualism to them that didn't seem to exist anywhere else. Hearing this record was a landmark event for me. I credit it as the biggest thing that made me want to play music."[2]

Bethel, a green and pleasant suburb, was pretty much a bummer for a young, aspiring "punk" kid; hardly anyone even knew what "punk" was, and most who did thought it sucked, with the same kind of knee-jerk inevitability of the infamous "Disco Sucks" demonstrations of a few years later. One fellow student at his high school, Harold Paris, shared Moore's love for punk and for Patti Smith, and the two would attend occasional shows together, and spend hours hanging out and listening to records and reading rock magazines. New York was only 60 miles away, a place vivid in their imaginations, conjured from glossy clippings hoarded in scrapbooks and fleeting school trips to the big city.

"I was impressionable and she came on like an alien," remembered Thurston, of his fascination with Patti Smith, in an interview he conducted with her in 1996. "The first time I met her was in 1975 in a magazine. It was two poems about three wishes: rock'n'roll, sex, and New York City. Her photo was stark – no disco colour flash. It was anti-glam, nocturnal staring eyes, black leather trousers. She was skinny and smart. She posed as if she were the coolest boy in the city. And she was. I could only imagine her world through her poems: telling, truthful, dirty, hopeful. I wanted to meet her and take her to a movie, but she was so unobtainable and fantastic. I could only entrust my faith to the future. The future would allow me to have a date with Patti Smith, or at least hang out with her."[3]

In the years before the internet offered music fans the opportunity to shop at record stores across the globe and find kindred spirits on online messageboards with whom to debate subjects like the best Sonic Youth album, being a fan of such a relatively obscure and subterranean subculture involved a considerable investment of time and effort, tracking down records, finding out information about the artists, and making connections with like-minded souls sharing your penchant for ugly noise. As with all such endeavours, the hunt was very much part of the fun, and with an enviable, infectious enthusiasm that endures to this day, Thurston immersed himself, driving to New Haven in the next county to pick up the records the department store wouldn't stock at Cutler's, and lose himself in their racks of rock magazines and fanzines. It was here that he bumped into J.D. King, an employee at a nearby arts supply shop, near the Velvet Underground section, striking up a conversation that would blossom into pen-friendship.

In November 1976, Thurston and Harold Paris lit out in the Moores' careworn Volkswagen Beetle – the archetypal Seventies American teenager's runaround – and made their way blindly to the Big Apple, in search of the seedy underground landmarks they'd read so much about. Miraculously, they bumbled their way to Max's Kansas City, where they managed to catch a performance by Suicide, that night supported by The Cramps, relocated Californian hellions whose unsettling, darkly sexual music worshipped malevolent Fifties rockabilly, psychotic Sixties garage-rock, and exploitation movies. Playing their very first show that night, they were fronted by black-clad contortionist singer Lux Interior; their gothic burlesque doubtless unsettled the two rubes from Bethel, something they similarly doubtlessly attempted to conceal.

The confrontational antics of Suicide's Alan Vega proved a step too far, however. The duo were playing at full-on earbleed volume, saturating the stage in bright green light, as Vega – dressed in a fright-wig, streaming tears, and with theatrical scars painted on his face – wandered into the audience and began assaulting anyone within arm's reach, smashing glasses and licking people's faces. Thurston and Harold left midway through the set, a little disturbed by what they'd seen – but not so much that they didn't begin to make regular weekend pilgrimages to the city, including one memorable visit for New Year's Eve in 1976, which Thurston spent tripping on mescaline at New York's Palladium as John Cale, Television and Patti Smith performed.

"By the time Patti came onstage I was cool," he wrote later. "I almost lost it during Cale, *seriously*." The show climaxed with an all-star onstage jam through 'My Generation' featuring David Johansen and Fred "Sonic" Smith. "And then they were all gone, except for Patti and Fred. The MC5 were very heavy for me; I was even wearing a Sonic's Rendezvous Band [Smith's post-MC5 outfit] button, which I still have. There was all this chaos onstage, and everybody split, but they stayed. Both were wearing guitars – and it wasn't like they were scraping and fuzzing out feedback insania – they just stood there shoulder to shoulder, with a high, clear ringing Fender pickup feedback coming out of the amp… Patti leaned her head on Sonic's shoulder and the audience just stood there like me, grubby, sweaty, full of pot and shit and post-acid blowout, and I recognised that as a defining moment of what I wanted to do with my life."[4]

1976 had been a tumultuous, traumatic year for Thurston; he had graduated high school that summer, an event overshadowed by the untimely death of his father from a brain tumour, which affected him deeply. He signed up for classes at Western Connecticut State University, but received a letter from King, who had relocated to New York with some fellow Rhode Island School of Design graduates with the intention of forming a group. King invited Thurston to live in the communal loft the four band members were sharing at 85 South Street, to play bass with them. Thurston had proved highly proficient at the flute in grade school, until he was told he'd have to wear a bow tie when he performed, at which he quit in disgust. Early attempts at the electric guitar had proved frustrating; his older brother seemed much more of a natural guitarist, coaxing Hendrixian wail out of the practice amp at every opportunity, assuming possession of the axe soon afterwards. It took the fast-riffing power chords of The Ramones and The Sex Pistols to lure Thurston back to the instrument, digging the ease with which he could ape their guttural roar on his cheap guitar.

King described his aesthetic as "punkadelic": he envisioned the band somehow fusing garage-rock with genres he believed kindred with punk-folk-rock and psychedelic rock. Thurston began crashing at the loft every weekend, eventually electing, with his mother's moral and financial support, to move there in early 1977, taking with him the sunburst Fender Stratocaster as a farewell gift from his brother. He fit in well with his new room-mates: King was also 6′6″ tall, while bassist Bob Pullin was a towering 6′10″. Jarringly average-sized drummer Dan Walworth rounded out the quartet, who played their first show in late 1977 as Room Tone at a loft party nearby.

Moore's first weeks in New York were a halcyon whirl of drunken nights out in East Village: leaving Max's late one evening following a show by transsexual Warhol alumnus and provocative punk performer Wayne (later known as Jayne) County, Thurston and friends bumped into Joey Ramone, leader of the The Ramones, who then led them the short walk to CBGB. At that venue, later, Thurston would absently bite his lower lip while watching Patti Smith, only for Patti to bite her lip back at him in response, a connection he would never forget.

Soon, however, he would be possessed of an unshakeable sense that perhaps he had arrived just a little too late to join the party that drew him there. "All the bands I came to New York to see were gone," he recalled. "I went to New York pretty much to see Patti Smith and Television, and they were on major labels, and major labels just did not give them the time of day, because they didn't immediately do anything. So Television floundered, Richard Hell floundered, Patti got married and just left, Blondie became a disco band and were huge. . ."[5] Inspiration came in the form of the new music happening in the underground, No Wave. "It was the next generation of the downtown music scene, all these new kids from art schools moving to New York and taking over the scene. Blondie became radio-friendly, so they created this real harsh, nihilist music called No-Wave. It was atonal, chord-less noise rock played by these weirdo personalities."[6]

Now a regular fixture in the audience at CBGB and Max's, Thurston was a swift convert to this new music, while never recanting his love for Patti and Television and The Voidoids. No Wave was fracturing into two loose factions. On one side were the abrasive East Village bands – Mars, DNA, The Contortions and Teenage Jesus And The Jerks – that had been showcased on No New York. On the other side was a slew of groups whose music was a touch more cerebral, less extreme – but no less striking – than their East Village kin. There was a palpable enmity between the No New York set and the groups operating from neighbouring SoHo, including The Gynaecologists, Theoretical Girls (featuring Glenn Branca and Jeffrey Lohn), and Red Transistor (featuring guitarist Rudolph Grey and James Sclavunos). "They thought we were a bit artsy, and they were coming from more of the Velvets drug kind of thing," remembered Branca. "That was bullshit."[7] The SoHo groups later boycotted the rock clubs, choosing to perform at loft parties and galleries, establishing new and sympathetic venues for the music. Thurston was a fan of both factions, though he was initially cool on Teenage Jesus And The Jerks because of Lunch's acidly hilarious "barefoot hippy chick" comments about his heroine Patti Smith.

Thurston moved out of the loft to an apartment on East 13th Street, a neighbourhood shady enough that he avoided walking the streets after dark if at all possible. He met his $110 a month rent through a series of short-lived, low-paid jobs vaguely related to the arts, and the assistance of his mother. In his 2000 book *Alabama Wildman*, Thurston recalled being "bonkers, alone", spending his days searching the sidewalk for loose change so he could go and see outdated movies running at the St Mark's Cinema.

It was in the lobby of the cinema, a regular meeting place for downtown arts figures, musicians and "East Village Puerto Rican dudes", that he crossed paths with Richard Hell, taking a seat at a table Hell was sitting at with his girlfriend "as if I was a dishevelled poet punk hoping to impress them."[8]

Room Tone rechristened themselves The Coachmen at the end of 1977, in part as a knowing tribute to the countless forgotten garage-rock bands who took the moniker during the Sixties. As 1978 dawned, they began playing their first shows; in their short life, they would play CBGB, another local club friendly to underground bands called Tier 3, a series of private loft parties thrown by figures in the art scene, a club called the Botany Talk House in the floral district and, for one night only, Max's Kansas City. Of all the local venues they played, A's – an artist-run Lower East Side loft space under the aegis of Brooklyn-born multimedia artist Arleen Schloss, a pioneer of 'xerox-art', and Todd Jorgenson, conveniently a photocopy business owner – was perhaps as close as they got to a regular haunt.

The Coachmen sounded oddly timid and out of time with their downtown contemporaries, eschewing the dissonance, noise, anger and confrontation of No Wave in favour of a more studied, melodic sound. It was King's band, and his songs were taut, lean, hewn in the image of The Modern Lovers and early Talking Heads. A posthumous five-track EP released on New Alliance in 1988, *Failure To Thrive*, is hardly an illuminative artifact like The Neon Boys' EP: the guitar terrorism and avant tunings that would later make Thurston's playing so instantly recognisable have yet to influence his playing. The bright, chiming guitars anticipate early R.E.M., weaving a charmingly amateur pop from an ungainly bundle of odd chords, King's murmur submerged under the guitar. 'Thurston's Song', also sung by King, dissolves from a fizzing bustle of jangle into a measured passage of soloing from Thurston of a Television vintage – while no blast of the flavour of noise that would later become his trademark, you can almost hear the wind whipping through his stupid mop. A couple of years younger than his college-graduate bandmates, Thurston was still enthralled with punk rock, where the other Coachmen had more middlebrow "arty" tastes.

In late 1978, Thurston had a brush with an infamous luminary from London's punk rock scene. Shortly after joining The Sex Pistols in 1977, troubled brute bassist Sid Vicious had met Johnny Thunders, touring with his Heartbreakers across the UK supporting The Clash and The Damned; Thunders goaded the impressionable Vicious into trying heroin. The Heartbreakers exited the UK leaving Nancy Spungen, a notorious and damaged groupie, in their wake; Spungen first fixated on The Sex Pistols' brilliant, sardonic leader Johnny Rotten. Perceptively, Rotten deflected her advances and – in a move he would later regret – shoved her in the direction of Vicious. In the months that had passed since, The Sex Pistols had unravelled during their American tour, and, following some ill-conceived final Pistols sessions without the exiting Rotten in London, Sid and Nancy had decamped to the Chelsea Hotel, living out the sordid final chapters of their lives in a haze of heroin abuse.

Ensconced in New York, Vicious had played a couple of live shows with The Idols, a backing band featuring local musicians and boasting a rhythm section of ex-Dolls Arthur Kane and Jerry Nolan, a former paramour of Nancy's. In October 1978, Nancy was found stabbed to death in the bathroom of their apartment, with Vicious as the main murder suspect. He would soon be arrested and held at Riker's Island prison on the East River, where he was allegedly gang-raped, before gaining release after his record label posted bail and fatally overdosing on heroin at a party to celebrate his freedom. In the weeks immediately following the murder, however, Sid roamed the New York nightclubs.

Thurston and his bandmates had gone down to CBGB to catch a performance by Judy Nylon, an artist and singer who won her place as a footnote in music history when she gifted a convalescing Brian Eno with an album of soothing 18th-century harp music, inspiring his later explorations in "ambient" music; Nylon's drummer was a friend of The Coachmen, and they could be sure to get a table. During Nylon's performance, as she was halfway into a brutal crawl through Elvis' 'Jailhouse Rock', a gaunt Vicious took a seat at The Coachmen's table. "He was the skinniest," remembered Thurston. "His skin was totally white. And he had those looks and mannerisms that you knew he just had to have. My dream was to start a band with him that would totally kill. He was down and out and I was ready to immerse myself in him. Total punk rock. But I was in an art-rock band. He was into heroin, murder and weird sex from after-hours hell. When he died it was one of the most intense moments of my life. I watched the TV reports like it was Kennedy being assassinated. I collected and have to this day every newspaper clipping there was."[9]

The Coachmen saw the new decade in at A's, playing as the bells tolled with Alan Vega as headliner. Later in January 1980, they shared a bill at CBGB with another New York art-loft band, The Flucts, who'd named themselves after the Fluxus intermedia art movement. Originally a college band formed by students studying at nearby Binghamton University, the group had reconvened in New York, led by guitarist Lee Ranaldo.

* * *

Lee Ranaldo was born in Glen Cove, a town on the north shore of Nassau, a densely populated and well-to-do suburban county on Long Island, east of New York City, on February 3, 1956. His mother was a pianist, and Ranaldo remembers "a musical environment… there was always music and singing in my house growing up."[10] Born to a large Italian-American family, Ranaldo's childhood was a blur of gatherings in big Brooklyn houses with his relatives, "Aunts, uncles, wine-drinking, bocce games – a great deal of the old country in that life," he would later write. He felt a certain distance from this background, however. "I suppose in many ways it ends with me and others of my generation. Finally, the old ways are seen as merely archaic, and no longer as a part of the warp and woof of life. It took three generations, but I can call myself 'American' fairly safely. Although I still have shadowy memories of an Italian heritage, the language is now gone, the great big families, even the home-cooked tomato sauces are going."[11]

The teenaged Ranaldo chafed at the constraints of life in Glen Cove, where he killed many hours idly speeding around deserted parking lots with the local gearheads. "I lived in suburban shelter until the time I was 18," he wrote in his journal. "A hellish vacuum. No communication with parents, no conception of their world, sadly we merely co-existed. As soon as I learned how to think, their teachings taught me somehow to turn it off and shut it up inside." He dreamed of being a writer, though his love for words was equally matched by his love for music; he grew up bathed in the sounds of Sixties AM radio, running the gamut of American pop and beaming The Beatles into the Ranaldo home when Beatlemania broke in America in 1964. American psychedelia was a particular passion, one that Ranaldo clung to long after punk revisionism declared war on everything "hippy".

Contemporary reviews of Television that compared them to The Grateful Dead – accurate as they turn out to be – were intended as backhanded compliments at best. From the exterior, The Grateful Dead seemed the apex of everything that was detestably "hippy", with their sprawling, indulgent instrumental jams, their addled mysticism and epic drug abuse, and a travelling nation of fans who gave up their lives to follow the band across America, many paying their way by selling acid to the communities that would spring up in the parking lots of venues before the Dead played. The stereotype obscured a group who, in those very psychedelic excursions, reached heights of improvisational reverie still to be eclipsed, indulging not themselves but their audience with fearless, adventurous, visionary music discovered in the outer regions of their imaginations. Alienated from the culture that surrounded him, the young Ranaldo would listen to The

Grateful Dead for hours, travelled to see shows by the group, even caught performances by side projects of the group's revered frontman, Jerry Garcia.

"Some of those shows still stand out as among the best I've attended, anywhere, ever," he wrote in August 1995, shortly after Garcia's death. "No bullshitting at their shows, no platform heels or mega light shows to mask the fact that this was just a group of ordinary mortals up there doing the best they could. Many nights they took us far over the rainbow with them. Those guys (and gal) from the Haight covered a lot of musical turf, a lot of history – and left plenty of avenues yet to be mined."[12] The Dead's open-minded, near avant-garde creativity was evident in Ranaldo's first experiments with musical instruments. "When I began playing electric guitar, and even banging on a piano before that, it was always obvious that setting notes free into the air has a magical quality to it. Something special happens when tones ring out, made by one's own hand. I always desired to make spontaneous creative tone poems with others, as soon as I learned to play. Like building castles our of cloud vapour – you build them up and then they drift off to the stars."[13]

While studying painting and print-making at Binghamton (he enrolled, however, for science classes), Lee turned on to the Beats; following an exploratory cross-country road trip the summer after his first semester, he read Jack Kerouac's highway odyssey *On The Road*. Kerouac's observations and vignettes suited a mind opened by such travels, resonating with the young Ranaldo; he soon immersed himself in the writing of the Beat poets, another interest that would endure. Allen Ginsberg was a particular inspiration, not only for his poetic works, but for his bravely outspoken, anti-establishment ideas on sexuality and drug-taking, a decade before the permissive generation would remove such taboos. For Ranaldo, Patti Smith represented a link between the worlds of poetry and rock'n'roll that would lead him towards punk.

Ranaldo would travel from Binghamton with fellow student David Linton to catch shows at CBGB and Max's Kansas City, the former struck by how down to earth the artists seemed, normal people like himself rather than the glittery gods playing the stadium rock shows. Soon, they formed The Fluks, with David playing drums, Lee on guitars, and two keyboard players, reforming after graduation in New York, as The Flucts. While their music has never enjoyed a commercial release (both Ranaldo and Linton possess live tapes, with vague plans for eventual release), they were an intriguing proposition, mixing piercing Farfisa din and Moog drone with guitar squall and tape loops, an idea inspired by the experiments of Steve Reich.

New York nurtured Ranaldo's taste for experimental arts. "A very powerful culture was brewing in the worlds of music and art," he remembered later, "which interacted with each other. You had many artists working in various fields, painters forming bands, guitar players making sculptures. It was a very high time when much great work was made. Many people were willing to experiment, try new things, and that was the character of the city which influenced us most. I wanted to become a part of that."[14] In the summer of 1979, shortly after they had moved to New York, Ranaldo and Linton attended a performance by "Meltdown, featuring Rhys Chatham", intrigued by a blurb in New York alternative paper *The Village Voice* promising "Steve Reich meets The Ramones", and the audacity of a group calling themselves Meltdown so soon after the worst nuclear power accident in American history, at nearby Three Mile Island.

The gig would have a momentous impact upon Ranaldo, and his nascent ideas about how he might express himself musically. As the show began, drummer Wharton Tiers manned a single hi-hat cymbal behind a wall of three guitarists: David Rosenbloom, Glenn Branca (a last-minute substitute) and – stood in the centre, high on Quaaludes and amphetamines, wearing Sixties psychedelic granny glasses – Rhys Chatham. The music they played was striking, Tiers beating eighth notes on the hi-hat as the guitarists struck their detuned guitars rhythmically, forming some grand, shifting chord with their amassed noise. As the din rose, Chatham – lost in the pounding, swelling sound – stumbled absently off the stage, blindly clubbing patrons and smashing glasses as he played.

"Something was going on inside the music that I couldn't put my finger on," remembered Ranaldo, years later. "Although the players seemed to be simply downstroking with flat picks across the length of the strings, amazing things were happening in the sound field above our heads. Overtones danced all around the notes, getting more animated, turning into first gamelan orchestras, then later a choir of voices, and finally a complete maelstrom of crushing sonic complexity, ping-ponging over the minimalist low notes of the rocking chord."[15]

After playing this single chord for over half an hour, Chatham led the group into a second, even more cataclysmic piece, which saw less hardy sonic travellers evacuate the venue. Those who stayed were treated to an assault of further monochordal noise, scoring a searing black-and-white slide show of five disturbing images selected by artist Robert Longo. Ranaldo was left reeling: "I had some sort of ecstatic experience there, listening to this strange music and watching these images. I say strange because on the one hand it was rock, really rocking out and familiar. But it had this other quality to it as well; something else was going on there. This was 'art' too. It was our entry into an amazing new world of music being created below 14th Street in lower Manhattan. I had never heard anything like it before, yet that night I felt it was something I'd been hearing in my head forever. Here it was, in front of me in the flesh, finally in real life."

Chatham's background lay in the avant garde. He'd worked as a piano tuner for La Monte Young, studied under Tony Conrad and Morton Subotnick, and composed works of his own that were ground-breaking and conceptual. One early piece, 1971's *Two Gongs*, lasted over an hour, as Chatham and friend played the titular gongs, the volume, tempo and intensity rising and falling, until the gongs scared up a near unbearable roar. Around this time, Chatham began programming shows at the Kitchen, a loft on Mercer Street in Soho. As the porous membrane that separated such "serious" music and the experimental rock music occurring in the underground clubs began to dissolve, Chatham was only one of a number of avant-garde composers looking towards rock for inspiration, and as a further arena for expression. The relationship was reciprocal. "Rock was pushing its boundaries to the limits, too," observed Chatham. "By 1980 it had became common practice for rock groups to incorporate noise into their sound palette, not as a mere effect, but as the whole piece! In New York the art world was embracing the new rock, it got to the point where it seemed that half the visual art world was going to the clubs, and the other half were actually in the groups! The breakdown of barriers separating the genres of art music, improvised music, and rock was complete."[16]

One of his fellow guitarists that night would further evolve Chatham's multiple-guitar theories. Born in Harrisburg in Pennsylvania in 1948, Glenn Branca studied theatre at Emerson College, an esteemed liberal arts institute in Boston. On graduation, Branca decamped to London, where his absurdist farce, *Scratching The Surface*, ran for two weeks in 1973. A year later, he returned to Boston and co-founded the Bastard Theater group with John Rehberger, operating out of a loft on Massachusetts Avenue. The Bastard Theater put on two well-received productions, with live score composed by Branca and Rehberger, and performed by the onstage cast. Simultaneously, the duo also wrote and performed music as The Dubious Music Ensemble, utilising avant-garde techniques and a broad selection of eclectic instrumentation, Rehberger specialising on saxophone, Branca on guitar.

Branca moved to New York in 1976, with an eye to bringing the Bastard Theater's confrontational approach to the downtown arts scene. A year later, he was collaborating with Jeffrey Lohn, a writer, musician and artist he'd met while hanging out at The Placenter, a loft space in Chelsea. A classically trained musician who abhorred most rock'n'roll post-Little Richard, Lohn was inspired by a Dead Boys show at CBGB to begin making music informed by, and in some ways resembling, this "punk" rock. The duo formed Theoretical Girls (their name suggested by their artist friend, Dan Graham, who invited them to perform at his shows), a quartet with Wharton Tiers on drums, Margaret Dewys on keyboards, and Lohn playing guitar and keyboards and singing. Branca again played guitar. The group played their inaugural performance at the Experimental Intermedia Foundation in early 1978, an arts support group and performance space on Centre Street, and began to play at local lofts and, until the SoHo boycott came into force, the rock clubs.

Lohn wrote the lion's share of the material, songs that infested the primal noise of punk with a post-modern anarchy. Their signature song, 'Theoretical Girls', was a swelling tease of an anthem, Tiers hammering at cymbals and tom as guitars revved and voices yelled "1-2-3-4" like malfunctioning android Ramones, their script a stuttering loop counting down to a power-chord "lift-off" that never arrived. Others, like 'Computer Dating', raced perilously before slowing to a molten, distended crawl; others still, like the martial 'US Millie', sounded like some missing link between twisted Sixties GI proto-punks The Monks and Talking Heads. A self-released single, 'Theoretical Girls', spread word of their experiments further than the borders of New York; indeed, The Theoretical Girls managed to travel to Paris in their lifetime, performing three shows there. By the end of summer 1978, Lohn signalled that he wanted to focus on work outside of the group, and that Theoretical Girls would continue as a part-time concern. Branca subsequently formed The Static, enlisting his girlfriend Barbara Ess (with whose group Daily Life Branca had previously played) on bass, and artist Christine Hahn on drums.

The songs Branca wrote for Theoretical Girls and The Static would see belated release in 1997, on *Songs 77–79*, via the Atavistic label. Tracks like 'Don't Let Me Stop You' built from a primal, repetitive riff to explosive epics of squalling, slaloming dynamism, Branca beginning to incorporate avant-garde techniques like alternate tunings and "third bridge" manipulations into the music, but with an approach steeped in the volume and attack, the very *physicality* of rock'n'roll, coining ideas he would pursue further with Chatham on the Meltdown piece, and throughout his career. Footage of a solo performance by Branca in Jeffrey Lohn's loft from 1978, included on Acute Records' 2003 re-release of Branca's The Ascension, is electrifying: in a blackened room, before a stark white projection screen, Branca shakes and thrashes wildly at a beaten-up telecaster (with 'Theoretical Girls' scrawled on its body), strangling an ugly-beautiful fracture of noise and busted notes from the neck, at one point licking his fingers as they traumatised the fret-board, camera flashbulbs popping away. "The funny thing was that the more outrageous the music became, the bigger the audience became," remembers Branca. "It became clear to me that I could do anything I wanted." Invited to perform at an Easter Festival at Max's Kansas City, Branca chose the event to debut a new piece he had composed, accurately entitled 'Instrumental For Six Guitars'. "It sounded fucking great and people loved it. I just kept working in that direction, on different tunings and stringings. It was a completely different approach to the whole system. It really only interested me if I was doing something I hadn't heard before."[17]

The Static parted ways at the end of 1979, when Christine Hahn moved to Berlin. Branca focused his energies upon further compositions for the guitarkestra he would assemble. In collaboration with Ed Bahlman, owner of a Greenwich Village record store called 99 Records, he started up a record label, named after the shop; Bahlman promoted shows and produced some groups, along with running 99. Bahlman and Branca were inspired by the example of the British independent labels that sold in the store's import bins, such as On-U Sound (run by punk-savvy dub producer Adrian Sherwood) and Rough Trade, a label run out of a West London record shop that would play a seismic role in British underground music. The British punk scene had sparked off a wave of independent labels, a D.I.Y. ethic that wouldn't really hit America until hardcore; without an infrastructure of small independent labels to chronicle the scene, much of the music of No Wave and its afterglow – music too fierce and uncompromising and resolutely, essentially uncommercial – was never documented for posterity.

Having convinced Bahlman that their venture would succeed, the first release on 99 was Branca's own *Lesson No. 1*. The mini-LP's two lengthy instrumental tracks, played by a group led by Branca on guitar, laid the groundwork for his subsequent symphonies, by turns deeply beautiful and scarifyingly fierce: a hurricane of sound teetering between harmony and cacophony, drawing strength from both. 'Lesson #1 For Electric Guitar' has an almost pastoral quality, gracefully shifting back and forth across two monumental chords from minimal, metronomic guitar chime, to lush and suffocating walls of multi-tracked, painstakingly exact strum, bass and drums scoring an earthy, primal dynamism, a visceral anthemicism. Second guitarist on 'Lesson #1 For Electric Guitar' had been Michael Gross, a sometime Fluct. 'Dissonance', on side B, was well titled; opening with a tight and twisted psycho-funk in The Contortions' vein, it revisits the atonal violence of Theoretical Girls and The Static, this time armed with layer after layer of multi-tracked, ricocheting, razor-edged guitar, Branca detuning and assaulting his instruments so they sound like tolling bells, resonant gamelan, phosphorent flashes of electricity illuminating the strobe-like din.

Early exposure to Branca's guitarkestra, a performance at A's, made a deep impression upon Thurston, who was struck by Branca's experiments with scordatura, the alternate tunings which, when combined with other, similarly or sympathetically "detuned" guitars, opened up the unexplored fields of sound his music uncovered. "I heard the electric guitar doing something I had thought about but never figured to execute," he remembered. "It was volume, dynamics, theatre, and artful rock'n'roll…full-on ROCK propulsivity."[18] That Branca was coining a vocabulary from unorthodox methods such as scraping guitar strings, or creating a "third bridge" by levering a screwdriver underneath the strings on the neck (yielding bell-like resonant sounds), was not lost on him either.

"I decided to play the guitar as if I existed in a pure state of mind and could attack it with flowing, mindful, sensitive energy/expression. I knew nothing of jazz, free-jazz, or any studied musical concept of improvisation. I had a ratty, skinny-lapel suit jacket (all East Village poor-boy punk rockers had one) and no job."[19] With The Coachmen about to unravel, Thurston began jamming with other local musicians, trying out his new, energetic, freeform approach, hammering and slamming his guitar with abandon while jumping recklessly and without heed to gravity. One such collaborator, both unnerved and impressed by his wild moves, was Miranda Stanton, an artist and keyboard-player then dating a friend of Thurston's.

The next Coachmen show, their penultimate, was at a performance loft owned by Giorgio Gomelsky, a Russian-born impresario who'd made his name putting on the first Rolling Stones shows in London in the early Sixties, and had recently moved to New York, to put on America's first progressive music festival. Miranda showed up for the performance, bringing her friend Kim along with her.

* * *

A decade and change later, as Kim Althea Gordon and her husband Thurston Moore were deciding what to name their first and imminent child, they absently toyed with the name Lolita. The idea tickled Gordon; her mother had given her a copy of Nabokov's tale of a middle-aged man's sexual obsession with a prepubescent girl when she was 12. "She was afraid I'd turn out like the character Lolita or something," Gordon remembered later. "She made it so black and white, you know, like if you read and you're intellectual then men will like you a lot and not just for your body. She was just afraid, because I was so sexually precocious and mature for my age, that I'd get pregnant by the time I was 13."[20]

Kim was born on April 28, 1953, growing up in Los Angeles, where her father, Professor Calvin Wayne Gordon, was Dean of Sociology and Education at nearby UCLA; her mother was a seamstress who worked from home. Kim describes herself as "a model child", if also something of a tomboy. She was schooled at the liberal, progressive University Elementary School at UCLA, an unorthodox laboratory teaching environment. "It was all about creativity, we used to make mud huts, spears and tortillas. It was all about learning through doing."[21]

Creativity and expression were very much a part of her home life too. She received private dance tuition and art lessons; she dreamed of attending art school from an early age. Her parents were avid jazz listeners, always playing records at home. However, when she was 12, Gordon says, "I wanted to be bad! My older brother, who I looked up to, was bad. He was very mean to me, and he later became schizophrenic in his early 20s, paranoid schizophrenic. He was really hostile."[22]

Her older brother, Keller, was three and a half years older than she was, a passionate music lover who nevertheless never played an instrument, educating his sister in the arcane magic of Bob Dylan, the electric thrill of rock-'n'roll, the star-scraping improvised excursions of John Coltrane and Ornette Coleman. "In the late Sixties he used to wear all white, carry a Bible and live in Malibu. He studied classical literature and wrote sonnets about maidens. It was very Renaissance Fair-like. His friends were like followers – almost Manson-like. All that stuff was in the air at the time. He had a girlfriend in high school who was killed by the Manson family."[23]

The Gordon family moved to Hong Kong in 1965, where they lived for a year; it was here that Kim met her first boyfriend. As a devotee of Roy Orbison's inconsolable balladry who would buy Beatles singles on the day of release and had recently transferred her affections to The Rolling Stones, it's unsurprising that her first beau was an English boy called Steve who claimed he was a drummer in a rock band. "I always seemed to have musician boyfriends," she reflected. "It took me a long time to figure out that I wanted to be able to play the music. I was really intrigued by it, even though I had no musical training." Later, a friend of Keller's played in a band that supported British Invaders Herman's Hermits when they played Hong Kong, with Kim in attendance; she would also get a taste of Hong Kong nightlife visiting the hotel bars, where Chinese girls wearing "weird party dresses" would sing Beatles songs.

On returning to California, Kim enrolled in a public school, a culture shock after the liberal laboratory school. "Somehow I ended up hanging out with the white trash, listening to Motown records," she remembered. "I was rebellious as a teenager. I would do stuff like stay out all night just for the hell of it, just cos my mom said I couldn't. I didn't completely become a juvenile delinquent, cause I come from a nice, academic, middle-class family." At 14, she was regularly taking the $10 Friday flight to San Francisco, where she would drop acid and catch bands like Jefferson Airplane and The Grateful Dead at the Fillmore; she never visited the Sunset Strip, however, a rawer and darker scene – her mother absolutely forbade her. A year later, Kim was arrested after she'd been caught smoking pot with her boyfriend in a cave on Tom Sawyer's Island, part of the Disneyland theme park in Anaheim. The indiscretion earned her a night in the clink.

Kim later ascribed much of her rebelliousness to her frustrations at the double standard between how she and her brother were treated; Keller's behaviour was excused as teenaged boisterousness, while Kim perceived that there were different expectations for her, because she was a girl. She saw the impact of the feminist movement and the sexual revolution in the divorcée friends of her parents, the women who were using their new-found freedom to discover the world and themselves. Kim didn't want to be simply a wife or a mother; she harboured ambitions to be an artist. She would spend hours listening to records by Janis Joplin; she later wrote that "listening to her voice, I knew it as a model for not being afraid to do something which may be considered ugly in order to create something entirely original – and beautiful. Women were creatively a little freer then – they had yet to be commodified as 'women in rock'."[24]

When she was 17, Kim took acid for the last time. "I was sick of having mind-expanding revelations," she recalled. "I knew it was artificial, so it wasn't fun. I couldn't wait to come down, so I could get on with my life."[25] She moved out to Toronto, Canada to study at York University, after her father convinced her that a bachelor's degree would prove more useful than the art school education she'd yearned for. At York, she studied under George Manupelli, a writer and film-maker who still teaches at the school, and who would later work as cinematographer on *Ladies And Gentlemen, The Rolling Stones*, a documentary following the group's 1972 American tour. Manupelli was also a founder of the Ann Arbor Film Festival, where Kim would make her onstage debut as a musician.

"I started playing music accidentally," she would explain. "The first band I was ever in was for an art project in school, and it was a crazy noise band."[26] The group of York students included a Canadian singer, two Chiliean exchange students, Kim, and William Winant, whose barrages of percussion (and the silences that followed) signalled whether a "song" was about to begin, or had just ended. Invited to play a party to celebrate the 1975 Ann Arbor Film Festival, their free cacophony proved a little too 'avant', even for the town that birthed The Stooges, and the group had the plug pulled on them. They didn't continue much further, rehearsals soon devolving into drinking sessions.

This, and a film project about Patty Hearst (then still on the run with her kidnappers, the Symbionese Liberation Front), would prove to be the highlights of Kim's tenure at York. Following an unsatisfying first year, she quit the university and enrolled at Otis College Of Art & Design. She thrived at Otis, studying post-conceptual fine art. She became enchanted with contemporaneous advertising for automobiles, which she interpreted as artistic objects. "The car brochures were like modern landscapes," she'd later explain. "There'd be cars sitting around and lakes and no people. They were eerily vacant, like modern De Chirico paintings or something."[27] Kim would paint shapes and patterns on the windows of these deserted automobiles and submit the finished works as originals, infuriating her painting teacher, who bizarrely accused Gordon of being a fascist.

In her final year, she befriended Michael Gira, a fellow Otis student. After his mother entered an alcoholic downward spiral following her divorce, Michael began experimenting with acid, aged 12, immersing himself in the burgeoning Californian psychedelic rock scene, groups like The Doors and Love. A wild and destructive kid, he was caught by police in possession of amphetamines and sent to live with his businessman father in South Bend, Indiana. After a year stifled in this white trash paradise, Gira moved with his father to Europe; hanging out and taking drugs with local hippies in Paris, Gira went on the lam, hitch-hiking alongside his tripped-out companions with a vague aim of ending up in Amsterdam. Following an acid-etched excursion at a rock festival in Belgium, where he saw Pink Floyd play, he was arrested for vagrancy and sent to Germany, where he worked at one of his father's factories, until going on the run again, eventually getting arrested selling hashish in Jerusalem. Released two months later, he was 15 years old; after a year in Israel, he returned to Germany and his despairing father, who shipped Gira back to California. There he dropped out of high school and spent two years working in factories and on building-sites, before returning to college and, eventually, Otis School Of Art. It was while filming a local concert at a nearby Elks Lodge (halls owned and maintained by the Benevolent and Protective Order of Elks, an American social club and fraternity, rented out for such private occasions) for a college project that Gira was sucked into the slipstream of three of the best Los Angeles punk bands – X, The Screamers and The Germs – thrashing and squalling at their prime.

After graduating Otis, Kim spent a couple of months in New York, feeling much more at home amid the grime of East Village than the walking cosmeticians' gallery that was Los Angeles. Fleeting exposure to the caustic noise of the No Wave only compounded her sense of kinship with the New York scene. She returned to California briefly, to earn enough money to finance the move east, to discover Gira similarly enamoured with the No Wave. Gira relocated to New York at the end of 1979; Kim followed him a few months later, driving cross-country with another friend from Otis, Mike Kelley. The pair had met after a lecture by artist Dan Graham, Kelley and Graham discussing punk rock as Gordon approached them; unbeknownst to her, Kelley had been in the audience at the Ann Arbor film festival some years before. The experience inspired his own musical experiments, including a tour of duty with Rocket From The Tombs.

Kim's intention had been to work as an artist in New York, but she found herself fast becoming disillusioned with visual art. At the dawn of the Eighties, the New York art scene was enjoying a boom period, young artists earning large amounts of money for their work. The creeping commercialism of the scene alienated Kim, and she was no longer confident that visual art would be the most rewarding medium for her self-expression. In her final year at Otis, she had been impressed by a fellow student's project, a fusion of conceptual art and an almost "punk" aural ferocity: a noise tunnel, in a warehouse full of airplane propellers. "It was just noise," she recalled, "but I had a feeling that what he was doing was more interesting than everything else that was going on."[28]

Kim's sense of ambivalence was aggravated by the still-vivid activity of what would prove to be the last days of No Wave. "I liked the immediacy of No Wave," she reflects, "because in my art, for example, I tended to overthink things, because I guess I knew too much about it. When I saw the No Wave bands, it just sort of struck a chord, no pun intended. The music was just very expressionistic in a way that I wasn't really into in art. It was hard for me to resolve the emotions of personal expression, and I had been approaching art in a more intellectual way – the music was kind of an extension of Warhol's Pop-ism to me, like instead of making art about popular culture, we were playing music to be within popular culture, even though we were really commenting about a subculture, at the time."[29]

Her deep thoughts about music and art found voice in *Male Bonding And Trash Drugs*, an essay written for respected New York journal *Artforum*, about the music and performance of Rhys Chatham; the title was derived from Gordon's fascination with the pre-show ritual of Chatham and his musicians, inhaling fumes from an aerosol underarm deodorant aptly titled "Locker Room" as a cheap high before taking the stage. "I was fascinated by it. So primal. It was just something that I wanted to be a part of. It wasn't penis envy... It was like, 'Oh, my brother has a train set. When am I getting mine?'"[30] Despite the high proportion of female musicians operating within No Wave, Kim still perceived rock as an essentially masculine arena, and took pleasure in her voyeuristic perspective upon it, as something alien, something other.

After her Los Angeles boyfriend, an artist called John Knight, requested he look after her while she was in New York, Dan Graham convinced her to pen the essay, saying she should contribute something to the arts community she was joining. Similarly, her first musical activity in New York was at Graham's behest. The artist invited her to accompany him on a performance of a variation on a piece he'd produced in 1979 at the Riverside Studios in Hammersmith, London. 'Performer/Audience/Mirror' was a conceptual piece, with Graham facing the audience, standing before a mirror stretching the length of the stage, parallel to the audience. Graham would spend the first five minutes describing his physical appearance in precise detail, while facing the audience; he would then describe the audience, "phenomenologically", for five minutes; for the final five minutes, he would face the mirror and describe himself, again. For the 1980 performance, at a festival curated by Christian Marclay at Boston's Institute Of Contemporary Art, Graham wanted to be backed by an all-woman group; Kim hooked up with Miranda Stanton and Christine Hahn to form CKM, though the performance itself was messily eventful.

"I played guitar but I hadn't had any lessons, I just taught myself," Kim recalled. "The lyrics were mostly taken from ad copy from magazines about separates and lipstick and *Cosmopolitan Girl*. We didn't have a particular look or costumes or anything. We were fairly punk rock-ish. We did the performance and one of us left to go to the bathroom, and we chatted to the audience; I don't think we successfully did what Dan wanted us to do, because we were so preoccupied with the playing. I was hooked on the experience, and have been playing in a band ever since."[31]

Kim spent the months that followed pursuing Design Office, an artistic concept where she would alter someone's living space in accordance with their personality; she would take a photograph of her work to be published in a Canadian art magazine alongside an essay she'd penned, deftly lampooning modern architectural publications. Her nights were spent at loft parties and nightclubs, in particular Tier 3, which she says she attended "religiously". Along with the downtown No Wave acts, Tier 3 offered a stage to groups from Britain's fecund post-punk scene. "Those nights were mysterious, lonely, and exhilarating," she wrote in her sleeve note for the 1993 re-release of The Raincoats' *Odyshape*. "I loved The Slits because of their boldness and that they actually had commercial songs, but it was The Raincoats I related to most. They seemed like ordinary people playing extraordinary music. They had enough confidence to be vulnerable and to be themselves without having to take on the mantle of male rock/punk rock aggression... or the typical female as sex symbol avec irony or sensationalism."[32]

Kim had yet to make a satisfactory connection with another musician, until she met Thurston Moore. He was immediately smitten. "Kim wore glasses with flip-up shades and had an Australian sheepdog named Egan," he wrote. "She had an off-centre ponytail and wore a blue and white striped shirt and pants outfit. She had beautiful eyes and the most beautiful smile and was very intelligent, and seemed to have a sensitive/spiritual intellect. She seemed to really like me. I definitely liked her but was scared as always to make a move. I was afraid to kiss her."

Kim was living in a sketchy apartment on Eldridge Street, in the thick of the art scene; Dan Graham also lived in the building, and had helped secure her the apartment. Thurston came over to visit one evening, playing a worn-out old guitar that used to belong to an associate of The Coachmen. Kim was impressed by his gonzo approach to musicianship, and much more. "He exuded this faith; he didn't really worry about the future," she remembered later. "And he would sleep until two or three in the afternoon."[33]

The apartment was sparsely decorated: "All she had was the guitar and a foam rubber cushion for sleeping. That night was the first time we kissed."[34]

"He had this sort of golden glow about him," said Kim, later. "He was younger than me, but I just thought, 'Oh *wow*...'"[35]

* * *

The Flucts ran aground some time late in 1980. Ranaldo and Linton soon found work playing with Rhys Chatham, performing a number of shows, including one at Tier 3 where Glenn Branca was in attendance. Lee had recently seen Branca at The Kitchen, his ensemble playing the pieces from *Lesson No. 1*, complete with a live sledgehammer "player" for a fearsome 'Dissonance'. Shortly afterwards, Lee called Branca on the telephone; remembering the young, anarchic guitarist from the Chatham show, Branca offered him a place within his group.

It would prove an enlightening, enthralling experience for Ranaldo, as Branca's new ensemble – now numbering four guitarists, including Ranaldo, within its arsenal – played a spate of New York shows before embarking on a tour of America in December 1980. Ranaldo learned much from Branca, not all musical; cannily, the composer/band leader had accepted an offer to play a relatively lucrative show at the Walker Art Centre in Minneapolis. This show effectively bankrolled the rest of the tour, as Branca and his musicians zipped across the country, taking full advantage of a $350 ticket offered by Eastern Airlines, which offered limitless travel over seven days (the 1978 Airline Deregulation Act was followed by a price war between airlines, yielding such attractive promotions).

"No one in America was ready for this music," recalled Ranaldo in his sleeve note for the 2003 reissue of Branca's first album, *The Ascension*. "No one was prepared when Glenn's group took the stage before a bank of ratty amplifiers and drums, for what would unfold… It was more than impressive. Beyond insane. It was really high art."[36] If Branca's multi-guitar pieces were so revelatory in New York, they must've been an absolute mind-fuck for audiences unfamiliar with the history and evolution of No Wave, which had yet to truly leak out of Gotham.

On returning to New York, Branca booked sessions for the sextet at Power Station, a former Con Edison power plant converted into an upper echelon recording studio by record producer Tony Bongiovi (cousin of Jon Bon Jovi). Branca struggled to preserve his vision, the engineers at the studio more used to working with the likes of Aerosmith, David Bowie and John Lennon than such avant fare. Ranaldo later noted that the album was "close mic'd, like a rock record", that it was missing much of the "Room Tone"; what the microphones *did* capture remains startling to this day. It opens with a queasy Contortions funk, soon swallowed by those four guitars, each individually and idiosyncratically tuned, building enveloping fogs of drone, or delivering explosions of bruising squall with Hitchcock's sense of suspense, or captured in screeching, screaming conversation with each other. A masterful monochrome painting by Robert Longo, of Branca dragging a prone besuited body, was the sleeve.

Branca's ambition and organisational skills saw his *Ascension* group embark on a similar tour of Europe early the following year. Soon afterwards, Lee joined + Instruments – a group led by Truss De Groot, a musician he'd met in Holland who'd relocated to New York – while remaining a member of Branca's ensemble. The drummer for + Instruments was David Linton, who'd met De Groot while touring Europe with Rhys Chatham.

Having unsuccessfully applied for a place in Branca's ensemble, Thurston began practising with a keyboard player named Ann DeMarinis and Miranda Stanton on bass, rehearsing at the loft of DeMarinis' boyfriend, renowned artist and architect Vito Acconci. When Miranda left the group, Kim stepped in, while Thurston tapped ex-Coachmen drummer Dave Keay for percussive input. The group took the name Male Bonding – a topic that held an abiding fascination for Kim – before changing to Red Milk for their first show, at A's on December 17, 1980. The show was not a success. The group renamed themselves The Arcadians, scoring a show at CBGB the following January. A week after that show, they found themselves playing a "Battle Of The Bands" at Inroads, a club on Mercer Street. Lee and David were in the audience and, before the end of the Arcadians' set, had snuck onstage, Linton playing percussion and Ranaldo sharing DeMarinis' keyboard (history does not record whether the group bested their opponents, Coup D'Etat, that night).

That spring, Ann announced she was leaving The Arcadians. The group would take another name before her final show that June, however, a moniker Thurston had come up with after fusing the names of two supercool underground icons, MC5 guitarist Fred "Sonic" Smith, and righteous dub pioneer Big Youth (Thurston had recently become enamoured with dub music, and would teach Kim rudimentary reggae basslines from a cherished Black Uhuru album as she familiarised herself with the instrument). The adoption of "Sonic Youth" marked the advent of a new era, as their concept for the group began to take more definite shape and their many different strands of influence began to coalesce. The very sound of Sonic Youth had yet to be defined, however; indeed, once they got hold of it, it would never stop evolving.

NOTES

1 *Alabama Wildman*, pg 3
2 *Spin* magazine, August 2002
3 *Bomb* magazine, Winter 1996
4 *Alabama Wildman*, pg 63
5 *Swingset* magazine, #3 2003
6 *Bomb* magazine, Winter 1996
7 *Vice* magazine, February 2007
8 *Alabama Wildman*, pg 4
9 ibid
10 Lee Ranaldo interview at http://www.sonicyouth.com/dotsonics/lee/ints/corregie.html
11 *Jrnls80s*, pg 65
12 *Online Diaries: The Lollapalooza '95 Tour Diaries*, pg 102

[13] Lee Ranaldo interview at http://www.sonicyouth.com/dotsonics/lee/ints/corregie.html
[14] ibid
[15] http://www.sonicyouth.com/dotsonics/lee/index.html
[16] http://perso.orange.fr/rhys.chatham/Essay_1970-90.html
[17] *Vice* magazine, February 2007
[18] http://www.nyfa.org/level3.asp?id=303&fid=6&sid=17
[19] *Alabama Wildman*, pg 3
[20] *Women, Sex And Rock'n'Roll: In Their Own Words*, pg 170
[21] The Observer, June 6 2004
[22] *Women, Sex And Rock'n'Roll: In Their Own Words*, pg 170
[23] *Grrrls: Viva Rock Divas,* pg 119
[24] http://legacyrecordings.com/janisjoplin/apprec.html
[25] The Observer, June 6 2004
[26] http://www.hernoise.com/interview_kim.htm
[27] The Guardian, Sept 30th 2005
[28] *Women, Sex And Rock'n'Roll: In Their Own Words*, pg 171
[29] http://www.ink19.com/issues_F/00_05/ink_spots/sonic_youth.shtml
[30] http://www.hernoise.com/interview_kim.htm
[31] The Observer, February 16 2003
[32] Odyshape reissue 1993 sleeve note
[33] The Observer, June 6 2004
[34] *Alabama Wildman*, pg 6
[35] NPR All Things Considered, broadcast June 12 2006
[36] The Ascension reissue 2003 sleeve note

CHAPTER THREE

Noisefest

"Let's face it, a lot of the music has just become noise."[1]

Robert Boykin, former owner of Hurrah's

"I called the event Noise Fest in reaction to what the Hurrah's jerko had said, and to reclaim the term 'noise' from its derisive status."[2]

Thurston Moore

The New York underground of summer 1981 was a dense, swarming, incestuous scene, where it seemed *every* artist was also a musician, who also did some acting, and wrote poetry, and built installations, and... There was a sense of a powerful, productive cultural energy within the city, one that these artists both fed, and fed upon. Thurston Moore, for his part, felt it; a resident of New York for almost four years now, he buzzed on the myriad cultural opportunities the city offered him, a passionate supporter of the No Wave scene and its radical, caustic sonic revolt. Fired by an enthusiasm that persists to this day, he was a tireless student of this music, a performer, a creator. He also possessed the energy, vision, commitment and desire to take on a number of seemingly less-explicitly creative (but no less crucial) roles, deeply involved in the perpetuation of the scene (and his group) as a lucid and vocal evangelist for this "noise" and, at the beginning of that summer, as curator of a festival dedicated to the celebration of the ever-evolving, ever-'free' sound of underground New York.

Not everyone involved in the scene shared Thurston's enthusiasm. Robert Boykin was owner of a midtown club called Hurrah's, a regular haunt of the East Village set (Ed Bahlman DJ'd there) that also played host to the likes of The B52s and Blondie, as well as a number of British post-punk groups, including The Slits and Young Marble Giants (Hurrah's would also have been the venue of Joy Division's New York debut, had singer Ian Curtis not committed suicide shortly before the tour). Boykin was not a fan of No Wave and its attendant arty and discordant sounds; in protest at what he perceived as the wilfully anti-commercial bent of the local talent, their passion for little more than "noise", he closed the club and voiced his dismissive opinion in an interview with the *Soho Weekly News*, one of New York's hip weekly newspapers. Thurston was incensed: "The Hurrah's dude thought there was nothing happening," he wrote later. "I knew there was."

White Columns was an alternative art space on West 13th Street run by Josh Baer, son of artist Jo Baer and a friend of Kim's, who had earlier curated an exhibition at White Columns where artists displayed record covers they had designed. Keenly aware of punk's symbiotic relationship with the art scene, Baer invited Thurston to curate a music show at the gallery, an offer the latter accepted with his trademark avidity. As Thurston began to dream up a list of possible performers for the festival, Branca introduced him to his old Bastard Theater cohort John Rehberger and Mark Cunningham from the recently dissolved Mars. With their assistance, Thurston compiled a line-up of disparate but united artists, and published a press release for the festival that spelt out his intentions in no uncertain terms.

"Noise Fest is a reaction to false claims made by the majority of rock/disco club owners and the overground music press," read Thurston's mimeographed screed. "The commercial, 'successful' sound of the 'Big Beat' British bands has seduced club owners and has diminished the range of music presented in the video/lounge circuit. The fact is there are more young, new, experimental rock musicians than ever before. The number of bands and their necessary progress is essential to Noise Fest and its main projection to unite."[3] Kim and Barbara Ess helped collate artworks by the various musicians for a related exhibition at the gallery, adding in the press release that "whether or not the work has any relationship to music remains open".

Ultimately, Thurston programmed more than 30 different bands to play across nine consecutive nights at the gallery through the second half of June, reflecting his own take on contemporary New York noise. His beloved Ut, a brilliantly acrid No Wave outfit comprising Nina Canal, Sally Young and Jacqui Ham, headlined the second night, while Glenn Branca topped a deafening bill on the 20th that also included fellow guitarrorist Rudolph Grey and former collaborators Jeffrey Lohn and John Rehberger. Referencing his interest in the burgeoning hardcore punk scene, Thurston later wrote that he "tried to get some of the new first generation hardcore bands, but they were so young they couldn't seem to dial the phone." After considering inviting The Beastie Boys, then in their earliest incarnation as egg-throwing brat punks, he selected The Primitives instead, a raging, full-on punk band with a 14-year-old mohawked singer who barked lyrics protesting newly elected President Ronald Reagan. Barbara Ess' Y Pants, friends of the group and possessed of a deliciously subterranean sound that echoed The Raincoats, headlined the Friday night, while Rhys Chatham presided over the preceding night, with support from Sonic Youth. Elliot Sharp, an avant-jazz composer and musician operating in the same orbit as John Zorn (another New York avant luminary), offered his services but Thurston couldn't find space on the Branca-night bill; other hopefuls were more lucky, such as Vietnam, a group who travelled from Georgia to play the event, and a band of Brooklyn unknowns called Fakir, who Thurston later remembered as "awesome, odd and sensual".

Some musicians performed in more than one group. A certain artistic promiscuity, a creative polygamy, was the order of the day; musicians would spread their talents and ideas across a number of groups, the better to satisfy their musically polymorphous ambitions. One such musician was Richard Edson, soon to assume the Sonic Youth drum stool in time for Noise Fest. Edson arrived in the city of his birth, New York, following a musical sojourn in San Francisco with plans to play drums; he didn't actually own a drum kit, but had in his possession his brother's beaten up bass guitar and a primitive Roland drum machine, with which he developed his earliest music. Yearning to collaborate with "serious" musicians, Edson's first musical experience in New York was with The Bumblebees, a loose and anarchic outfit led by Arleen Schloss, manager of A's. Debuting at the loft, The Bumblebees comprised Edson and a number of mostly non-musicians, friends of Schloss' along for the ride. The "peak" of their seven-song set was a piece based on William Blake's poem 'The Tiger', whereupon two girls would stride onstage and strip before painting tiger stripes on each other's naked bodies. The Bumblebees played several shows in New York, climaxing with a performance for a local cable access station, one of several channels on American television given over to "citizen media", amateurs and enthusiasts and crazies invading communal studios to provide content. In the sober light of the dingy television studio, remembered Edson, "the whole thing seemed sordid and depressing, and I felt sorry for the girls having to take off their clothes in such a cold and drafty place."[4]

With money he made working in the darkroom at the *Soho Weekly News*, Edson invested in a vintage drum kit and began playing with a group called Konk, a groove-based, multi-headed outfit drawing influence from funk, disco, Afrobeat, anything with an irresistible rhythm, which suited him perfectly. He also began drumming with a savage group called Body, some of whose members later formed Live Skull, a scarifying post-No Wave ensemble that later morphed into Come, whose smouldering, funereal blues underscored the later "grunge" era. Edson was a voracious devotee of live music and a regular at A's, where he saw The Coachmen play; he was impressed by Thurston, not least as he was the shortest of the group's ceiling-scraping frontline, and struck up a conversation with him after the show.

The two met again during one of Branca's massed Symphony performances, Thurston having recently been drafted into service, Edson playing percussion with the ensemble. Soon Kim, Ann and Thurston were rehearsing with Edson at Konk's rehearsal space in the East Village, their inaugural practice marked by the flecks of Thurston's blood as the guitarist's frenzied, string-strangling musicianship splattered across Edson's drum kit. Playing against the fearsome amplified squall, Edson would thrash and trash his gear as hard as he could to be heard above his bandmates. This perhaps explains why, shortly after their Noise Fest performance, Edson quit Sonic Youth.

The festival was a success, easily fulfilling Thurston's vision of "a watermark event in that community of disparate yet contemporary avant-garde, post-No Wave punk experimentalists [getting] to hang out, meet each other, and feel connected." There were reviews in the weekly New York press; when Lester Bangs called asking to cover the festival, Thurston invited the rock critic down to perform as The Lester Bangs Explosion, which might've actually happened had Lester not spent too long getting boozed up beforehand, arriving at the venue long after closing time. There was also an impromptu visit from actor John Belushi during one afternoon sound check. The comedian, star of anarchic sketch show *Saturday Night Live*, was a devotee of antisocial noise; he would later build a sound-proofed music room into his Hollywood home to facilitate his penchant for playing punk records at deafening volume and, shortly before his drug overdose death in 1982, finagled LA hardcore band Fear a slot on *SNL*, inadvertently gifting mainstream America its first televised moshpit riot. Thurston recalled Belushi being impressed by "but not fully sold" on the Noise Fest aesthetic.

For Noise Fest, in addition to their respective performances with Glenn Branca's ensemble and Rhys Chatham, Lee Ranaldo and David Linton played as Avoidance Behaviour, a most intriguing set that opened with Lee playing solo noise guitar while David sat at the back of the venue, manipulating loops drawn from Lee's scree and threading them back into the din, the guitarist doing the same for the drummer's percussion afterwards. To attend Noise Fest, Ranaldo and Linton had reneged on a planned + Instruments

European tour at the last possible moment; as a consequence, Truss De Groot lost the money she'd paid for airfare. The decision meant that, after an album and a single, Ranaldo and Linton were no longer members of + Instruments.

It was during Noise Fest that Kim first suggested to Lee that he jam with Thurston; the week following the festival, the trio reconvened at White Columns for their first rehearsal together; Barbara Ess played bongo drums. Early in July, after this sole rehearsal, Lee, Thurston and Kim first performed together as Sonic Youth, at the Just Above Midtown/Downtown Gallery. In the absence of a drummer, Thurston thrashed alternately at his guitar and a snare drum; their setlist contained embryonic versions of songs that would soon form the group's early repertoire.

They played a handful of shows around New York as a trio, honing their raw and misshapen songs. Still without a drummer, they filled the percussive vacuum with their inventive experiments on the electric guitar, introducing techniques such as thrusting a drumstick underneath the strings on the neck, thus introducing a "third bridge" that enabled the guitar to more resemble percussive instruments like bells, gongs and chimes; for the song 'Burning Spear', Ranaldo would "play" an amplified power drill, run through a wah-wah pedal, radically manipulating the tone of the resultant noise.

In September, however, they invited Richard Edson back into the fold, in anticipation of their performance at Music For Millions, a festival showcasing underground groups held at the New Pilgrim Theatre in the East Village. A cassette recording of the show, later appended to the 2006 reissue of the group's debut mini-LP, captures the songs in a raw state: 'Burning Spear' lopes at brooding half-speed, razor guitars chiming until the song is swallowed by Ranaldo's set-piece, the drill amplified to a nigh-unbearable white noise that sounds like it could reduce teeth and bones to fine powder. 'Cosmopolitan Girl', a hangover from CKM, hurtles with inventive menace, guitars creaking and scratching behind Kim's eerie cry, sounding almost like 'Poptones'-era John Lydon. Most impressive is 'Destroyer', a song that would soon disappear from the SY setlist, gliding along like a No Wave echo of Television's spiralling epic 'Little Johnny Jewel', Lee and Thurston entering into extended garbled conversation, their contusive guitars spewing spidery scrawl and splintering like shattered glass. If this was, as Robert Boykin had it, just "noise", Sonic Youth were fast proving that there was much innovation to be wrought within these outer realms.

★ ★ ★

Ed Bahlman passed on the opportunity to sign Sonic Youth to his 99 Records. The label had enjoyed much success with its subsequent signings, groups operating on the more dance-orientated fringe of the New York underground: the Bush Tetras, featuring former Contortions guitarist Pat Place; Liquid Liquid, whose icy agit-funk would later serve as backing track for Grandmaster Flash and Melle Mel's anti-coke salvo 'White Lines (Don't Do It)'; and ghostly funk sisterhood ESG, whose elemental grooves proved ripe for sampling by the hip-hop generation. While Edson's drumming nailed Sonic Youth's squalling carcass of noise to a tighter beat, Bahlman couldn't see a place for them on 99.

Josh Baer, owner of White Columns, had no such qualms. In collaboration with Branca, he founded his own label, Neutral Records, and signed Sonic Youth for the label's inaugural release. With a budget of $2,000, the group entered Radio City Studio in the bitter December of 1981. Located in the Rockefeller Centre in midtown Manhattan, the studio was a remarkable venue for a group such as Sonic Youth to make their debut recording. It was located above Radio City Music Hall, a majestic theatre built by millionaire philanthropist John D Rockefeller Jr in 1932 as a "palace for the people" to host performances by Arturo Toscanini and his NBC Orchestra, featuring a magnificent Wurlitzer organ with pipes that took up 11 separate rooms; 30 Rockefeller Plaza was situated a little further down the block, the NBC television studio complex where many of the country's most successful television programmes were taped, including *Saturday Night Live*. A 24-track studio with state-of-the-art technology, Radio City Studio had also been the birthplace of debut albums by Blondie, The Ramones and Richard Hell & The Voidoids. Edson didn't remember the group being particularly overawed by their surroundings. "We didn't take it too seriously," he wrote later. "We were just making an album. What was the big deal? It was nothing more than documenting what we were doing and what we did."

The five tracks they recorded and mixed over those two days were issued in March 1982 as an eponymous mini-LP, Neutral's maiden release. In his slender notes for the 2006 reissue, Thurston recalls his intention for the album to open with a struck E chord. However, "being immersed in underground reggae at the time," he wrote, "I embraced the replacement of the E smash with the strike of the drum – a primitivist announcement to the world, or so I reckoned as a young romantic no-New Yorker." With Kim's sidewalking bass carrying the six-note melody, and Edson building a taut rhythm from closed hi-hat rattle and tight snare rasp, 'Burning Spear' (named for roots reggae pioneer Winston Rodney, who performed under that name) had a very vaguely "reggae" sensibility, contrasting with the resolutely avant, experimental flavour of the guitars – chiming a twisted gamelan song until the closing 20 seconds or so, when they explode into a climax of scraping scree – and the genius conceit of Ranaldo's amplified drill, kicking in at 1:34 with a rushing white-noise roar that sets hairs on end. The eerie prowl of 'I Dreamed I Dream' anticipated later Sonic Youth tracks like 'Hallowe'en' and 'Flower', a slow and sludgy dirge overlaid with Lee and Kim's murmured vocals, the latter spitting out a couplet of "working youth, fucking youth" (the group had designed a flyer for a show at Club 57 just before Noise Fest, with "Fucking Youth" as a not-entirely-practical variation on their name; Kim and Miranda had also contributed a 45-second piece entitled 'Working Youth' to a compilation LP slipped inside the December 1981 issue of New York art magazine *Just Another Asshole*, also containing solo tracks by Thurston, Lee and Ann DeMarinis). Kim also noted, with dispassion, that "many people suffer from impotence", a sentiment jarring with the track's dark, sexual menace.

When the group's back catalogue was re-released through Geffen Records in the Nineties, *Sonic Youth* was the sole album not included in the reissue programme; until the 2006 remaster, it was perhaps the most elusive, least-heard of all their albums proper. In many ways, they don't quite sound like themselves yet: for all their innovative "third bridge" experimentation, Lee and Thurston have yet to explore the vast sonic possibilities of the alternate tunings, the scordatura that Branca and Chatham had unlocked. Meanwhile, Richard Edson plays in a unique style unlike that of any of the group's subsequent drummers, his taut rhythms and high-tuned tom rolls composing edgy urban rhythms for the guitarists' noise, evoking a little of the dancefloor discipline of Konk. It would also be some time before Sonic Youth returned to a studio quite as grand or technologically advanced as Radio City Studio; indeed, the recordings that followed would scare up a fierce, murky, chaotic power from their relatively "lo-fi" sessions.

The mini-album was a modest critical success, winning mild praise and only gentle scorn in whatever corners of the press would review such an obscure release. Sonic Youth were greatly pleased with their debut recording, however; it was an especially confident release for a group who'd been playing together for barely two months. For Edson, it was a peak he wasn't interested in besting. Shortly after mixing the album, he announced his decision to leave the group and dedicate his time to Konk.

"I was very comfortable playing these two diametrically opposed musical forms," he wrote later. "Still, I knew that someday I might have to choose between one or the other... My heart was closer to the multiracialgrooveclecticism of Konk." Edson continued to play with Konk before branching out into the world of acting, with a starring role in 1984's *Stranger Than Paradise*, the second movie by cult director Jim Jarmusch. Further film work followed, including roles in *Good Morning Vietnam*, *Tougher Than Leather* (a vehicle for hip-hop pioneers Run DMC) and Spike Lee's brilliantly combustive take on race relations in Eighties New York, *Do The Right Thing*.

Edson's final show with Sonic Youth took place at The Mudd Club, an ice-cool nightclub in the TriBeCa neighbourhood founded in 1979 (with assistance from Anya Philips). "It was my swan song, and easily the best show we ever did," he wrote. "We never played as well, or as loosely, yet with so much power and feeling." In contrast with Konk, Sonic Youth were chaotic, messy, noisy and disturbing, but those very qualities were a great part of their charm and effect; for his last show with the group, they aligned with Edson's dill-perfect sense of rhythm one final time, with powerful results. Not everyone was quite so moved, however; an attending member of Konk whispered to Edson afterwards, "These people are squares."

⋆ ⋆ ⋆

Bob Bert was 22 when he moved to New York in 1977, taking an apartment on 23rd Street, paying his monthly rent of $115 with money he earned as a fine-art screenprinter. He'd grown up no more than 10 minutes' drive from Manhattan. "I lived near the Capitol Theatre in Passaic, New Jersey, which opened in 1972," he remembers. "I was always going to concerts and saw so many hot, hip shows. I also travelled to see shows at the Fillmore East in New York.

"I was always drawn to music," he continues. "When I was nine, The Beatles were on the Ed Sullivan Show, which most American families watched every Sunday night. I took drum lessons for a year at the age of 12, got a cheap set and banged away in the basement driving my family crazy. I jammed with some pals from junior high school doing songs like 'Dirty Water' by The Standells, and Cream covers. Even when the British Invasion was first happening, I was checking out the alternatives, like The Mothers Of Invention, Captain Beefheart, The Fugs, Dylan, The Byrds, jazz and, of course, the Velvets."[5]

At the age of 18, Bert moved out of his parents' house and gave up playing the drums to concentrate on becoming a visual artist. Studying at the New York School Of Visual Arts, he caught shows by The New York Dolls and Wayne County And The Backstreet Boys, and first ventured into CBGB in 1975.

"The first night I went there," he recalls, "Patti Smith and Television were performing and there were maybe 15 people there," he recalled. "That was the ultimate, mind-blowing shit for me! I went there four or five nights a week and saw *everything*: the first Ramones shows; The Heartbreakers, when Richard Hell was still with them; Talking Heads, when they were still playing as a three piece; the Voidoids' first show, The Cramps, Suicide... Still at this point, I had no concept at all about ever being more than a fan, no thought about being a musician."

Bert's first contribution to punk culture was as a visual artist; spying an advertisement in the back pages of the *Village Voice* inviting contributions from "punk-influenced artists", he visited the Nonson Gallery in Soho with a portfolio of his work. The gallery gratefully accepted one of Bob's lithographs, transposing the head of transvestite Warhol superstar Holly Woodlawn (the Holly Lou Reed sang about in his 'Walk On The Wild Side') onto a woman's body. The piece was exhibited in a group show that also included works by Joey Ramone (who contributed a framed toothbrush dappled with red paint, hung on the ceiling, which he titled 'Bloody Gums'), and Jean-Michel Basquiat, a painter and later Warhol collaborator who played in a noise group called Gray with film-maker/provocateur Vincent Gallo, and who was then going by the name of Jean Samo, a reference to a series of graffiti works he painted in the late Seventies, signing off as "SAMO", meaning "same old shit".

It was at Nonson that Bob met his future wife, artist and musician Linda Wolfe. They began dating on January 1, 1980, soon deciding to move in together. "She lived in Jersey City and I was still in New York," remembers Bert. "She didn't want to live in NYC and I didn't want to live in Jersey City, so we compromised and moved to Hoboken.

"There was this strange punk character that lived next door to us called Peter Missing. One night a few months later, we were at this local club, hanging and drinking; the band didn't show up so Linda said, 'Hey, Bob can play the drums!' So Peter, myself and a dude named Jeff Holiday drunkenly took over the stage. Jeff played guitar, I drummed and Peter spouted his poetic ramblings and banged an electric kalimba."

The impromptu performance proved strangely fortuitous: in attendance at the bar that night was a patron named Pat Clarke, who had booked shows for shambolic-savant British post-punk mavericks The Fall whenever they toured America. Clarke dug the trio's messy, drunken din, and proceeded to book them a number of live gigs in the city. They called themselves Drunk Driving. "Part of our schtick was bringing all this confetti and garbage and flinging it all around the club, which, of course, pissed off the club owners," recalls Bert. "Drunk Driving ended for me when, during a live gig, I got clocked in the head with a hardcover book. Peter Missing went on to form the Missing Foundation, causing havoc wherever he went. He was the originator and creator of the upside-down martini glass graffiti that still litters the world. After living for quite a long time in Germany, he can still be found on the streets of NYC peddling his talents."

Bert imbibed deeply of the No Wave scene as it erupted, and loved what he saw and heard. He was a devotee of Ed Bahlman's 99 Records, regularly shopping in the store, and coming to trust the record label's roster of acts like the Bush Tetras, ESG and Glenn Branca, whose *Lesson No. 1* album rocked Bob's world. "I read in the alternative musical rag the *New York Rocker* that Glenn was starting his own label called Neutral Records with a partner and the first release was gonna be by a band called Sonic Youth," remembers Bert. "Soon after, I saw the debut Sonic Youth mini-album in the shop window of a Soho record store called Rocks In Your Head. I took it home, threw it on and immediately dug what I heard."

Bert heard echoes of Public Image Limited, John Lydon's scabrous, scarifying and anarchic "communications company"-cum-group, within the grooves of the Sonic Youth mini-album, and later saw the Richard Edson line-up play twice, at CBGB and The Mudd Club. "Not long after that, I saw a flyer in Rocks In Your Head that read 'SONIC YOUTH NEEDS A DRUMMER'," adds Bert. "I took it home with me – I still have it – called them up, auditioned, and got the gig. They were all pretty much the same then as they are now, still real cool folks, only 26 years younger." At the audition, Bob and Thurston recognised each other from the audiences of countless late-night New York nightclub scenes; finding they shared much in common with Bob, Sonic Youth swiftly offered him the drum stool, upon which he gladly planted himself.

Bert's style differed greatly from the rigourous, groove-orientated clip of Richard Edson. "My drumming skills were limited back then," he admits. "But the No Wave scene had made me realise that concept was better than skills. Who would you rather listen to, Eric Clapton or Arto Lindsay? My approach was to combine the rock skills of Heartbreakers/New York Dolls drummer Jerry Nolan with the primal, tribal action of DNA's Ikue Mori and the groove of ESG." Nevertheless, the heavy rhythmic atmospheres Bob Bert laid down would become a crucial element of Sonic Youth's fractured ambience.

Bob played his first set with Sonic Youth on November 3, 1982 at CBGB, where the group shared the bill with Don King, an avant-skronk group featuring Mark Cunningham and Lucy Hamilton of Mars and Duncan Lindsay (brother of DNA's Arto), and Swans, a group led by Michael Gira delivering a brilliant, grinding, mercilessly heavy and painfully slow noise. The groups played before a modest crowd, but this didn't dampen Bob's enthusiasm. "Lydia Lunch and Arto Lindsay were in the audience; I couldn't believe that I was playing at CBGB in front of some of my idols... I was in heaven."

> "The vibe was fresh and, though mirroring the nihilism of No Wave, had notions of forward positivity."[6]
>
> Thurston Moore

Bob joined a group deep in the process of writing new material, woodshedding songs that would mark a radical departure from what came before and shape the sound of all Sonic Youth music that followed. This new sound would be born of necessity, but would open up the gateway to a universe of sonic possibilities; they're still exploring the outer reaches to this day.

Poverty was the mother of Sonic Youth's invention. The members were making precious little money from the group, making ends meet via a series of part-time jobs; the benevolent Todd Jorgenson, co-owner of A's, employed various members at his copy shop, along with many others of New York's community of starving artists and musicians. They painted peoples' apartments, while Bob found work creating silkscreen prints of Andy Warhol works alongside printmaker Rupert Smith, a job he held until Warhol's death in 1987.

They couldn't afford new guitars; they couldn't even afford serviceable old guitars. Their meager budget could just about stretch to cheap, rotten thrift-store guitars, worn out with maltreatment, damaged and dysfunctional. Those guitars that Lee and Thurston managed to string and just about get into tune would soon fall into discord, the tuning pegs loose and useless. "They really sounded *horrible*, especially when you tried to play normal guitar with them," Moore would remember later. "But they sounded *great* if you got a drumstick and put it under the strings."[7]

Lee and Thurston were already familiar with the concepts of scordatura explored by Glenn Branca and Rhys Chatham, having played in their ensembles and still being awed by their earlier, revelatory live experiences. Emboldened and inspired by these composers' example, Sonic Youth's initial "make do and mend" approach evolved into an ethos akin to, "if life gives you lemons, make lemonade". They made virtue of their instruments' shortcomings, restringing and modifying and detuning and "hot-rodding" until they uncovered the unique "voice" of every busted and bruised axe that fell into their hands. As the process developed, some guitars would be unique to certain songs, untouched for the rest of the rehearsal or set.

In abandoning traditional tuning and taking such a radical approach to the electric guitar, Sonic Youth were in a sense unburdening themselves of the weight of a quarter of a century's worth of rock history, and the inherent limitations that came with that, claiming for themselves a clean slate, an empty page. They couldn't make their guitars sound like Eric Clapton's even if they wanted them to; they could only make the unfamiliar and alien noises the group discovered within them. Casting themselves adrift from the constraints of tradition, Sonic Youth were able to sculpt a noise that sounded new, bizarre, thrilling, just as mainstream rock'n'roll was reaching a formulaic nadir. "We're not playing in your typical guitar tuning," said Lee in reference to this freedom, "so we're pretty much just making it up as we go, as far as the sounds we're creating. Oftentimes a song will be inspired by a certain block of sound someone creates."[8]

This fresh batch of new material would soon get a thorough road-testing. A couple of weeks after his first gig with the group, Bob Bert loaded his drums into the U-Hual trailer and clambered inside a cramped rental van as Sonic Youth made their first, faltering steps outside the rarefied, avant-friendly atmosphere of New York, to cities where the few kids in the audience had little or no frame of reference for the noise that confronted them, caught up in their own, very different, localised punk phenomena.

Michael Gira, whose Swans would be sharing the bill and travelling alongside the Youth, dubbed the tour "Savage Blunder", which would prove somewhat prophetic. The tour was broken into two legs. The first saw the bands spend the third week in November 1982 travelling down through the southern regions of the East Coast of America, stopping off at North Carolina, Georgia, Washington DC and Maryland. The second leg, later the next month, was financed by a lucrative offer to perform for the Walker Arts Centre in Minneapolis at the nearby 1st Avenue Club, Lee following Branca's lead and booking a tour around the date that traced a path through the Midwest, via The Stooges' hometown of Ann Arbor.

Their touring circumstances were resolutely unglamorous; Kim's later published tour diaries were dubbed "Boys Are Smelly", while non-smoker Bob Bert remembers endless hours spent "stuffed in a shag-carpeted van with a U-Haul attached, floating in a nicotine cloud." The musicians' endurance of such iniquities was bolstered by a shared sense of purpose. "We definitely felt a kinship with Swans," continues Bert. "Both bands had a sound that could only have come out of the art-damaged streets of New York. No band on the planet was as loud as early Swans, and I'm not too sure what the kids in the South or Midwest made of us. It was very memorable for a first tour, Mike Gira jumping into the pogoing crowd at the original 40 Watt Club in Athens, Georgia, and punching out a guy for dancing. It was like the opposite of James Chance a couple of years before, beating up people for not dancing!"

The main cause for this schism separating the Savage Blunderers and their audiences was a crucial disconnect between both sides' concept of "punk". The New York musicians had been privy to the malevolent ferment of No Wave, operating with minds blown by the high-volume avant experimentation of Branca and Chatham. However, these radical paradigm shifts were mostly felt only within the boundaries of Manhattan, leaking slowly and fitfully to the outlying states. In these exterior regions, "punk" was (if recognised at all) still a short-hand guarantee of the kind of gleefully dumb, hi-octane thrills of The Ramones, which Sonic Youth and Swans certainly weren't offering. In other cities, younger punk kids brought up on their own, fiercely localised "hardcore" scenes arrived at the shows expecting that genre's more simplistic thrash; Washington DC was then in the grip of its infamously abstinent Straight Edge subculture, an ethos neither band on the tour could get behind.

The tour opened on a sour note at the Cat's Cradle in Chapel Hill, North Carolina. Despite a lively local punk scene, Sonic Youth and Swans found themselves playing before "six jeering cowboys", the ambience that of a dreary redneck bar. Gira attempted to provoke the patrons by introducing a song as a meditation on the topic of "getting butt-fucked by a cop". "We waited around to see if Harry Crosby, the English bass player for the Swans (who was drunk as anyone) would feel the need to defend their honour," recalled Kim in her diary. "But nothing happened, a fitting end to a stupid evening. All 10 of us piled into the van, and the Swans fought among themselves. Morale was very low, tempers short, and our expectations not as high as Mike's, which is why they were screaming at one another. One night Mike and his drummer started strangling each other and calling each other "dickhead" and "asshole". Meanwhile everyone else is crammed around them trying to mind his or her own business, being really cool."[9]

The following night, at The Pier in nearby Raleigh, Thurston recounted the sorrowful story for a more appreciative audience, whose calls for an encore were repaid with a Sonic Youth and Swans "jam-fest". There were highlights, however, not least meeting deposed Stooge Ron Asheton and his partner Niagra at their basement rehearsal space in Ann Arbor; Niagra sang with Destroy All Monsters, a group she formed with Mike Kelley in 1973, later morphing in 1976 to a line-up featuring Niagra backed by Asheton and MC5 bassist Michael Davis.

Exposure to the furious, disciplined, lightspeed rattle of the drummers on

Sonic Youth. **(FRANS SCHELLEKENS/DALLE)**

Late Night in the Bowery, during the Summer of No Wave, 1978:
l-r: Harold, Kristian Hoffman, Diego Cortez, Anya Phillips, Lydia Lunch,
James Chance, Jim Sclavunos, Bradley Field, Liz Seidman. **(GODLIS)**

"Lydia always wanted Teenage Jesus & The Jerks to sound like rough sex, like a hate-fuck. I could relate to that, having recently been deflowered by her." – Jim Sclavunos. l-r: Jim Sclavunos, Lydia Lunch and Bradley Field. **(GODLIS)**

The man whose music John Cage would define as "Fascist":
Glenn Branca, 1981. **(LAURA LEVINE)**

Richard Edson, filming Jim Jarmusch's *Stranger Than Paradise*, 1983,
with Eszter Balint and John Lurie. **(GOLDWYN/EVERETT COLLECTION/REX FEATURES)**

Sonic Youth's tour-mates for the appropriately-titled Savage Blunder tour, Swans; M. Gira, seated. **(LAURA LEVINE)**

"I saw a flyer in Rocks In Your Head that read 'SONIC YOUTH NEEDS A DRUMMER'. I took it home with me – I still have it – called them up, auditioned, and got the gig." – Bob Bert. **(CARLOS VAN HIJFTE)**

SY show at Maxwells club in Hoboken, New Jersey. 1981. **(LINDA WOLFE)**

Hanging out backstage during the Savage Blunder tour, 1982: l-r: Michael Gira and Harry Crosby (Swans), Thurston Moore and Lee Ranaldo. **(COURTESY OF BOB BERT)**

Thurston Moore onstage. "I love anyone shy, and Thurston was shy, and tall, and blonde, and looked like Opie Taylor." – Lydia Lunch. **(STEPHANIE CHERNIKOWSKI/REDFERNS)**

Sonic Youth, Holland, during their first European tour in 1983. **(ERNEST POTTERS)**

Thurston flips the bird – Sonic Youth pose for the press during their first European tour, 1983. **(CARLOS VAN HIJFTE)**

Sonic Youth onstage with several of their thrift-store guitars, during the first European tour. **(CARLOS VAN HIJFTE)**

A photo shoot from 1984, around the time of recording 'Bad Moon Rising' – the last SY album with Bob Bert on drums. **(PETER NOBLE/REDFERNS)**

"I was looking at these posters everyday and thinking, well, I'd really like to be in a band like Sonic Youth, something unique." Steve Shelley, at his kit, 1985. **(CHARLES PETERSON)**

"When I began playing electric guitar, it was always obvious that setting notes free into the air has a magical quality to it. Something special happens when tones ring out, made by one's own hand." Lee Ranaldo, live. 1985. **(CHARLES PETERSON)**

"Listening to Kim's approach to bass, you can tell she didn't learn licks off records. It's intuitive to her." – Mike Watt. SY live in NY. 1986. **(EBET ROBERTS/REDFERNS)**

Kim on a skateboard, in front of Spinhead Studios (during recording of 'Made In USA'), North Hollywood. 1987. **(DAVID J.MARKEY)**

early hardcore records he'd purchased had left Thurston dissatisfied with Bob's more primal, heavier style. "He was getting a little frustrated that I couldn't play like the hardcore guys, and that my cheap childhood drum set wasn't up to snuff," remembers Bert. "When we returned from the Midwest, there was a gig coming up at The Mudd Club and I couldn't understand why I wasn't being called to rehearse – Sonic Youth rehearsed at least three times a week around that time. A few days before the show, I got a call from Kim telling me I was out of the band because 'the chemistry wasn't right'. I was bummed. They played the show at The Mudd Club with a new guy – I think his name was Tom. I didn't go to this show, but I heard that they were joined by Jeffrey Lee Pierce [leader of Los Angeleno death-punks The Gun Club] for an encore of 'I Wanna Be Your Dog.'"

★ ★ ★

Tom Recchion, an alumnus of the Los Angeles Free Music Society, a collective of experimental, mischievous musicians based in California during the early Seventies, would not linger for long on the Sonic Youth drum stool. His replacement was a veteran of the New York underground club scene, former Teenage Jesus & The Jerks bassist James Sclavunos.

By the time Teenage Jesus split in 1979, Sclavunos was already playing with Lydia Lunch in her next project, Beirut Slump. "My favourite description of Beirut Slump," recalls Lunch, "was that we sounded like 'a slug crawling along a razor blade.'"[10] Lunch wrote all the music and played guitar, while bassist Liz Swope and her violinist brother, Bobby "Berkowitz" Swope, sang lyrics Lunch had collected from homeless people in the street. Beirut Slump rehearsed for a year but parted ways after their third show. Scalvunos followed Lunch into 8-Eyed Spy, a swampy blues group smeared with the seamy murk of No Wave, a corrugated clatter of rumbling bass and drums, sick horns, strangled guitar and Lydia's declamatory, sensual yell.

While still unhinged, 8-Eyed Spy were a decidedly more palatable proposition than Teenage Jesus, winning press praise for fevered live sets peppered with choice cover versions such as The Strangeloves' 'I Want Candy' (also covered by London New Wave group and Malcolm McLaren protégés Bow Wow Wow), a couple of Sixties standards from Seattle garage-rock pioneers The Sonics and early Americana romantics Creedence Clearwater Revival, and a thoroughly sinful, wanton shimmy through old Willie Dixon/Bo Diddley blues 'Diddy Wah Diddy'. Before they could record an album, however, bassist George Scott III died suddenly, and the group immediately disbanded. Lunch left New York, living for a while in Los Angeles and then London, before returning to New

York in the company of Jim Thirlwell, a subterranean musical maverick with a fascination for noise and No Wave. Through Richard Edson, she was finally introduced to Thurston, the boy upon who she'd gazed across the subway tracks years before.

"I love anyone shy, and Thurston was shy, and tall, and blond, and looked like Opie Taylor," remembers Lunch (Opie was the youthful star of distinctly "Apple Pie" Sixties sitcom *The Andy Griffith Show*, played by Ron Howard, who would later win fame playing Ritchie Cunningham, archetypal all-American teen lead of nostalgic, retro Seventies sitcom *Happy Days*). "I was fucking crazy about him, and I still am – he's one of my favourite people in the world. He's incredibly enthusiastic, and incredibly cool; I asked him once if he ever gets angry, and he said 'yeah', and I was like, uh huh, yeah, sure. *I'll* show you angry. I can make him blush in 30 seconds! I love it..."

Lydia thought Sonic Youth were, "Fucking awesome. The live shows I saw during that period remain the best I've ever seen. That period, when they were just building up their 'hurricane' guitar thing, was just bliss. It's so sexy. I was struck by how sexy Thurston was – maybe it was the way the guitar hit his body, I don't know, it was like something was just *leaking* out of him. The dynamic between him and Lee is very interesting too. In some senses, they seemed like the next step past Television."

Soon after they met, the duo played out a spoken word performance – the first in a long and successful career for Lunch – at Life Café, a restaurant on the corner of Tompkins Square Park that was a legendary bohemian hang-out. Days before, Lunch had beckoned Thurston to take a walk with her; as they strolled, she told him the story she was planning to perform. "He responded to every line by gasping 'Oh, really?!' and 'What, really?!'" laughs Lunch. "His reactions were so perfect, I decided that was how we'd do the performance: I'd tell the story and he would react just like that. We did it unamplified, so people had to walk up close to us if they wanted to hear it. Thurston was my straight man."

Lunch then played a handful of shows in New York backed by Richard Edson on drums, Thurston on bass, Pat Place (ex-Contortions and Bush Tetras) on guitar, and Sclavunos finally getting the opportunity to squawk on sax; the group also entered the studio to record some tracks, and completed a short tour. "I thought Thurston was a cool guy," recalls Sclavunos. "Lydia first suggested that I play drums for Sonic Youth, and then Thurston approached me about it. I said, sure, why not... And boy, did I live to regret that [laughs]. I don't regret it at all, it was just all a lot more complicated than I first realised."[11]

Sclavunos was a New York native, born and raised in Brooklyn. "It was very different to how it is now," he remembers, "a lot more violent and unpredictable, as was the whole city, I suppose. Back then, people just didn't go to Brooklyn – somewhere like Williamsburg was inconceivable, off the map. People just didn't take that train ride, let alone settle here. It was considered quite a dangerous place, and rightly so. When I was about 12, some guy with a handgun just walked up to my friend on the street and stole his guitar from him.

"I can remember, back in grammar school, starting to feel the divide between my musical tastes and those of my schoolfriends during a debate about Jimi Hendrix, who they described as 'the nigger'. I guess I wasn't 'normal', whatever a 'normal' kid is – I have issues with that word. My frame of reference, musically, was not 'normal' – it was increasingly esoteric. I was really into Frank Zappa when I was younger; that led me to obvious connections like Beefheart, but also, on the inside sleeve of the first Mothers Of Invention album, there was a list of incredible avant-garde luminaries – everyone from Eric Dolphy to Krzysztof Penderecki to Xenakis, all this music outside the realm of rock'n'roll. Soon, I was listening to stuff like Ornette Coleman, and actually *enjoying* it, believe it or not. And I found some other people who kind of liked that thing, and we formed a really awful band..."

By 1982, however, Sclavunos had become uninterested in the New York scene. "I was a self-taught drummer, my first gigs were arty noise bands. As I became more familiar with the instrument, I became capable of doing different things on it, and I wanted to explore different avenues of musical expression. I was starting to get gigs with people like Alex Chilton when they passed through town. That was new and exciting to me – I had never imagined myself playing that kind of music; when I had the opportunity to become acquainted with these things, I found them quite novel. But I wasn't unexcited to be in Sonic Youth – they were a great live band, they were really exciting to watch. They were a lot less 'toe-gazey' then than they became thereafter. There was this one number, 'Burning Spear', where they had this dilapidated set of tubular bells onstage; Thurston set about attacking it in the middle of the song, and the whole thing looked like it was about to fall over on him. But he set about it with such gusto and ferocity that it made for pretty good stage spectacle."

Sclavunos played only a couple of shows with Sonic Youth before the group began six weeks of rehearsals at Michael Gira's place for their next recording session, decamping to Fun City Studios, a basement studio on East 22nd Street run by Wharton Tiers, to begin recording what would become their second album, *Confusion Is Next*. Neutral's cash-strapped coffers struggled to cover the sessions, which were ultimately funded by friends of the group based in Switzerland. As evidenced by Lee's first phone call to Tiers, included on the group's *Candle* EP in 1989, the group initially planned to record two tracks for a cheaply produced seven-inch single; Thurston was currently enamoured by the upsurge in low-budget, DIY seven inches released by the early hardcore bands of the period, and wanted to release a Sonic Youth record with a similar aesthetic. However, the group's wealth of new material dictated the project be extended to EP and then, later, album length.

Confusion would be the first album produced by Tiers, a Philadelphia-born musician who moved to New York in 1976, drumming with Theoretical Girls and working with performance artist Laurie Anderson. Fun City Studios was a modest operation, especially compared to Radio City Studio. "I had certainly worked in better studios at that point," recalls Sclavunos. "Radio City was a pristine-looking, beautiful studio, the likes of which don't exist in New York any more, where you felt guilty if you sat down on a piano bench in your dirty jeans, and the microphones were not to be touched. It was very 'old school'. Wharton was about as disrespectful of that sort of thing as possible."

The studio was located in a basement flat, Tiers' recording equipment cramped in under a low ceiling. "It was very makeshift," adds Sclavunos. "Things got tense when we got in the studio. My reservations were mostly technical; it was clear to me that some basic things were not quite up to snuff. They didn't have any adequate monitoring system, so they didn't really know what kind of mixes they were getting. They wanted it to be a very bass-heavy record, but they did all their mixes on a system that didn't represent the bass very well. And then they went to a mastering studio and added even more low-end. When we got the first pressing from Neutral, I put it on my turntable and the needle went skating across the record – it wouldn't stay in the groove because there was so much low-end. Whenever I made a cautionary comment about, say, monitoring through speakers with blown cones, they dismissed me as a fuddy duddy, which got a bit tiresome. It was frustrating, because I saw a lot more potential for the music."

The sessions dragged on for several weeks, and were fraught with occasional technical disasters, resulting in several lost takes. But the group responded vividly to Tiers' unusual recording environment; without Radio City's 24-track recording desk at their disposal, the group pushed Tiers' 8-track tape recorder to its very limits, creating an album that's sublimely claustrophobic, a cloud of bad feeling that envelops and threatens to smother. Their aforementioned lust for low-end is a master stroke – unlike the sometimes brittle and often clear sound of Sonic Youth, the guitars on *Confusion* roar and howl with a primal, animal ferocity: detuned, restrung, with drumsticks thrust through the necks and screw-drivers scraping the strings, they summoned a dense, dark wall of sound, hurtling and splintering into Sclavunos' skull-quaking drums.

Kim's bass glowers in the foreground of first track '(She's In A) Bad Mood', guitar scrawl building a tension released in violently explosive, cacophonic crescendos, a burnished sense of dynamics that pervades through the album. For 'Protect Me You', Thurston tolls his guitar like an ominous gong, Lee playing an uneasy, sloth-like bassline (his only contribution on the instrument in the Sonic Youth catalogue), Kim's disquieting, mantric vocal murmuring of a girl quickly maturing, begging protection from the demons that come in the night, erotic anxiety painted in chill, gothic tones. It was a theme furthered by the scarifying 'Shaking Hell', guitars scything like a slasher-flick soundtrack and wailing alarm, before slowing to a panicked pulse, Kim screaming "Come closer and I'll take off your dress/I'll shake off your flesh"; sexual contact played out as prurient horror-movie nightmare, to unsettling effect. The panicked, clanging disco of 'Inhuman' strobed with bursts of alien guitar noise before crumpling into a glorious wreckage, while 'The World Looks Red' hammered together a primordial throb from angular abrasions. On both songs, the very physicality of Lee and Thurston's performances bled into their pick-ups, their fingers throttling sounds like twisted metal from their amps. 'Confusion Is Next' regaled in the very oppressiveness of Sonic Youth's din, Thurston's declamatory vocal spelling out a nonsense manifesto with absolute, unhinged sincerity, the group pounding out a junkyard din that raced and slouched to its whim. The album closed with 'Lee Is Free', a passage of free-form guitar play Ranaldo recorded at home, plucking strands of weird neon light from the air around him.

More so than *Sonic Youth*, *Confusion Is Sex* betrayed the influence of Branca, both in the adventurous tunings and methods deployed, and its sense of mass and velocity, a kinetic energy where the droning guitars sculpt great dive-bombing arcs and collide with each other, recalling the similarly abrasive rush of Theoretical Girls. But while *Confusion* saw the group explore further their avant influences, it is at least as visceral as it is cerebral, an unashamedly "punk rock" record, as the group's impassioned mauling of The Stooges' 'I Wanna Be Your Dog' attested. Recorded on the second night of the Savage Blunder tour, with Bob Bert hammering a death-rattle rhythm and Thurston bruising at a low-tuned bass, Kim inverts the gender of Jim Osterberg's predatory lyric and subverts the sensual pout of his vocal, screaming the kink-riven come-on with utter abandon, her holler echoing off the walls and ceilings. "The performance is absolutely unstable," wrote critic Greil Marcus in his liner note to the 1995 reissue, "three minutes of panic, and it still bubbles like a witches' cauldron; it'll dissolve anything. This was a kind of fire nobody was playing with in 1982 and 1983 – not that I heard, anyway."[12]

Bob Bert caught Sclavunos' two New York shows with the group. "I thought it was great, but I mentioned that I didn't think James pounded hard enough to be heard above their volume," he remembers. "I also said that I thought my approach for 'Making The Nature Scene' was groovier." The group invited Bert down to Fun City to record the primordial dirge-funk, which he'd played a large role in developing, marking his studio debut on a Sonic Youth record.

Sclavunos' tenure with the group was not without its tensions. He was dating Truss De Groot (they would soon marry), and she was still angry at Lee about the + Instruments European tour he abandoned to join Sonic Youth. "I totally did not know about this," adds Sclavunos. "Neither of them mentioned it to me before I joined the band. They waited a good two months before it came up, I guess they were trying to be 'civilised' about it. It added to the tensions that were going on during the recording sessions.

"It had been a very brisk mating ritual, a couple of live gigs and we were in the studio. We didn't have much chance to let the dust settle and get to know each other better; we were working. Ordinarily with a band, you'd have played with them for months before you'd go into a studio together. What I did was more akin to what a session musician would do. And I think it kind of affected the dynamic."

Sclavunos left the band shortly after the *Confusion* sessions. Of his former band-mates, he remembers Thurston as "very enthusiastic: he just radiated this energy and positivity about music, and music's possibilities, and what they were going to do as a band. Kim came across as much more intellectual, and more reserved. She always seemed to measure her statements carefully, and wasn't prone to outbursts of enthusiasm – which isn't to say she wasn't enthusiastic, that just wasn't her style of conveying her ideas.

"Lee was kind of hyper and nervous, a little bit reactionary – he was always the first, if he thought something was not the way it should be, he wouldn't hesitate to speak up. I think he was monitoring very closely what he thought the band should represent. I guess I got on most poorly with Lee back then, but he's probably the one I've been most in touch with since then. I run into him every now and again, and it's always good to see him.

I don't know if he's changed much. That's how I remember him. He wasn't a mellow guy back then [laughs], but he seems pretty mellow these days.

"I was just in an awkward position, between this band I just joined but didn't really know personally, and my wife, who I *did* know personally. I guess if I'd gone into it better informed, or maybe I was taking too many drugs at the time to know what was going on around me... Either way, I might have dealt with it differently."

★ ★ ★

Following his exit from Sonic Youth, Bob Bert had begun rehearsing with a couple of other New York musicians, Karyn Kuhl and Alice Genese. (Kuhl would later find modest fame with punk/metal group Sexpod, while Alice now plays in Psychic TV, the avant-industrial project of former Throbbing Gristle figurehead Genesis P. Orridge.) "My skills were rapidly improving," he remembers. "One day at work I got a call from Thurston, saying that they had just wanted to give James a shot, and asking if I wanted to come to a practice and jam. When I did, they were impressed with my improved kick-ass beats."

The group had signed on to play at another noise festival at White Columns. Speed Trials was a five-night event promising "Music and performance from NYC & Beyond" throughout the first week of May 1983, featuring shows from Lydia Lunch, Live Skull, The Swans and The Beastie Boys, followed by a party on Tuesday, May 10, with appearances from New York playwright and performance artist Eric Bogosian and a scabrous noise-punk band from San Francisco called Flipper. Sonic Youth played the opening night, Wednesday, May 4, supporting British punk mavericks The Fall; their drummer that night was Bob Bert.

"The band received their copies of *Confusion Is Sex* that night," he recalls. "After we played, we went to the bar across the street where I was told that the next day Thurston and Lee were going to Europe to tour with Glenn Branca, and while they were there they were going to set up a Sonic Youth tour. They asked me if I would be willing to go over there and tour with them. I made them promise me that it wouldn't cost me anything, and that they wouldn't fire me again."

NOTES

1 *Soho Weekly News*

2 Sonic Youth myspace.com blog

3 Noise Fest press release, reproduced at http://www.sonicyouth.com/mustang/cc/noisefest81.html

[4] *Sonic Youth* 2006 reissue sleeve note
[5] Author's interview, March 2007
[6] http://www.sonicyouth.com/history/ographies/thurstonleavenotes.html
[7] NPR *All Things Considered*, broadcast June 12 2006
[8] ibid
[9] Boys Are Smelly, from *The Village Voice Rock & Roll Quarterly* 1988
[10] Author's interview, February 2007
[11] Author's interview, March 2007
[12] *Confusion Is Sex/Kill Yr Idols* 1995 reissue sleeve note

CHAPTER FOUR

Kill Yr Idols

"Having played every song we knew, Thurston and Lee were still on stage exchanging feedback. A small riot broke out and there were some fires in the audience. It was an insane scene."

Bob Bert

On January 1, 1983, Thurston and Lee joined Arleen Schloss, Barbara Ess, Michael Gira and the rest of Glenn Branca's ten-piece ensemble onstage at the Brooklyn Academy Of Music, for the world debut of Branca's latest work, *Symphony No. 3*. Subtitled 'Gloria – Music For The First 127 Intervals Of The Harmonic Series', the piece followed a recent performance of a work by Branca, *Indeterminate Activity Of Resultant Masses*, which had won an impassioned response from John Cage, the godfather of modern composition. "My feelings were disturbed," said Cage at the 1982 New Music America festival in Chicago. "I found in myself a willingness to connect the music with evil and with power. I don't want such a power in my life. If it was something political it would resemble fascism."[1]

Such delicious evidence of his music's power to provoke accompanied a building respect for Branca's work from corners of the mainstream and the establishment, winning him a heightened visibility, and the opportunity to bring his radical new music to such hallowed stages as the Brooklyn Academy and, in May/June 1983, to audiences in continental Europe. This tour would prove to be Lee and Thurston's final sortie with Branca, however. Sonic Youth were beginning to chafe under the constraints of Neutral Records, which was struggling as any new independent record label catering to esoteric tastes might. Furthermore, Thurston was sensing a distance between his goals and Branca's, a crucial divergence of sensibilities. Moore had found an early hardcore gig flyer, advertising the ferocious fare with the tagline "The Sex Pistols weren't enough!". Intrigued by their moxie, tickled by the hyperbole, he showed the flyer to Branca, who shot back with "The Sex Pistols were more than enough!"

"That's when I knew I had to break away from the old men of the scene,"[2] remarked Thurston, later. According to Branca, Lee and Thurston promoted their group during their performances with his ensemble, spray-painting "Sonic Youth" on their jackets, their guitars and, in a gesture that infuriated the composer, the stage. In their defence, they had to *somehow* advertise the June shows they'd booked for Sonic Youth while playing the venues hosting *Symphony No. 4*.

"The first European tour was a wild, trailblazing experience," remembered Bob. It wasn't his first journey to Europe, having vacationed in Paris, Amsterdam and London on his own in 1977. "I was in London the week that the Sex Pistols album was released. I went to see The Heartbreakers at The Rainbow Theatre. Here was a band that I saw a ton of times in NYC and now they were playing this huge place with a large, fake city block as their stage backdrop. Johnny Thunders threw a brick though the fake pawn-shop window at the end of the show. There was manic, hardcore pogoing and spit flying everywhere, way different to a night at Max's."

Bert travelled 24 hours by plane and train, on his 23rd birthday, to make the first show of Sonic Youth's maiden European tour at Lausanne, in Switzerland, where he was met by Catherine and Nicolas Ceresole, the Swiss friends of Kim and Thurston's who'd helped finance *Confusion Is Sex*. After a quick stop at a nearby McDonald's for some comfort food, the group walked straight into the venue, La Dolce Vita, and up onstage, for their debut show outside of American soil. The show was a resounding success, the audience responding to Sonic Youth's destructive dervish and alien tones with lusty, destructive approval, lovingly hurling their beer bottles at the stage. "Having played every song we knew, Thurston and Lee were still on stage exchanging feedback," remembers Bob. "A small riot broke out and there were some fires in the audience. It was an insane scene."

The group crawled their way around Europe, taking advantage of cheap InterRail passes that granted them unlimited travel on trains across the continent; financially it made sense, but Sonic Youth's mission was complicated by the 13 guitar cases and Bob's snare drum and cymbals forever trailing them. Wisely, they booked time between shows for travelling, which also gave them a chance for a little sightseeing. The tour snaked through Austria, Germany and the Netherlands, the group returning to New York feeling triumphant. In their hometown they were just beginning to enjoy some recognition, but were still struggling to fill venues, and had experienced mostly disinterest and confusion from audiences in the outlying States. In Europe, however, the group were rapturously received by music fans utterly unfamiliar with Sonic Youth's milieu, but utterly enthused by their roaring, beautiful din. "We got a good reception pretty much everywhere," remembers Bob. "No one had heard anything like us before."

Throughout the tour, Sonic Youth befriended kindred spirits across the Atlantic. Having seen a video of one of their live shows early on in the tour, the group visited Einstürzende Neubauten – a German experimental group who utilised sheets of metal, building tools and cement mixers for their exhilaratingly percussive music – in their West Berlin studio while they were recording their album *Halber Mench*. The Youth also connected with The Ex, a Dutch anarchist DIY collective whose inventive din embraced skronk-jazz, wild improvisation and a primal punk-rock energy, and whose furious creativity spilled out across the sides of countless albums and seven-inches they released on myriad European indie labels. Bob remembers their period with The Ex as perhaps uncomfortably intimate: "We had to sleep snuggled together on their freezing floor in the swamplands of Holland. But I was fucking blown away by their DIY records and pamphlets; it was only 1982 but their output and approach was incredible."

The group spent the rest of the summer playing occasional shows in New York, headlining a hardcore benefit show for the Vancouver Five (an anti-capitalist militant group who'd been arrested for the bombing of a porno store) at Charas New Assembly Hall on East 10th Street on August 13. At the end of the month, they played a disastrous show at a club named Storyville in Boston; organized by Gerard Cosloy, editor of pioneering hardcore fanzine *Conflict* and a passionate fan of confrontational noise, the show had the misfortune to be scheduled the same night as a performance in Boston by David Bowie, who snared much of the Youth's potential audience. What patrons did turn up to the show responded to the group's music with a vehemence that unsettled Kim.

"Gerard Cosloy, Jimmy Johnson [editor of *Forced Exposure*, another influential Boston 'zine], and this drunken fan-boy were just about the only ones there," she wrote in her tour journal. "During the first song the fan-boy picked up this broken drumstick that had flown onto the floor and threw it back. It speared into my forehead. At first I thought it had bounced off Thurston's guitar; shocked, I didn't know whether to cry or keep playing, but then I just felt incredibly angry. It took a long time to resolve that incident, cos it really made me feel sick, violated, like walking to the dressing room after a set, having some guy say, 'Nice show', then getting my ass pinched as I walk away.

"I blamed it on the music for a while, because it did draw fans who really want to see you hurt yourself. It's not that I don't share similar expectations; there's beauty in things falling apart, in the dangerous (sexual) power of electricity, which makes our music possible. But what was once a hazy fantasy has since clarified itself. I don't want my blood to be entertainment."[3]

At the end of October, the group returned to Europe, where they'd enjoyed such a rabid reception months before; they spent a month playing shows around Germany, Austria, Switzerland, Italy and Holland. Their final show on the continent, at Open Ontmoetings Centrum in Venlo, Holland, was later released as an official "bootleg" through the Sonic Youth fan club, capturing the roaring turbulence of these early European shows and revelling in their dark, atonal noise. The next show, the last of the tour, would be their first in England, playing at The Venue, a big club near Victoria Station in central London.

"England, although no bigger than some states in the US, had four weekly music papers, *NME*, *Record Mirror*, *Sounds* and *Melody Maker*," explains Bert. "We needed to impress the press." The Youth opened for SPK, an industrial band from Australia; after a falling out with fellow support act Danielle Dax, the group was forced into the opening slot, with only 25 minutes to play. "We went onstage and everything went wrong. Thurston strummed his guitar and it fell apart, so he started sliding the monitors all over the stage. The drums were falling all over the place. It was just a mess... We were still playing, and this big wooden curtain came down on us. We were so bummed, thinking we blew our big chance to conquer London."

The group glumly flew home the next morning; the tour had ended on a sour note, in the very place where they had needed to shine brightest. Beautiful noise is in the ear of the beholder, however; having little experience of Sonic Youth's music, or the No Wave aesthetic they were springing from, the British rock critics had thrilled to the pure anarchy and uncompromising chaos of the Sonic Youth set. The Venue show won them their first rave reviews in the influential British music press.

* * *

As Sonic Youth embarked on their first tours of Europe, finding allies and welcoming audiences thousands of miles away from the streets and slums that provoked their noise, Thurston was becoming ever more obsessed with the latest wave of American musical extremism, hardcore. As the name suggested, hardcore boiled punk rock down to its most primal, intense, violent essence, gilding its raw, direct, lightning-fast riffs with barked, rabble-rousing lyrics and drums that rattled at double time. "All the songs were 30 seconds long, played as fast as humanly possible, and released on seven inches that came with detailed, hand-written or typed lyric sheets," remembered Lou Barlow, an early hardcore convert living in Massachusetts, who would later tour alongside Sonic Youth with his group Dinosaur. "It matched my energy level, my anger level."[4]

Thurston first discovered hardcore while rooting through the fanzine racks and seven-inch tubs of the hip New York record stores. "I started getting into it when I saw the records at the Rat Cage. Kids started making records," he recalled. "I just thought they looked so good, because they were so cheap, with the econo Xerox sleeves folded in half, 20 songs on a seven-inch. There was a certain energy to it that really drew me in. And then I listened to them, and they were amazing, like this abstract noise in a way – they were so primitive, no frills."[5] There were some hardcore groups in New York, not least the early incarnation of The Beastie Boys, friends of the Youth. But Thurston's first true taste of the music came when he saw an early New York show by Minor Threat, in 1982.

Based in Washington DC and fronted by shaven headed 18-year-old skateboarder Ian MacKaye, the quartet were figureheads of their bustling, insurgent local punk-rock scene, though their example would prove an inspiration (and a template to imitate) for hardcore groups the country over. Their most crucial contribution to hardcore might have been the formation of Dischord Records, a label co-owned by MacKaye and Threat drummer Jeff Nelson, dedicated to chronicling the hardcore groups of DC, a motley bunch of angry teens playing Ramones riffs at lightspeed and railing against any available figure of authority.

Minor Threat's lyrical content was a touch more complex, though MacKaye's personal choice to reject alcohol, drugs and casual sex (expressed in the lyrics of their track 'Straight Edge') unwittingly birthed an abstemious and occasionally violent punk subculture named after the song. As MacKaye said during their second recording of 'Out Of Step', a similarly moralistic Threat anthem, "This is no set of rules, I'm not telling you what to do; all I'm saying is, there's three things that are so important to the rest of the world that I don't invest as much importance in", but this nuance was lost on much of his audience. Beneath their blind youthful idealism, MacKaye's lyrics reveal a deep-seated fear of adulthood, of tainting the purity of their adolescent outlook with the compromises and hypocrisies they perceived in adult life – the vulnerability that fuels their fury. Songs like

'In My Eyes' and 'Filler' seethe with near-Freudian panic at the corrupting influence of intoxicants and sex; honour and trust were constant themes, and betrayal the most heinous of sins. This idealism ruptured with a growing disillusionment borne of increasing violence within their rambunctious audience moshpits, inter-band tensions and conflicting musical directions. There was a bleakness to their last songs, a bitter, newfound sense of irony to 'Salad Days'' sign off lyric: "They call these the salad days/what a fucking lie".

Focus on MacKaye's lyrics should never obscure the white-heat brilliance of Minor Threat's music, their jackhammer riffs played with a discipline that would impress James Brown, turning on a die; their absurdist 63-second dash through '12XU' (a track by British punk group Wire that had become a much-covered standard for the DC hardcore bands, much the same way 'Louie Louie' had for the Sixties garage hordes) unleashed the chaos seething beneath their martial rattle, the corrugated guitars reduced to an inchoate, guttural bark.

Minor Threat could trace their nosebleed thrash directly back to the arguable pioneers of hardcore, a group of four former jazz-fusionist Rastafarians who, inspired by The Sex Pistols and The Dead Boys, played brutal, primal punk rock at breakneck speed. Unlike most punks, Bad Brains had musical chops honed on the jazz circuit, and could throw in lightning-quick tempo changes when the mood took them, also slipping deep, soulful roots reggae tracks into their set.

In 1979, a blanket ban of the group by DC's local venue-owners necessitated their relocation to New York, where they proved a formative influence on early Beastie Boys, recording their debut album for New York's ROIR label and a second, *Rock For Light*, produced by Ric Ocasek of The Cars.

Shortly before their exile, the group had found themselves without a rehearsal room and, thanks to a van break-in while on tour, without any equipment. MacKaye immediately volunteered Bad Brains the gear that belonged to his earlier group Teen Idles, along with vocalist Nathan Strejcek's parents' basement as a rehearsal room.

"Bad Brains were the fastest, greatest band in the world," remembers MacKaye. "They'd meet us from our high school and we'd set up in the basement and rehearse for an hour, them sitting on the sofa watching us play. Then we'd all switch places. Watching them work was so inspirational, it just made me realise the key to everything is to work really hard, and never sell yourself short." MacKaye put these lessons into practice with Minor Threat, who mapped out pioneering expeditions across America, playing at local community halls as they were too young to legally play nightclubs, and with Dischord, which continues to thrive 25 years later. His hometown proved a great inspiration for his DIY spirit: "One lesson I learnt was, if you live in Washington, don't ever ask for permission, because the answer will always be 'no'. Go about things on your own, and do it under the radar."[6]

Part of the thrill of hardcore was a sense of simultaneous localised scenes across the country all drawing upon a similar frame of reference, but developing in radically different ways. All over America, hardcore scenes flourished wherever there were enough disgruntled kids with a penchant for antisocial noise: Texas boasted both the provocative, anti-authoritarian Dicks and rabidly eclectic funk-punks The Big Boys; Detroit had Negative Approach, whose muscular attack was formidable. The West Coast hardcore sound developed from the early auto-destructive attack of The Germs, through the profane polemics of The Dead Kennedys, to the acrid, dystopian din of Black Flag.

The Dead Kennedys' signature tune, 'California Uber Alles', painted an ugly picture of a state ruled by the draconian, baton-wielding LAPD, overseen by Governor Jerry Brown, in singer Jello Biafra's eyes a dangerous hippy-fascist who represented everything wrong with the baby-boom generation. The members of Black Flag suffered constant police persecution throughout their career, like The MC5 before them, their gigs regularly disrupted and band members harassed by cops. They responded by penning blackly hilarious, devoutly antisocial and often bleakly violent songs that gave twice as good as they got, and starting a record label, SST, that would support both the California punk scene and, later, hardcore groups across the country. Most importantly, they were one of the first hardcore groups to regularly tour outside their hometown, living in constant squalor and on punishingly tight budgets and negotiating community halls, nightclubs and squat parties across the country (and, later, abroad) in a shitty van. In their wake, America's nascent hardcore scene flourished.

Guitarist Greg Ginn formed the group in 1976 in his hometown of Manhattan Beach, California, burning through musicians averse to his fearsome work ethic before their line-up solidified, with Keith Morris on vocals and Chuck Dukowski on bass. Called Panic, they renamed themselves Black Flag on the suggestion of Ginn's brother Raymond Pettibon, an artist whose pulpy, venomous and unnerving pen-and-ink drawings would grace many later Black Flag record sleeves. They began organizing gigs at alternative venues across the state, nightclub owners unimpressed by their blackened, brutal attack. Two years after their 1978 debut EP, *Nervous Breakdown*, on Greg's own SST label, Morris quit the band following disagreements with Ginn and mild drug burnout. His replacement was Ron "Chavo Pederast" Reyes, who was himself replaced by Dez Cadena who, soon after, stepped sideways to rhythm guitar, ceding the microphone to a recent migrant from Washington DC, Henry Rollins. Rollins, who would soon tattoo the group's distinctive "four black bars" logo on his torso, fronted the group when they recorded their still-striking debut album, *Damaged*, in 1981.

Opening with the rallying cry of 'Rise Above', *Damaged* spoke to a disenfranchised American youth, grown cynical and distrustful of authority on a childhood diet of drugs and rock'n'roll and Nixon and Vietnam. Loathing of themselves and others saturated the violent riot of 'Police Story' and the sneering disgust of 'Six Pack'. But while Black Flag's corrosive barrage barreled along at terminal velocity, the avant brilliance of Greg Ginn's musicianship steered them away from slavishly following a hardcore blueprint they helped coin, his spiralling, spidery flurries of atonal guitar running headlong into juggernaut riffage. Kim Gordon caught Black Flag in California shortly before heading down to New York in 1980; she remembered being struck by Ginn's guitar playing most of all, and the way he seemed to be playing the instrument so the notes sounded like they were being played backwards.

Black Flag ran afoul of a corporate dalliance as *Damaged* was released. Sensing commercial potential in this burgeoning new youth phenomenon, Unicorn Records, a subsidiary of MCA Records, offered to distribute the album. Following MCA executive Al Bergamo's disgusted description of *Damaged* as "an anti-parent album"[7], Unicorn reneged on this deal, and the group entered into an extended legal dispute that barred them from releasing records as Black Flag for several years. In the interim they began recording a backlog of material that would see release after the Unicorn dispute was resolved, concentrated on the running of Ginn's label SST – an extension of Solid State Transmitters, a company he formed in high school selling spare parts to ham radio enthusiasts – and toured heavily and constantly. They established a somewhat legendary nadir in touring conditions (according to Rollins' bleakly entertaining tour journals, *Get In The Van*), as well as a network connecting America's disparate hardcore scenes and the many potential venues that would welcome their sound, if they could only power their crummy vans the distance to reach them.

Thurston felt empowered by these young hardcore entrepreneurs, by their energy and idealism, by their can-do DIY attitude. His love for the scene was tinged with a little envy, however. "There was no such thing as hardcore at my high school," he rued in an interview with Ian MacKaye in

2003. "That culture did not exist. I was really envious when I was older, living in New York, when I saw bands Ian's age. A lot of it was just songs that were really emotional, real heart-on-the-sleeve sort of things, and songs that were really taking to task authoritarian measures. How come when I was 18 I didn't have the wherewithal to go out and sing against local and civil injustice? People like Ian came out of punk rock knowing that they could do it themselves, without having to adhere to this model of professionalism that existed in the rock'n'roll industry. It was completely amazing, it was so subterranean. Even by punk-rock standards, 'punk rock' was still a professional gig.

"I started seeing this whole other generation of bands taking punk rock as a musical form. At that time my age group was like, 'punk rock's over, Sid's dead, New Wave sucks'. But then all of a sudden punk rock's being reintroduced through this new generation. That was really shocking to my age group in New York. I remember friends my age being like, 'Who are these kids? Don't they know punk rock's over?' It was a real affront, in a way. They were wearing leather jackets with writing on 'em; it was like, 'What is this, London '77 again?' New York was *not* London '77. New York was *artists*. But I thought it was totally exciting. Even internally in Sonic Youth, I remember Lee asking me why I was going to those gigs. I knew that it was really potent and it was really connected, seeing bands like Black Flag and The Dead Kennedys playing every little donut shop on the map."[8]

Thurston's love of hardcore's pulse-quickening rhythms had motivated Bob Bert's first exit from the group, and Jim Sclavunos didn't share Thurston's ardour either. "I found it *laughable*," he says. "I lived up the street from [legendary NYC hardcore venue] 7A, and they all looked like a bunch of bozos for me. There was too much human contact, it felt too homoerotic for me – if I'm going to get down like that, I'll go to the Anvil and bring some lube with me. I did not find it musically interesting; I found it really tedious. The ethic of straight-edge didn't appeal to me. The dress code didn't appeal to me. Hardcore seemed to be too much of a music of zealotry and rejection. It was almost abstract-expressionist – fling a can of black paint all over a record, and turn that into electrical frequencies from a guitar – that's the kind of energy it was putting out there... I'm not really knocking it, it just wasn't my thing. But Thurston was quite enamoured by it, and trying to make some alignment between Sonic Youth and the hardcore movement."

Thurston immersed himself deeply in hardcore culture, joining in the scene's vibrant Xeroxed dialogue with *Killer*, a fanzine filled with his record reviews and show reports and interviews with hardcore bands, which he circulated to like-minded zine editors. With his band-mates resisting his attempts to turn Sonic Youth in a more explicitly "hardcore" direction (which might've pleased the punk kids who erroneously attended their gigs expecting a group like hardcore stalwarts Reagan Youth, or any of the zillion other hardcore bands with "Youth" in their name), Thurston joined Even Worse, a hardcore outfit cast in The Beastie Boys' image, playing four shows with the group. Finally, seduced by the hardcore DIY ethic, he released a cassette collage of recordings from Sonic Youth's early shows, a radical spool of feedback and found sounds, fragmentary, distorted Sonic Youth favourites and passages of abstract noise entitled *Sonic Death*, the debut cassette release on his new label, Ecstatic Peace.

"I always wanted to put records out," remembered Thurston, later, of his tireless drive during these years. "I wanted to be in a band, I wanted to put records out, make books… I wanted to do everything. I just wanted to be a part of anything that was about creative expression. Being a New Yorker, there was a history of that anyway. I moved here when people were playing not only in clubs but in people's apartments and loft spaces and galleries – the art world was very on top of the music world, because everyone lived in the same neighbourhood. There was no real separation, there was a lot of shared aesthetic."[9]

One hardcore band that shared Sonic Youth's broadened sense of aesthetic were The Meat Puppets, a trio from Arizona whose ragged, chaotic and absurdly comic punk rock had won fans in the owners of SST Records, who released the group's eponymous debut LP despite their many diversions from the hardcore archetype. "We were pretty much a punk-rock band, I think," offers singer/guitarist Curt Kirkwood, who formed the group in 1980 with his brother Cris on bass and childhood friend Derrick Bostrom on drums. "We tried to play things fast. I think we also liked to play things really shitty. We could play our instruments well, pretty much, we just liked to be irritating."[10]

Though the group initially styled themselves after the sounds of Bostrum's collection of early punk seven inches, Kirkwood had a rich musical background to draw upon, being a fan of art-rock, prog, jazz, even heavy-rock acts like Thin Lizzy. In between their own feral, chaotic hardcore originals, the group would throw in familiar covers, misshapen by their enthusiastic, purposefully anti-musical interpretations. They held no truck with punk rock's scorched-earth, year zero approach. "I remember playing with The Angelic Upstarts in about 1982, and we covered 'Can You Hear Me Knockin'' by the Stones, a really horrible, shitty version of it. We had probably done some hard drugs or something beforehand. The Angelic

Upstarts guy came onstage, and he was militantly knocking us, going, 'No more rock'n'rolling stones, this is 1982!' Big fuckin' deal, whoa, 1982!"

The group won a reputation in Arizona for their surreal, confrontational live shows. "We were sick of the yuppie crowds," Kirkwood remembers. "We'd go through the women's purses while they were playing, pour people's drinks over 'em and stuff, really upset people. There was a great Phoenix punk-rock scene, based around drugs and the most ludicrous kind of partying – not sleazy-street dope and shit, but really cool. I mean, if there's a good use for heroin and cocaine, these people found it." After the Puppets opened up for Black Flag when they came through Arizona, SST offered to release the group's debut, but while the association with the label ensured something approximating countrywide distribution for the release, it also allied them with a hardcore scene they were fast outgrowing, drawing audiences expecting typical SST hardcore fare.

"There was an unspoken machismo sort of ethic, a boys' club thing, in punk rock at the time," Kirkwood recalls. "I like loud music, but it's not a requirement for me. Let Metallica do that kinda thing; I remember hearing their first two albums and thinking, 'They have a handle on it, I'm not going to scream any more'. I did it, it was fun, it was mistaken as 'hardcore'... It was meant to be artistic, it wasn't meant to be taken as aggressive. But we played shows with Black Flag, Fear, TSOL, and got lumped in with all that. It attracted a bad crowd."

The Meat Puppets' first national tour stopped off in New York at Folk City, in December 1982, headlining over Sonic Youth. Bostrum missed the Youth's set, already sick from touring and yearning for the wide open spaces of Arizona, but Curt made sure he caught their set. "I'd heard Glenn Branca, I knew what was going on in the Lower East Side scene," he recalls. "I knew where those guys were coming from, to a degree. I could tell we shared certain influences, that Lee was a Deadhead, immediately. There's not a lot of Deadheads who'll come out and admit that in punk rock, he's one of the few. There's no harm in that, it's a privilege to have had a band like The Grateful Dead in your life, that's something that only comes around once every thousand years. That's why his guitar playing has this beauty to it, kinda like a dandelion in the junk pile of New York City."

* * *

Moore had enough hardcore punk-rocker spirit within him that when John Picarella, a reviewer at the *Village Voice*, filed a scathing write-up of a less-than-stellar Sonic Youth show, he responded in kind. Moore directed his first missive, a venomous letter-to-the-editor dripping with black humour and stinging wit, at Robert Christgau, the head of the music section at the *Voice*, whose incisive reporting had won him the title of "Dean" of rock criticism. As the biggest and most influential of the city's alternative weekly papers, the *Voice*'s support of New York's underground music scene was crucial to its survival, being too marginal and obscure at that point to win space in mainstream rock magazines like *Rolling Stone*. With the tunnel vision of a 'zine-writing zealot, Moore interpreted Christgau's commissioning of such negative coverage as an act comparable to Robert Boykin petulantly closing Hurrah's, and deleterious to the scene; his ire was voluble enough to further fuel the lead track off the next Sonic Youth release.

They had performed a memorable show at New York's Danceteria in the summer of 1983, playing the main stage alongside Swans while Lydia Lunch performed in a side-room. The group played a number of new, as-yet unrecorded songs, for what they vaguely planned as their next full length; for one, a fearsome tornado of swirling detuned guitars and scorched, unsettling vocals, Lunch joined the Youth onstage. Promoter Ruth Polsky drunkenly paid Lunch twice for her performance, and the group used their extra $500 to finance another short session at Fun City Studios. This time, Wharton Tiers would record Sonic Youth live and direct to two-track tape recorder, the latest step in a continued devolution of recording technology since the group exited the 24-track Radio City Studio.

The three songs recorded at this session essayed an even darker, more malevolent intensity than *Confusion*. 'Kill Yr Idols', a riposte to Christgau, was as close to a hardcore song as the group had yet penned, its brutally simple, lunging riff punctuated by occasional noised-out breakdowns, and a lyric by Thurston that doubled as a refutation of naysayer critics and a call to fellow musicians to better their inspirations, to throw off the shackles of rock history and make a noise of their own. "I don't know why you wanna impress Christgau," he snarled, "Aw, let that shit die, and find out the new goal." Thurston preached "Sonic Death!", promised "the end of the world"; certainly Lee and Thurston's guitars sounded apocalyptic, each player taking a separate channel of the stereo mix and assaulting their instruments with screwdrivers and drumsticks, bruising and twisting a barbed squall entwining Kim's bass.

Kim sang lead on 'Brother James', her lyrics filled with shadowy religious imagery, giving the song a seductively dark tone. Again, the guitars sound immense, tolling like great iron bells, notes bending and squirming and swooping, their maverick squalls interlocking to stir up a whirlwind of noise swirling ever faster, seemingly to oblivion. By comparison with these tracks, 'Early American' was almost abstract, the taut, lashing rhythms and screaming guitars giving way to a broodingly primeval rumble, guitars droning with portent and crashing dramatically; at its centre lay a delicate, off-kilter Kim Gordon lullaby, sinister in such a context, followed by a tense, doomy coda.

These tracks formed the group's *Kill Yr Idols* EP, coupled with a cacophonic live take of 'Shaking Hell', which, in its chaotic, frantic way, bested the studio take (which was also included on the EP, along with 'Protect Me You'). To coincide with their second triumphant overseas tour (and perhaps signal ambitions beyond Neutral Records), it was released through Zensor Records, a label based in Germany that would soon re-release *Confusion Is Sex* and distribute it throughout Europe.

'Kill Yr Idols' inaugurated a couple of Sonic Youth constants, not least in the abbreviation 'Yr', a shorthand that would proliferate through later song titles and Sonic Literature. The conversation between Lee and Thurston's guitars was developing in vocabulary too; when he caught the band in 1982, Curt Kirkwood noted their interplay, describing them as "two very different guitar players; Thurston had a very angular approach, while Lee's playing was cool, sublime." The sounds these two guitars could wreak as a composite, as evidenced on 'Kill Yr Idols' and 'Brother James', were powerful indeed, a signature sound they would often call upon and evolve, known by fans and contemporaries as "the hurricane".

Though he was later won over as a vocal and loyal supporter of Sonic Youth's cause, Christgau wasn't immediately impressed by the brilliantly focused spite of 'Kill Yr Idols', especially when the group released a live take on *(Over)Kill Yr Idols* (a seven inch released on friend and zine editor Byron Coley's Forced Exposure label) re-christened 'I Killed Christgau With My Big Fuckin' Dick'. "They actually *did* call for my death," he said, later. "There are nuts out there, you know. I listed that seven inch in my top 10 singles, only at [wife Carola Dibbell]'s suggestion. I called it 'I Killed Christgau With My Big Fucking Dick And Now It Don't Work No More'."[11]

NOTES

[1] http://media.hyperreal.org/zines/est/intervs/branca.html
[2] *Confusion Is Next*, pg 82
[3] Boys Are Smelly, from *The Village Voice Rock & Roll Quarterly* 1988
[4] Author's interview, January 2005

[5] Watt From Pedro radio show, February 14 2007
[6] Author's interview, October 2002
[7] *Sounds* magazine, 1981 http://www.micksinclair.com/sounds/bf.html
[8] *Swingset* magazine #3
[9] Watt From Pedro radio show, February 14 2007
[10] Author's interview, Februrary 2007
[11] Salon, http://archive.salon.com/ent/music/int/2001/05/09/xgau/index.html

CHAPTER FIVE

Like A Hurricane

> "Honey, I'm an American. It's our generation. When you're 10 years old and the Manson family killed the Summer Of Love, it makes a big fucking impact. Race riots happened outside my front door. There was strife, Vietnam, riots at Kent State University. Not until I was older did I realise what it all meant, but I knew how it made me feel – excited, horrified, terrified, thrilled. So my father's car got smashed, so fuckin' what? Too bad he didn't get smashed!"[1]
>
> Lydia Lunch

In early 1984, Lydia Lunch found herself stranded in London, following a failed romantic and creative liaison with Nick Cave, debonair and unhinged frontman of destructive Australian punks The Birthday Party. She had no money, certainly not enough for a plane ticket back to New York; she did, however, have possession of a carrier bag laden with reels of tape from a session she'd recorded in New York, shortly before decamping to Britain. Rescue would come in the form of Paul Smith, a draughtsman and music fan who earned a living illustrating Coventry Council bus timetables.

In addition to sketching buses, Smith worked for Doublevision, a video production company owned by Cabaret Voltaire, a group from Sheffield who experimented with electronic music of an avowedly industrial, punk aesthetic. As these were still early days for the video cassette retail industry, Smith struggled to get attention for Doublevision's releases in the influential British music press, so the company branched out into releasing soundtracks from their projects as albums, winning some media coverage and introducing Smith to key members of the British music industry, such as Pete Warmsley of independent distribution company and record label Rough Trade.

Another ploy was inspired by an interview Lydia Lunch gave to *Sounds*. Talking to journalist Edwin Pouncey, Lunch explained the concept behind 'Fifty One Page Plays', which she had conceived with Cave. Sensing an intriguing potential low-budget video project in these short pieces, Smith called Lunch and arranged a meeting. "But she'd just split up with Nick," he remembers. "She couldn't do the project. Instead, she sat at the table and drummed her fingers, and began telling me this story she'd written. It was fucking mesmerising, Lydia performing at me, up so close."

Smith approached his friends at Rough Trade about Doublevision possibly releasing a Lydia Lunch spoken-word record. "They thought it was a great idea," he continues. "The guys in the warehouse said her music would sell really well too, but no record label was willing to deal with her. And I thought, that's funny, she was very nice to me, as Lydia can be. We started up the Widowspeak label together, and I suggested releasing her music. She said, 'None of my records ever fucking sell, I don't know why you're suggesting it, but I do have *this*.' And she pulled out these two reels of tapes from a plastic carrier bag, this mini-album. She hadn't finished the vocals yet, but all the music was all done." Lunch and Smith travelled up to Cabaret Voltaire's studio in Sheffield to clean up the tapes and re-record some vocals. "She terrified the Cabs with her approach; she had to clear her valves before each take, so there was much hawking of spit onto the studio floor. Cabaret Voltaire were all good northern lads, but they thought Lydia was a bit *hardcore*."

The mini-album would soon be released as *In Limbo*, six tracks of slow, discordant disquiet, scored by Thurston's bleak basslines, Jim Sclavunos' seething, deeply noir sax, and Lunch's uneasy, unsettling vocals. To her delight, Doublevision paid Lunch enough to secure a flight back home, and soon she was back on the streets of New York. Crossing paths with Thurston one afternoon soon afterwards, she told him of the imminent release of *In Limbo*, and of Paul Smith, the guy she'd met in England who'd been so enthusiastic about her music, making sure to hand him Smith's postal address.

* * *

Sonic Youth played few shows in 1984. In August, they travelled up to the Nova Scotia School of Art & Design in Halifax, Canada to take part in a symposium, discussing the group before a gathering of students. Later that night they played in the college cafeteria, but despite blanketing the city with flyers, a nearby hardcore show drew most of their potential audience. Playing to an audience of eight, they performed a set list drawn heavily from new material, its psychotic fury accented by the clatter of stolen trashcans pummelled by the group onstage.

Mostly, they preferred to write and rehearse in a basement room in the Plugg Club, on 24th Street, owned by Giorgio Gomelsky. Once they'd developed a full set of songs, the group approached Martin Bisi as producer for a proposed album. Bisi was a young producer/engineer who'd founded his own studio in Brooklyn, B.C., with the assistance of Brian Eno and Bill Laswell (a Detroit-born musician and producer who, on arriving in New York in 1978, played in his own avant-funk outfit, Material, along with working with Eno and David Byrne on *My Life In The Bush Of Ghosts*, their postmodern 1982 exploration of world music and sampler technology). Working together, Laswell and Bisi developed and produced 'Rockit', a track by jazz pianist and former Miles Davis collaborator Herbie Hancock that blended his fusionist jazz with the new street sound blaring out of New York, hip-hop. Bisi also worked on albums by John Zorn, Elliot Sharp and improvisational guitarist Derek Bailey.

"New York is simply huge," says Bisi. "If you compare it to any other city at any time, there's just always more of almost *anything*. Most cities get known for spawning only one distinctive scene at a time, but in New York there are usually many scenes co-existing. Music is social. I've always been drawn to cool scenes: in their freshness they seem revolutionary, and music becomes part of their respective languages. I was one of the few people who crossed over between so many of those scenes." Bisi represented an intersection between many New York musical subcultures of interest to Sonic Youth, his experience in hip-hop a particular attraction. "Hip-hop had tons of street cred, everybody on the downtown scene was looking to see what they could nibble off of hip-hop."[2]

Where *Kill Yr Idols* had captured Sonic Youth live to tape, without overdubs, they used these new sessions as an opportunity to explore the possibilities of the studio. "They were in the studio for a marathon two and a half weeks," remembers Bisi. "They were long sessions – back then, everyone assumed you had to kill yourself trying to make a record. The recording approach was to experiment, and to do lots of overdubs, try weird treatments." Some of these effects were achieved via inventive, primitive methods; one loop they recorded, for example, required such a long amount of tape that Bisi had to thread it through several cymbal stands. The mixing sessions were similarly anarchic, "multiple-hands-on and spontaneous, with moves being done on the fly, like a performance in and of itself."

To mask the long gaps between songs when they performed onstage – while Lee and Thurston exchanged, retuned and restrung their modified guitars – the group had begun playing pre-recorded tape-loops through the PA system. The album that would surface from these sessions, *Bad Moon Rising*, would raise this method to a high art; save for the gap between the end of side one and the beginning of side two, the album runs as an unbroken suite of music, mysterious and wraith-like segues of noise, feedback, found-sound and drone bridging the distances between where one song ends and another begins, subsuming the listener in a thick, stoning fog.

Bisi says the album has "a very urban, kind of cold, New York No Wave edgy vibe." It's an album that imagines the skyscrapers of New York leaning in like the great redwoods of some dark, haunted forest, recording all the ghosts and ghouls within, its industrial clanks and twisted textures pulling together to create something very alien, very unfamiliar, where you can't quite trust your ears. It opens with haunting, eerie chimes, swiftly swallowed by a rousing symphony-for-treated-guitars, echoing Branca at his most anthemic; the roaring motif soon erupts into black noise, scrubbed guitars spitting raw distortion, speaker cones splintering, Bob Bert pummelling every cymbal and drum-skin within arm's reach. The chaos ebbs away, replaced by those chiming guitars again, only more ominous now: Bert's skittering drums chase an urgent beat, Lee and Thurston scraping new sounds as Kim sings with a morbid shiver. This all occurs within the four or so minutes of first track, 'Brave Men Run'.

Over the half an hour that follows, the noise shifts from uneasily meditative, mantric chime, to free-form guitar excursions operating on the outer planes, to cold, alienating soundscapes eked from broken amplifiers, tribal drums and serrated machine grate, to disorientating tape cut-ups. Things don't sound as they should – a diffuse ghost of Iggy and his Stooges, stuttering through a distorted jump-cut of their 'Not Right', hazes into view, just long enough that afterwards you wonder whether you imagined it. The lyrics encompass dystopian howls, dippy but profound acid-fried love poems, and coldly psychotic, murderous incantations, darkly humourous in places, uncomfortably exhilarating in others. You can sense the group revelling in the dark, disorientating ambience they stir up, a bleak mischief.

The album's title was a signal towards the apocalyptic mood contained within. 'Bad Moon Rising' was a hit in 1969 for Creedence Clearwater Revival. As Creedence's rootsy swamp-rock stood in counterpoint to the incense and peppermints of psychedelia, so the lyrics to 'Bad Moon Rising' ran contrary to the lysergic optimism of the era; though an infectious and upbeat strum, it was, at heart, a blues warning of rough times ahead, an unmistakable allusion to the violent tensions that underscored the late

Sixties. 'Bad Moon Rising' was a massive jukebox bar favourite and true Americana, from its heady freeway chug, to its acknowledgement of a dark undertow running through the country's culture. In many ways, the Sonic Youth album that shared its name was a slice of contemporary Americana, reflecting the turbulent, conflicted mindset of its generation.

1984 found America still reeling from the upheavals, the profound tectonic shifts in its culture over the previous 10 or 20 years: presidents murdered and presidents disgraced, the civil rights movement and the violent suppression of student war protestors, Woodstock and Altamont, and the unshakeable images of bloodshed and destruction beaming in from Vietnam, the bodies returning in flag-draped coffins, the scarred survivors abandoned to a fate of unforgivable neglect. The country had elected a Republican government that sought to demonise the social revolutions of the Sixties, to set the progressive society in reverse; its president was former Hollywood actor Ronald Reagan, an appropriate choice for a country so fatally besotted with escapism. Hardcore punk responded to the Republican authoritarianism with spittle-flecked polemic venom, Reagan their figurehead of hate. Sonic Youth's reply was more subtle, more nuanced, less explicit; but within its air of dark alienation, its potent psychosis, lay just as much of a political statement. The America evoked by *Bad Moon Rising* is a country of violence and bloodshed, of serial killers and psychotic murderers.

"America was in such a dark period at the end of the Sixties," remembers Lydia Lunch. "I was only young, but I was aware, something's not right. America was desperate, was diseased by the wrongness of war, was being lied to, was aware. In the Seventies I think a lot of people felt, 'How did we let the possibility of the Sixties disappear without real fuckin' change?' That left such anger and disappointment within people of my generation. This was America, and already we could see what a fuckin' lie it was. And New York was really just an ignored wasteland at that point. Nobody cared."

'Death Valley 69' closed the album on a cacophonic, gloriously unhinged high. The music had been written while the band were rehearsing at Michael Gira's bunker space on Avenue B, a swirling swarm of railing, screaming guitars that buzzed at such fierce velocity that they recalled the frantic, surf-guitar brutalism of Link Wray and Dick Dale, The Ventures' '2000 Pound Bee' run rampant across a detuned, post-No Wave soundscape. For all the avant-garde terror techniques the group explored throughout the album, 'Death Valley 69' heavily echoed primal heavy metal in its nightmare riff; at London's ULU in November 1985, Thurston introduced the song as by Alice Cooper. Ranaldo and Thurston's guitars howled in dark harmony with each other, a wall of noise that was breath-taking, and not a little scary. "That swirling guitar sound, which I think is a trademark of theirs, was called 'the hurricane' by some people back then," remembers Bisi. "You can hear 'the hurricane' on 'Death Valley '69'."[3] Over this hurricane, Thurston and Lunch sang lyrics they'd written during a bus ride to her apartment in Spanish Harlem, on the topic of Charles Manson and his murderous Family.

The group weren't the first punks to cut a track in reference to a serial killer; New York trash-rockers The Chain Gang recorded their lo-fi classic 'Son Of Sam' at the height of the killer's reign in 1977, the product of an obsession that would lead them on an ill-fated quest to capture the murderer themselves. And even before Sonic Youth wrote 'Death Valley '69', the Manson mythos was irretrievably entangled with the culture of rock'n'roll. An unemployed ex-convict, he'd auditioned unsuccessfully for TV's prefab pop group The Monkees, later befriending Beach Boy Dennis Wilson, who was impressed by the strange, beautiful women who forever followed Manson. The relationship would soon founder, Wilson abandoning his home to Manson and his family of followers as they moved in to stay for a year.

Manson's unhealthy obsession with stardom and rock'n'roll only devolved after his attempts at pop stardom were rebuffed; 'Cease To Exist', a song he'd offered to Wilson, was heavily rewritten before appearing in the nether regions of a later Beach Boys album. Reading awful portent in the obtuse lyrics of The Beatles' 'White Album', Manson predicted a coming race riot, and instructed his followers to commit a series of brutal crimes, which peaked with the bloody murder of pregnant actress Sharon Tate and her party guests at the Hollywood mansion she shared with husband Roman Polanski. As surely as the murder of Meredith Hunter at the Stones' Altamont gig, the Tate murders signalled the bloody end of the hippy dream, the newly aspirant rockers in nearby Laurel Canyon living in fear that they might be Manson's next victims.

Lydia Lunch ascribes her youthful fascination with the Manson atrocities to "my typical teenage bloodlust, a general hatred that was so strong the only thing that could redeem it was someone who wanted to *kill everyone now*. Manson's one of America's great poets, if you've ever read any of his parole interviews. He had a *small* problem with killing other people, but if he could have found a way to channel his poetry, well... Maybe there'd still be a few more Hollywood superstars around today."

Thurston and Lunch's lyrics were almost hallucinatory, snatches of dialogue from some imaginary Manson bloodletting, the violence and gore underscored by some dark and irresistible carnality. "Say 'I love it!'" screamed the chorus, in manic reverie, "Now! Now! Now!" An ominous middle section saw another, climactic reappearance of the ominous chimes from the album's opening moments, Thurston and Lydia's delirious jump-cut poetry unspooling murderous details with the leering prurience of exploitation auteur Roger Corman's camera lens. The language is sensual, almost erotic, of sand in mouths and sun in eyes. The moment of bloody impact is played out in slow motion, with murky sado-masochistic overtones, voices lost in twisted ecstasy moaning, "And then I had to hit it... hit it... hiiiiiiit iiiiiiiit...", before the hurricane tears back in, Lydia's chilling death-scream dovetailing into the climax.

Although he didn't know it yet, *Bad Moon Rising* would be Bob Bert's final album with the group. "Over the years, a lot of people have come up to me and said it is their favourite Sonic Youth record," he reflects today. "I always joke and say, yeah, but if you ran into Steve Shelley you would probably be saying *Daydream Nation* or *Evol* was your fave SY record. The album has a certain pastoral quality, which I love. And I got to work with Lydia Lunch, which was a dream come true. I think *Bad Moon Rising* stands apart from every other Sonic Youth record; whether you see this as a good or bad thing, it's just a matter of taste. I see it as a *good* thing, naturally..."

> "I understand that the show will be held outdoors at a remote desert location under primitive conditions and I expressly assume any and all of the risks arising out of my attending the show."[4]
>
> Liability Release form signed by patrons of the Gila Monster Jamboree

1984 was a year of domestic bliss for Sonic Youth. That summer Kim and Thurston were married in a traditional Catholic wedding in Connecticut; also that year, Lee wed his girlfriend Amanda, and Bob married Linda Wolfe. In December, the group travelled out to Los Angeles, where they stayed with Kim's parents, hung out with her brother Keller, and played their first shows on the West Coast. The opening date would prove an unforgettable experience.

The Gila Monster Jamboree was the brainchild of promoter Stuart Swezey, whose Desolation Centre organisation specialised in arranging concerts in unusual locations. He put on a show on a barge featuring The Meat Puppets and The Minutemen, an eclectic punk group from San Pedro. "It was a party boat with a hundred people and a bar, floating real slow around Long Beach harbour all night," remembers Curt Kirkwood. "That was amazing."

The Jamboree was the second of three guerrilla festivals Swezey organised in the Mojave Desert. Savage Republic, Los Angeleno post-punks fusing drone, tribal industrial rhythms and hypnotic, psychedelic guitar noise, headlined the first show alongside The Minutemen. "We rented out two school buses and a generator and played on the dunes of a dry lakebed,"[5] remembers Minutemen bassist Mike Watt. The third show featured German avant-industrialists Einstürzende Neubauten. Sonic Youth performed at the middle show, on the night of January 5th, 1985, sharing the bill with The Meat Puppets, Los Angeles teen-trash rockers Redd Kross, and a local psychedelic punk group called Psi-Com. "We went to this weird goth guy's house the day before, to check out the drum kit I'd be borrowing," remembers Bob. "The place was full of wild reptiles. He was the singer of Psi-Com; years later, I would realise he was Perry Farrell, of Jane's Addiction."

"Gila Monster was a pirate thing," explains Kirkwood, "the kind of thing Meat Puppets used to play in Arizona, where people would bring kegs. But Stuart did it on a much larger scale." The generator and crappy PA system were set up at Skull Rock, a knoll deep in the Mojave desert, eight miles from Joshua Tree. The operation was entirely illicit, conducted as far under authority radar as possible; for $7.50, attendees received tickets with directions to a booth in nearby Victorvillle, where they would be given a map directing them to the location. "The last stretch of road to the concert site will be on unmaintained, rocky dirt road," warned the handout. "Your car should be in good repair – especially your suspension and spare tyre."

"It was well lit, because it was full moon," remembers Kirkwood. "Clear viewing, you can go hiking around, you don't need a flashlight or nothin'. It's real nice. You were surrounded by the desert, you kinda had to sneak in. There was slippery stuff going on all around; there were 500 people there, and I think a lot of them were on LSD. There was this bizarre feeling of paranoia. Loads of people were just sitting there going, 'woooah, woooah', tripping in the desert, all these punk rockers from LA. It was a pretty SST-heavy affair. Like I said, we're all friends, Redd Kross, Sonic Youth, all the attendant freaks from SST. It wasn't real loud, it was pleasant."

The Meat Puppets had recently released their second LP, *II*, on SST Records; a marked progression from the gleefully inept thrash of their debut, the album cross-pollinated elements of Americana – country, bluegrass, folk and psychedelia – that rarely figured in the hardcore blueprint, playing with a hazy, stoned, punk approach delivering strange, charming, utterly unique sound. Eschewing hardcore's unwelcoming roar won The Meat Puppets the tender ear of the press; *Rolling Stone* critic Kurt Loder described *Meat Puppets II* as "one of the funniest and most enjoyable albums of 1984"[6].

Favourable attention from such mainstream organs merely exacerbated the group's sense of displacement within the hardcore scene. They hardly shared the movement's gung-ho approach to politics, the line, "I'm sick and tired of living in Nixon's mess" from the deliciously lazy 'Lost' their sole contribution to the discourse. Coming from privileged (but profoundly damaged) backgrounds, and loving the non-competitive lifestyle and dippy, psychedelic punk scene of liberal Phoenix, they were unlike most bands on SST. "I remember when the *Rolling Stone* review came out," remembers Kirkwood. "Punk-rock bands didn't get reviewed in *Rolling Stone* back then, Black Flag had never been reviewed. We were in DC, and I remember the Flag crew saying, 'Did you see this shit? Fuckin' Meat Puppets, those fuckin' queers? Fuck that shit.'

"We did six weeks with Black Flag in 1984. It was awful, just awful. I wore a three-piece suit, and grew my hair down to my ass. Oh, and I dyed it bright blue. I looked *good*. But people were fuckin' spitting on me every show, like *hundreds* of loogies. I was fuckin' kicking people in the face, it was full-on combat. I don't want shit thrown at me, not many people do. I've had to have work done on my teeth, cos they got fucked up by people doing shit to me early on, hitting me with the mic-stand and all that stuff. I'm just really not that rowdy."

In many ways, a group as cerebral, as avowedly "arty" as Sonic Youth were just as unlikely signees to SST as The Meat Puppets, but as the group played several more shows around Los Angeles in the company of SST luminaries ("Henry Rollins stood front and centre at the Loungerie Club, checking us out," remembers Bob), Thurston began harbouring fantasies of Sonic Youth finding a place on this label he so admired. "SST was always pushing the boundaries without losing the aesthetic, putting out records by Saccharine Trust, The Minutemen, The Meat Puppets," he remembered. "It was incredible. And Black Flag were so instrumental to the scene, touring across America and playing everywhere. For me, it was obvious that SST was the vanguard label."[7]

Thurston had caught a show by The Minutemen during an earlier trip to Los Angeles, sneaking into Californian nightclub The Music Machine by pretending to be a local journalist. When the Youth played the Anti Club, The Minutemen returned the favour. "Me and [Minutemen singer/guitarist] D Boon were pretty blown away," remembers Mike Watt. "We thought *we* were trying adventurous stuff – we were influenced by Wire and The Pop Group, we'd grown up on Blue Öyster Cult and Creedence and T Rex – but I gotta tell you, when Sonic Youth came along, we felt like Chuck Berry! Thurston was putting screwdrivers into his guitar, they were playing strange tunings. I remember they had a book full of their tunings, before they had roadies. They didn't have cases for their guitars either, they just slung them in the van, under a shelf. It had a pretty profound effect on us: like, wow, these cats are light years ahead of us. I didn't know anything about Branca and all that, until I spoke to Thurston."

Thurston had already struck up a faltering postal relationship with Watt. The Minutemen ran their own label, New Alliance, distributed by SST, and had released a 7″ and LP entitled 'Feeble Efforts' and *Mighty Feeble* respectively, compilations of avant and experimental music from underground LA; Thurston loved these records so much that he wrote to Watt. "What really tripped me out was, he'd seen the Voidoids a bunch," adds Watt. "Richard Hell was my first punk-rock hero, a bass player who led his own band. Thurston had seen him in person, had seen a lot of shows in New York City; his first-hand accounts were mind-blowing. That first night we just talked and talked and talked, and I couldn't get over it, his knowledge of music... And it continues, whenever I talk to him, I'm still learning."

While on the West Coast, the group stopped by Radio Tokyo, a local studio often frequented by Black Flag, to record a couple of new songs with producer and studio owner Ethan James, a former member of Sixties proto-metal psychedelicists Blue Cheer (whose brutishly loud blues rock din was a distant Californian echo of The MC5), who later produced many crucial West Coast hardcore albums. 'Hallowe'en' evoked the doomy lull of *Bad Moon Rising*, a muted tremble of tambourine and tom-tom, deeply psychedelic guitar rasps coiling about a Kim Gordon vocal inspired by a Black Flag performance and, in particular, frontman Henry Rollins. Confusion, sex and a whole jumble of other nebulous themes lurked in the foreground, as Kim's lyric dissected and drank in Rollins' performance – and, more so, the erotic thrill of being a voyeur of said performance – with similar acuity to her lauded essay on a Public Image Ltd show at New York's Ritz, published in *Artforum* in 1981 as 'I'm Really Scared When I Kill In My Dreams'. "And I don't know what you wanna do, and you're looking at me with your big dark eyes, and you're rubbing your body," murmurs Gordon, but the focus is as much on her response, their interaction, as his actions, unravelling the seduction of performance, and Gordon's attraction. "It's the devil in me, makes me stare at you," she whispers, "Fucking with me, as you slither up to me, your lips there, slipping, twisting at my insides, and singing on."

It was dark at Skull Rock by the time Sonic Youth started playing. "The High Desert can get real cold in the Winter at night," warned the directions to the Jamboree. "We recommend you bring extra sweaters, jackets, gloves, hats, etc." The group had clearly heeded the advice, Kim wearing thick black leggings under a dress, under a hooded top pulled over her head, while the boys wore thick sweaters over warm flannel shirts, their heavy boots leaving footprints in the desert sand. A camera crew were on hand to film the event, tripping audience members staggering in front of the lens and standing there for a while, oblivious. Still, the crude footage captures some sense of this anarchic event.

They opened with a brutal lunge through 'Brother James', Kim soon ditching her bass to holler with hands clutching the microphone, guitars swooping and squalling about her while, for a snarling 'Kill Yr Idols', Thurston throttled his beat-up thrift-store Telecaster with glee. During a brief tune-up lull, Kim called for "one beer for the band, one sip," while Lee asked the crowd gathered in close around them whether everything sounded "totally fucked up?". A yelled reply of "No!" signalled a swing through some *Bad Moon* material: the kaleidoscopic bruise of 'Brave Men Run', a dizzying 'Death Valley 69' that almost buckled under its chaotic attack. The psychedelic love poesy 'I Love Her All The Time' bubbled up from a din of strobing, inventive guitar abuse, Thurston rubbing and striking a drumstick thrust under his strings with another drumstick, and singing while the camera gazed on Kim, bathed in purple floodlight and punching away at her bass with severe focus. For 'I'm Insane', Lee hammered at an old automobile wheel-hub by way of percussion; 'Flower', another song recorded at Radio Tokyo, opened with Kim accompanied only by Bob's drums, Lee and Thurston off in the shadows, hastily preparing their guitars.

"I remember a bunch of bonfires scattered amongst the crowd," says Bob. "It was a fabulous show, a surreal and chilly night." As droning, howling tape loops from *Bad Moon Rising* screamed from the PA system, Sonic Youth lurched into a final, savage career through 'Burning Spear', Thurston and Lee scaring up fierce and caustic din with their guitars, screwdrivers, drumsticks and power-drill, collapsing moments after the first verse into chaos, band members crouched in the sand beating strange noises out of their instruments, before the stuttering, distorted voice of Iggy Pop singing 'Not Right' materialised into earshot. Sonic Youth's maiden voyage to the West Coast had been a success, forging a connection they'd failed to make during the Savage Blunder, initiating a dialogue with the wider underground scene in America. But their debut performance was a resolutely one-way conversation, flooding the Californian desert with the artful chill, the kinetic might of their super-evolved New York No Wave.

"People started getting stuck on their way out," laughs Kirkwood, of the messy Gila Monster aftermath. "Others got too stoned and just hung out at

Skull Rock. The cops showed up at dawn, just as the sun was coming up, and the stragglers got arrested. I'm sure we got paid, but I'm sure it wasn't much. Money was never an issue, we never made crap from touring, especially not back then."

> "At that point the UK scene was touting the death of the electric guitar, and Sonic Youth, in a New York minute, wiped that concept out. They encouraged Blast First! to bring over Big Black and the Butthole Surfers to further the explosion of recognition for the new US underground. Things have not been the same since."[8]
>
> Thurston Moore

Shortly after *Bad Moon Rising* was completed, Thurston sent a cassette with six tracks from the sessions in a package to Paul Smith in England. Accompanying the cassette was a yellow Post-It note upon which Thurston had nonchalantly scribbled, "I guess I'll send one of these to everyone in England".

"I liked the idea that he spent his days making these cassettes for people," smiles Paul Smith. He liked the music contained on the cassette even more. Smith was a veteran of the British punk era; while working at a record shop in Mansfield, Nottinghamshire in 1977, he'd made sure the store stocked copies of The Buzzcocks' *Spiral Scratch* EP, the first punk record released on an independent label in the UK. He caught The Clash at their early peak, but had actually turned up to see the support act, Suicide, embarking upon a poorly received, spit-flecked UK tour.

"I'd never ever seen an audience react so badly," says Paul. "This hail of gob, screams of 'Get this band off!' I think they managed to play four songs. It was brilliant. I thought, fuck, I'm going to see that again tomorrow!" Later, he immersed himself in the music of Cabaret Voltaire and Throbbing Gristle, avant-garde electronic music with dark industrial overtones. "To me, it's all 'pop music'. It might not be popular, but its 'pop'. Richard H Kirk believes his Cabaret Voltaire are a dance band, they're deep into soul music. The culture I came from was the Midlands, really working class. We all grew up with the Northern Soul weekenders; part of it was the music, part of it was the drugs. All my mates had ended up working in the pit, and that was our weekend.

"When I listened to the cassette, Sonic Youth's music made total sense to me," remembers Smith, of what he would later describe as "a Blakeian vision" that converted him to Sonic Youth zealotry. "It was a fantastic experience, something that really spoke to me at that time. I thought the greatness of this music was obvious, that everyone else could see what I saw. To be honest, weirdly enough, I always saw them on a major label. I really thought my involvement with the group would amount to playing the tape to people, and whoever first said they wanted to release it I would give Thurston's number. That would've been it. But no one wanted them."

Richard H. Kirk vetoed a release through Doublevision, deciding Sonic Youth too "rock'n'roll" at a time when the British pop scene was retreating from such old-fashioned relics as guitars in favour of the possibilities offered by the synthesiser. So Smith called up every contact he'd built within the London music scene, visiting all the successful independent labels that had sprung up during the fertile punk era, imprints like Rough Trade, 4AD and Mute, proffering the cassette. He played it to A&R people at the major labels, anyone and everyone who could possibly have done something with the music. Eventually, his friend Pete Warmsley, tiring of Smith's constant barside spiels about this amazing band from New York and all the clueless record labels who weren't interested in signing them, suggested Smith start his own label and release *Bad Moon Rising* himself.

"Sonic Youth hadn't heard from me much since Thurston had sent me the tape; the expense of calling up America was frightening at that point, and I was struggling to pay my mortgage," remembers Smith. It's easy to forget, in an age of affordable mobile telephones, internet and email, just how complicated and expensive transatlantic communication was only two decades ago. "But I called them. Lee answered the phone, and he offered the rights to release the album for $10,000, an unheard-of amount of money. They had no fucking idea. They eventually signed for £500, which meant I had to skip two mortgage payments, with permission from my then-wife."

Now possessing the master tapes and the right to release the album, Smith had Warmsley draw up a distribution contract for his new, as-yet-unnamed label. "That's how little I'd thought it all through," he reflects. "I hadn't even thought of a name for the label." Smith christened the imprint Blast First!, after author and painter Wyndham Lewis' short-lived literary journal *BLAST*, and by February 1985, less than six months after he first received Thurston's cassette, was preparing to release the label's maiden release, *Bad Moon Rising*.

"The group sent the artwork in," remembers Smith, "and for the back sleeve they'd submitted some pictures of Lee and Bob when they were younger, with big curly hair. I said, this is a total mistake; people are going to think it's a reissue of an old Seeds record or something. They'd also sent me this promo photo with them standing before the horizon, Kim wearing her 'little red riding hood' thing. It was a lot more 'modern', so we used that.

Apparently, no one had ever had a conversation with Sonic Youth from a marketing point of view; we needed to make sure it would sell, and those hippy photos were the wrong image to put across." The front cover was a shot of the New York skyline at dusk, taken from some nearby shore, the sunset melting from orange to purple; in the foreground stood a jack-o'-lantern, its pumpkin head aflame, straw poking out of flannel-shirted arms tied to a cross... a perfect evocation of the album's nocturnal thrill, its uniquely urban flavour of American Gothic.

Via Richard Boon, former manager of The Buzzcocks and Smith's friend since the *Spiral Scratch* days, the latter was introduced to Pat Naylor, who worked in the Rough Trade promotional department. "Pat was a punk original," remembers Smith. "She was also a friend of Kim and Thurston's, she'd stayed in their apartment in New York. We met up in the pub and I said, 'You know them, you've seen them play, you should be their press agent'. She said, 'I fuckin' hate people with beards'."

Nevertheless, Naylor accepted the offer from the bearded Smith, soon penning their first UK press release, an account of a Sonic Youth gig she'd seen where she noted how Thurston got all tangled up in his wires, and Kim's powerful onstage presence. Smith also soon took receipt of a bulky package couriered over from New York: an exquisitely presented, colour-photocopied compendium of all of Sonic Youth's press coverage to date, painstakingly collated and produced by Thurston while working at Todd's Copy Shop.

Britain's music scene sustaining four high-selling music weeklies, the press still had enough influence on its readership to make or break groups, and with four titles publishing every single week there was more than enough space to devote to groups floating beneath the radar of television, artists who struggled to get radio play beyond the benevolent, quixotic and questing Radio 1 DJ John Peel, whose show long served as a haven for the unlikely and the unique. Support from the press would be crucial to selling a group like Sonic Youth in the United Kingdom.

"Pat's approach was completely different to the Rough Trade press officers, Scott Piering and Claude Bessy, who were pretty 'out there' and aggressive," says Smith. "She told me, 'You're obviously an idiot, so you stay away from the press, leave it to me'. Her general attitude towards journalists was that they weren't good enough to write about her band. She liked Edwin Pouncey, though." Smith estimates that Pouncey's *NME* review of *Bad Moon Rising* sold 5,000 copies of the album overnight, swiftly recouping his initial investment.

Newly anointed as a record label mogul, Smith spent his lunchtimes in a pub round the corner from Rough Trade's offices in Collier Street, north London, soaking up tips, stories and advice from his friends in the London music scene, people like Richard Boon, Rough Trade PR Claude Bessy (a refugee from the LA punk scene who sometimes wrote under the pseudonym Kickboy Face) and Rob Gretton, a co-founder of Manchester's Factory Records and universally respected manager of Joy Division and New Order. "Rob was an enormous influence on me personally, somebody I miss an enormous amount," says Smith [Gretton passed away in 1999]. "He completely straightened my head out with regards to the responsibility of the manager/label owner, and I could never thank him enough for that. He said, 'This is fucking serious, you are now responsible for these peoples' lives, until they don't want you involved any more'. That made me feel this very adult sense of responsibility. It was the schooling I needed."

Smith met Sonic Youth at London's Heathrow airport in March of 1985, as they embarked upon their third European tour. "I'd seen photographs of them, so I knew what they looked like, but they didn't know what I looked like," remembers Smith. "Thurston was tall, he was easy to recognise. They had shitloads of guitars with them. I walked over and said 'Hi'. I asked them if they wanted to change some dollars into pounds, and they got in a huddle and, between the four of them, scared up about $22. I don't think it changed into much more than a tenner."

Smith remains incredulous, over two decades later. "They'd paid for their own one-way tickets over from New York, arriving with no way to get home and barely enough money to feed themselves for the next couple of days. It really shook me up; I'd never seen a band just throw themselves into another country and hope somehow it would all be all right. They didn't have a credit card between them, either. It was a mixture of confidence and naivety. They were very emotionally serious, very committed to the fact that this was what they wanted to do, and they would do whatever it took."

For Sonic Youth's performance at London's Institute Of Contemporary Arts, a progressive arts centre located just up the road from Buckingham Palace, on Wednesday March 20, the group were supported by Tools You Can Trust, a manic and cacophonic Mancunian group with an avowed passion for No Wave, and a duo performance from Frank Tovey, an eccentric electronic-music pioneer from Leeds, and Boyd Rice, best known for the industrial noise he purveyed as NON. Perhaps aware of the importance of the impending show, Thurston was struck with a pervading sense of panic beforehand. "He'd had an attack of nerves," remembers Smith. "He got the fear; he was shaking, it was like he had the flu. If you look at photographs taken at the gig, in practically every shot Thurston's wearing a different shirt. He'd taken the stage wearing all the shirts he'd brought with him, like eight shirts or something, because he felt so cold; as he got going and started to feel better, he peeled them off. Some idiot wrote that he thought Thurston was trying to make a 'statement', but he wasn't. Years later, this bigwig from the ICA used to go around saying he'd seen the group shooting up smack before the show... I set him right on that. Thurston was lying there shivering, but that was from *fear*, not drugs. There's this very English mindset which always wants its rock groups to behave like The Velvet Underground. And Sonic Youth aren't anything like that. They smoked a bit of pot maybe. They couldn't drink to save their lives. They didn't 'get' the whole English pub culture."

Sonic Youth took to a stage decorated with jack-o'-lanterns, a tip of the pumpkin to *Bad Moon Rising*'s iconic sleeve. Smith handled sound for the group, as the only person present with an idea of what their avant tangle of noise was "supposed" to sound like. He felt hugely anxious for them. "The friend whose flat I stayed at when in London had seen the group's previous London show, at The Venue," he explains. "He said they were shit. But I had great fun up on the sound desk; I treated it like a big stereo, panning the guitars across the stage. I remember being upstairs in the balcony at the ICA, and I swear, my jaw was on the floor, at the *intensity* of it..."

Sonic Youth were a shock to the system for a London live scene that could only muster the comparatively puny Jesus and Mary Chain by way of competition for the group's brutally artful attack. "I'd seen the Mary Chain, William Reid standing there with his back to the audience, the weight of the world on his shoulders, making his racket. I'm a fan, but it's very *English*, very non-confrontational. The Youth were completely in your fucking face. Thurston was this huge guy, whacking the shit out of his guitars, and the noise they made was *fantastic*. I loved Kim's lurching bass playing, it wasn't 'technically good', but it was emotionally brilliant. She was doing this weird, very sexual frug. It was so striking, this petite girl handling a massive Thunderbird bass, having to throw her whole body weight into it to get what she wanted out of it."

The group's set was balanced equally between *Bad Moon Rising* material and earlier songs; during 'Shaking Hell', Kim inadvertently fell off the stage, but kept playing along. "During our sets at the time," recalls Bob Bert, "we left no space for audience response until the very end of the set. It was one continuous piece of unbroken music, like on *Bad Moon Rising*." The group had their tape-loops all primed, so the noise didn't stop.

"They'd been kicked off a few stages in their time," laughs Smith, "so they'd planned their set so you couldn't stop them once they got going. I quite clearly remember that gig being full at the start, and nearly empty at the end. I met Pat at the bar afterwards and said, 'That was awesome, but people left in droves!' She said, 'It doesn't matter, all the people who stayed were journalists!'"

One journalist present at the ICA show was Mark Sinker, a young writer then freelancing for *NME*. "I was already aware of Sonic Youth, because Chris Bohn and Don Watson had mentioned them in their special 'Noise' issue of *NME* a couple of years earlier," remembers Sinker. "I think Bob Bert must have sensed his time with the band was running out, because I remember him playing as if his life depended on it. It was very exciting, it felt almost like a force of nature. What really struck me was that the sound was mutating out of something very together, and yet very chaotic. I'd never seen anything like that, except in the realms of improvisational music, and that would have been almost a chamber music set-up, without amplification. There was more sticking drum sticks behind strings and banging them than there was 'straight' playing of guitar. I was just so excited by it."[9]

Another patron who withstood the sonic assault until the very end was Mick Harvey, former guitarist with The Birthday Party who had recently formed The Bad Seeds with frontman Nick Cave. The group had their first British tour looming at the end of April, and Harvey felt Cave needed "a kick up the arse", and that Sonic Youth supporting them for the tour would have the required effect.

* * *

Three nights later the group played Woolwich Polytechnic, booked by Student Union Entertainments Officer Lee Gurney, a musician with connections to the punk-rock scene. In the audience for the show was Jerry Thackray, a sometime musician who performed as The Legend!, which was also the title of his fanzine. "I was going to between 160–200 shows a year at the time," Thackray remembers. "I'd seen Sonic Youth's earlier show at The Venue; I think they were out to alienate people, and they succeeded." A devoted follower of the burgeoning early Eighties cassette culture, where fast-evolving home-taping technology offered musicians an affordable means of distributing their music unhindered by record labels' A&R filtering process, he'd purchased a copy of *Sonic Death* from the Virgin record store on Oxford Street, at a booth dedicated to cassette culture manned and stocked by Jim Thirlwell.

"The soundman had a party he wanted to go to, so he'd told the band they had a definite curfew," remembered Thackray. "But the band refused to leave the stage. So the soundman clambered up and started dismantling the microphones as Lee and Thurston were singing into them, and taking them away. Bob just continued drumming, and everyone else continued playing their guitars, and they did this for 20 minutes. It was just one of the most incredible things I'd seen, just *so* 'Fuck You!' They also played 'Death Valley '69' that night. I was a huge Lydia Lunch fan, had been since I was 16, but I knew fuck all about Charles Manson. The obsession a certain sector of the American indie scene has with serial killers is just juvenile, quite frankly. But that's a fucking amazing song. It's just a sheer rush of adrenaline when that scream comes in. Or is it a guitar? Maybe it's both."

The Youth played a show at London's famed jazz and punk haven The 100 Club on the 26th, supported by relocated NYC No Wave group Ut, before leaving for three weeks of shows booked across Europe, taking in the Netherlands, Belgium, Italy, Switzerland and Germany. "I was getting a little tired of touring for six weeks at a time, sleeping on cold, dirty floors and not making any money," remembers Bob. "Paul Smith was freaking me out, with all his future plans for Sonic Youth. I pictured myself never being home. He kept saying, 'I'm gonna make you as big as The Birthday Party!', which is pretty funny, when you think about it."

They hooked up with The Bad Seeds on April 23, exactly a month after their triumphant ICA show, at The Powerhouse in Birmingham. "It was The Bad Seeds' first tour," continues Bob. "Roland S Howard was in the band for the tour and they would encore with some Birthday Party songs. They were ultra-amazing, and still are."

"Those shows exposed them to a *big* audience," beams Smith. "The Youth kicked The Bad Seeds' ass every night, except for the Hacienda in Manchester, when the scary acoustics of that venue overwhelmed my abilities as a soundman. Other than that, we were slaughtering them. The kids who were going to the shows really wanted to see The Birthday Party, and The Bad Seeds were quite a different proposition. Sonic Youth had a similar mad physicality to The Birthday Party, so we scored quite an audience off the back of that. A lot of bands would've baulked at playing with a group as great as Sonic Youth were then. But Mick Harvey felt Nick Cave *needed* to see the Youth, to get off his arse.

"I remember that first afternoon I met them," continues Smith. "We rode the Tube back into town, carrying all the guitars with us. Thurston subsequently told me that when they met me, he was disappointed because I was the same age as them and wore ripped jeans; he'd been hoping he was going to meet some sort of a 'businessman'. Because he gave me a list of 22 bands he hoped I would sign immediately. His real hope was that they'd gotten signed to a 'proper' label, and that I would handle all these bands."

The list contained the names of groups Blast First would subsequently release in the UK, a cross section of Thurston's favourite sounds emanating from Noise America. In the years that followed, the label would build a formidable roster of groups from the American underground, sating British audiences unmoved by their country's more tepid local produce, hungering for the profane avant chaos the Blast First! label reliably offered. "The artists we signed, people like Steve Albini or Gibby Haynes, they were all lovely people but they had their own vision of the world," explains Smith. "That was the stuff that interested me.

"Thurston arrived with a whole wave of music. Collectively, they're all very interested in music, in other bands, and they've done a lot to create a network for these groups. In America, that's phenomenally hard. It was such a different time. There was no internet, mobile phones didn't exist. Touring involved telling someone you'd see them in six weeks, and maybe you'd get a phone call from a hotel room en route. America didn't even have an 'alternative' chart – that was part of the struggle.

"As Blast First! grew," Smith adds, "the people who came to work for us had a certain amount of 'attitude'. There's a lot of walking wounded, as a result of the Blast First! experience. We all get along well now, but for years people would leave and not want to talk to me again. And I completely understand that; we used to have some full-on, stand-up arguments. But those arguments sprang from a passion. Because I was on this weird zealot's mission.

"So that was all very fortuitous, all very wonderful… And then they went off and recorded that slew of albums. Thinking about it now, I get quite teary about it. At that moment in time, they were unstoppable."

NOTES

[1] Author's interview, February 2007
[2] Author's interview, March 2007
[3] Author's interview, March 2007
[4] http://www.sonicyouth.com/mustang/cc/sy010585e.jpg
[5] Author's interview, February 2007
[6] *Rolling Stone* #420, 1984
[7] Watt From Pedro radio show, February 14 2007
[8] http://www.sonicyouth.com/history/ographies/thurstonleavenotes.html
[9] Author's interview, March 2007

CHAPTER SIX

EVOLution Summer

"People tell me these are bad times to be young… I've never known them to be better. Taking into account the young's boundless enthusiasm for mischief, the opportunities afforded are endless."[1]

Biba Kopf, *NME* review of Hüsker Dü's Zen Arcade

The mid-Eighties would prove a watershed era for hardcore and the American underground, tectonics shifting and radical new sounds emerging. On the West Coast, Black Flag finally closed the book on their legal entanglement with Unicorn and set about releasing the backlog of material recorded during their enforced hiatus. In the absence of any new material since 1981's *Damaged*, these releases seemed a quantum leap from that album's blunt brilliance, to the new and unfamiliar places Greg Ginn's insaniac guitar playing and Henry Rollins' fury-laden Bukowski-on-Ritalin lyrics were taking hardcore. *My War*, *Slip It In* (both 1984) and *In My Head* owed as much to Black Sabbath as any previous Flag reference point, the group unafraid of kicking out some intense, agonisingly slow jams, toying with Jazz-Fusion-esque time changes and a heaviness akin to Metal.

1984's *Family Man* album – a side of instrumental Flag music, heavy on Ginn's murderously lyrical, skronk-laden guitar playing, and a side of Rollins' spoken-word poetry – made for uncompromising, brilliantly uneasy listening. But a vocal portion of the moshpit didn't dig their fast-developing complexity, their blackened and burnished poetics; after years locked in combat with the cops and the major labels and local club owners, Black Flag had to open up another front, deflecting attacks from the more stubbornly closed-minded corners of the hardcore community.

SST continued to flourish under the aegis of articulate, opinionated LA-born A&R man Joe Carducci, releasing epochal slabs of vinyl (even if the straight press wouldn't recognise them as such until years later) and fashioning an aesthetic encompassing an impressive cross section of the American hardcore scene. The groups sharing the SST imprint were every bit as uncompromising and creative as Black Flag, though few shared their dystopian, dark blues.

San Pedro's The Minutemen released their early records through their own label, New Alliance (co-founded with Martin Tamburovich, an ex-member from an earlier Minutemen line-up), which was later absorbed by SST. The Minutemen themselves signed to SST for their most respected releases, capturing the band's urgent mess of poetry, politics and fiercely punk groove, with never an ounce of fat on their tunes' wiry carcasses. Comprising upstart drummer George Hurley, force-of-nature bassist Mike Watt and charismatic eternal flame of enthusiasm D. Boon on guitars and vocals, The Minutemen's peak was perhaps their never-sprawling, always-lean twin set *Double Nickels On The Dime*, 81 taut minutes of scattershot genius, ranging from the considered polemic of 'Political Song For Michael Jackson To Sing', to the charming chime of latterday *Jackass* theme 'Corona', to the napalm-spitting fury of 'This Ain't No Picnic'. *Double Nickels* also found space within its four black vinyl sides for covers of tunes by Van Halen, Creedence Clearwater Revival and Steely Dan, saluting their non-hardcore roots, along with tunes written by Joe Carducci, Henry Rollins and avant-metal labelmates Saccharine Trust, and even finding enough space to include a three-horn salute from the band members' automobiles.

New Alliance also released the early recordings of a hardcore trio based out in Minneapolis, in the Midwest. Hüsker Dü's speed-freak earliest recordings proved they could do 'hardcore' faster than the pack, their aptly-titled *Land Speed Record* live set from 1982 still a genre landmark: 17 songs in 26 nose-bleeding minutes, its apex the tumbling-down-stairs chaos of 'Bricklayer', which somehow packs two verses, two choruses and a fret-melting guitar solo within its 53 seconds. Compared to their Minneapolis rivals The Replacements – a drunken, shambolic and in many ways heart-breaking punk outfit whose bar band roots/influences shone through their careworn riffage – Hüsker Dü were a fearsome, disorientating, exhilarating experience. They signed to SST for 1983's mini-LP *Metal Circus*, drawing back from the full-on thrash of yore to allow a chiming pop sensibility to come to the fore, while their 1984 cover of 'Eight Miles High' showcased the sophistication of guitarist/singer Bob Mould's art, wrapping the Sixties psych classic's melancholic jangle within his own heavily distorted, high-treble guitar rasp, high-speed flurries of notes making some cosmic, amp-melting connection between The Byrds and the genius, modal squawking of John Coltrane that originally inspired the song.

In many ways, Mould and singing drummer Grant Hart were a Lennon/McCartney for the hardcore era, and their fractious, competitive relationship fuelled the exhaustive creativity of their 1984 double album set, *Zen Arcade*. A perfectly Townshendian teen-opera detailing a young punk's descent into the urban subterranea, *Zen Arcade* encompassed brutalised hardcore, acoustic anguish, achingly beautiful pop (Hart's haunting eulogy for a junkie hooker, 'Pink Turns To Blue', is the best of a brilliant bunch) and a closing 14-minute jazz-core instrumental that suggested the entire narrative was just a dream (a plot device the writers of TV soap *Dallas* would appropriate a couple of years later).

Double Nickels On The Dime and *Zen Arcade* shared a rave review by critic David Fricke in *Rolling Stone* magazine, proclaiming that "the chances they take and the earnest fury that drives them not only challenge the 'no future' dictum, they are the blueprint for a brave new music."[2] In between the coasts, brain-scrambling and unpalatable noise also thrived, twisting hardcore roots into gnarly new shapes. Touch & Go Records began life as a punk fanzine published out of Michigan, co-edited by Tesco Vee, frontman of local hardcore group The Meatmen. Aided by Corey Rusk, bassist with Ohio's Necros, Vee founded the label to release the music produced by their bands and others, including inspired Michigan brutes Negative Approach.

By the mid-Eighties, the label had relocated to Chicago, bravely handling the output of a gaggle of troublemaking, acid-gobbling Texan freaks named the Butthole Surfers, whose anarchic hardcore had swiftly mutated into a garbled, genius squelch of ugly psychedelia, inchoate noise, black-hearted humour and bilious parodies of classic rock riffola. Towering iconoclast frontman Gibby Haynes was the most deeply fried of the bunch, fire-breathing ringmaster for House of Horrors live shows that pulsed to the endless beat of double stand-up drummers King Coffey and Theresa Nervosa, as guitarist Paul Leary perverted the axe-hero archetypes and Haynes fed his vocals through the transmogrifying 'Gibbytron' while stolen autopsy footage flickered behind them. The Buttholes purveyed grim and luridly hilarious cabaret, a phantasmagoria sewn together from prime American trash.

The humour plied by Big Black was of a markedly more bitter flavour, their songs impossibly bleak punchlines that provoked more winces than laughter. Uniquely for their era and milieu, the Chicago trio featured a primitive drum machine within their rhythm section, the human elements

– Santiago Durango (formerly of Chicago punks Naked Raygun, who also fielded early member Jeff Pezzati), Dave Riley and vocalist Steve Albini – wielding guitars pitched to such a shrill and rasping level of distortion that, along with the digital pulse of their Roland TR-606, lent their noise a most industrial, urban chill. Big Black were signed to Homestead Records, a label run by *Conflict* fanzine's Gerard Cosloy, an underground-rock aficionado of such savagely hilarious acuity that his influence would reign over indie-rock for years afterwards, via his later New York-based independent label Matador Records.

The sleeve to *Atomizer*, Big Black's 1986 debut album, painted the Earth at the mercy of a disintegrating ray like that wielded by Marvin The Martian in Warner Bros' Duck Dodgers cartoons. The subject matter was of a stark contrast, telling tales of an America where small towns sheltered barely underground child abuse rings, where seedy thrills forever lay in too close reach, where self-immolation is the only way to spend your Saturday night; the same kind of America evoked by the movies of David Lynch and, indeed, by *Bad Moon Rising*.

In Washington DC, the increasingly violent meathead quotient of audiences had forced the once-vibrant local hardcore scene aground. "It was like having these great picnics," remembers Ian MacKaye. "Then suddenly a bunch of skinheads turn up at the picnic and start beating the shit out of people, and every time you have a picnic they show up. So we just started another picnic, with food they don't like to eat. We started making music which didn't appeal to skinheads. Embrace, Rites Of Spring, they changed the course of events. Here's something that's real deep and meaningful that's not gonna sound like Minor Threat."[3]

Many of the surviving groups from the initial spurt of DC hardcore dissolved, reconstituting in new line-ups under new names, playing music that steered their creative momentum away from the frantic slam-dance of early hardcore towards new, more complex and sophisticated directions. The summer of 1985 was christened "Revolution Summer" to celebrate this era of metamorphosis, of renewal, with new voices surfaced within the DC scene having a powerful effect on its subsequent direction. Chief amongst these was Rites Of Spring, fronted by Guy Picciotto, a most balletic punk-rock frontman whose raw, painful howl personified perhaps the first music to win the description "Emo". His contemporaneous statement, that "To hurt yourself playing guitar while falling around onstage is far more noble than to be sitting weeping to yourself somewhere,"[4] sums up the heroic romance of his group's hemorrhaging squall perfectly.

From self-pressed seven-inches with Xeroxed sleeves, to double albums that won plaudits from the mainstream press, the underground was caught in a fit of revolution, of evolution. It was, as Biba Kopf wrote, doubtless a great time to be young.

> "I had talked to Thurston on the telephone and said, 'I'm gonna leave Michigan, I'm either gonna move to San Francisco or Austin, Texas.' Thurston said, 'You don't wanna move there, people always need a drummer in New York.' He didn't need a drummer, because he had Bob Bert back then."[5]
>
> Steve Shelley

Hailing from Lansing, Michigan, The Crucifucks were an archetypal young hardcore group, ferocious and antagonistic – their sacred-spliced-with-profane moniker alone enough to provoke a conniption or three in the Bible Belt – with a fine line in Molotov-juggling polemic, titles like 'Cops For Fertilizer' and 'Hinckley Had A Vision' indicative of their radical lyrical stance. The group had recorded a self-titled debut for Alternative Tentacles, the San Francisco hardcore label founded by Dead Kennedys vocalist Jello Biafra and guitarist East Bay Ray, and, in the grand tradition of early hardcore bands, had traversed the country in a beaten-up van, touring the clubs, youth halls and basement parties of America.

In 1984 they swung through New York to play CBGB, with Thurston and Lee in attendance. After the show, the duo met and hung out with The Crucifucks, Ranaldo agreeing to produce their next EP in the near future. However, the group imploded before they were able to make good on Lee's offer. Drummer Steve Shelley also played in another local group with his old friend Tim Foljahn, Spastic Rhythm Tards. In contrast to The Crucifucks' SST-flavoured hardcore spree, SRT drew influence from the British post-punk scene, groups like The Slits, Joy Division, Gang Of Four and Rip Rig And Panic. "That music was closer to my heart," he admits, "and probably closer to where I wound up."

Spastic Rhythm Tards weren't enough to keep Shelley in Michigan, however, and he began to contemplate a move to a bigger city: San Francisco, or maybe Austin, Texas. Late one night, while debating his options with Thurston, a regular telephone-buddy since The Crucifucks' CBGB show, the latter suggested he move to New York, which was more happening, and where bands always needed drummers (as Sonic Youth could attest).

Initially, Shelley baulked at the suggestion. "I was from a small town, Midland; if Michigan is a mitten, we're the middle finger. I was much more comfortable thinking about moving to somewhere like Austin, where I'd met people like The Dicks and The Big Boys." To help him get a taste for New York, Moore invited Shelley to "house-sit" the apartment he shared with Gordon, while the group flew to Europe to play their show at the ICA. Shelley drove over to New York in his beat-up old van, his drum kit piled in the back, with former Crucifucks bassist Marc Hauser for company. As Sonic Youth booked more shows in Europe and accepted Mick Harvey's offer of support on the Bad Seeds tour, so Steve and Marc's stay in the Big Apple was extended, and extended, and extended. "We were having a great time in New York, checking the place out, being young guys who'd never really spent more than a day or two in New York," remembers Shelley.

Shelley auditioned with a couple of local groups while in town, but had yet to find musicians he felt a true connection with. He wasn't looking for just another band to play drums with; inspired by this new city, his ambitions for what he wanted out of music were growing. *Bad Moon Rising* had just been released in the US, on Gerard Cosloy's Homestead label, and Kim and Thurston's apartment was artfully cluttered with promotional gear, posters, stickers, press sheets and promo photos.

"I was looking at these posters every day and thinking, 'Well, I'd really like to be in a band like Sonic Youth, something unique'," he recalls. His dream came true when Sonic Youth returned to New York at the end of April 1985; Bob Bert had announced he was leaving the band, and the group offered Shelley the Sonic Youth drum stool. "No audition, no anything… I was in!"

The group played one final full show with Bert after their return from Europe, a set at the Pyramid in New York. Steve took a seat in the front row and soaked it all up; it would be his first, and only, Sonic Youth gig as a spectator. "It was just fantastic," he recalls, "a wonderful set. I was sitting in the front row, watching them play, and I couldn't believe that I was going to be a part of this. I went backstage, in the basement of the Pyramid, and I met all these New Yorkers, Lydia Lunch. It was just overwhelming. It was a very fortunate time."

"I actually like to think of my final show as the last date of the Bad Seeds tour, at the Hammersmith Palais," smiles Bob Bert, warming to the memory. "Mark E Smith, Jeffrey Lee Pierce and The Jesus And Mary Chain were all there… I'd decided I needed to branch out aesthetically; it was a very amicable split, and I never imagined I'd still be answering questions about it all 22 years later."[6]

In the aftermath of Bert's exit from Sonic Youth, he would play in a number of local groups – indeed, he still does, along with editing his luscious print zine *BB Gun*, alongside his wife Linda. The first of these groups was inspired by a fib Thurston told a British music journalist that got printed, publicising a non-existent band featuring Bert and the Youth's lighting operator, Suzanne Sasec, called Bewitched. Bert would use the moniker for his subsequent electrifying, experimental recordings. He would also soon join a group who marked a "next generation" of New York noise vanguard artists, Pussy Galore.

Bob appeared with Sonic Youth again on June 12 at Folk City on Bleecker Street, an area of New York legendarily thick with record stores. The show was part of Music For Dozens, a festival curated by music journalist Ira Kaplan, who would later find fame with his own group Yo La Tengo. Posters promised a "special psycho-acoustic set with special psycho-guests", also offering "free admission if you're naked". The "special psycho-guests" were King Coffey and Theresa Nervosa of the Butthole Surfers, each manning their kettle drums in opposite corners of the room; at the other corners, Steve Shelley and Bob Bert sat behind full drum kits. The show opened with a couple of *Bad Moon Rising* songs – 'I'm Insane' and 'Ghost Bitch' – played with this set-up, the four drummers sending a tribal call and response from one to another. "There were strobe lights and Richard Kern films splashing behind the band," remembers Bert, "creating a complete aura of psychedelia." These segued into an extended noise jam of loops and drums and drone, before Bert and the Buttholes left the stage, and the Youth continued to play a short four-song set equally split between old and new songs.

Sonic Youth spent the summer of 1985 rehearsing the *Bad Moon Rising* material with Steve, and hammering a fresh batch of songs into some kind of shape. The first of these was a lyrical pop song that spelt death for "the California girls", before collapsing in on itself and melting into a seismic, meditative drone. Bob played one last show with the group at the Peppermint Lounge on July 5, sitting in for Steve on a couple of songs before enacting their transition live onstage. Lydia Lunch joined the band for 'Death Valley '69'.

The group also shot a promo film for the song – although the gore so gleefully depicted in the short endured it rarely got shown on MTV, defeating its promotional purpose. Still, the clip is a wonderful piece of film-making, responding to Sonic Youth's fierce hurricane of bumblebee guitar and bloodshed with inventive, perverse brilliance. The director was Richard Kern, a photographer and film-maker who made explicit, erotic art films starring figures like Lydia Lunch and Henry Rollins, and was a friend of the band's. Concluding the year's transitional theme, both Bob and Steve star in the clip, the former performing in the earlier half of the film, the latter towards the end. This performance footage peppers a loose-to-the-point-of-unhinged narrative that nevertheless touches on the many layers of subtext (barely) contained within the song, setting them aflame on Super 8mm. Filmed in a style redolent of Roger Corman's exploitation flicks, it was a lurid, unforgettable video. Steve's take on the premise is winningly hazy: "We're kind of acting like Manson Youth: we're supposed to be Long Island kids who're into Satan, who think Satan's totally cool, or something."

Lung Leg, an actress and model who was for a while a Kern regular, opens the clip in tight close-up, eyes black, plump lips turned up into a snarl, black hair framing a psychotic scowl. Primitive pinwheel effects are intercut with footage of the group dancing in a round, caught in some eerie psychedelic reverie, like cult members. Cut to: a pick-up truck, that gnarly symbol of redneck Americana, swerving through scrubland; the Sonic Youth in the back, dressed like hicks, toting shotguns. Kim, in lurid rock tee, shark's tooth necklace and thick brunette bangs, loads and aims hers with glee; she's done this before. Scenes of violence and wild abandon erupt, as Lydia and Thurston's voices screech into the foreground, stirring unrest. Cut to: Lee caught in strobe flicker, blinking into the lens and holding a sign with "Rise" daubed in some dark fluid. A camera dollies roughly towards a house, finding the aftermath of a self-inflected gunshot wound spread all over a nearby table. The camera veers woozily to the left, to find Ranaldo, disemboweled, his innards twisting through a blood-soaked shirt, sprawled on the floor. Throughout the deserted, graffiti-daubed house we gaze upon gushing corpses littered across the floor and slumped in bathtubs. Cut to: shadowy footage of the band in concert, Bob Bert bathed in scarlet light, Thurston a mess of golden hair holding his guitar to the sky, his body tautly violent, twisting in the murk. A split-second of Lung Leg, snarling and clawing at the camera. Cut to: footage of warheads dropping, footage shot from underneath the wing of a warplane, over the song's unsettling middle section (to remind us the Tate murders weren't the only bloodshed in the Sixties). Lung Leg snarling and clawing again, this time her face smeared with blood. An evil leering face twists in and out and in and out of the darkness. Lung Leg, riding an escalator with a paranoid stare, like Travis Bickle in the last reels of *Taxi Driver*. "Hit it..." A switchblade opens. "Hit it..." A shotgun is loaded. "Hit it..." Now she's walking through a peace rally, strolling with purpose behind two cops, scowl on her urchin face.

The cuts come faster now: scenes from a hippy love-in; Lung Leg retrieving the switchblade from her garter; Thurston scrubbing a blue Telecaster; Lee shaking the neck of his guitar, so it might snap; Lung Leg snatching at the camera lens; riot police gassing and beating peace protestors. As the song swings into its final chorus, the images repeat again, in and out of cycle, jump-cutting with violence as a missile rockets across the ocean, finding its target and blowing a massive splintering gash in the hull of a warship. By the end of the clip, Lee and Thurston are on their knees, scraping at their guitars so furiously the strings might snap away, spent after that orgy of destruction. So powerfully, Kern's film fetishised a cornucopia of gore, sex and transgression, bloody murder presented as orgiastic feast, psychotic violence sexualised, military might played out for sheer thrill, dovetailing with the chaotic violence of a Sonic Youth live performance in amongst it all. Perfectly, it evoked their inspired tangle of violence and sex and confusion, their powerful fetishisation of "darkness", the passages of disquiet and terror hiding within their early music. But 'Death Valley '69' would prove a "bottoming-out" for their fascination with this nihilistic theme. The mood of Sonic Youth's music was about to shift; as their molten, boiling dirge 'Flower' put it, "Love" was the word.

⋆ ⋆ ⋆

August brought Sonic Youth's first national tour since the Savage Blunder; booked by Gerard Cosloy, the month-long hike took in Ohio, Missouri, Wisconsin, Minnesota, Illinois, Oregon, Washington, California, Texas, Georgia and Philadelphia. It was their most ambitious trek across the continent yet. "I knew a lot more people on that tour than the rest of the band did," remembers Steve, "because I'd been to all those cities in the Midwest and the South, where they'd only really hit pockets before. We played with a lot of bands I knew from my days with The Crucifucks."

With their ears pressed firm enough to the ground to sense every last rumble of life within the nation's sonic subterranea, the group booked an enviable selection of bands to open for them when they played; the Youth got to catch some of their favourite acts playing live, while the bands enjoyed the positive exposure and kudos the Sonics' approval engendered. Over the course of the tour, the group shared the stage with feral Michigan punks the Laughing Hyenas, metallic hardcore hybrids Die Kreuzen, Rites Of Spring, The Minutemen, and Austin's Scratch Acid (featuring David Yow and David Sims, later of The Jesus Lizard), a heady cross section of the ever-shifting underground as it stood then.

In Seattle, they witnessed the early flowering of a scene that would, only a few years later, gain a fleeting access to the mainstream denied to the hardcore scene (and, certainly, the New York No Wave). The Pacific Northwest had proved a fertile breeding ground for garage-rock in the Sixties, cult groups like The Sonics and The Wailers and The Ventures jamming in carports around Washington state; 15 years on, groups like The U-Men spliced their energy with the manic, destructive abandon of The Birthday Party. A subsequent generation of groups, however, would draw their inspiration from punk rock and suburban stadium rock, essaying both with a seductive mixture of knowing distance and genuine affection.

Sonic Youth hit Seattle halfway through the tour, playing the Omni Room at Gorilla Gardens. Their support that night was Green River, a ragged, raging group whose name referenced both a Creedence Clearwater Revival song and a Seattle-based serial killer who murdered at least 48 women in the early Eighties. "It was a matter of local pride," laughs founding guitarist Steve Turner, over their choice of name. "Why call ourselves Ed Gein? We had our very own mass-murderer in our own backyard."[7]

"There was a really twisted sense of humour in mid-Eighties punk rock," adds singer Mark Arm. "Big Black, Butthole Surfers and Sonic Youth were all writing stuff about mass murderers, weirdoes, and how freaky America was under Reagan. The hardcore era had been about openly attacking Reagan; this was more observational, about how the real shit is *really* surreal."[8]

Arm won the group the slot through tirelessly lobbying the promoter, a friend. He was already a Sonic Youth fan, owning copies of *Confusion Is Sex* and *Bad Moon Rising*; he placed their brutal, alien sounds in a similar context to Savage Republic, Californian kindreds who also supported Sonic Youth on this tour. "You could tell it was a 'punk rock' thing," Arm remembers. "I was into *anything* that referenced The Stooges, and they covered 'I Wanna Be Your Dog' and dubbed that sliver of 'Not Right' somewhere in *Bad Moon Rising*. But it was going in a different direction – it was an exciting new thing."[9]

Arm remembers Thurston, ever the insatiable record collector, asking him if he owned a copy of the sole five-song seven inch released by Solger, a first-generation hardcore group from Seattle and a formative influence on Green River. "I got his address and mailed him my copy," continues Arm, "assuming I could pick up another copy at the record store, no problem. This wasn't the case. I asked him to mail me a copy of *Kill Yr Idols*, because it was an import and hard to get hold of. But he never did!"

Shortly after the tour, Sonic Youth headlined CBGB for the Homestead Records showcase at the New Music Seminar, an annual industry festival held at venues across New York. Also playing at the show was a new signing to Cosloy's label, a trio from Amherst, a sleepy collegiate town in Massachusetts, called Dinosaur. The group's roots lay in hardcore punk – indeed, bassist Lou Barlow and guitarist J Mascis met in Massachusetts hardcore group Deep Wound – but they drew considerable influence from country and from classic rock, former drummer Mascis playing his guitar like a trap kit, stamping on pedals and scraping a beautiful, bruised squall perfectly offset by his laconic drawl. The group's 1985 debut was a beguilingly odd thing, deftly warped songcraft rubbing shoulders with inarticulate, raging riffage.

Sonic Youth were instantly smitten. "The bands coming up through the Eighties were mostly shying away from what they perceived as the 'hippy' mannerisms," remembers Ranaldo, an ardent fan of those selfsame sounds. "And then Dinosaur came along, combining hardcore with the most beautiful elements of Sixties rock." In the months that followed, the group would introduce Dinosaur to producer Wharton Tiers, who would record their sublime second album *You're Living All Over Me*.

Having ventured out into the wilds of America and liked what they'd found, the group returned to Europe for a tour split between festival appearances and their own headline shows. Paul Smith came along for the Pandora's Box festival in Rotterdam, rubbing shoulders with the likes of Einsturzende Neubauten, The Bad Seeds and The Gun Club; the festival also offered Smith the chance to meet one of the groups on Thurston's list, the Butthole Surfers.

"Sonic Youth were friends with many of these groups," says Smith. "I remember sitting at a long bench in the hospitality area backstage, and the Buttholes kept asking each other, 'What time is it?' I didn't realise it until later, but they were trying to work out when to drop their acid, so it 'came on' as they hit the stage. They went out and played this fucking stunning show… I'd taken acid as a recreational thing when going to gigs, but the idea of actually *playing* on acid blew my mind. The Youth seemed to be presenting the Buttholes to me with a disclaimer, saying we *do* know them, but we're not *like* them."[10]

For their triumphant return to the UK, the group played two momentous shows in Brighton, down on the south coast of Britain. It was a city rich with pop culture – mods and rockers had fought pitched battles at the seaside resort in the Sixties, later inspiring Pete Townshend's rock-opera *Quadrophenia* – and Sonic Youth played there twice on November 8. The afternoon show took place on a makeshift stage on Brighton's pebble beach, a red-haired Kim flanked by the two guitarists, clad in blue denim like any dutiful American, a banner reading "Jesus Is The Answer" flapping beneath their feet by way of ambiguous, ironic statement. Under a heavy, overcast sky, punctured with ruptures of autumnal sunshine, the group raged eloquently, playing another, similarly inspired set at the nearby Zap club later that night.

"The Brighton Beach gigs were my idea," says Smith, who was reading *Guitar Army*, John Sinclair's account of managing The MC5, at the time. "I had always been interested in the Sixties as an era of activity, and how music relates to that. It was quite obvious that they were ambitious. They weren't the sort of musicians who couldn't get off the couch: they knew it was going to be a fight, they were prepared for a fight, they just wanted allies. I didn't know much about the music industry, but I knew more than they did."

The group had planned to release 'Hallowe'en' b/w 'Flower' as a 12″ single in the UK to coincide with the tour, but had run into trouble with their distributor. Rough Trade objected to the record's sleeve artwork, an image of a topless girl from a glamour magazine that Thurston had earlier used in the pages of his fanzine, *Killer*. The group didn't back down. As a result of the dispute, Blast First! left Rough Trade distribution, finding shelter with British indie label Mute, home to the phenomenally successful Depeche Mode, and run by Daniel Miller, who founded the company in 1978 to release 'Warm Leatherette', the pioneering debut single by Miller's experimental electronic pop project, The Normal.

In response to Rough Trade's veto of the 'Hallowe'en' single, Claude Bessy clambered onstage moments before the group's performance at the University of London on October 30, to issue an impassioned onstage tirade. "In these day of AIDS, and Ethiopia and all that shit," spat Bessy, "you would think a major alternative record company would have better things to do than worry about the shape of our bodies. So, I thought I'd let you know, next time you go and buy a record, and you think you're really alternative and groovy, remember it's just like the other side, except it's a bit stranger. There's no fucking culture there, you know. There's just as much censorship."[11]

⋆ ⋆ ⋆

Returning to Los Angeles in December, the group played a winter solstice show in the company of Swans and Saccharine Trust, closing out a year spent forging important connections with the wider American underground, completing their first circuit of the underground railroad that Black Flag had pioneered, and making a profound impact upon the influential music press in London. That same night, in Tucson, Arizona, Minutemen singer/guitarist D. Boon was killed in a car accident.

The Minutemen immediately disbanded, silencing one of the most endearingly inventive, humanely political groups of the hardcore era. "It pretty much destroyed me,"[12] says Mike Watt, who had lost not just a bandmate, but also his best friend since his childhood, with whom he'd shared the journey to punk rock.

"D. Boon and me, our dads were working people," remembers Watt, son of a sailor. "Nothing *wrong* with that, but we didn't have the grounding in the arts that people like Thurston had; his pop wrote music. The whole punk scene was really intense for us that way ... The Seventies punk scene in LA had a lot of people from the glam and glitter scenes, the 'arts'; they were much different to the people we knew in San Pedro. Having grown up in the Sixties, when the Seventies came along, it was nothing like we thought it was going to be. It was kind of 'lame-ass'. The punk scene was the underground counter-culture we were always looking forward to when we were growing up. Through this little scene in Hollywood we discovered what was going on in England, buying import seven inches for $2 at this Long Beach store called Jet Of London. We didn't know anything about these bands, we would pick them by record sleeves, by how funny the song titles were. Like The Pop Group – we didn't know anything about them, but their name was worth the gamble."

In the aftermath of Boon's accident, Watt stopped playing music; it was too painful, he didn't feel the desire. Early in 1986, he drove his girlfriend Kira Roessler, former bassist with Black Flag, to Yale University in Connecticut; on his return journey, he stopped off at Thurston and Kim's apartment, on Eldridge and Christie in the Lower East Side. So began a ritual, every time Watt passed through New York en route to Connecticut; Kim and Thurston even gave him a key, in case they were out of town. "It only had a window on either end, it was like a long hallway," laughs Watt, of their cosy apartment. "It had a table, and if you flipped up, there was a tub under there! The only hatch was the head, you know? Everything else was this one hallway. So you had to take a bath in front of everyone! Staying at their pad in New York for a week or so at a time, that's how I really got to explore New York. They were very generous to me."

Early in the spring of 1986, the group returned to Martin Bisi's studio to record their next album, *EVOL*. The unconventional B.C. Studios left Steve Shelley impressed and bemused. "Martin Bisi had this really weird set-up with the mixing board," he remembers. "It's in the room, where you would put the drumkit, or something; he has his mixing board right out there, so there's no glass wall between him and the musicians. Martin enjoys that."

Bisi says he played a larger role in the sound of this new album than on *Bad Moon Rising*. "On *Bad Moon*, the ideas for guitar layerings and amp tones were all theirs. On *EVOL*, I had a bigger effect on the mixing and direction of the final sound; I think it was me who pushed the record into sounding more 'Eighties'; wetter, prettier, lusher. I went for an obvious 'Eighties', big sound kinda thing. And there are MOR songs in a hooky, traditional sense on *EVOL*."

While nothing off *EVOL* could be remotely described as Middle Of The Road, the album stepped away from the blackened din of *Bad Moon Rising* towards a more traditional sense of songwriting, and a broader palette of melody. For Bisi, this sound sat better with the group than the more self-consciously savage tones of *Bad Moon*.

"Like, at the time, I didn't get the connection between The Stooges and Sonic Youth," he begins. "It seemed like they wanted to make a strict 'punk' connection. I drew a distinction in my mind between the downtown arty, bourgeois , avant-garde-ish noise bands, and the punk/New Wave stuff going on. I didn't really imagine Sonic Youth hanging out at Max's Kansas City; that crowd was more working class and 'traditionalist rock' in a sense: short songs, no sweeping soundscapes or experimenting. There was a slight rift between us, because I thought some of their sonic experiments were *pretty*, and that that should be brought out in the recordings. They were a bit reluctant on that point, though they didn't fight me too hard on it. But they wouldn't have wanted to use the words 'pretty' or 'beautiful' to describe their music. I'm almost certain they never did."

For Thurston, the main influence behind any perceivable 'prettification' of the Sonic Youth sound on *EVOL* was their practise space, described by Steve as "a cruddy old basement" off Halston St, owned by their friend Ruth Polski. "Rehearsal spaces really affect the way you play," he explains. "When we wrote *EVOL*, we were rehearsing in this 8 x 10 ft square, concrete room that was so live and noisy. When we were in there playing, the only way we could really hear each other was maybe to play stuff that was more melodic. And the songs came out really melodic."[13]

With the discordant segues of *Bad Moon Rising* shorn clear, *EVOL* was a set of deftly off-centre pop songs, candyfloss surface a perfect offset for the darker centre. 'Tom Violence' loped to the whipcrack lull of the Velvets' 'Venus In Furs', reverb-swollen guitars tolling as Thurston murmurs of leaving home "for experience" and all that entails. For the sleeve of a later single release of 'Starpower', Thurston would pose cradling a sitar in his crossed legs, hands splayed across his face, marker-pen eyes scrawled on his palms, looking for all the world like Rolling Stone Brian Jones. The song itself was elegant, sultry psychedelia, detuned guitars ringing in eerie harmony. Early versions from live tapes featured Thurston on vocals, but Kim's take on the album gives a delicious twist to a lyric concerning the sexualised relationship between audience and performer, singing with innocent determination

"Starpower, over me/She knows how to make love to me". 'Green Light' offered more woozy psychedelia, Thurston plucking a fluid melody from a maze of 'I Love Her All The Time' guitar scrawl and intoning a nonsense poem in stoned sing-song.

An experimental mood pervaded the sessions; for Kim's ominous lullaby 'Shadow Of A Doubt', Bisi spent a long day working on the startling explosion of overlaid vocals midway through the song. "I remember being *particularly* involved in that crazy vocalscape," he remembers. "At the time I thought that it was my 'fault' that it took so long, but later I realised that it was worth it."

Another song, 'In The Kingdom #19', would be composed from snippets of studio jams. The bassist on these sessions was Mike Watt. "Thurston said I should play," remembers Watt. "I came in and jammed with Steve Shelley, and they recorded that." Bisi and the group later cut these takes together into some loose narratives of rhythmic tension and combustive explosion, Lee and Thurston spraying guitar scree and taped drone over the top. Finally, Lee read a poem he'd begun writing on the first night of the Savage Blunder tour, a surreal tale of "death on the highway" enlivened by the lit firecrackers Thurston threw in the vocal booth during the take (you can hear the brittle crackle of gunpowder and Ranaldo's yelp of terror on the final track; the sound of Lee attacking Thurston in enraged retribution is sadly inaudible).

If most of *EVOL* found the group tangling boldly with more traditional song structures, the last third of the album was altogether more daring. The gently turbulent piano and Kim's chalky vocal on 'Secret Girls' emerged from mordant industrial clanking, while chilling tape drones – manipulated screams played at the audience of the Gila Monster Jamboree – announced the deathly rattle of 'Marilyn Moore', Thurston drawling his vocal across slurred lyrics detailing a torturous obsession, with shadowy Hitchcock-esque overtones. The closing 'Expressway To Yr Skull' was their bravest leap yet, into a vast, rushing and, in a very real sense, unending wave of noise.

Golden, chiming chords strum the introduction, swelling with glorious, anthemic weight, as Thurston taps again into the dark Manson mythos, gleefully announcing plans to "kill the California girls", this murderous spree painted in terms of some blissful oblivion. Toying with fragments of rock arcana – the song's title itself is both a nod to the Buddy Miles Express album of the same name, and the Stax soul classic 'Expressway To Your Heart' – Thurston sings of a "mystery train", barrelling towards the titular Expressway. This mantra is repeated three times, mirage-like guitar-song materialising from the ether, before 'the hurricane' stirs up, guitars swirling as Steve stirs up a dervish on his kit, Kim hammering her bass like a bell, guitars raising and swooping in panic, before slamming into a slow melt of dreamy, churning guitar tone and gently burbling amp noise. In these dying moments, the song pulls tender, prone melodies out of what most groups believe the sonic detritus of rock – the crackle, the fuzz, the machine noise. The vinyl release closed out with a "locked groove", ambushing the needle into a never-ending, eternal loop of drone.

Neil Young, who could stir a pretty mean hurricane of noise from his own guitar, later described 'Expressway To Yr Skull' as the greatest guitar song of all time. While the group had previously explored both the violent and soothing possibilities of abstract noise throughout their catalogue, 'Expressway' encompassed both ends of that spectrum – the apocalyptic blitz that follows the final words sung, and the resulting, elegantly cascading fallout that gently dissipates across the final minutes – in tandem with a lilting song-section of a "classic" hue. It would prove a landmark within the Sonic Youth songbook, a cherished set-closer for many years and a powerful influence upon groups following in its dreamily corrosive wake, a gateway beckoning towards the wild creative possibilities of feedback, drone and amp-tone. "The whole 'free noise' thing Sonic Youth explored on 'Expressway' was a crucial influence on Mogwai," says that group's guitarist and *de facto* leader, Stuart Braithwaite. "For our first 10 rehearsals that was pretty much all we did, make abstract noise, until we worked out how to write some songs. There's something really freeing and enjoyable about making a lot of noise, and making it so it becomes soothing, in a weird way."[14]

Lung Leg, heroine of the 'Death Valley '69' clip, scowls out from the cover of *EVOL*, Richard Kern's lens capturing his favourite starlet in a vicious cat-scratch pose, a teasing cocktail of allure and recoil. This dichotomy played out across the album, its title "LOVE" spelt backwards, its lyric sheet speaking of whipcracks that feel like kisses, of violence as a gateway to bliss, of the potent erotic bond between strangers encoded within the audience-artist relationship. In mainstream American pop culture, the trend was towards clarity, literalness, a deadening blatancy. In a landscape where Bruce Springsteen's 'Born In The USA', a searing lament for the betrayal of the working man and the squandering of young lives in a futile war, could be so wilfully misinterpreted by Republicans as a rousing anthem saluting all that was *good* about America, Sonic Youth elected for irony and ambiguity, exploring the vast, multi-textual grey distances between language and meaning, illuminating seductive shadows of doubt.

Still, the group retained a genuine fascination with the popular culture, with the mainstream that defined the subterranea they operated within. On the sleeve of *EVOL*, 'Expressway' was purposefully retitled 'Madonna, Sean and Me', in reference to pop's rising Material Girl and her surly-sexy bad boy beau Sean Penn. By 1986, Madonna Louise Veronica Ciccone had already won acclaim for her first cinematic lead in *Desperately Seeking Susan*, a comedy using a Hollywood approximation of the New York underground as its backdrop, and featuring Richard Edson in a minor role, while her second album *Like A Virgin* and subsequent hit single 'Get Into The Groove' made for pop as brilliantly brash and confident as her media-saturating image.

"I first found out about Madonna from Kira," says Mike Watt, who shared the Youth's fixation. "I saw a weird parallel with Ronald Reagan's regime, not that she was an acolyte of his but just some symptom, some paradox. I put a sticker of Madonna on my bass, which made some people upset. Fuck, I remember having a beard on tour and weirding people out. Things were getting a little orthodox in punk rock, so she was a provocative thing to embrace. But if your slogan is anarchy, you have to live up to it! I found out that the Sonics knew all about her, because she lived in New York City, and they had mutual friends, like Mike Gira of Swans."

Thurston later described Ciccone Youth, a project between Watt and the group, as "an idea born from the fact that Madonna, who at one point was making out with a friend of ours, had become a superstar on the cover of *Time* magazine."[15] In a later interview with *Cosloy Youth* (a punk zine titled in tribute to a grumpy editorial Gerard Cosloy ran in *Conflict*, bemoaning all the copycat zines that had sprung up since *Conflict* began publishing), Kim and Thurston filled in a little more background on their relationship with La Ciccone.

"When she used to play around New York, we always hated her, cos she's such a jerk," explained Thurston. "There's this guy she used to go out with we know, she used to sit on his lap, the whole time like looking around. . ."

"She was *so* much the babe on the make," added Kim. "She'd be making out with this guy one second and then looking around..."

"And when she first got signed to Sire we were just kinda like, 'Oh no', and when her first single came out we used to *laugh* at her. We'd always be at a club and she'd be playing, and we'd go, 'Let's leave before Madonna comes on.' And then all of a sudden, she started writing *really* great songs."[16]

The Youth paid early tribute to the Material Girl by playing her music over the PA as they switched guitars. The plan for Ciccone Youth took shape during the sessions for 'In The Kingdom #19', at Before Christ. "That was the first time I'd played bass since D. Boon got killed," remembers Watt. "Before that, I didn't want to hear myself playing without him. I played Kim's Ovation bass, some of the notes pinched because the strings resonated so much." Still, Watt regarded playing Kim's bass as something of an honour. "I've always cited her as a great influence on my bass-playing. Listening to Kim's approach to bass, you can tell she didn't learn licks off records. It's intuitive to her. Their studio approach was all about creativity and experimenting, they turned me on to so many new things, I got so much confidence. At these sessions I said, 'Hey, I should start recording'. Thurston named it; it was going to be a seven-inch, I'd do one side and they'd do the other side. We'd do Madonna songs!"

Watt chose Madonna's relatively little-heard second single, 'Burning Up'. "Though I did it with an apostrophe," chuckles Watt. "*Burnin'*." The sinister, whispering funk of his cover was a home-recorded demo, only meant to sketch out the idea for his track. "I had to be very quiet, because I was living in a little one-room apartment; I just wanted to give them an idea of what I wanted to do. I recorded it on my four-track and mailed it off to them; they liked it, so I rerecorded it with Ethan James at Radio Tokyo, with Greg Ginn playing lead guitar. But they used the demo!"

Following Watt's lead, Sonic Youth entered Before Christ to tape their contribution to the Ciccone Youth 7″, a dirgy squall through 'Into The Groove' enlivened by haunted syn-drums, Thurston's megaphone drawl, and bursts of Ms Ciccone's original vocal bleeding through the tracks. "'Into The Groove-y' was a bit chaotic from a technical point of view," remembers Martin Bisi. "We laid their tracks directly over the Madonna song. We did two mixes of it, one had a lot more of Madonna's track in it, and that's the one I liked because it was more like a dance remix. I wasn't really thinking about copyright issues back then."

For Watt, the experience with Sonic Youth renewed his love of music; soon, with former Minutemen drummer George Hurley and Minutemen-fanatic singer Ed Crawford, he would form fIREHOSE, continuing The Minutemen's glorious gospel of spiel against rock'n'roll's tendency towards "mersh", Watt and D. Boon's term for the creeping spectre of commercialism.

"What Sonic Youth spoke to the scene was possibilities," says Watt. "Because that was what it was about from the get-go for us – the possibilities of the punk scene. And then some homogeneity came in, some orthodoxy, and it seemed it was going the way of all things human, starting to get all ossified. And then here comes Sonic Youth, to reopen the world of possibilities – you can do whatever you want, it's *your* band. Punk ain't a style of music, it's a way of doing things, letting the freak flag fly."

"In those days, it was like a gang – you had your band, and you had the other band that you're with for a week or two. We toured with a lot of SST bands back then, Dinosaur's first records were just coming out; that was a blast. We'd gone to Europe in '85, before *EVOL*, and played all these crazy festivals with a lot of bands that were my heroes, back then. Those days were pretty eye-opening, all the music that I got to see, travelling in different countries. A lot of fun, a lot of new experiences."

Steve Shelley

EVOL would be Sonic Youth's first release for SST Records; while Gerard Cosloy was a dear friend to the group, his Homestead label couldn't compete with the allure of Thurston's most beloved hardcore imprint. SST had been considering signing the group since their first visit to California, but Joe Carducci used his power of veto, believing the label should consolidate its strengths and concentrate on its local hardcore scene. With Carducci's exit from the label in 1986, there was nothing to hinder this marriage between East Coast artcore and West Coast hardcore, a union of grubby hands across America, emboldening Sonic Youth's ambitions.

"When Carducci left, Greg Ginn wanted to reach out to bands from further out, bands they'd toured with all over the world," remembers Thurston. "We were the first people they called. We were recording for Gerard Cosloy's Homestead, we really didn't have any ambitions at all beyond making a record, and getting a gig here and there. Ginn called, asked if we were interested in making a record and, if so, maybe we could utilise their touring company, Global."[17]

Straight after completing the *EVOL* sessions, the group drove out west for two low-profile shows in Texas. Austin's Continental Club began life in the Fifties as an upscale supper club, a lustre its current owner restored with a comprehensive overhaul in the later Eighties. In April 1986, however, it was another past-its-prime stop-off for the Underground Railroad spanning Hardcore America.

"We just wrote some new songs and we never played 'em before in front of people," grinned Thurston, by way of introduction. "So… you guys are the 'guinea pigs'." He wasn't being entirely accurate – a number of the *EVOL* songs had been debuted at earlier shows, in raw form – but the set opened with six songs from the freshly recorded album in sequence, the brutal chime of 'Tom Violence' silencing the chatty crowd, a dark elegance to its sinful lope. The eerie music-box music of 'Shadow Of A Doubt' followed, Thurston and Lee veering from their disciplined clip to stir up the mid-song cacophony.

The songs were still a little new to the group; after a false start before 'Starpower', Thurston (who sang the tune that night) barks, "This is not a rehearsal!" Certainly, they sound more confident on a crushing blast through 'Kill Yr Idols', a caustic scour of barbed guitars honed by years on their set list. 'Expressway To Yr Skull' was the set's peak, however, segueing from eerie, wispy psychedelia into a bellowing, roaring, ecstatic rage of white noise, Steve racing to demolish his kit, Lee and Thurston's guitars ever climbing, until the final blissful wave, the group drawing a symphony of subsonics from their murmuring, prone instruments. Following 'Expressway''s joyous, epic ride, even an ultra-violent 'World Looks Red' and a profoundly chaotic 'Confusion Is Next' felt like afterthoughts.

The following month, the group flew over to Britain for the first European tour in support of *EVOL*. After playing a couple of out-of-town dates supporting The Bad Seeds, this would prove Sonic Youth's first foray to the outer regions of Britain, beginning in Brighton, where they headlined another show at the beach after planned show-closers Psychic TV had to pull out. From there, the group ricocheted between Britain and the European continent, leaving blown minds in their wake. In Manchester, they were supported by local punk heroes The Membranes, an anarchic group who were like Mancunian kindred of The Minutemen, with enough cred in America to enjoy the production services of Big Black's Steve Albini.

"A friend of mine from college was helping Paul Smith bring them over for this first proper British tour," remembers Membranes frontman John Robb. "Blast First! was a pretty new operation then, so we helped out with a list of phone numbers of venues across the country. On the night of the gig at the Boardwalk, we played three songs before Sonic Youth came on to help pump up the ticket sales, as we had a bit of a following at the time; we were actually quite hip then, and were 'bigger' than Sonic Youth, although not for much longer," he laughs.

"They seemed older than us – they didn't look older, just seemed more grown up, like they were your older punk-rock brothers and sister, even though they were only about a year older. Thurston had a big box of guitars on stage, 14 guitars of all different tunings in a flight case. That seemed amazing, as every band like us in the UK had one guitar and no spares."

Robb also published a fanzine out of his Manchester flat, *Rox*, and was clued in to the New York No Wave, having been one of 10 attendees at a Lydia Lunch show at the Hacienda in the early Eighties. He also recognised the influence of friends and tourmates The Ex, from Holland. "There must have been some cross-fertilisation between the two bands' sounds," offers Robb. "Terrie from The Ex has done some amazing things with his guitar over the years. Sonic Youth didn't come out of a void; there was a lot of experimentation at the time, people were fucking with guitars, changing the way they could be heard. Nowadays the post-punk scene is remembered as being the Gang Of Four and nothing else, but there were countless bands messing with sound at the time. Sonic Youth, though, had their own take on things."

Returning to New York at the beginning of June, the group played a date at CBGB before pealing out in Steve's shabby van, crammed in amongst their gear with their lone crew member, lighting technician Suzanne Sasec. The tour took a more leisurely route through the outlying states than the Youth had yet undertaken, aided by SST's experience in booking national hardcore tours. They fell afoul of SST's limited distribution, however, playing shows in towns where their records couldn't be bought, a frustration that would linger throughout their career on independent labels.

The tour itself was, however, a success, audiences responding to Sonic Youth's newfound sense of melody and classic structure, still thrilling to the unalloyed violence and menace of the earlier material, and left slack-jawed by the screaming amplifier symphonies of 'Expressway'. Opening for the group at these dates were a selection of their favourite new groups: Saccharine Trust, fIREHOSE (Mike Watt jumping on vocals for 'Starpower'), Green River. For the opening show of the tour, at the 9:30 Club, famed venue for the Washington DC hardcore scene, they were supported by an early incarnation of Pussy Galore, an offensive and atonal No Wave/hardcore hybrid co-fronted by Jon Spencer and Julie Cafritz. Soon, the group would decamp to New York, where they were joined by Bob Bert.

"One night I was at the Cat Club seeing Einsturzende Neubauten and ran into Kim and Thurston," remembers Bert. "I was getting itchy to play again and asked them if they knew of anyone needing a drummer. Kim mentioned a band that just moved to town from DC called Pussy Galore, and then introduced me to them since they were standing a few feet away from us. They were about 10 years younger than me, had jet black hair and black leather motorcycle jackets. I checked out their seven-inch *Feel Good About Your Body* and totally dug it.

"A few nights later I was standing outside CBGB and Jon Spencer came over and handed me a copy of *Groovy Hate Fuck*, which they had just pressed up. I asked them if they needed a drummer and Jon wrote his phone number on it. Sonic Youth was way into Pussy Galore and supportive. When I first got together with them they said that they wanted to record the

Stones' *Exile On Main Street* album, as a response to Sonic Youth's long-threatened cover of The Beatles' 'White Album'. I thought this was brilliant. We whipped it out in like a week and it was a limited edition of 500 cassettes. The cover art was a collage imitating the Stones' artwork, with a picture of Steve Shelley, which I think freaked him out a little at the time."

During the tour, Paul Smith finagled his first trip to America, catching up with the group as the played the Metro in Chicago. "We all met up with Steve Albini," remembers Smith. "We were walking down the street on our way to a Mexican restaurant, and in the space of two blocks, about four or five guys from the other side of the street shouted, 'Fuck you Albini!' I thought, fucking hell, people really *hate* this guy. We got to the Metro, and there was a poster on the wall, saying, 'Do not let this man in the building under any circumstances'. The Youth said, 'Steve's on our guest list, and if he doesn't get in we won't play'. They said, 'Fine, don't play, but we're not letting Steve in'.

"He and Santiago Durango were coming over to London two weeks later, to find a label to put Big Black's record out. I told them that I would be away, but they could have the keys to my flat in London if they needed somewhere to stay. Albini eventually got in touch and asked if I wanted to release it." Big Black's records were hereafter released in the UK by Blast First!, winning them a vital and supportive new audience.

While travelling with his beloved charges, Smith was upset by the indignities forced upon them by touring on such a tight budget. "The band were touring in a *van*," Smith remembers. "We had a conversation about possibly releasing a double 10″ of live tracks. They were struggling to make ends meet, they weren't making a lot of money; it was exactly the right time for them to release a 'bootleg'. Someone was going to bootleg them anyway. I've always believed you might as well bootleg yourself and keep the money. If someone's bootlegged you, it really means you're 'happening'; but they're stealing your money. So do it yourself, semi-'officially'.

"But they didn't get around to it, it didn't get done," he sighs. "I said, 'You should have fucking done this, there's a big opportunity here, plus you really need the fucking money!' I was really conscious of the fact that they were going back with the next month's rent, but couldn't afford any food. I don't want Thurston Moore to be worrying about that, I want him to be thinking about what he *should* be thinking about, which is writing songs, doing his thing."

Accompanying the group for many of these dates was Dinosaur, soon to record their second album, their debut for SST. While the shows were unforgettable, Lee joining the group for a cover of Neil Young's 'Cortez The Killer' in Buffalo, Sonic Youth were soon acquainted with the unusually tense atmosphere that pervaded their tour-mates' camp. "Back in those days, it was hard to get three sentences in a row out of J," remembers Ranaldo. "There were a lot of things bubbling under the surface between them that none of them wanted to deal with in any way."[18]

"We weren't the 'bonding' types we wanted to be,"[19] agrees J Mascis, dryly. "We had too much time on our hands, which I spent picking Lou's life apart. I think we pushed Lou over the edge."[20]

"Rock bands are generally miserable people, I knew my rock'n'roll history," laughs Lou Barlow today. "You didn't have to get along, that was a 'hippy' ideal. Rock'n'roll was about a bunch of ambivalent people getting together, hating each other and playing loud, nasty, hateful music."

The dynamic fuelling Dinosaur was certainly unique, bassist Lou Barlow in worshipful awe of Mascis' talents, Mascis in turn brushing those affections away with a very older-brotherly disdain, drummer Murph caught in the middle. Their touring tensions reached a miserable peak on the Sonic Youth tour, an exasperated Mascis telling Barlow, "You're living all over me!" This memorable turn of phrase formed the title of the group's 1987 album, synthesising the myriad influences Dinosaur had absorbed. Ranaldo accompanied the group on backing vocals for opener 'Little Fury Things', a lush, tuneful blaze of restlessly fiery guitar and sleepy melody. Their blend of hardcore's sense of dynamic, the noise experiments of Sonic Youth, and an unabashed love of Sixties relics like country-rock, considered outré and passé by the underground, won widespread acclaim.

The searing guitar heroics of J Mascis, the former drummer who played his axe like a trap kit, stomping pedals and thrashing at his guitar, drew particular mention, his old-school Marshall-stack roar threading together fragments of acid-rock, Sabbath sludge and noise abstraction. Bassist Lou Barlow, meanwhile, contributed closing track 'Poledo', a chilling mess of ghost-folk, found sound and eerie tape recorder trickery, utterly 'lo-fi' in execution. Barlow had recently discovered the joys of weed, to the bemusement of the ever-abstemious Mascis and reformed wild-man Murph, and would lose himself in stoned reverie listening back to their sessions. He became so lost in worship of Mascis' talent that he soon lost the confidence to volunteer his songs to the group, and their relationship deteriorated further.

The tour ended in August, Sonic Youth resting for two months before their next jaunt. While they'd enjoyed a positive reception from their audiences, the rigours of the road were leaving their mark, and the daily struggle with PA systems, faulty equipment, and dealing with the idiosyncrasies of each different venue had left the group in need of recuperation.

Following his return from the Sonic Youth tour van, Paul Smith had set

SY, posed 1987. **(DAVID J. MARKEY)**

Kim during filming of Dave Markey's short, *Astro Turf*, 1987. **(DAVID J. MARKEY)**

Kim and Thurston during filming of *Astro Turf*, 1987. **(DAVID J. MARKEY)**

"That first night we just talked and talked and talked, and I couldn't get over it, his knowledge of music... And it continues, whenever I talk to Thurston, I'm still learning." - Mike Watt, with Thurston on Ray Pettibon's couch, 1988, during filming of *Weatherman '69* (A Ray Pettibon film) **(DAVID J. MARKEY)**

SY posed, 1989. **(IAN TILTON/SIN)**

1989 at Ray Pettibon's house. l-r: Joe Cole, David Markey, Kim Gordon.
(COURTESY OF DAVID J. MARKEY)

1989, at Ray Pettibon's house, Hermosa Beach CA. An impromptu jam,
l-r: John Press, Thurston, Steve McDonald and Jeff McDonald (Red Kross) **(DAVID J. MARKEY)**

Steve Shelley, August 20, 1990. **(KEVIN CUMMINS)**

1991: The Year Punk Broke, live in Ireland. **(ED SIRRS)**

Courtney Love meets her pin-up, Kim Gordon, 1991. **(DAVID J. MARKEY)**

"It was almost like Mudhoney were on a trail of carnage, they were completely living out the life of the kind of rock'n'rollers they were supposed to be. They were constantly fucked up, constantly on the edge of chaos and collapse and all that stuff." – Lee Ranaldo. Steve Turner of Mudhoney with Steve Shelley, 1991. **(CHARLES PETERSON)**

"Kurt would say afterwards, 'I really want my next album to sound like you guys.' I'd say, no, that would be a *bad* idea." Kim Gordon, with Kurt Cobain, 1991. **(CHARLES PETERSON)**

"I decided to play the guitar as if I existed in a pure state of mind and could attack it with flowing mindful sensitive energy/expression." Thurston on stage at Endfest, 1992.
(CHARLES PETERSON)

the planned/aborted bootleg into motion. "I thought, fuck it, I'll do this myself," he remembers. "Stupidly, I had to make a nice job of it, maybe too nice, not 'bootleg'-y enough. I picked all the tracks because I'm a big Sonic Youth fan, I've got all these live tapes and I've listened to them, and I knew the tracks I wanted to hear – like that version of 'Expressway' with the really long ending that isn't on the studio version. All those tracks deserved to be released. It was a lovely little document of that era. And I made it a nice package, because it deserved to be a nice package – finally I get to play Sonic Youth's designer."

Encased in glossy sleeves decorated with eerie flaming jack-o'-lanterns, *The Walls Have Ears* collects tracks from their 1985 Hammersmith Palais set supporting The Bad Seeds, with Bob Bert on drums, their second Brighton Beach show, and their set at the University Of London, including Claude Bessy's rabble-rousing introduction; a quality product, an obvious labour of love. In his book *Bootleg: The History Of The Other Recording Industry*, Clinton Heylin makes a case that the best illicit releases prove that artists sometimes aren't the best judges of their own artistic output. *The Walls Have Ears* is such an album, unloved by its creators, but a crucial and electrifying document of the group at their live best, playing with violent and ecstatic abandon. The take of 'Expressway' Smith cites takes that song's meditative bliss in directions the studio version only hinted at.

"I pressed up 5,000 of them, and the idea was to sell all of them on 'export', meaning the distributors who bought them were paying for them immediately," explains Smith. "The boys who worked at the warehouse, who I'd been buying beers and getting into shows on the guest list all these years, knew what it was when it came in, and worked extra hard to ship the thing that night. I was away at the time. They did such a good job for me that it arrived in New York much faster than I thought it would.

"My plan was to go in the next day, knowing that they would be about to hit the shelves, and I could give them the money and say, look what I've done for you. None of the money was for me. But the guys shifted it overnight, it got to New York. Gerard Cosloy and I had a little competition going on between us sometimes, about who was Sonic Youth's 'best buddy'. Gerard opened up his copy and thought, wow, this is fucking beautiful, and called Thurston about it.

"They'd had their chance to do it and dropped the ball," sighs Smith. "I swear to God, it was just to get them the money. It would have been something like 12 grand, a lot of money, which they received. It looked too nice, that freaked them out a bit. There was a review which described it to the effect of, 'The ultimate Sonic Youth record'. That didn't go down well.

"I'd been over-enthusiastic, too clever for my own good. It hadn't occurred to me that they would get upset. I thought they'd be, 'Cool, thanks for the money'. Steve had just joined; Steve's a very innocent soul. He was hitting the big time, joining the Youth. I remember going to the airport, picking them up and going to the office. It was just one of those great days, every phone was ringing, people calling about Sonic Youth, quite exciting, I have to say. Suzanne Sasec said it was like something out of a movie. I think that was the moment when Steve realised just how big a deal Sonic Youth was.

"Steve saw me as being more part of 'the business' than I actually was," continues Smith. "Our office was in the Mute Records building, it didn't look very 'indie'. There were 'pop stars' hanging around, Depeche Mode were visiting that day. One time, when I was visiting New York on business, they came to see me at my hotel room. I offered them room service, saying it was on EMI's tab, but when Steve saw the price list he was absolutely outraged. He said, 'It's like $8 for an orange juice! I'm gonna go down the store and buy one from the corner'."

* * *

Following their summer tour, Lee Ranaldo quit his day job. "There are going to be major changes in daily life for me now," he wrote in his journal. "More time for my work. My thoughts right now are long and involved, too detailed to come out in a succinct page or two. I'm really looking forward to pushing ahead."[21]

Their fall 1986 tour with Mike Watt's fIREHOSE, subtitled the Flaming Telepaths tour, was a mostly joyous experience for the group, enjoying some of the best audience responses of their career, and reconnecting with their brethren across America. Most nights, Mike Watt would join the band for an encore of 'Starpower', sometimes staying on to sing vocals on a closing cover of the Blue Öyster Cult's 'The Red And The Black'. The tour van hit Texas in November, where they played Liberty Lunch. "The Buttholes came too," remembered Ranaldo. "Texas, and Austin in particular, feels so comfortable. People are really interested in the music, and up for turning up to party and groove and listen. So different from some areas where people don't seem to know why they've even come to the show. We stayed at the house Gibby, Paul and Jeff live in. It's pretty cool, with their recording studio in a yard by the highway; something that wouldn't be possible in New York City."

As the Flaming Telepaths jaunt wore on, the group got in synch with their weird daily schedule, grabbing sleep whenever and wherever they could, building up energies to be unleashed on the stage, the moment every day built towards. Ranaldo remembers Thurston waking up only moments before the group's show at Einstein A-Go-Go on November 14. "It was a set for sleepwalkers," he wrote. "We wound our way as though through uncharted territory, taking liberties at every turn, in confused fusion with purpose. Even with the poor PA and the small stage it was one of those nights where somehow the stars were right; somehow the room tone was up high. It was a screaming maelstrom."

When the tour arrived in New York on November 22, the group got an unpleasant taste of their hometown's infamous lawlessness. Before their show that night at Irving Plaza, Thurston's beloved yellow Gibson Marauder, the guitar on which he'd originated 'Expressway''s tender drones, was stolen. He played J Mascis' guitar instead, precluding a planned jam through 'Kill Yr Idols', Ranaldo racing to detune the guitar before curtain. The encore was similarly disastrous, a post-'Starpower' pigpile upon Watt, busting his already fragile knees; he played bass through 'The Red And The Black' that night, singing from a barstool. The group closed out the year with a performance at Artist's Space in New York on December 5, improvising drone as accompaniment to Mike Kelley's poem/performance piece, 'Plato's Cave, Rothko's Chapel, Lincoln's Profile'.

In March 1987, the group reconvened to record their fifth album, *Sister*, at Sear Sound Studios. Founded and run by Walter Sear, a grand figure within the recording industry, Sear Sound was a proud throwback at this dawn of digital recording technology, offering warm analogue sound recorded on 16-track tape, processed using old-school valve and cylinder technology. "We kind of expected that record was gonna sound a little different," remembers Steve Shelley. "We were still learning how to record, how to get our live sound down on tape." Later, the group would have qualms over the drum sound in particular but, to these ears, Sear Sound's vintage set-up perfectly captured the erudite clip of Shelley's drumming, eschewing the tribal bruise of Bob Bert's echo-y pummel for a taut, "pop" sensibility that powered the songs.

Every Sonic Youth album to date had marked a paradigm shift in their sound, from the brittle No Wave of their debut, to the murky horror of *Confusion Is Sex*, to the atonal swamp drone of *Bad Moon Rising*, to *EVOL*'s darkly psychedelic pop. *Sister*, however, would prove an unmistakable sibling to that last album, a further step in the evolution of their songcraft. The roaring, inchoate noise they could stir from their gear was still present, focused to dramatic bursts, like the firework of frazzled din that rises triumphantly from the pristine chime of 'Schizophrenia', or the distended coils of neon feedback oozing through the outro of 'Pipeline/Kill Time'.

There was more method to their chaos now, a discipline that was audible and thrilling. No longer fighting against their thrift-store equipment, they'd achieved a fluency in their guitars' unique foreign tongues, which, though broken and detuned and distorted, sang in a voice both strangely familiar and deliriously alien. Their sense of structure was tighter, though still stretched to inventive lengths; the lush, sad chords and inventive percussion of 'Beauty Lies In The Eye' stirred a mood akin to some broken-hearted Brill Building ballad, churning guitar turbulence accenting a bereft lyric, bemoaning a spent (and perhaps misspent) life, Kim murmuring mocking come-ons through the outro: "Hey cool thing, hey fox, c'mere".

The influence of hardcore was clearly recognisable; where before, Sonic Youth had "rocked" via their chaotic volume, and the fearsome ambiences evoked, *Sister* was an album of crystalline riffs, orchestrated jags of guitar that thrilled in ways more similar to "classic rock" than the group's typical No Wave, arty milieu. 'Catholic Block' was a case in point, its rushes of discordant guitar racing at Minor Threat velocity, matching a gleefully psychotic lyric that proved that Thurston, like every good Catholic boy, knew the threat of damnation only makes the sin taste that much sweeter. Still, traces of their East Village roots bled through to the fore, not least on 'Stereo Sanctity', which closed with a speaker-shredding climax of squalling detuned guitars – the hurricane – swooping and slaloming in unison, with a very real and powerful physicality, a roller-coaster Branca symphony fed through the pop prism.

"'Tuff Gnarl' is a classic rock'n'roll lyric, like 'Tutti Frutti'," says Mike Watt, of his favourite track off *Sister*. The deliciously offbeat bubblegum-pop of 'Tuff Gnarl' eked a sleepy-eyed melody from psychedelic chime and Kim's warm, rolling bass, Thurston sing-songing a lyric cut together from sentences excerpted from the pages of *Killer*. These lurid knots of garble conjured vivid images of "fatal erections", "hard-tit killer fucks", and the "saving grace" that was "Sonic hip-hop". Its dense spiel of playful code – assembled according to the random "cut up" method favoured by SY icons like David Bowie and William S. Burroughs – would befuddle the unconverted and, indeed, many of the converted; but a dedicated few, like Mike Watt, would find meaning in the tangle.

"Something I think gets overlooked about SY's music are Thurston's words," says Watt. "He writes some of the most profound, most beautiful lyrics, I just love 'em. They're on, like, a Roky Erickson level of sublime, they're just fuckin' intense, you know? They get my mind going. I remember visiting their house, when they were working on *EVOL*, and their lyrics would be spread out across the deck, written on the back of flyers – it reminded me of Raymond Pettibon, the way his art's filed 'horizontally'. I was like, 'Whoa! Look at this!' I think it was 'Starpower'... And it was just scribbled on scrap paper! It was beautiful stuff."

The album cover was a group effort, a montage of group-selected photographs the sleeve notes claimed were "from public domain, jacked from the sonic matrix": a ringed planet; a naked boy toddling across a suburban lawn; steers gazing from heather; sleeping dogs; a shooting star; a half-naked girl sprawled on a bare wood floor. Not all of the images were as public domain as the group had assumed; Richard Avedon threatened to sue over the unauthorized use of a portrait he shot of a young girl, later blacked out on the sleeve, while fear of legal reprisals from the Walt Disney Corporation over a photograph of their Magic Kingdom led the group to scrawl over the image with a sharpie pen, obscuring it with the UPC barcode.

The liner notes thanked a litany of Sonic luminaries, further evidencing the depth and breadth of the group's cultural roots. Kudos was gifted to Mike Watt, J Mascis, artist Dan Graham, film-maker Richard Kern, authors James Ellroy and Raymond Carver, Lee's son Cody and wife Amanda, and Kim and Thurston's cat, Kitty Magic. Also thanked was Philip K. Dick, though he wasn't alive to acknowledge this. A science-fiction author, Dick's works were visionary, hallucinatory and, above all, thoroughly humane stories haunted by his own turbulent life, marked by drug abuse and enduring angst over his dead twin sister, perished at six weeks; this boiled over into "visions" he experienced in his later years. Dick's 1968 novel *Do Androids Dream Of Electric Sleep?* had formed the basis for Ridley Scott's mesmerising, existential future-detective film *Blade Runner*, in 1982.

But it was Dick's later works, those written after the intense visions he experienced in the early months of 1974, that inspired Moore most. *Valis* and *Radio Free Albemuth* were directly influenced by the episodes Dick had experienced, triggered by a visit to his house by a deliverywoman sporting a brooch that, he believed, first inspired the visions. These books found Dick sharing a theological dialogue with literary alter ego Horselover Fat, discussing religions and philosophies and indulging in existential speculation. Sonic Youth's 'Schizophrenia' and 'Stereo Sanctity' would reference these works, lifting entire sentences intact for lyrics, and daubing the album's inner sleeve with imagery relating to Dick's universe, enveloping the writer within their nebulous, ever-expanding web of arcane, cool references.

The chill clatter of the abrasively industrial 'PCH', Steve hammering at a huge sheet of metal for percussion, perfectly suited Kim's leering lyric, perhaps the voice from a car offering a trip to the forbidden pleasures beyond

Los Angeles' Pacific Coast Highway. A joyfully ramshackle rocket through 'Hotwire My Heart' by San Francisco's Crime – classic skuzzy rock'n'roll of a Seventies CBGB vintage – affirmed the group's punk credentials, while 'Cotton Crown', an elegant, wasted duet between Kim and Thurston, possessed a hazy, opiated glide, akin to the Velvets' first album. The venomous clatter of 'White Cross', echoing *Bad Moon Rising* in its horror-movie ambience and chainsaw guitars, dashed at a vicious hardcore pace, bringing the album to an ear-ringing, dazed close.

Released in June 1987, *Sister* enjoyed an impressive critical reception, building upon previous advances in media visibility. Writing in the *New York Times*, Jon Pareles praised the album's "tight song structures, driving rhythms, and new emphasis on lead guitar," comparing Sonic Youth to jazz innovator Ornette Coleman and recognising them as "re-imagining sound itself, what it can do, what it can be. Their innovations are cutting across genre categories, and that's as it should be."[22]

Meanwhile, having survived the fatwa Thurston issued against him (reports of his death, following assault by a noise rocker's penis, proved unfounded), Robert Christgau awarded *Sister* a perfect "A" grade in his influential *Consumer's Guide*, a record reviews column running in the *Village Voice* that graded releases like term papers. Since grazing the Youth with "C" grades for their first two albums (*must try harder!*), Christgau had been quite impressed by the progression since *Bad Moon Rising*, albeit with severe reservations. "Despite all their apocalyptic integrity and unmediated whozi-whatsis," he wrote, "the achievement of their first halfway decent record is strictly formal: simple, rhythmic songs that neither disappear beneath nor get the better of the clanging and grinding of their brutal late-industrial guitars. Whatever credibility the guitars lend to their no doubt painful but nonetheless hackneyed manic depression is undermined by their usual sociopathic fantasies, and in the end the music isn't ugly or ominous or bombs bursting midair. It's just interesting."[23]

'Death Valley '69', their most sociopathic of fantasies, received a scowling "D" grade in the *Consumer's Guide*. *EVOL*, however, initiated a recommencement of civilities between the two parties ("... the good parts are so good that for a while there I thought I was enjoying the bad parts..."), setting the scene for Christgau's unabashed, unequivocal embrace of *Sister*.

"Finally, an album worthy of their tuning system," cooed the Dean, "keeping a distance from the insanity they find so sexy and not letting their slack-jawed musings drone on too long. Hence, those with more moderate tastes have space to feel the buzz and a chance to go on to something else before boredom sets in. With the California punk cover acknowledging their debts and the bow to coherent content safeguarding against that empty feeling, their chief pleasure, as always, is formal – a guitar sound almost unique in its capacity to evoke rock and roll without implicating them in a history few youngish bands can bear up under these days."

NOTES

[1] *NME*, September 1 1984
[2] *Rolling Stone*, February 14 1985
[3] Author's interview, October 2002
[4] *This Band Could Be Your Life*, pg 381
[5] The Watt From Pedro radio show, March 17 2007
[6] Author's interview, March 2007
[7] Author's interview, July 2002
[8] Author's interview, July 2002
[9] Author's interview, February 2007
[10] Author's interview, March 2007
[11] *The Walls Have Ears* "bootleg" album
[12] Author's interview, February 2007
[13] http://www.indexmagazine.com/interviews/kim_gordon_thurston_moore.shtml
[14] Author's interview, April 2007
[15] http://www.sonicyouth.com/history/ographies/thurstonleavenotes.html
[16] Cosloy Youth #1, January 1988
[17] The Watt From Pedro radio show, February 14 2007
[18] Author's interview, January 2005
[19] Author's interview, January 2005
[20] Author's interview, January 2005
[21] *Jrnls80s*, pg 75
[22] *New York Times*, July 5 1987
[23] http://www.robertchristgau.com/get_artist2.php?id=1280

CHAPTER SEVEN

Daydreaming Days In A Daydream Nation

"I always thought what I wanted to do in Sonic Youth was put forth the idea that a song can be whatever you make it. Like on those D. Boon stickers where it says, 'Punk Rock is whatever we want it to be' – to me, that was punk rock. A song can be whatever you make it, if it has a certain vibe that you feel is right."[1]

Thurston Moore

As the sessions for *Sister* drew to a close, Sonic Youth let loose the relative constraints of their newfound sense of song craft with a ramshackle experiment, exploring sounds outside their arty enclave. For anyone who wasn't a teenager in America in the Seventies, the mammoth success of Kiss, New York's grease-painted purveyors of base heavy metal, is befuddling, beyond the schlocky kitsch appeal of their stage show. Kiss lacked the blues chops and lofty ambitions of Led Zeppelin, or the sinful groove of Aerosmith, their main competitors among the stadium-rock classes. Their music was big, dumb, loud and simple, gracelessly macho riff-boasts like 'Strutter' and 'Love Gun' the kind of single-entendre spectacle that went over best in the echoey suburban arenas that were their stomping grounds.

Throughout the Seventies, America gave the world a slew of second-tier heavy-rock acts (most of whom found little success outside those United States of Riff), groups whose blues-based ruts of guitar play, lumbering swagger and throaty yelling comprised a mostly blue-collar rock subculture. Which isn't to say that there weren't untold pleasures hiding within the epic fourth side of Grand Funk Railroad's 1970 live album ('Into The Sun' will fry your synapses), or that a cultured record collector like Thurston Moore didn't hold a guilty fascination for what is sometimes derided as "butt-rock". But still, this music was the contrast against which punk-rockers of Thurston's generation defined themselves; the records they studiously *didn't* select from the Columbia House music club brochure. There was nothing thrillingly transgressive, intriguingly dark about this music, certainly not compared to more arch, cerebral, knowing artistes like The Stooges, The New York Dolls, the Velvets, groups priding themselves in a subtlety, a complexity of attack missing in stadium rock. The generation that followed, however, would be mostly weaned on this mainstream mutation of the original rock'n'roll virus, tempering their ironic adoption of the odd stadium-rock move with a very genuine love for this noise, in spite of or because of this perceived "dumbness". After all, were these gonzo stadium groups not a logical extension of the garage-rock explosion – bar-band rockers rising up through the circuit?

Certainly, there's something wickedly subversive about 'Master-Dik', that misbegotten afterbirth from the *Sister* sessions. The project began with Steve Shelley sat at his drum kit, headphones on, playing grooves to fit the loops Lee Ranaldo was playing through his cans. These loops were specially chosen fragments from the Kiss catalogue, selected for their greasy riffs, or some particularly ridiculous vocal from frontman Gene Simmons. Afterwards, Lee and Thurston cut these loops of Steve duetting with Kiss together to form a loose, messy groove, over which Moore grabbed the microphone and indulged in his first on-tape rap.

'The Royal Tuff Titty' was Thurston's newfound rap alter-ego, a personality he would explore further on Sonic Youth's later recordings as Ciccone Youth. Doubtless influenced by the divine braggadocio of New Yorker LL Cool J, rap's reigning superstar of the day, Tuff Titty's persona proved a perfect fit for the lusty exhortations of Kiss, celebrating his own self and begging all assembled to rock with him and taste his love. Indeed, by the second verse Tuff Titty was playing the cock-rock star in excelsis, "coking up the boards, tripping anywhere", before a distorted loop of Simmons leering "you bet she's lookin' good" melted into the foreground, surrounded by screaming Sonics guitars, Thurston declaring "We're Ciccone!", in proud celebration of the Youth's nascent alter ego and his allegiance to the Cult of Madonna (whose subsequent reign would help sweep Kiss into the pop margins). The Kiss loop changes as Thurston clears his throat, Gene yelling "I know!" over and over, Tuff Titty mimicking his lame ass rock, slurring that "Gene Simmons is an ugly mother..." as growling low-end bass enters the mix and the squalling Sonics guitars swallow the speakers, Thurston lost in babbled poetics.

Then, one last verse, Tuff Titty throwing a prima donna rock star tantrum: "London fuck, you're pissing me off... Won't you please let me rock you? I'm just a boy with nothing to do", before the twisted Sonics hurricane tears the track to oblivion, with a tape-loop coda of chiming church bells, recorded by Lee. In just over five minutes, Sonic Youth had tried on some stadium-rock moves, to see how they felt for a while, before employing their avant-garde attack to render dull mainstream fare like Kiss irrelevant. The four young musicians of Sonic Youth didn't feel the need to hire make-up artists or firework shows to thrill their audiences; dressed down but electrified, seducing minds as well as engorging sexual organs, Sonic Youth delivered the sublime to a tight budget, on a nightly basis.

* * *

Following a tradition they'd begun with the first *EVOL* tours, the group set out shortly after completing the *Sister* sessions for some shows in New York and the surrounding states, playing mostly material from this as-yet-unreleased new album. The first show, at Maxwell's in nearby Hoboken, New Jersey, was somewhat disastrous. The audience, confronted with the new material, heckled the band and called out for 'Expressway' and 'Inhuman', tunes they knew. The group, meanwhile, grappled with technical malfunctions, sound problems, errantly tuned guitars and all manner of false starts, detracting from the laser-guided precision of the *Sister* songs. The following night was more successful, Dinosaur playing support.

Sonic Youth spent the rest of April and May playing around New York, Philadelphia, Ohio, Rhode Island and Washington DC; at a gig in Buffalo, in upstate New York, they were supported by locals Shady Crady, later to metamorphose into star-gazing New York noise-a-delicists Mercury Rev. In June, they shipped out to Britain for their *Sister* European tour, opening on a good omen, a guest appearance from hero Iggy Pop for an encore of 'I Wanna Be Your Dog'. Hair slick and black, clad in whip-tight midnight pants and high-collared black leather jacket, Iggy prowled and preened, as Kim bopped, one arm holding the mic-stand, hollering the age-old Stooges lyric with venom. Watching footage of the show at London's Town and Country Club, its hard to imagine how Thurston didn't just explode with pride, writhing around at the lip of the stage, scraping his guitar against the monitors while his hero Iggy Pop crouched with a predatory stare at his young offspring, in awe of the hallucinatory noise they were stirring from his decades-old song.

The seemingly impromptu collaboration, inspired by the lucky coincidence of Sonic Youth and Iggy's band sharing the same London rehearsal rooms, left a deep impression on the younger group. "I was amazed that he was so professional," wrote Kim, of her iconic proto-punk mic-partner. "He expressed the freakiness of being a woman and an entertainer. I felt like such a cream puff next to him. I didn't know what to do, so I just sort of watched."

"It's a big fuckin' jammed event," wrote Lee, in his tour journal. "Super crowded, smoke-filled, and fairly unbearable. I'm leaving the talk about the coke snowstorms and the hash out of all this because it's basically uninteresting stuff: who was high on what, or how many people were crammed in the men's room trying to get a line, or who had the acid in their matchbox. It all went down, and I was caught in the flurries when possible, I admit it, but what else was there to do to break the monotony and feel the razor's edge? That shit's all beside the point. We have no infatuation with that stuff, just a giggle, as the Fabs would have said."

In England, the group came up against the sharp end of the media they'd so successfully courted in the past. "Interviews have been weird all along this tour," Lee wrote. "People refuse to believe we don't have some big new statement to make, or that it's really all encapsulated in the music. They want from us what it is we're 'into' now, what's our concept; they refuse to believe us when we say we're still just doing what we do, trying hard and making songs. There's all this about *Sister* being '*EVOL II*', and everybody is so ready to peg us in a slot and set us adrift. 'Ah so that's SY! Now we've got them!' Stupid crit think."[2]

Interviewed by the Stud Brothers, a confrontational duo of writers from *Melody Maker*, the group deflected unwelcome "socio-political" questions by filming their interviewers with Super 8 cameras, following one of the Studs into the bathroom. Smith felt the press often distorted his group to fit their own prejudices. "Kim's astigmatism is widely misread as her being really 'West Coast cool'," he laughs, "but *she really can't see very well.* Kim's also a stunning-looking person, and the vibe she emanates is a very interesting one. There weren't a lot of women in music at that time; Danielle Dax, Siouxsie, a few others. It's weird, nobody ever talks about Kim's sexual power; it's not like we had to sell it, it was obvious."

Kim had noticed journalists' reluctance to engage with her, mentioning it when interviewed by *Cosloy Youth* zine. "They describe everyone in the band except for me, and I get the feeling that they don't know how to deal well with women unless they conform to a really specific, conventional stereotype. I think it's difficult to project an image that's different, that's also honest. It's hard to project something that's not stereotypical; it involves something more personal, putting more of 'yourself' out there. You're not protected. People have their style so 'stylised', to protect themselves."

Mark Sinker, interviewing the group in 1987 for a feature in *NME*, appreciated the sexual nature of Sonic Youth's allure, grappling with the subject in his piece. "Kim wrote a piece in *Artforum* some years earlier which engaged with ideas about sexuality in the pop performance," he remembers. "It's something which is brought to the fore whenever you have powerful woman performers in rock, because the audience is mostly male. What's interesting is, it also applies at a slightly unconscious level on the relationship between young adolescent males to older male performers. What's exciting about it is, the sexual allure is quite ill-defined; you don't know whether it's a mixture of wanting to *be* this person, or wanting to sleep with them. That was something that was very potent in their performances, although my figure of attraction was always Thurston rather than Kim.

"The way we discuss sexuality has become more explicit since the Sixties," continues Sinker, "but it's become about defining and fixing an identity. And what is interesting about performance is that the audience and the performers are allowed to be playful with their identities, and go through the pleasure of imagining other kinds of relationships and negotiations. That's hard to write about, precisely because it's unformed; you can't define flirtation. Performances are less about consummated sex than they are about flirtation, and that one of the things that the people in the audience are doing is flirting with other possibilities of themselves, as manifested or encouraged or affirmed by the performer, and that that's something you can do in that space. You can pretend, get carried away with your feelings."[3]

The group were very much about flirting with seductive, undefined fantasies, their new album full of songs about splintered identities and alternate realities, and recognised Sinker as a kindred spirit, even forgiving a disastrous first interview where his Dictaphone malfunctioned and agreeing to be interviewed again. "They were very tolerant of my slightly weird enthusiasm for them," he recalls. "I found their interplay very entertaining and amusing, in a way I found the byplay of some bands to be tiresome and laddish. They were very friendly, and quite happy to do this weird thing, giving interviews to complete strangers with microphones who were likely to be dicks. The Butthole Surfers are also very friendly, but they are very playful about leading the interviewer up the garden path. Sonic Youth weren't like that at all; they took the process quite seriously, were quite idealistic about the same things that I was.

"There was this form of idealism about them, latently, as a force," remembers Sinker. "I was very starry-eyed about the idea that it had some kind of potentially political dynamic, which would be what the Sex Pistols *should* have been. There was a good reason why punk 'happened', but it had become a real shibboleth, where not knowing about the past was a badge of your intellectual distinction. I'm a bit 'old school' about knowledge, that seemed like a silly way to think about things. I was unusual, in that I was 'punk rock' but not averse to the Sixties. They were the same way; they were a bit older, they were historically aware of what had gone before, *interested*."

"I was just starting to discover a lot of American bands that would subsequently become very important to me," remembers Keith Cameron, later a respected writer for *NME* and *Mojo* but in 1987 a recent graduate living in Edinburgh. "I'd become fascinated by the underbelly of American society; I studied some American history in university, and some modern American political history as well. The decay of the hippy dream in the Sixties is obviously a fairly tasty subject, and the Manson killings were ghoulish and bizarre and, to this day, unfathomable. To find any rock song [like 'Death Valley '69'] that, however obliquely, dealt with that whole tale was interesting. That's all obviously stuff I found out after I first heard it. My initial reaction was, what a *brilliantly* scary song."[4]

Cameron saw Sonic Youth for the first time on the *Sister* tour, a revelatory experience. "I had no idea how they made the sounds on the records," he remembers. "I was so caught up in the excitement of seeing them, a band that unusual and yet so powerful, face-to-face. As people, they seemed incredibly glamorous, in comparison to everything else that was going on. The previous year I'd seen Hüsker Dü, another life-changing gig. I was really into R.E.M. These bands all shared a sense of otherness, and the sounds they made spoke eloquently. These seemed to be dealing in a *real* Americana, something apart from the generic term for horrible country music that it's become. It seemed that these bands could almost tell you as much about American culture as reading *Rolling Stone* at that time, or watching American movies. As I got deeper into it, I realised that so much of what Sonic Youth did was informed by and feeding from and subverting elements of American pop culture. There was a whole lot more there than just weird-tuned guitars."

While the group were blowing the minds of audiences across Europe, their own experiences were often more mundane, the numbing tedium of extended periods of touring and promotion echoing scenes from Rob Reiner's parodic rockumentary, *This Is Spinal Tap*. "We get to the radio station in Geneva very late," wrote Kim in her tour diary, of the June radio session in Switzerland that would later be excerpted on the B-side to 'Master Dik'. "We started complaining about having to do the show when we found out we weren't getting paid. And it's the same old story about how we'll end up with a high-quality recording, but we already know it's gonna be lame because it's a dead room and we'll be playing in front of five Swiss people bobbing their heads and smiling politely. So of course, they have a great spread of pâté, cheeses, and smoked ham. We feel like slobs surrounded by this plush equipment and stark beige environment, quiet as a bomb shelter. From the first note it's a disaster. Thurston starts whispering obscenities over the intro to 'Cotton Crown'. We feel like jerks, so pretty soon Thurston is swearing new lyrics to all the songs, and no one stops us."[5]

Late arrival at the venue for their Munich date ended in a pitched battle between Sonic Youth and "German egoist assholes" who refused to let the group play. "A long-winded fight ensued as only the Germans know how to stage," wrote Lee. "We ended up in front of the crowd, Thurston and me on top of the van playing 'Master-Dik' out of the blaster, him blowing his police whistle and me announcing the whole fiasco to the crowd waiting to get in, just to keep the record straight and cause some ruckus. We played some rap tapes and sold T-shirts and posters in the parking lot, talking to some disappointed people who'd actually come to see us."

The group returned home at the end of July, resting up throughout August before touring across America through September and October, with a typically impressive list of opening bands: drug-drenched Virginian anarchist noise band The Happy Flowers (the Youth incorporated a cover of the Flowers' 'Mom, I Gave The Cat Some Acid' into their set by way of tribute); big-hearted Oklahoman psychedelicists The Flaming Lips; New York SST-signed acid rockers Das Damen; Scratch Acid; Live Skull; Californian friends fIREHOSE and Redd Kross. In Atlanta, Kim and Thurston stayed at the home his older sister Susan shared with her husband and four children. Kim remembered waking up to "food flying around the room and babies crawling all over us. I know many people think we indulge in twisted sex and ingest massive amounts of drugs on tour, and of course we do. But I'll always remember Susan, standing in the driveway with the kids and waving goodbye."

Most nights on this tour, the Youth would spend their encore spiritedly hurtling through a handful of affectionately chaotic Ramones covers, captured for posterity on *Hold That Tiger*, an "official" bootleg of their show at Chicago's Metro on October 14. The bootleg, recorded by a fan using microphones suspended above the venue's balcony seating area, captures in rough fidelity a typical set from the tour, drawing heavily from *EVOL* and *Sister*. Following a colossal, psychedelic 'Expressway' and a positively feral, dissonant 'Pacific Coast Highway', the Ramones set is a final burst of careering, reckless energy and "1-2-3-4" countdowns, the Sonics' screaming guitars blasting out the infectious, dumb chords, closing with the hard-riffing ramalama of 'Beat On The Brat', Thurston yelping with audible glee over the final power chords.

"The band is really good, and the people are all fine and sane," wrote Ranaldo in his journal, that summer. "We argue and we get all pent up on the road and everyone is grumpy and no one gets what they want often enough, but that's beside the point. After all this time we've got a system down, however imperfect, with which to deal with all the stress, and what we do together is stronger than all the folly and personal differences. It's something very good, and big, and somehow very right."

* * *

The original mix of 'Master-Dik' would see release as a bonus track on the CD release of *Sister* (the first time a Sonic Youth album was released simultaneously on vinyl, cassette and the fast-rising compact disk format). A second mix, with Steve's live drums replaced by primitive synth drums (the 'Beat Box' mix, now sounding awkward and dated compared to the original), was released late in 1987 as a 12-inch single, much to Paul Smith's distress.

The B-sides in particular rankled with Smith, a raw run though The Ramones' 'Beat On The Brat', and a sequence of shorter fragments that comprised 'Master-Dik Parts 2 & 3', eschewing the conceptual smarts of the lead track for a formless and mostly baffling handful of vignettes that mostly demystified the band: a mind-numbing interview conducted in a foreign language; a sliver of onstage babble from an off-night on tour; a messed-up run through The Beatles' 'Ticket To Ride' that morphs into a New York Dolls rockout topped by some Tuff Titty lines; abstract studio noise; warbly guitar improvisation; some a cappella Tuff Titty raps; and a coda of bonus beats and ambient birdsong. These B-sides caught Sonic Youth at their most impish and self-indulgent.

"I fought them tooth and nail over 'Master-Dik'," remembers Smith, who released the EP at budget price. "Basically, I thought it was half a record, so we had to charge them half the money. That was a big fight; they were on tour, so it was conducted via lots of late night phone calls, with them saying, 'But Paul, you don't tell *us* what to do, we tell *you* what to do.' And me replying, 'Yeah, I know, I know you *think* that, but in this case you're *wrong*'. It doesn't stand up as their brightest musical moment. I encouraged the wackiness that was Ciccone Youth: it had a concept to it, *great*. But the B-side to 'Master-Dik' was a fucking mess. I was disappointed in them. But they wanted to put it out."[6]

Tensions were growing between Smith and his charges, not aided by the misunderstanding over *The Walls Have Ears*. "I always said that I started the label for them," explains Smith, "but somewhere along the line they interpreted that to mean Blast First! was *their* label. Which it wasn't. Blast First! grew, primarily, out of Thurston's genius list, but there were releases they weren't involved with. That bothered them big time." Following the success of *Bad Moon Rising*, Smith had begun to receive an onslaught of demo tapes. The first he opened was from a British band called Head of David. "That was one of the few times I actually found something I loved via a demo tape," laughs Smith. "These bands send you their tapes, asking for your honest opinion – but they don't want it. The first time I sent someone a letter along the lines of, 'This is what I think is wrong with your band, but good luck to you', they sent me back a sheet of wallpaper with, 'This is what's wrong with your record label' smeared in shit."

Smith signed a number of groups without Sonic Youth's approval: Head of David, New York noiseniks Big Stick, and symphonic students-of-Branca Band of Susans. Smith alleges Sonic Youth were unsupportive of his signings, Thurston drubbing Band of Susans in the press (which doubly stung Smith as he was married to their bassist, Susan Stenger). Their hostility to his other signings pained Smith. "I almost didn't go to Mute because of Sonic Youth," he says. "I had no money, Blast First! had no money, Sonic Youth had no money. But I almost didn't do the deal with Dan Miller because the only band on the label he didn't like was Sonic Youth. He *loved* Head of David and Big Stick, weirdly enough. Head of David, God bless 'em, got me that deal. He said, 'I don't really get this Youth thing.' He finally saw them the second time they played the ULU, and he came up to me afterwards going, 'I *get* this now.' But up till then, he was saying, 'We'll just do the deal without them.' And I said no. Not without Sonic Youth."

"Thurston Moore, he big and strong/He write the dynamic song"
'Sonic Yoot', Swanic Youth

Late in 1987, college radio DJs started playing an obscure seven inch with a sleeve design in the blocky, utilitarian style of Swans' record covers, purporting to be a collaboration between that group and their erstwhile tourmates, Sonic Youth. A cloying calypso track serving as a paean to our favourite guitar abusers, it was in fact the work of an impish writer from *Maximum Rock'n'Roll*, zine bible for the hardcore scene, and Peter Holsapple, a member of New York power-poppers The dB's and sometime associate of R.E.M. With a B-side, 'Swan Jovi', that took a swipe at New Jersey's favourite poodle rockers, Swanic Youth was painfully punsome, definitely sub-Al Yankovic, but the presence of such a parody record was testament to how high Sonic Youth's star had risen through 1987.

A genuine Sonic Youth alter ego, Ciccone Youth, rose again early in the new year. The sessions arose from the long-proposed and highly ambitious plan to cover The Beatles' self-titled 1968 album, popularly known as the 'White Album' because of its plain white sleeve, in its entirety. Recorded as the Fabs bailed upon the psychedelic riot of preceding years, the 'White Album' was a two-disc set of raw, subtle, damaged creativity, by turns as ugly, noisy, sweet, sad and weird as The Beatles ever got, and certainly worthy material for interpretation via Sonic Youth's transmogrifying guitars.

"I was totally in love with the idea of recording the 'White Album'," laughs Steve Shelley. "I'm a complete Beatles freak, ever since I was 12 years old. We talked about it, but we never really did any of the work. I thought we could really have done something interesting." However, the Youth's local noise nemeses Pussy Galore – East Village Stones to SY's Beatles – rained on their parade with their rough, lo-fi approximation of the Stones' *Exile On Main Street*, facilitated by newly added guitarist and resident Stones freak Neil Hagerty, who taught the band the songs, despite considering *Exile* to be the weakest of all Stones joints. "That kinda took the wind out of our sails," sighs Shelley. "We didn't really need to make that statement, they already did it."[7]

The Whitey Album would eventually comprise the earlier Ciccone Youth single along with the experiments they recorded with Wharton Tiers in January 1988, a wiry tangle of non-sequiters, primitive beatbox experiments, bursts of spoken word and found sound, and bratty rap, along with Kim's karaoke cover of Robert Palmer's creepy Eighties anthem 'Addicted To Love', recorded at a kiosk in a local shopping mall and accompanied by a video shot under similar circumstances, Kim dancing before a montage of military footage. Much of Ciccone Youth was similarly smart, subversive fare, though the album would baffle many attuned to the more classically structured Sonic Youth compositions of recent times. Akin to Sonic Death, *The Whitey Album* is a dense jumble of electrifying textures and squalling, atmospheric instrumentals, offset by moments of playfulness and perplexing in-jokes.

"It's inspired by working with Eighties pop things," explains Steve, "like Kim singing karaoke, or us fooling around with samplers and beatboxes. That stuff was really happening back then, but not in our world; it was all in the hip-hop world. We never set out to make a 'hip-hop record'. We got together and we didn't write *anything*, we went over to Wharton's studio and came up with the ideas. Whenever I talk to Lee about it, he says it's like an Eno record. I like *The Whitey Album*. I would probably edit some of it, if I could turn back time."

Ranaldo's observation was accurate; some of the most intriguing tracks, like the abrasive 'March Of The Ciccone Robots', the disorientating street-funk of 'Macbeth', and the eerie, chilled rumble of 'Platoon II' recall Eno and David Byrne's *My Life In The Bush Of Ghosts*, forcing something broken and beautiful from the sequencers and drum machines. On *The Whitey Album*, Ciccone Youth are the ghosts within the machine, malignant human viruses disrupting the rote rhythms, forging blackened industrial clunk funk from the scrape of plectrum against metal strings, lost in caverns of dub, not developing these experiments into "proper" songs but rather inviting the audience to share in this indulgent chaos.

Smith convinced the group to leave the newly completed *Whitey Album* on the shelf, to be released after the next "proper" Sonic Youth album, which they began writing that spring. Following their increased confidence with traditional forms of songwriting structure, evident on the skewed but still perfect pop of *EVOL* and *Sister*, this new material took a brave step forward. Sonic Youth songs had typically been composed of two sections – the "song" part, and the "noise" part. Once their earlier compositions slalomed into the "noise" section, there was rarely any chance of them escaping before fade-out. These new songs, however, would embrace a new complexity, composed of multiple parts, segueing from song to noise to exultant instrumental passages with a chutzpah that would impress the ghosts of progressive rock that still lingered in the larger venues the Youth played. Having recorded their most oblique, perplexing and potentially impenetrable music since *Sonic Death*, and doubtless emboldened by the unabashedly classic-rock leanings of tour-mates like Dinosaur, their new music embraced classic-rock conventions with a refreshing absence of ironic distance (still subtly rewiring them in the process).

When the group played a handful of small shows around the New York area, debuting this new material in its entirety, with no old favourites to soften the blow, they hadn't played before an audience since the last American *EVOL* tour, the previous autumn. Tapes of their show at CBGB on June 24 depict these songs in late embryonic stages; lyrics for some of them are entirely different, and gibberish-heavy; others, like 'Cross The Breeze', are sung by Thurston but will become Kim songs on the album. Still, the music is pretty much intact, the songs noticeably longer than before, shifting through different but united passages before expertly crafted climaxes.

There was a bitter truth behind Thurston's improvised couplets for that evening's version of 'Hyperstation'. Although signing to SST was a hardcore dream come true for Thurston, the group's experience on the label proved frustrating. While their touring circuit was taking in ever more obscure locations, and their press profile was expanding outside of the New York radius, to nationally respected press outlets, Sonic Youth's records remained hampered by SST's limited distribution. As many SST bands discovered, the label might book you to play a town where none of your vinyl could be found. Indeed, many outlying stores were more likely to be stocking imported Blast First! pressings than SST releases of Sonic Youth albums. Another harsh reality for such a relatively successful group signed to an independent label was that they often found SST lagging behind in royalty payments, the group's profits helping to subsidise the label's less successful signings. At CBGB, Thurston summed up his feelings plainly: "SST owes us money/it's really something funny".

"We really became part of the family, but it started getting destroyed from within," says Thurston, of the disintegration of their relationship with the label. "There was a lot of personal conflict, political conflict. SST changed when Black Flag stopped touring and Greg got more involved with the day to day business." Years later, the first issue of their self-produced fan-club zine *Sonic Death* reprinted a letter from the Sonics' law firm to the label, terminating their contract due to "consistent failure to pay Sonic Youth... Demand for such payment has been made repeatedly over the past several years by the group and their accountants." Thurston deleted SST's name in the document, replacing it with "Kitty Poo Records", scribbling over his lawyers' company name and writing "good guys" underneath.

"It was Thurston's love story," says Paul Smith. "He was heartbroken at the time. I don't think he's ever really spoken much about it, but he should do; it would reflect a little better on Blast First! if he did. *We* didn't put out his record and not pay him, *we* didn't screw him over. If you read the interviews at the time, Thurston was in fucking seventh heaven that these people were putting out his records, that he was part of the 'revolution'. No one over there seemed to have worked out that the Black Flag guys really wanted SST to be about *their* band, didn't want any bands who were bigger or more popular or more influential than Black Flag. The Youth only just scraped onto the label; Chuck Dukowski certainly wasn't a big Sonic Youth supporter. But the Sonics really wanted to be on SST, and those guys saw it as an opportunity to make a bit of money. I always felt sorry for them, for Thurston, because it was a kid's dream that was destroyed by people who should know better."

It was a familiar story; a number of SST's signings are now in legal dispute with the label, to recover their master tapes, large portions of the catalogue in dire need of remastering and repackaging. The music industry is built upon ripping off artists in such a fashion; the independent scene, for all its myths to the contrary, doubly so. That's why exceptions to this rule are so noteworthy, like Corey Rusk's Touch & Go, or Ian MacKaye's Dischord or, indeed, Blast First!

Smith was the antithesis of the fast-talking Indie Label Proprietor archetype. "Someone like Tony Wilson from Factory Records could do the accounts on his shirt cuff and decide he didn't owe the bands anything," he says. "Then he'd buy everyone a drink and get away with it. I had none of Tony's glamour or charm, I came from a more solid place. We discussed everything, down to the amount of money we'd spend on ads, and where they'd be placed. It was an equal discussion, not the record company telling them what to do.

"The Youth, quite sensibly, never wanted to get into a position where they were owed money by only one record label," continues Smith. "We distributed their albums all over the world, but we always had to deal with an American label, and these labels were always paranoid that we would release an album two weeks before them and flood the market with imports. I went over to SST and had a meeting with Greg Ginn and Chuck Dukowski, some time in 1988. We were huddled round a tiny table, but the distance between us seemed wider than the 6,000 miles I'd just flown to be there. They were the biggest bunch of arses I'd ever met. They thought I was some English wimp or something. 'Yeah, but we lived on a dollar a day when we were in Black Flag'. Every conversation was about living for a dollar a day when they were in Black Flag. I wanted to tell them to shut up… That Sonic Youth don't need to *do* that…"

In July, the group decamped to Greene Street Studios, a New York recording facility with an impressive history. "It was located in a then still up-and-coming section of New York, Soho," remembers Nicholas Sansano, who worked as staff engineer at Greene Street. "It was very much outside the mainstream in every way possible. The studio played host to everyone from Nico, to Philip Glass, to Public Enemy, to James Brown, to Run-DMC, to Kurtis Blow, to Afrika Bambaataa… I am leaving out so, so much. This place should be written about… It was very special."[8] A victim of the rejuvenation of New York, and the rent increases that followed, Greene Street closed its doors in 2002.

Born in the Bronx, Sansano was a perfect match for Sonic Youth. He spent his teenage years lost in punk and prog-rock, studying piano and composition at Berklee College Of Music, earning money in a soul covers band. At Greene Street, he began working with the Bomb Squad, the innovative and radical production unit behind hip-hop's militant polemicists, Public Enemy. "I think Sonic Youth were attracted by all the hip-hop that was going on there at the time," says Sansano. "The group came down and I played them some of the music I'd been working on, Public Enemy's 'Black Steel In The Hour Of Chaos', 'It Takes Two' by Rob Base… I played no heavy rock, all hip-hop, and perhaps something off an album I had just finished called *The Smell Of A Friend*, a prog-ish thing with John Grieves, Anton Fier and some of the Golden Palominos. I guess they liked what I played. It was after this meeting that I took the time to research and educate myself about how influential they were to so many of my contemporaries. I was never what we call a 'hipster', I never followed hot trends. I was and remain open to any and everything."

Paul Smith fully supported the budget increase incurred by recording at Greene Street. "We spent a bit more money, to raise the production values," he remembers. "My view was always that a Blast First! record had to be able to stand next to a Madonna record and not seem cheap and 'indie' by comparison. Being the Youth, they went into the studio and recorded a double album, which cost double the money. They were unsure about it, but I thought the world can't get enough of them so, as a Sonic Youth fan, a double album would be perfect. You always read about record companies telling their artists to cut double albums down to a single album. We didn't do any of that bollocks. It just meant more Sonic Youth music out there, which was exactly what I wanted."

"We'd been playing together live for a while," remembers Steve, "and the songs were all growing these long intros and long outros, with a long jam in the middle. All the new songs were long songs. It got to a point where we knew it wouldn't all fit on one LP, that it was gonna be a double album, so we started playing with the idea of, what is a double album?" Fitting with the more epic, extended, "classic rock" feel of this new material, the resulting set of songs would be released as a gatefold double album, a format synonymous with the more ambitious/pretentious end of the mainstream rock market, the records lazy rock critics cite – distended multi-disk sets from the likes of ELP and Yes, the conceptual conceits of the buffoonish Rick Wakeman – when conjuring straw-man arguments against prog-rock.

By contrast, the songs Sonic Youth cut for those four sides of vinyl would, despite their length, be the most purposeful, flab-free, focused music of their career, but still they toyed with the trappings of progressive-rock excess; each member adopted a personal runic symbol, printed on the album sleeve, in imitation of the runes that composed the title of Led Zeppelin's mammoth-selling fourth album. "We were fooling around," adds Steve, "trying not to be too serious about putting out a double album. I guess the only people we knew who had put out double albums at that point were Hüsker Dü and The Minutemen."

Sonic Youth spent three weeks recording the album at Greene Street. "We had a very limited amount of space," remembers Sansano, "and we had to set up for loud, live performance. I was worried that we couldn't achieve proper isolation between the instruments to correctly record them. I set the band up in the round, drums in the middle, the band surrounding Steve. There were partitions between them, but they had large glass inserts, so they could see each other. I was young and knew that we were in the wrong type of place to do what we were doing, that we didn't have enough money… But we were pulling it off, nonetheless. I never said no, to overloading things, combining things, processing things. We fine-tuned guitar sounds, came up with some creative layers in overdubbing, discovered effects that worked. If you are open-minded and tasteful you can stretch the envelope as far as you wish.

"You have to remember that I was also recording Public Enemy at the time," adds Sansano. "To make *that* work on tape, we had to make all our own rules."

> "It's an anthem in a vacuum on a hyperstation/daydreaming days in a daydream nation"
>
> 'Hyperstation'

Daydream Nation is an album alive and enraptured with the romance of being young and making music, as poignant and earnest a tribute to this music as The Velvet Underground's deathless 'Rock'n'Roll'. While still unafraid to stir righteous white-light rock'n'roll from the darker corners of American culture, and exploring the shadowy side of sexual relationships, *Daydream Nation* captures a group drunk on the exhilaration of being in a rock'n'roll group, gathering strength from the weird new Americana made by their contemporaries, absorbing this spectrum of fresh perspective, heady from the fusion of presumed-archaic classic rock signatures and inarticulate post-punk noise perfected by their friends Dinosaur.

Of all the groups Sonic Youth had played with while criss-crossing America, they shared a special kinship with the combustive Massachusetts trio; J Mascis' radical employment of the resolutely old-school Marshall stack guitar amp set-up, responsible for Dinosaur's roaring onstage din, would prove influential on generations of indie rock groups. "People would go buy the exact same equipment J used, the same amps and pedals," remembers Lou Barlow. "J embraced the Marshall stack as something that could be *expressive*, not some bludgeoning heavy metal crap. *Rolling Stone* published some crappy '100 Greatest Guitarists Ever' list a while back; Kurt Cobain was in there, Kevin Shields, even Frank fuckin' Black, but not J. And he was so fucking influential. He was the progenitor of that style."[9]

Dinosaur's somnambulant frontman would cast his lazy shadow over much of *Daydream Nation*, most notably inspiring the lyrics to the album's opening track. As befits an album so optimistic in its general tenor, 'Teenage Riot' opens with gentle lilts of sunshine guitar, Kim conducting a playful, childlike dialogue with herself, before the endearingly ramshackle guitar lick rises from the glow, a scruffy but spritely strum. 'Teenage Riot' is the sound of rock'n'roll pumping from college dorms and suburban basement entertainment rooms, the touring life of a punk-rock musician beckoning, with a chance to see the world from this unique perspective if the hero can just tie a tangle of notes tight enough to write a hit.

'Teenage Riot' evokes the purgatorial haze of the "slacker" existence: so much *potential* they're left only dazed and confused, asking, like Mick Jagger in 'Street Fighting Man', "What's a man to do?" It's a song dizzy with opportunities to squander, a lazy call to arms, Thurston singing, "It's getting kinda quiet in my city head/takes a teenage riot to get me out of bed." Underneath lies a charmingly naïve belief in the power of rock'n'roll, of this underground music, of pop culture as a whole, as some kind of positive, rejuvenating force. Mascis stalks the song, a mysterious outsider figure "running in on platform shoes, with Marshall stacks to at least just give us a clue", the hero with a zero painted on his hand. 1988 was election year, the end of punk figure of hate Ronald Reagan's reign in the White House; accordingly, Sonic Youth almost called their new album *Rock'n'Roll For President*, with Mascis their preferred candidate for Head of State. The message was classic rock'n'roll, some talking 'bout their generation. A band-produced music video for the track cut together flailing band performance, on-the-road levity and footage of heroes like Patti Smith, Mark E Smith of The Fall, Iggy Pop, underground comics creator Harvey Pekar, Black Flag, Dennis Wilson of The Beach Boys, Neil Young, Sun Ra, Mike Watt, Joni Mitchell and William S. Burroughs, offering forth a most personal canon of alternative genius.

'Silver Rocket', the second track, wrote the Youth's new approach to songcraft large, its initial 90-second burst of hurtling panic-rock running headlong into a slick of garish, abstracted noise: scraped strings roaring like crashing jets, spumes of frothing feedback, oily pools of detuned tangle, wah-wah pedal turning screes into screams, guitars that sound like sirens and alarms. The song builds again, riding a martial snare-drum barrage to emerge intact, unscathed from the dissonant wreckage, a gesture that seems to ooze a cool confidence, a swagger akin to that of a lion tamer, establishing the Youth's mastery of such sonic chaos. It's a trick they'd pull off again and again over *Daydream Nation*'s four-sided circus, most notably on 'Total Trash', where Thurston's bubble-gum nonsense poem gets chewed up by a noise section awash with echo and delay – an almost "dub" soundscape that sends guitars skittering like someone just tossed a barrelful of marbles and ball bearings across the floor of the studio – emerging from the other side as some bizarre new mutated self. On 'Eric's Trip', the noise played out as a narrative device, signifying the mind-altering effects of the heroic dose of psychedelics swallowed by the narrator, dramatising lyrics Lee lifted from Andy Warhol's cinematic document of weird scenes at the Chelsea Hotel, *Chelsea Girls*.

Elsewhere, songs shifted from section to section, 'Cross The Breeze' morphing through pastoral chime, fast-revving punk-rock, prog-thrash explosions and back again, its central riff twisting through these changes before slowly evaporating away over a long, meditative coda. The final track, 'Trilogy', was indeed three separate songs sharing only their title and similar guitar tunings (they would often be rehearsed together as a block). A lysergic, sensual parade through the lurid underbelly of the urban sprawl, 'The Wonder' was named after crime writer James Ellroy's pet name for Los Angeles, a jagged, detuned squall that melted into a swarming, humid mess of guitar noise. The languid, burnt-out lullaby of 'Hyperstation' was seemingly composed from the still smouldering embers of the previous song, as myriad multi-tracked guitars painted shapes in neon, forming a vortex of noise, as Steve Shelley played a raga rhythm. 'Trilogy''s closing part, 'Eliminator Jr' (named in tribute to Dinosaur, who had recently had to append 'Jr' to their name following a lawsuit from a touring group of Sixties survivors calling themselves The Dinosaurs, and also bearded Texan rockers ZZ Top, whose *Eliminator* album this rasping, brutal rocker roughly echoed) delivered a rude-awakening after 'Hyperstation''s dreamy reveries, its fierce, electrified riffage closing the album on a bluntly feral note.

In 'Hyperstation' the album found its title, the song an autobiographical tale of a noise-rocker zipping about his own personal New York of nightclubs and recording studios and rehearsal spaces, spending his nights tripping on acid and getting beaten up by jocks, his existential blues summed up by a howl of "I totalled another amp". Despite – or via – the lowlife details (there's "bum trash in the halls" and his "place is ripped"), there's a definite romance to Moore's lifestyle as presented in 'Hyperstation', a low-rent glamour abetted by Michael Lavine's photography of the group on the inner sleeve, hanging out on some deserted street corner with neon halos glowing in the distance and loitering about a load-in bay. By contrast, Kim's lyrics furthered themes of sexuality and identity running throughout her songbook, 'Kissability' playing upon the power-dynamic of the Hollywood casting couch, 'Eliminator Jr' all snarling carnal hunger, for the "poor rich boy coming right thru me". Elsewhere, the influence of contemporary science-fiction writing could still be felt, from 'Silver Rocket''s space-age pyrotechnics, to 'The Sprawl' taking its name from the Boston-Atlanta Metropolitan Axis urban development featured in William Gibson's novels.

"I can still remember the feeling I had when we were mixing 'Trilogy'," says Nicholas Sansano. "It felt incredibly fulfilling, like an affirmation of sorts. One day a friend of the studio owner was speaking to me and said something to the effect that he couldn't believe records like *Daydream Nation* and Public Enemy's *A Nation Of Millions* were all being recorded here, that we had entered into the history books of recording and pop culture. I began to feel a certain amount of pressure. It's hard to replicate the one-two punch of Sonic Youth and Public Enemy.

"I was young and idealistic and had no agenda other than to make the best record I could make," he continues. "The band and I did not have a sense of how difficult the task we set out to accomplish actually was. An equal combination of naivety and talent made it happen, a couple of weeks in a small studio doing whatever we could to make it come together. There were no extreme financial expectations, no extreme expectations at all; the only pressure was our personal motivation and pride. I equate the experience of recording the album with innocence, and although no one knew it at the time, the success of this album marked the end of innocence for independent music."

The finished double-album made good on every chance taken, the group's discordant, broken guitars approximating the more rapturous elements of classic rock, forging their own dynamic, newly anthemic sound from the fallout. Not all their fans were impressed, including Lou Barlow, Dinosaur bassist, who concluded the new Sonic Youth music was "boring". But such voices were decidedly in the minority. Encased in Gerhard Richter's luminous candle paintings, *Daydream Nation* was Sonic Youth's boldest, bravest and most ambitious statement yet. They had taken on the hoary old double-album format, and triumphed.

"Everyone's doing them nowadays," dead-panned Thurston in 1988. "I think it's a new trend. It's an excuse for us to expand the actual object, see what we can do with it. It's an actual gatefold sleeve. I've always liked the gatefold thing, I guess; they get kinda boorish though, after a while. This one also has a poster inside."[10]

* * *

To ensure *Daydream Nation* didn't suffer the same distribution problems that had handicapped earlier Sonic Youth albums, Blast First! opened an office in New York, Daniel Miller of Mute brokering a deal with Enigma, an American label affiliated to Warner Bros, to distribute the album.

"We'd never asked to handle America," remembers Smith, "and in retrospect it was a bad thing for me to do, because then they were 'surrounded' by me. They came to us with only eight weeks before the album was coming out in the UK and I had to put a company together to handle that. I got Ray Farrell from SST to come to Blast First! – Ray's a god amongst men when it comes to working in the trenches. I got Ann Liman, who had been at Factory in New York. They were the sort of people we needed, who were willing to work all hours. We were all doing the same thing, we'd all go to the bar together and hang out. It was a close time.

"We did what we did everywhere else in the world, finding enough money to get ads, flying journalists out to interview the band. None of the American indie labels were doing that then. Pat Naylor had left Blast First!, exhausted. Evil bastard that I am, I bought her a ticket to travel around America. She loved it, and on her return journey she came back through New York. I told her to come work for me. I got her back. It was quite calculated and evil, really. We sat down with a map of America and worked out where all these remote towns were, so she could work the regional press. We spent the money on those guys in a way no one had to date. We ferociously went after *Rolling Stone* – *ferociously* – because it was the logical place they had to go, for the whole thing to work. I'm not just talking about Sonic Youth, the whole *thing*. Nothing was going to move forward unless we engaged the mainstream."

From the first moment he'd heard Thurston's tape of *Bad Moon Rising*, Smith had fervently believed Sonic Youth belonged on a major label. Certainly, there was nothing about the way *Daydream Nation* sounded that suggested it was inferior to products released by the major labels. The mainstream press' response to the album would validate all his wildest claims on Sonic Youth's behalf; *Rolling Stone* awarded the group their first review, with a relatively glowing (but in retrospect miserly) three and a half stars, while Peter Watrous of the *New York Times* described the album as having "the sort of exploratory power of late pieces by John Coltrane or Grateful Dead jams… Fitting into the group's obsession with the Sixties, the tunes follow a hallucinatory experience, from the realism of the everyday to a more abstracted version of reality, back to the words and the concrete. It's the contrast between the gorgeous music and the knowing, wonderfully sequinned gaudiness of the lyrics, so desperate for sordidness, that gives the band its ample power."

"Literally, as soon as the reviews landed on powerful people's desks, my phone was ringing and Ahmet Ertegun was calling me," remembers Smith. "I'm a huge music fan, so, *fuck*, it's Ahmet Ertegun! Ten minutes later, Tommy Mottola's secretary called up and said, I've got to go see him for a meeting. All these people whose biographies I'd read and studied were calling up, saying, 'I've always been a fan', all that bullshit. We'd been through it before, though. After Robert Palmer's brilliant piece on *Sister* in the *New York Times*, major labels had requested copies. Invariably, it was some kid in the post room who didn't want to buy the record, but sometimes it wasn't, and in those cases they'd ring up afterward and say, 'This isn't the record that was reviewed in the *Times*, is it? You must've put the wrong record in the sleeve, this is just really noisy stuff.'"

NOTES

1 The Watt From Pedro radio show, February 14 2007
2 *Jrnls80s*, pg 115
3 Author's interview, March 2007
4 Author's interview, February 2007
5 Boys Are Smelly, from *The Village Voice Rock & Roll Quarterly* 1988
6 Author's interview, March 2007
7 The Watt From Pedro radio show, March 17 2007
8 Author's interview, March 2007
9 Author's interview, January 2007
10 *The Catalogue*, October 1988

CHAPTER EIGHT

From Here To Infinity

"Sonic Youth played to people who'd grown up on punk rock and hardcore, and were looking for something else. They were a band for the curious; the kind of punks who only wanted to hear hardcore were left by the wayside. When we opened for Sonic Youth, we were playing to open-minded people."[1]

Mark Arm

By the time they'd finished recording and mixing *Daydream Nation*, Sonic Youth had spent almost an entire year off the road. In October 1988, they undertook a brief European tour culminating in two sold-out nights at London's venerated rock venue The Astoria, supported by Dinosaur Jr, Wisconsin hardcore survivors Die Kreuzen, and Steve Albini's post-Big Black project Rapeman (provocatively named after a Japanese erotic manga) whose sole LP, *Two Nuns And A Pack Mule*, included a song titled 'Kim Gordon's Panties'. The group also recorded a session for John Peel's cult show on BBC Radio 1, doffing their caps to the genial, tireless supporter of obscure noise by taping four songs by his most beloved obsession, post-punk mavericks The Fall.

Two weeks later in Boston, they began a tour that would trace a circuit across America for the rest of the year, reacquainting themselves with an underground scene that had evolved somewhat in the period Sonic Youth had spent in the woodshed. Many of the original hardcore bands had dissolved by 1988, most notably Black Flag, who played their last show in the summer of 1986, the culmination of a gruelling tour that aggravated tensions already brewing within the group; lead singer Henry Rollins formed his own hard-rock Rollins Band and branched out further into spoken-word recordings and publishing his writing, while Glen Ginn invested his time in SST. Hüsker Dü, meanwhile, had left SST for Warner Bros, but despite the coruscating, cerebral punk of their major label debut, 1986's *Candy Apple Grey*, and 1987's ambitious double set of mature, turbulent pop, *Warehouse: Songs & Stories*, the already tenuous relationship between Bob Mould and Grant Hart couldn't survive label pressures, the suicide of their manager David Savoy, and Hart's increasing substance-abuse problems. The group dissolved early in 1988, Mould going on to an acclaimed but frustrating solo career with Virgin Records, Hart forming ill-fated power-trio Nova Mob, whose two fine albums would fall victim to their label's subsequent bankruptcy.

Dinosaur Jr had also signed to Blast First! for their third album, *Bug*, thanks to Sonic Youth. "Kim played me a cassette of theirs in my apartment in New York," remembers Paul Smith. "I didn't really get it, but a couple of tunes stuck in my head. Later, I called Kim and asked if I could pop over and collect the tape, that I'd changed my mind, and she said 'It's under your pillow, sucker.' Which I thought was very confident and sweet of her."[2]

The album would prove to be the original line-up's final release, however. Emboldened by a new relationship with the woman he would later marry, Barlow entered into a passive/aggressive war with J Mascis, undermining live shows and contributing no songs to *Bug*. Indeed, Mascis recorded much of the album alone, perversely inviting Barlow to sing lead vocals on album closer 'Don't', a deranged dirge whose sole lyric was "Why don't you like me?", yelled over and over until Barlow was coughing up blood. Shortly afterwards, Mascis made Murph tell Barlow that the group had split; secretly, Mascis immediately reformed Dinosaur Jr with a new bassist, and began touring in support of their new album.

A spirit of regeneration was also in the air, however. As Revolution Summer faded, Ian MacKaye hooked up with bassist Joe Lally and drummer Brendan Canty to form Fugazi, a group that would further Minor Threat's politicised idealism, while expanding their frame of reference to embrace shades of funk and dub within their rhythm-heavy, pulverising punk. Former Rites Of Spring frontman Guy Picciotto joined the group shortly before they recorded their self-titled debut EP in late 1988, his sinewy stage presence and spidery vocals brilliantly complementing MacKaye's blunter attack. Eschewing all forms of merchandising, remaining staunchly independent, and selling records and concert tickets at rock-bottom prices, Fugazi furthered the DC hardcore philosophy, via their actions and some of the most adventurous and compelling music punk ever offered.

In Olympia, an egalitarian college town in Washington State, a vibrant, inclusive and politicised punk scene had grown up around K Records, a label formed by scenester, musician and producer Calvin Johnson, whose group Beat Happening had plied a most beguiling, subterranean pop. Pro-gay, pro-feminist, anti-aggression, the K scene was dismissed by detractors as "twee", but its influence would be felt across the underground for years to come, most visibly via a tattoo on the forearm of the following decade's defining rock hero.

Neighbouring Seattle was also home to a vibrant local scene. A city stranded in the Pacific Northwest, where it rained more often than not and the ailing logging industry was only one reason for its perilously high suicide statistics, Seattle would offer up a slew of bands who fused the alienated attack of punk rock with the muscular riffage of heavy metal and other stadium-rock affectations. Sub Pop, a local label run by Bruce Pavitt and Jonathan Poneman and growing from Poneman's *Subterranean Pop* fanzine, would release much of this local product and, by following Sonic Youth's lead and actively courting the influential and curious British press, deliver it to the world at large. One Seattle group, Soundgarden, would pay sly tribute to Sonic Youth on their SST-released debut album, 1988's *Ultramega OK*, excerpting a distorted, manipulated sliver of 'Death Valley '69' just before their 'Nazi Driver', echoing *Bad Moon Rising*'s similar abuse of The Stooges' 'Not Right'. This track followed a cover of Muddy Waters' 'Smokestack Lightning', revealing the group's molten heart sheltered by a jacket hewn of heavy-metal denim.

Sonic Youth took two groups from the Pacific Northwest along as support for a couple of shows on the tour: Screaming Trees (whose psychedelic garage-rock would evolve into a wracked, beautiful metallic blues as lead singer Mark Lanegan wrested power from guitarist Gary Lee Connor), and Mudhoney, a new group fronted by ex-members of Green River. Guitarist Steve Turner had quit Green River shortly before their 1986 show with Sonic Youth, after clashing with what he described as his bandmates' "ridiculous ambitions"[3]. Shortly after recording their debut album, *Rehab Doll*, in 1988, bassist Jeff Ament and guitarist Stone Gossard quit Green River, forming Mother Love Bone with legendary Seattle extrovert Andrew Wood, a group with an openly commercial sound, more akin to cock-rockers Whitesnake than The Stooges.

"I went to some show, shit-faced drunk and so happy," recalls Mark Arm, who met friend and local drummer Dan Peters standing in line for the bathroom. "I said, 'I gotta slip in front of you, I gotta puke! By the way, Green River have split up. BAAAARF!'"[4] Weeks later, Mudhoney (their name stolen from one of Russ Meyer's sexploitation movies, signifying a fascination with lurid trash culture) were playing their first rehearsal, reuniting Arm with Turner. That summer, they released their debut seven inch, an inspired rasp of bad attitude, gross humour and buzzsaw Stoogian punk-rock, 'Touch Me I'm Sick'. Though they weren't calling this music by such a name yet, the giddily haywire single was pure "grunge", from its belched opening seconds to its final sludgy climax, produced by local engineer and unwitting architect of the "grunge" sound, Jack Endino.

"Bruce Pavitt knew Sonic Youth pretty well," remembers Arm. "He sent a copy to them straight away, and they seemed to dig it. They took us out on tour, which was great for us, otherwise we might have been toiling out in the Midwest for years." The group returned from the first-ever tour as Mudhoney, across the East Coast, jumping on the second half of Sonic Youth's American *Daydream Nation* tour, touring the West Coast down to Texas. "There was a huge difference between us playing by ourselves, and us playing with Sonic Youth," adds Arm. "We were playing to a lot more people, and most of those people seemed pretty receptive to what we were doing. Whereas, when we'd toured on our own, we played to a handful of people in Lexington, Kentucky and got paid $14, six bottles of pop and a pack of cigarettes."

The boys of Mudhoney bonded well with Sonic Youth, many shows ending with a ragged take of 'Hallowe'en' or a chaotic cover of 'I Wanna Be Your Dog', Arm, Turner, Peters and bassist Matt Lukin joining in on vocals. "I have super-fond memories of that tour," says Arm. "We played a place called Night Moves in Orange County, after the Bob Seger song. Matt was completely hammered, and afterwards he tried to wrestle Kim in the parking lot." At the suggestion of Bruce Pavitt, the two groups cemented their kinship with a split seven-inch released on Sub Pop and Blast First!. Aided by Das Damen guitarist Alex Totino, the Youth taped a raw and loose take of 'Touch Me I'm Sick', Kim savouring every guttural yowl. Mudhoney, meanwhile, tackled 'Hallowe'en', rewriting its wraithful slog as sulphurous Alice Cooper riffage, Mark Arm having a ball singing Kim's lust-poem for Henry Rollins.

"Who's sexier, me or Kim Gordon?" laughs Arm. "Was it weird to be singing the words she wrote about how sexy and hot Henry Rollins is? It was super-funny, and that was one reason for doing the single. We were more excited by the whole idea of mutual admiration; we were getting validation from them, and maybe they were getting some from us, a band that was less experimental, more vomit'n'rock'n'roll [laughs]."

Arm says the group spent a fair amount of time mulling over which Youth track to cover before settling on 'Hallowe'en'. "The bassline somehow starts turning into 'I Wanna Be Your Dog' towards the end," he laughs. "We knew we wouldn't be able to replicate their tunings, but we could definitely play that. Sonic Youth's choice was easier, we'd only released two songs at that point. I thought the natural choice for them would've been 'Sweet Young Thing'. But then I've never been very good at picking out the songs people will gravitate towards. I thought 'Sweet Young Thing' was the A-side and 'Touch Me I'm Sick' was the B-side. I'm sure Steve felt the opposite, because one riff was his, and one riff was mine."

Another guest-star appearing during the *Daydream Nation* tour was musician and friend Don Fleming, who took the stage at Traxx in Charlottesville, Virginia, for a closing medley of 'I Wanna Be Your Dog' and The Stones' 'Jumping Jack Flash'. Born in Adel, Georgia, Fleming moved to Washington DC in 1980, bitten early by the hardcore bug and playing in his own group, The Velvet Monkeys. "I grew up on rock'n'roll, but once punk happened, I was like, 'Fuck Yes! Fuck Zeppelin! Let's go!'" laughs Fleming. "That's where the good music's coming from. I was very into Dischord Records and the whole indie scene, it had a thriving DIY ethic. There was a lot of weird art-rock bands in DC at the time, and The Velvet Monkeys were one of them, but we played shows with our friends Minor Threat and Government Issue; what was cool with those bands was that they were open-minded, hardcore wasn't all they were interested in. It's good Ian MacKaye was the papa of the DC hardcore scene, because he had the right moral compass. A lot of white-boy punk scenes devolve into fascism; maybe that's more than likely when you've got a bunch of macho guys who wanna bang heads."[5]

Fleming first made contact with Sonic Youth after hearing *Hard Rock*, a cassette released on Ecstatic Peace featuring spoken-word material from Lydia Lunch and Michael Gira. "I didn't really know about Thurston at the time," says Fleming, "but I made him copies of some cassette releases on my label Big Circus, local bands recording in their dorm rooms. Sonic Youth struck me as very much a New York thing: they're cool, they've got guitars, and they reminded me of Philip Glass, playing repetitive things in unusual tunings." Fleming had played shows with Sonic Youth in 1987 as a member of B.A.L.L., a group of malicious rock satirists led by himself and Mark Kramer, an idiosyncratic composer and musician who served as bassist with the Butthole Surfers for a while in 1985, and whose Shimmy-Disc label released similarly wayward talents like Ween, Japanese noise excursionists Boredoms, and gory metal absurdists Gwar. The tall, blonde-haired Fleming, who could easily pass as Thurston's brother, soon struck up a close friendship with the group. "I just remember doing those first shows, finally seeing Sonic Youth play and thinking, wow, they're really fuckin' good!"

As the New Year dawned, the group made a brave expedition out to the Antipodes, beginning a short tour that saw them play lands very distant from the East Village, triumphing nonetheless. In Australia, they were joined onstage by former Birthday Party guitarist Rowland S Howard for 'I Wanna Be Your Dog', while support act The Verlaines, a turbulent and wonderful group from New Zealand, forged an important connection between American indie rock and the vibrant scene surrounding New Zealand indie label Flying Nun. From Australia, the group detoured behind the crumbing Iron Curtain to play shows in Moscow, Leningrad, Kiev and Vilnius. The tour then moved on to Japan, where the group played two shows in Tokyo and one in Kyoto; the country's fascination with an exotic western art form like rock'n'roll – even a relatively subterranean strain like Sonic Youth – was considerable. In Tokyo, the group met and befriended the Boredoms, an avant-rock collective from Osaka who had been pursuing sometimes-baffling, often-transcendent noise experiments since the early Eighties, and whose remote noise would soon gain an international audience, thanks to Sonic Youth's patronage. Indeed, later that same year Boredoms leader Yamatsuka Eye would collaborate with John Zorn for his *Naked City* project.

Guests for the Soviet section of the tour were Paul Smith and, representing British music weekly *Sounds*, Keith Cameron. "To this day, it's probably one of the best assignments I ever took," beams Cameron. "They'd been approached by a promoter based in Lithuania, who was a huge fan of Sonic Youth. He made an enquiry via Paul Smith, and Paul arranged it with this guy. Sonic Youth were obviously interested in playing unusual places. It was a weird experience for them; they seemed quite tired, it was right at the end of four months' solid touring.

"The places we visited were still part of the Soviet Union. It was insane, an unreal situation, a jarring experience. The social and political fabric of the country was beginning to fray. In Moscow, they played in a huge function room in the hotel where they were staying. According to the laws, audiences weren't allowed to stand up at gigs. But at this gig, kids were beginning to flout these rules. There were a bunch of 'anarcho punks' down the front slam-dancing. The guys in the uniforms with the guns were meant to be keeping an eye on the audience, but they weren't doing anything. You could tell it was an uneasy atmosphere. We heard that six months earlier, those people would've been arrested.

"Then we got to Kiev, in the Ukraine. The further away from Moscow – from the centre of power – we got, the more unhinged things became. To this day it's one of the most out-of-control, amazing gigs I've ever seen. I'm sure Sonic Youth had never played to a crowd going that wild for some time, either. They played a lecture hall in what looked like a youth centre, the Kiev Centre Of Youth. If Wham! had been playing to a room full of teenagers, I don't think there could have been a more adrenalised atmosphere – it was absolutely insane. The kids went mad, as much because they were seeing a rock group from the west, as necessarily for the specifics of what Sonic Youth were doing. I don't think many of the audience knew who they were, maybe a very small handful. They were an American band playing in the Soviet Union, that was enough to get people out. I didn't see any *Confusion Is Sex* T-shirts in the moshpit."[6]

In downtime, Cameron got to explore these strange cities with the group, sharing their experiences. "It was the first time I'd met them," he says. "They were all really nice, considering that it was a very strange situation. After the gig in Moscow, we ended up round someone's flat; Lee and I attempted to smoke a joint, but because they were so completely freaked out that it would be discovered by the authorities, we had to stand on the cistern of the toilet and blow the smoke out of a window."

Cameron also went record-shopping with Thurston; the guitarist's long-running vinyl collecting habit was already something of legend. "I like the artefact aspect of collecting," says Thurston, in explanation of his most beguiling obsession. "That's the only reason I started Ecstatic Peace, to create artefacts. I'm not into getting involved in the record industry at all."[7] Their Soviet crate-digging expedition proved mostly fruitless, however.

"I think we eventually found a department store that sold records," laughs Cameron. "At that point there was only one record label in Russia, Melodia, run by the State; they'd put out compilation albums by 'approved' western acts. It was weird, some of the bands that got approved: there were lots of Beatles albums, Led Zeppelin, Creedence Clearwater Revival, but also Yngwie Malmsteen and Rainbow."

For Cameron, there was a certain symbolism to the group playing the penultimate dates of the *Daydream Nation* tour in the crumbling Soviet Union, a land caught in the midst of a violent and chaotic metamorphosis. "It seemed appropriate," he observes, "to be ending the *Daydream Nation* tour in a nation that had been daydreaming for so long. It seemed to appeal to them. Though I didn't know this at the time, that was their last album before signing to a major label. You could tell that they were realising they were going to have to *do* something, in terms of how far they could take this. They were becoming increasingly popular, their music increasingly... not *conventional*, but employing more conventional rock 'tools'. It seemed natural for them to maybe try and reach a broader audience.

"At that point, you have to remember that the prospects of a band like them signing to a major label didn't seem likely. The idea of Sonic Youth being on a 'major' still seemed like an adventure. Their integrity was fairly ingrained, they weren't young, they didn't seem like they'd be naïve enough to believe that they'd become rich overnight, or that they'd suddenly become pop stars. They'd created their own parallel universe, anyway, their own little world, in which they were, in the eyes of themselves and their fans, stars already. You knew they weren't going to be seduced by any of that stuff. And you could tell they were too smart to fall for any of the traditional pitfalls in the music industry. If any band of their milieu, culturally, was suited to signing to a major – and surviving the whole experience – you'd put money on it being Sonic Youth."

> "Weirdly enough, I always saw Sonic Youth on a major label. I'd grown up with labels like Island, who would've picked up on that kind of music. From the start, I thought of it as a temporary thing, that they'd end up on a 'proper label'. Obviously, as I got more involved, I thought we'd all move to a proper label."[8]
>
> Paul Smith

Filmed while Sonic Youth promoted *Daydream Nation* for British television channel ITV's long-running and respected arts documentary strand *The South Bank Show*, *Put Blood In The Music* documented the riotous underground music scene via the impressionistic direction of film-maker and video-installation artist Charles Atlas. The film, identified by austere presenter Melvyn Bragg as "very much a New York artefact"[9], jump-cut between footage of loud, noisy, beautiful New York in full bristling bloom, a riot of fire-engine sirens, hip-hop blasting from shoulder-slung ghetto blasters, noise pouring out of every basement doorway and corner. Over this visual din, Atlas superimposed talking heads of myriad figures from the underground scene – Branca, Chatham, Ikue Mori, rock critic David Fricke, Lydia Lunch and many more, sermonising on the wonderful and gnarly sounds emanating from New York. Lunch described the city eloquently as "loud, violent, non-stop energy... I can't live without it."

The movie interspersed this footage with segments focusing on two very different figureheads within the American underground: John Zorn, a composer whose shadowy, dissonant and richly textural albums drew upon free jazz, avant-garde and a million other nebulous elements for their considerable impact; and Sonic Youth. Martin Bisi suggests the group were uncomfortable with this formal alignment with Zorn. "Bill Laswell was dismissive of indie rock because it lacked serious musicianship, while John Zorn thought it was too conventional," he remembers. "Sonic Youth, on their part, hated being associated with stuff like Zorn. They wanted to be seen as 'punk rock', not a part of the avant-garde. One of the reasons they were so psyched about Steve joining was that he came from the DC punk scene."[10]

Still, despite their reservations, *Put Blood In The Music* offers a fine and flavourful overview of the band, including footage from Kern's 'Death Valley '69' video, and some thrillingly anarchic live footage of *Daydream Nation*'s choicest moments. If some of the interview segments seem slightly awkward, the group numbly deflecting weak questions about the UK music scenes, their own goofy vignettes illuminate a playful sense of humour, an irony, which interviewers often missed. The movie opens with Ranaldo consulting a tarot-card reader as to the group's future, before Thurston clownishly shows the cameraman around his record collection; later, Thurston shoots Steve Shelley in the stomach for playing a sluggish beat. "New York has been home to many highly influential musicians and musical genres," intoned Bragg. "In the Eighties, its difficult to identify any one avant-garde musical sound likely to develop into a major movement, as the scene is so fragmented, it almost defies definition." However, by the time of the show's broadcast, Sonic Youth were already making the climb up to "major" status.

The division between "mainstream", major-label approved rock'n'roll and America's independent music scene was somewhat membraneous, especially as the Eighties closed. While signing to a major label – and deliverance from perennial financial instability and the toil of the working hardcore group – was still a hash-pipe dream for most operating within the underground, some groups had managed to leap the divide. Following a sequence of acclaimed records that blended the politicised Americana of The Byrds with edgier post-punk leanings and a keen blend of earnest integrity and larger ambition, Athens, Georgia quartet R.E.M. left indie label IRS and signed with Warner Bros for their 1988 album *Green*, confidently transferring their intimate, intense charms to the wider open spaces they were playing. But for every success story like R.E.M., there were plenty more groups like Hüsker Dü and The Replacements, whose sorry experiences in the straight world suggested the mainstream was infertile ground for such idiosyncratic artists.

Still, there was a certain restlessness within the Sonic Youth camp, aggravated by growing tensions with Paul Smith that had surfaced while in Japan and Russia, following the release of *The Whitey Album*. "Sonic Youth and I used to laugh at all the Eighties business-speak babbled by the guys at

Enigma," remembers Smith. "They were always talking about 'upcharges'. I saw our ads as a personal way of communicating with our audience, often hiding little messages in them. So the *Daydream Nation* ads in America had a little tag running along the bottom, reading 'Upcharge? What Upcharge?', which was our little message back to Enigma, ha ha. By the time of *The Whitey Album*, we were having trouble negotiating an actual contract with Enigma, it wasn't signed off. The 'heads of agreement' were not in place. So my stupid tagline for the Ciccone Youth ads was, 'Give good head'. Thurston got tremendously upset about this, said it was childish, toilet-wall humour. And I said, hang on, you're the guy who wrote 'I Killed Christgau With My Big Fucking Dick' and 'Tough Titty Rap'? Up until that point I always felt our relationship was a two-way street, but here I felt like it was, 'We're the artists, you're just the businessman'. And I've never been a businessman, and I've never wanted to be a businessman.

"In retrospect, I could tell they were getting fed up with me. But had it not been a British-run label putting *Daydream Nation* out there at that time, I honestly think Sonic Youth could've missed their 'shot'. You look at the amount of money we spent around that time… Thurston hated Enigma because they were very 'LA', guys in Hummers with long mullet haircuts. But they were prepared to do the job, they had the clout, and they did a good job, under our direction."

Smith's belief in Sonic Youth hadn't waned, and his mind was on the group's future, the next great step after the success of *Daydream Nation*. "I remember a discussion with Richard Grabel, a lawyer who represented indie bands for Grubman Indursky & Schindler, about the group's future," recalls Smith. "I was having conversations with other major labels on Sonic Youth's behalf, weeding out the ones who I didn't think offered the control the group would need over their output. I was hoping Blast First! could be brought along as a production company, so we could be that little office that protected them from the cruel world. Grabel laughed, said they'd be lucky to get signed at all. I said, you're absolutely wrong: whoever gets Sonic Youth gets the gateway to the whole American underground. If the Youth moved to a major, it'd open the doors. He said I was up my own arse."

* * *

Even as Smith worked to secure a conduit between the group and the mainstream, Sonic Youth busied themselves with their many subterranean, extra-curricular activities. In keeping with the incestuous scene from which they sprang, the bond within the group was strong enough to endure the members exploring relationships outside Sonic Youth. Lee had released his debut solo album in 1987, *From Here To Infinity*, on SST. A bravely experimental work, the vinyl copy of the album was composed as a series of loops and locked grooves of guitar noise, so each band of manipulated amplifier static would ensnare the helpless needle until the listener moved the tone arm (the less satisfying CD release consisted of edited loops, recordings of the vinyl being played). He had opened a number of Sonic Youth shows throughout 1987 with his *Infinity* set, playing loops and noise backed by Steve on drums.

Shortly before the *Daydream Nation* tour began, Kim had collaborated with Lydia Lunch on a project named for one of their favourite authors. Harry Crews is a cult novelist whose work operates on the more brutal edge of the Southern Grotesque school. "We were both reading a *lot* of contemporary American fiction at the time, and both fell completely in love with Harry Crews' writing," remembers Lunch. "Somehow, along with drummer Sadie May, we formed a band based around his books." As you might expect from the artists involved, and their inspiration, the music was corrosively uncompromising, electrifying noise, siring a short European tour, from which their *Naked In Garden Hills* LP was culled. "It was a blast," says Lunch. "Kim's fun to collaborate with; very cool, easy-going."[11]

Thurston, meanwhile, seemed in perpetual motion, recording another collaboration with Lydia Lunch, *The Crumb*, as well as contributing noise guitar to the self-titled debut of Honeymoon In Red, Lunch's group with Rowland S. Howard, joining Jello Biafra for a Suicide tribute album, enlisting with Don Fleming's Velvet Monkeys after he moved to New York, and adding extra noise to Dutch friends The Ex's *Joggers & Smokers* LP with Lee. En masse, the group backed Velvet Underground drummer Maureen Tucker for her 1989 album, *Life In Exile After Abdication*.

Another of Thurston's external projects indicated a new interest in the fiery outer reaches of jazz music, a collaboration with Jim Sauter and Don Dietrich, saxophonists with terrorising noise-jazz trio Borbetomagus. Sauter and Dietrich had both grown up in Nyack, a village in upstate New York, and had been friends since meeting at summer camp. Aged nine, Dietrich took up the saxophone, getting thrown out of the school band every year for disrupting proceedings.

"We had to play Tchaikovsky's '4th Symphony'," remembers Dietrich. "About halfway through, the first run began to sound suspiciously like Albert Ayler. The band-leader stopped the band and put his glasses down to the tip of his nose, banged his baton on the stand and said, 'Dietrich, if you wanna play that kinda stuff, I suggest you go off and join a hippy tribe!' But I never was much for hippy tribes..."[12]

Out in remote Nyack, rock'n'roll leaked slowly into Dietrich and Sauter's world. "We lived in a very conservative, white-bread middle-American community," says Dietrich. "I was a huge fan of The MC5, and Hendrix, but it was hard to find the albums. Jazz records were *completely* alien; I didn't learn about free jazz, the stuff that really piqued my curiosity, until later on, in college."

Dietrich and Sauter spent all of their spare time listening to whatever records they could find, immersing themselves in jazz and the more outré permutations of rock; while a sculpture major at Parsons School Of Design in Manhattan, Dietrich played in a group specialising in hour-long improvisations based around MC5 tunes. In New York, the duo met guitarist Donald Miller, whose vast record collection exposed them to the New Music, the avant edge of jazz, inspiring ideas of their own. "We decided, OK, we like what Evan Parker's doing, but why can't we do it with a roaring rock aesthetic, the monster guitar of Hendrix, or Velvet Underground on 'I Heard Her Call My Name', or something with a Beefheart sensibility?"

When Borbetomagus performed, Miller's screaming noise guitar howled in dissonant union with Sauter and Dietrich's horns, through a special technique the duo had developed in their youth called 'Bells Together'. "We approached these things innocently," remembers Dietrich, "because we were very young. We were trying to disrupt things and make weird sounds. We had the wacky idea of joining the horns and created a sound that, to our very young and uninformed minds, was unusual. Little did we know at that point that we could turn it into an art form of sorts. What we created with two instruments was a new instrument."

For *Barefoot In The Head*, released on Sonic buddy Byron Coley's Forced Exposure label in 1990 but recorded by Wharton Tiers two years before, Thurston deputised for Donald Miller over 40 minutes of improvised scree, matching those Bells Together for full-blooded attack and relocating them within similar soundscapes as the segues from *Bad Moon Rising*. "Jimmy Johnson and Byron Coley at Forced Exposure had this idea that it might be interesting if we jettisoned Donald Miller for a moment and substituted Thurston," recalls Dietrich, "to see what kind of dynamic that would have on the proceedings. It sounded like an interesting experiment. We had no idea at all of what Thurston sounded like; I think *Bad Moon Rising* was the only record that I'd heard of theirs, which really didn't tell me much as to what I might expect from his playing. I remember several six packs of

Rolling Rock, I don't think Thurston was drinking but I *know* Jim and I were imbibing. We just laid the tracks down, sent them back, and Byron named the songs."

Kim once spoke of playing jazz records to Thurston early on in their relationship, to his general bemusement; by the mid-Nineties, however, he would contribute a shopping list of fine, obscure, ear-splitting improv albums for publication in The Beastie Boys' in-house zine and bible of slacker cool, *Grand Royal*, preaching (in a hepcat spiel apeing the totally gone, Beat-poetic sleeve note style of Impulse or ESP Records) that "no matter how you listen to it JAZZ is ostensibly about FREEDOM. FREEDOM and the MYSTERY surrounding it. And, like MUSIC, it is an ABSTRACT. Its SHAPES, FORMS (SOUNDS!) are DISTINCT and PERSONAL and SENSITIVE to each player's DESIRE. And the DESIRE is INFINITE."[13] These sessions with Sauter and Dietrich were an early indication of Thurston's burgeoning interest in the outer reaches of jazz, making a connection with an entirely subterranean, fierce and thriving avant-jazz scene operating in parallel with the Youth's own milieu.

"Had Thurston improvised with sax players before?" laughs Dietrich. "I don't know. When you're making love to a woman, you don't think about who she was with before you. But I think it's a pretty good record."

* * *

In the spring of 1989, Sonic Youth returned to Europe for the final leg of the *Daydream Nation* tour, with Mudhoney in tow, the latter establishing a standard of on-the-road debauchery that easily outpaced the older, more austere headlining act. "It was almost like they were on a trail of carnage," laughed Lee Ranaldo later. "They were completely living out the life of the kind of rock'n'rollers they were supposed to be. They were constantly fucked up, constantly on the edge of chaos and collapse and all that stuff. Mudhoney were just real heavy dopers and boozers, and they would go at it until literally they were not able to be conscious any more."[14] Europe's lusty response to Mudhoney's chaotic, gleefully raucous garage-rock was an early indicator of the kind of reception Seattle's home-stewed noise would enjoy when it finally leaked outside of the Pacific Northwest.

The tour kicked off with another Peel Session, four tracks of loose, wayward instrumental exploration sounding like the sort of jams from which *Daydream Nation* was hewn. One song, echoing the percussive, rushing panic and neon-noise explosions of 'Silver Rocket', was entitled 'Major Label Chicken Feed'; another was called 'Corporate Ghost', titles suggesting that the business matters awaiting the group in New York, at the tour's end, were playing on their minds.

"We got a call from Tommy Mottola's office, to come in and see him at Black Rock," recalls Paul Smith. Mottola was in charge of Sony Music and was one of the industry's enduring larger-than-life figures, for a time married to his protégé Mariah Carey. "It was the biggest farce I've ever been privy to in my life, a missing scene from *This Is Spinal Tap*. We waited for Tommy with Richard Grabel and Allen Grubman, one of the senior partners in his law firm, in the office of Dave Blue, Columbia's head of East Coast distribution, a real nice guy who'd been with the company since the Fifties, a *serious* motherfucker. Mottola eventually arrived, in a black-and-white checked suit and long mullet haircut, the full-on record company boss thing, and sat behind his big desk, with Grubman sat cross-legged on the floor, looking up at him. Mottola said, 'OK, Sonic Youth, great to meet you, love your work, always been a fan. In this desk, I have a button that I can press to make you guys stars. I, Tommy Mottola, am pressing that button for you now… What do you have to say about that?'

"There was dead silence; the Youth said nothing, I was stifling laughter. I wasn't overawed by the situation at all. Tommy asked if we had any questions, and when no one else replied I brought up artistic control, noting that CBS had been involved in some disputes. He came back with some bullshit about how the artist has 'complete control'. So I told him about a friend of mine signed to CBS who had had his record taken off him, remixed and released against his wishes.

"Mottola, head of CBS, God Of The Whole World, went into this weird panic, stuttering 'Uh, that happened before I worked here. *Dave*, were you here then?' 'Uh, I wasn't involved in that project, I think you'll find that was *Bob*.' This weird panic went across the room. The meeting ended and I travelled down in the lift with the group. It was a nice sunny day when we hit the street; I looked up at Thurston and said, 'So?' And he replied, 'At least I know what the face of the devil looks like. Forget about that, dudes.' We all split, they went off to see a movie.

"Years later, someone who worked at the firm told me that Grubman walked back to their offices, directly across from Black Rock, and said to Richard Grabel, 'Who the fuck was that guy embarrassing Tommy Mottola? Get rid of him.' I had just stepped on the landmine, offending the powerful mogul and his music biz lawyer mate, who worked across the road from each other."

Mottola wasn't the only industry heavyweight interested in Sonic Youth; Ahmet Ertegun, one of the most respected label owners in the history of the music business, who'd midwifed and nurtured the careers of godlike talents like Ray Charles, Aretha Franklin, Led Zeppelin and other greats signed to his prestigious Atlantic label, also stroked the group's collective ego in the aftermath of *Daydream Nation*. "Wily fox that he was," grins Smith, "after the meeting Ahmet said, 'I've decided to walk home. You guys take my limo, the driver will take you wherever you want for the rest of the night.' They all piled in the car and beckoned me in, but I said, 'It's all right, been there, done that.' I was making a bit of a statement to Ahmet, that I knew what he was doing, knew his style. You'd like to think artists as intelligent as those I work with wouldn't be taken in by that sort of thing; but you'd be amazed at how well it works. Little things like that remind me of how we were on different wavelengths.

"They came round to my apartment a short while later to talk about filming a video," continues Smith. "Bob Lawton, their agent at the time, came with them. The meeting about the video was two sentences long, 'OK, you want to do that? We'll get the money sorted.' And then Bob said, the other thing is, you're out, we're off to sign to Geffen. Nobody from Sonic Youth spoke to me. They were sat on a couch and two chairs; Thurston pretended to be asleep, somewhat famously. None of them would give me eye contact, the corners of my apartment were apparently *fascinating*. They never actually said anything to me, which upset me. They were leaving Blast First!."

Despite the growing tensions, Smith had not anticipated such an abrupt end to his relationship with Sonic Youth. "Pat Naylor said she saw it coming," he says. "I didn't. There was a great amount of pressure, they were quite frankly probably bricking it; they were nervous not to miss their *opportunity*. I always thought it was important that they had ambition, I just never imagined that turning against me."

The exit of Sonic Youth was only the most severe of several wounds Blast First! sustained in 1989. "The label crashed, this fantastic six-week period when I went from hero to zero," recalls Smith. "Big Black broke up. The Buttholes signed to Capitol Records. Dinosaur Jr broke up, ostensibly to get rid of Lou, but they broke up. And now the Youth were shipping out. Not the best six weeks of my life, I have to say.

"I called Dan Miller at the London office, went down the corner to buy a bottle of wine and a meatball hero sandwich, and went on a good month-long bender," Smith smiles. "God bless Gibby Haynes. When he found out, he called me up and said, 'The fuckers'. Gibby got on a plane from Austin and came up and stayed with me for two weeks. There's no way you can't have fun with Gibby in New York when you've got nothing to do; we went out and had a whale of a time, most of which neither of us can remember." At the opening of an exhibition of works by artist Robert Williams, who had painted the controversial sleeve for Los Angeles rockers Guns'n'Roses' phenomenally successful *Appetite For Destruction* album, Gibby and Paul happened upon Sonic Youth, being interviewed in front of TV cameras in a corner of the tiny gallery. "Gibby strode across the room, and yelled at 'em, 'You fuckin' buy Paul a Mercedes Benz!! I *know* he can't drive, but it's the thought that counts!!' They were pretty shocked. I stood there thinking, well, *someone's* got to say what I sort of, kind of wanted to say."

On his return to the UK, Smith faced grim prospects. "Simon Edwards, then head of Rough Trade distribution, sat me down in the pub and said, 'So, here's the thing. Your label's all over with, it's a fucking disaster. What I'm thinking is this: just lie low for five years, bring it all back in five years and it'll be great.' Weirdly enough, round that time The Mekons' *Rock'n'Roll* tape fell in my lap, and I played that, liked that, met them, liked them, and then I was back into it again."

Adrift from Blast First!, Sonic Youth would soon sign to a major label, a move that offered them financial stability, international distribution, and promotional support that, even bolstered by Enigma, Smith's label could only have dreamt of. In tandem with an unexpected and potent rupture in the barrier between the underground rock scene and the mainstream at the dawn of the Nineties, that major label would help bring Sonic Youth's music to shopping malls, to MTV, to arenas and stadiums. Perhaps they could still have achieved all this with Blast First!, ploughing revenue back into the British indie label that had supported them at a most crucial juncture? The point was soon moot, the subsequent collapse of Enigma Records ensuring *Daydream Nation* went out of print in America until its reissue in 1993. Still, whatever the state of their relationship by 1989, the group was bidding farewell to one of their most constant, enthusiastic friends, whose support had had such a potent effect on their career. Though Smith couldn't register it at the time, it must have been a similarly painful decision on their part.

"My attitude *was* loose cannon," admits Smith. "I was into the idea of *using* the machine; that's the British approach towards punk rock. Once we'd got those amazing reviews for *Daydream Nation*, they could have done whatever they wanted to.

"If the only thing I did, by their understanding, is help move them towards being full-time musicians, you can put that on my gravestone and I'd be perfectly happy. I'd much rather have Thurston Moore playing guitar than selling oranges on the street. I'd sooner have Kim writing and playing bass than painting walls. I'm still delighted by how they've continued to continue. Obviously, it's impossible to imagine what record they might have made after *Daydream Nation* if they hadn't signed to a major. They did. One of the things, in that sense, which I'm proud of, is we got them to a major label. We just didn't get a chance to stay in there."

The connection between Smith and Sonic Youth remained broken for some time afterwards, although they are friends again now. "I think in the end, Sonic Youth were just sick of me," he reflects. "They're not saints, nobody is. People say don't work with your heroes, but in a lot of cases I have. Sun Ra was *the* most wonderful person in the world to work with, 300 years old and from Saturn, too. Lee Perry, also a lovely man. He *did* hex me for a couple of years, but then he lifted it. Which was nice."

* * *

Ultimately, Sonic Youth signed with DGC, a subsidiary of Geffen Records, the successful imprint run by music mogul David Geffen, whose Asylum label had been one of the behemoths of the Seventies, releasing albums by all-conquering cocaine cowboys The Eagles. Behind such success stories, however, Geffen had a reputation as a label owner willing to nurture talents he believed in, borne out in the career of Jackson Browne, to name one such artist. His Geffen Records imprint, founded in 1980 to release records by Donna Summer, as well as John Lennon's final album *Double Fantasy*, struck gold later in the decade when Guns'n'Roses sold the glamour and sleaze of Sunset Strip to a rock audience desirous of new young libertines in the Rolling Stones mode, but also won negative press when it sued Neil Young for releasing "unrepresentative work", following several unsuccessful experimental releases the ineffable maverick recorded for the label.

Sonic Youth welcomed the material comforts the deal with DGC provided, sweet respite after years of financial struggle; moreover, they savoured the opportunity Geffen offered to enter a mainstream culture they'd flirted with, explored and paid tribute to throughout their career, a fascination with the world parallel to theirs but that remained ever disconnected. They'd taken great pleasure in toying with Madonna and Kiss, these vast pop icons whose personae and music were carried via radio waves and television transmissions, saturating at the speed of light a landscape Sonic Youth had crawled across in a beaten-up van. Signing to a major levelled the playing field somewhat, allowed Sonic Youth to engage with this audience not already tuned to their previously obscure frequencies, to seduce innocent ears into their frame of alternative reference. As Paul Smith had suggested, success for Sonic Youth would open a gateway for the groups following in their wake, the breakthrough that the underground had long strained for – even if this wasn't openly professed – and deserved. This success was by no means guaranteed, however, and indeed it would be another group – friends and acolytes of the Youth – who would make the initial crossover, allowing "punk" to "break" 16 years after the CBGB heyday.

"We have a great contract," commented Lee later, in an interview with Princeton New Jersey radio station WPRB in 2002. "We had established who and what we were by the time we signed to a major label. We had our own identity very firmly established at that point. And no matter what the label thought was going to happen, we didn't have many preconceptions about what was going to happen with us. Labels are all about distribution and that's how we saw it; they were going to get our records in *every* store. The first year or two was a little rocky, getting adjusted to having a lot more money to make records with and stuff like that. Whereas before everything was scrimp and save, all of a sudden you have these guys hanging around saying, 'Well, if you have to put another 25 or 50 thousand dollars into it, just go ahead.' It was a weird mind-set. They were totally wasteful of money. But we knew who we were and we knew what we were all about and we just kept being who we were."[15]

The newfound responsibilities of life as a group signed to a major label would lead to a reshuffle within the Sonic Youth organisation. They had never employed a manager before, organising contracts and tours themselves, with Paul Smith adopting further roles as and when necessary. With Paul gone, another friend stepped into the managerial breach, albeit in the loosest of senses. "They needed someone to tell the venue owners, 'We need a bottle of whiskey!'" laughs Don Fleming, Velvet Monkey and Sonic Buddy, nominally the group's manager as they negotiated their move to the majors. "It was a blast, a real fun time; they kept dragging me around, telling people, 'This guy's our manager, talk to him.'"

Subsequent to Fleming's tenure as manager, the group were represented by the management company that handled Living Color, leading lights of the Black Rock Coalition, featuring the prodigious talents of guitar wizard Vernon Reid. Finally, they settled on the services of John Silva and Danny Goldberg of Gold Mountain management, whose connection to Sonic Youth would help deliver them a number of powerful new clients. Fleming was still playing manager in November 1989, however, when the group recorded their segment for *Night Music*, a television show produced by Hal Willner, a music producer famed for high-profile, star-studded tribute projects dedicated to musical greats like Nino Rota, Charlie Mingus and

Leonard Cohen. A year later, Willner would invite the Youth to contribute stray noise to *Dead City Radio*, an album featuring the work of Beat poet and Sonics idol William S. Burroughs. The selection of guests on that segment of *Night Music* attests to Willner's broad, brave and inquisitive tastes: provocative avant-garde diva Diamanda Galas; singer-songwriter Daniel Lanois (also producer for Eighties megastars U2); and activist folk duo The Indigo Girls.

"Now here's Sonic Youth, with their manager Don Fleming on keyboards; the song is 'Silver Rocket'..." The words were spoken by saxophonist David Sanborn, whose mellifluous and buffed smooth-jazz sound tracked Eighties yuppie lawyer dramedy *LA Law* and had made him a millionaire. About as far removed from Sonic Youth's frame of reference as was possible, Sanborn nevertheless betrayed a frisson of excitement as he introduced the group's first song.

On a stark stage recalling the set of hip sketch comedy *Saturday Night Live*, the group looked amazing: Lee dressed down like a collegiate Springsteen playing a hot-pink Telecaster; Kim in hot pants, patterned leggings and purple leather jacket, mauling her Gibson Thunderbird bass; "Bizarro-Thurston" Don Fleming hammering at an electric piano, in a black leather long-coat and neon-blue Stetson. The real Thurston, garbed in retro-futuristic green anorak and looking not unlike Luke Skywalker, peered through straw-blond fringe as he snarled his words at panic tempo, the camera drinking in the fidgeting chaos of Sonic Youth liveage, Lee skittering dangerously about the stage, Kim pogoing with splayed, booted feet, in time to the beat. Even with the advent of 24-hour music television, performances like this were unusual for broadcast television, which had barely blinked at the punk phenomenon, lulled by more saleable, easier listening artistes. And then came the noise section.

As Thurston spat the lyric "*Burnin' a hole in yr pocket*", he bit hard on his bottom lip and swung his guitar backwards, staggering towards his amp and frantically scrubbing at the pick-ups, left hand throttling the neck of his guitar as he carved out a vicious sonic boom. With Lee crouched down, operating on his prone guitar, and Kim punching ugly noise from her bass, Thurston slammed the head of his guitar into the stage; it screamed in response, ululating as he tried to drive it through the floor. Steve Shelley thrashed at every cymbal and drum to hand, conjuring a tempo-quickening tattoo from the chaos, as Thurston hoisted his guitar to the skies, like Sun Ra drawing in transmissions from the heliocentric worlds, enacting a gracefully clumsy ballet of instrument abuse not seen since Hendrix first sprayed lighter fluid over an entire generation's concept of what a guitar could sound like. As Thurston launched his six foot plus frame from the speaker stacks across to the monitors at the lip of the stage, the group were emitting alien sounds that must've unsettled the pets of any household tuned into the show.

More impressive still than this freakish din was the ease with which they glided back into the song, a breathtaking feat of daring worthy of a circus high-wire act, Thurston hurling himself hard into Lee as they began playing the riff again, barely breaking tempo for a final dash to the feedback-splayed climax, Kim a bopping mop of blonde hair, like Janice the lead guitarist of The Muppet Show's in-house band The Electric Mayhem. Their guitars rang ever so raggedly out of tune for this final lap, Thurston throwing himself flat on the ground at the last kerrang.

For the show's closing number, Sanborn introduced a fevered thrash through 'I Wanna Be Your Dog', members of The Indigo Girls and the *Night Music* house band playing with an abandon that suggested Sonic Youth's ferocious 'Silver Rocket' had infected all assembled with their gleeful anarchy. Dressed in a faded Kiss tee, Kim convulsed at the mic, frenetic and bold like an indie Madonna, a female Iggy, but mostly *like Kim Gordon*, as a session musician dressed in a lurid blue shirt playing a keytar frugged behind her, suited sidemen thrashing alongside the Sonics, Sanborn blurting murderous free skronk during the instrumental break. "During his solo I ran over with my flute and starting blasting away on it into his mic," laughs Don Fleming. "None of it was pre-planned; I can't play the flute at all, it was a friend's flute. I threw it on the ground, and we tried to bust it, and it flew up in the air! Afterwards, he came over and said, 'I loved our duet, man! You were playing all these crazy high notes, I was really into it!' Even David Sanborn was into the scene and a little bit of the chaos."

It was testament to the confidence and ability of the group at this point that, performing at both of their seemingly polar extremes, their most traditionally song-like and most violently abstract, they could still charm such a group of musicians, boding well for when their music met other unfamiliar ears. "It's like Neil Young's respect for the group," explains Fleming. "Certain musicians who don't pay much attention to a lot of current music do 'get' it, or appreciate them or respect them. That's just a testament to how strong Sonic Youth are, how good their music is. Even in a mixed crowd like the one at *Night Music*, everyone was psyched to be playing with Sonic Youth."

"People assumed, 'You're on a major label so you're gonna suck now.' Looking back, I don't think it matters so much. We really just wanted more distribution, some funds, and we were curious to see what our songs would sound like with a bigger budget. It was kind of an experiment."[16]

Kim Gordon

Save for a show at New York Ritz in July, supported by regular touring buddies Mudhoney and The Laughing Hyenas, plus Old Skull (a group whose members were all nine years old, and whose songs were foul-mouthed anti-Reagan hardcore screeds), Sonic Youth played no more shows in 1989 after the *Daydream Nation* tour and the split from Blast First! Mostly, they worked on their new material, the songs that would form their major label debut album, finding a step forward from the quantum progression that was *Daydream Nation*, easily their most successful album to date.

For Steve Shelley, Sonic Youth's graduation to the majors meant upgrading his old drum kit. "I'd been playing an old Pearl kit I'd brought with me from the Midwest," remembers Shelley. "I'd had that Pearl kit for a while, *nobody* plays Pearl, except maybe Peter Criss of Kiss! We'd just signed to DGC, and J Mascis took me shopping for a new drum kit on 48th Street. I'm from Michigan, I'm a pretty conservative person, a 'thrifty' person. The sales guy asks, 'What price range are you looking at?' And J replies, 'Money is no object.'"[17]

In November of 1989, the group headed to Waterworks, a studio in the meat-packing district of New York, to record *Blow Job*, a rough 8-track sketch of the songs that would form their major label debut album. The title, enough to raise the blood pressure of their new paymasters, was taken from a T-shirt owned by Thurston, featuring a Raymond Pettibon illustration of Hollywood diva Joan Crawford in her role as the titular heroine of classic noir *Mildred Pierce*, with the word "Blowjob?" scrawled underneath. Also along for the ride, to ease their first steps in the major arena, were J Mascis and Don Fleming, as producers of this demo.

The songs that unfurled from this session were very much fully formed, differing only in details from the versions that would ultimately be released. These songs furthered the developing lyricism of Lee and Thurston's tangle of guitar, nurturing an emotional vocabulary that gave their noise a growing poignancy. The classic-rock stylings of *Daydream Nation* were present, though tempered by a more brutal, lean and to-the-point "pop" sensibility: there were no trilogies this time, and passages of ugly/beautiful noise were carefully metered out, to heighten their effect, roaring from the bruised melodicism. Sonic Youth's mutated sense of conventional songwriting and structure was played to the fore, with the thrilling, self-destructive abstraction of title track 'Blowjob' an anomaly: a brooding, turbulent instrumental strum that seemed to exist only for the purpose of exploding into fiery fragments at 1:40, Thurston's distorted scream played at bloodcurdling volume as instruments were ceremonially battered. That the song restarted, only to so brattishly disintegrate several more times, somewhat diluted its impact, a mistake remedied at the later sessions.

The final sessions for the album took place once again at Greene Street early in 1990, with Nicholas Sansano returning to co-produce, for a repeat of the *Daydream Nation* magic. Also in the studio, again, were J Mascis and Don Fleming, as consultants and vocal producers. "I don't know why we were there," laughs Don. "J was handling drum sounds, and I was there to deal with vocals." It's a role Fleming has repeated for Sonic Youth on a number of their subsequent Geffen releases. "I always get called in during the last week of recordings, because they don't record any vocals until it's time to mix. I love it."

Another guest in the studio was former Television guitarist Tom Verlaine. "He came by for one session," remembers Lee, "but he didn't do anything. He just stayed for like six hours and smoked about a million filterless cigarettes and left them all over the floor."[18] Perhaps his visit inspired the group's haywire career through The Neon Boys' 'That's All I Know Right Now', cut with Wharton Tiers later for the B-side to the 'Kool Thing' single.

With her instantly recognisable, powerfully unconventional timbre, an erudite burr of a purr that would only evolve and mature over the following years, Fleming says Kim Gordon's vocals in particular were a pleasure to record. "She tries a lot of different approaches with her vocals. A lot of vocalists, you can't get them to sing a song a different way, they're convinced the way they hear it in their heads is the only way. But Kim is just *free*," he laughs. "And it's great, because I get so much more fun stuff to work with. It *is* experimental, she's fearless. Most people are afraid they're going to fall off the horse if they try something crazy; but she does that all the time."

Kim's 'Kool Thing' was inspired by her experience of dealing with the heads of record labels as she helped negotiate Sonic Youth's graduation to the majors. "I was trying to deal with the labels on a day-to-day basis, and it got incredibly frustrating," she says. "You end up talking to all these people who will only have fake conversations with you, because you're an 'artist', which means that you're supposed to be incredibly fragile. It was the most extreme because I'm a girl, and dealing with this on a daily basis was making me hysterical. 'Kool Thing' came out of that experience."[19]

Rapper LL Cool J, hip-hop's Long Island-born heart-throb hard man superstar, then enjoying the first of several peaks in an enduring career, was another inspiration – or more specifically, Kim's disappointment when meeting LL to interview him for a magazine some months before. "The song was inspired by a white woman's fascination with this beautiful black guy," explains Steve Shelley, of a lyric Kim expertly composed from song titles and lyrics in the LL Cool J canon: name-checking the radio he couldn't live without, his panther strut, and his ability to "rock" things, such as bells and beats. Within this paean to his strength and fortitude Kim posed a pointed question about the place of women within hip-hop's revolutionary thrust, touching upon both tensions surrounding women's liberation and its relationship to the black nationalist movement of the Sixties and Seventies (a tangled and painful subject that the Womanist writings of Alice Walker, Toni Morrison's *Beloved* and Ntozake Shange's *Sassafrass Cypress & Indigo* only begin to unravel), as well as hip-hop's swift adoption of rock'n'roll's chauvinism in its leering, over-sexualised treatment of women in lyrics and videos.

"Hey Kool Thing, c'mere," she called, "Sit down beside me… Are you gonna liberate us girls from male white corporate oppression?" Representing hip-hop in this symposium upon some Equality Of Oppression was Public Enemy frontman Chuck D, again recording at Greene Street alongside Sonic Youth, finishing his group's fractious third album, *Fear Of A Black Planet*. Recorded later, Chuck offered some cool-sounding platitudes, spoke of a "fear of a female planet", and rapped encouragement to Kim's cause, but his contribution falls a little flat. Indeed, Chuck's earlier press interviews, in particular a discussion with *Melody Maker* journalist Simon Reynolds in 1987, suggested he perceived the woman's role within the revolution as a mostly servile, domestic one, a stance his contemporaneously recorded "pro-sister" anthem 'Revolutionary Generation' didn't clarify. Kim remains hopeful however, deciding "when you're a star, I know you'll change *everything*", an interesting statement from an artist making her own first concerted step towards mainstream stardom.

'Tunic (Song For Karen)' was one of the new album's standout tracks; the Karen in question was the singing drummer of brother-sister pop duo The Carpenters. Kim's song – in part inspired by Todd Haynes' scandalous 1987 movie *Superstar: The Karen Carpenter Story*, which retold the events of Karen's life as performed by Barbie dolls – sung Karen's story with particularly deft insight, touching upon her dreams of rock'n'roll stardom, her struggle against society's corrosive expectations of a female pop star, and her ultimate death from anorexia nervosa in 1983. While these final scenes are played out with a grim kitsch akin to Haynes' film – Karen playing drums in heaven, jamming with Janis Joplin, Elvis Presley and Beach Boy Dennis Wilson – the song is coloured by a suffocating, almost gothic sadness, haunting the impassive cold-chill growl of the chorus, "you ain't never going anywhere". The lyric's exploration of body politics traces Karen's anorexia back to her mother's comment that she looked overweight on television, and the industry's smothering of a proposed 1980 solo album that damaged her already fragile self-esteem. The song was possessed with a melancholy perhaps similar to that which underscores The Carpenters' own music, rediscovered (with a pinch of irony) by "Generation X" following the song, and a subsequent Carpenters tribute album, where the Youth covered ghostly groupie lullaby 'Superstar', Thurston singing Karen's part.

The album opened, like *Daydream Nation* and *Bad Moon Rising* before it, with pastoral chime, before launching into 'Dirty Boots', Thurston toying with corny but sincere rock moves, its brisk strum joined by his lazily drawled vocals, declaring "it's time to rock the roll". All this is elegant preamble to a climactic rockout that elevated the Sonics' newly polished squall to stadium-slaying volume, Thurston howling, "I got some Dirty Boots, baaaaaaaby!" like some gloriously ridiculous rocker, as guitars screamed ferociously from both speakers. Elsewhere, however, the Youth were unafraid to record pieces that strayed far from their more structured recent material; 'Mildred Pierce' cut 'Blowjob''s aural firework down to a more immediate two minutes thirteen seconds, while 'Scooter & Jinx' was a minute of hypnotic drones eked from mortally wounded amplifiers, their most openly abstract piece of music since 'Lee Is Free' on *Confusion Is Sex*. "At one point," remembers Sansano, "we had such severe feedback coming from Thurston's amp that we literally shorted out the entire studio... The whole place shut down with a slow whirr that you normally only hear in cartoons and sci-fi movies."[20] Thurston, meanwhile, boasted to *Guitar Player* with pride that he had suffocated his amp by covering the fan on top of the cabinet with his guitar. The sounds you hear are the dying screams of that particular amplifier.

'Scooter & Jinx' was one of a number of songs derived from a particularly obscure and subterranean reference, a movie directed by Raymond Pettibon titled *Sir Drone*, starring Mike Watt, Sonics friend and road crew Joe Cole, and Kim's artist friend and sometime Destroy All Monsters musician Mike Kelley as teenaged punk rockers aiming for stardom, with characters named Scooter, Jinx and Goo. Lines from the movie would be endlessly quoted at Sonic Youth rehearsals; "When someone wasn't giving their all in practice, we'd say, 'Hey, you're side's getting a little New Wave!'," remembers Steve. "That movie was the inspiration for a lot of the titles and characters in the record. Also, Raymond did the album cover, and a lot of T-shirts and posters and singles sleeves for us at the time – just beautiful stuff."

The album's sleeve and title would be one front where the group and their new label would test bargaining positions. The group initially suggested Pettibon's "Blowjob?" illustration as title and sleeve artwork, which Geffen baulked at. The album would eventually be titled *Goo*, taken from Kim's caustic bubble-grunge tune, with another Pettibon illustration on the cover, depicting two teenage hepcats on the lam, both dressed in black shades and cool bowl haircuts and Velvets-esque garb, her smoking a cigarette, him copping a feel. "I stole my sister's boyfriend," read Pettibon's scrawl in the top right hand corner of the drawing. "It was all whirlwind heat, and flash. Within a week we killed my parents and hit the road." The sleeve oozed a dark, alienated cool – so seductive was Pettibon's image that young Sonics fan Patty Orsini would transpose the sleeve artwork as a mural on her bedroom wall, videotaping her efforts and sending them to the band (the footage can be found on the group's 2004 DVD collection of their Geffen-era promos, *Corporate Ghost*). Snuck in on the back sleeve, nestled next to the UPC bar code, was a little cartoon reading "Smash the PMRC", directed at the Parents Music Resource Centre, a committee headed by Tipper Gore, wife of future Democrat vice-president Al Gore, which sought to censor and sideline what it defined as "offensive" music (focusing its ire mostly on rap, the rebellious black art form that sold by the million to young white audiences).

Such gestures signalled a group defining their boundaries in such new, unfamiliar surroundings. Don Fleming says he could sense the tension, the pressure playing upon the group. "They were freaked out. J and I didn't care, we were there to have fun, and I think that's why we were there. I think everyone was playing it as cool as they could, but… Later, they established a relationship with the label where they would tell them, 'We're gonna make our record, you're gonna take it when we give it to you, because you don't understand it.' But, for the first couple of albums, there was a little more label involvement, although not much. The Youth were apprehensive that there *would* be. Geffen said, 'Let's bring in a mixing team'."

The mixdown was handled by Ron St Germain, an industry veteran who had engineered posthumous Jimi Hendrix releases, mixed records by synth pioneers Kraftwerk and Jean-Michel Jarre, and worked with the Black Rock Coalition, producing Living Color's 1988 debut album, a Vernon Reid collaboration with jazz composer Bill Frisell, and Bad Brains' *I Against I*, which fashioned a vibrant, metallic punk from the group's hurricane of hardcore and dub. This last album in particular impressed the Sonics. "It was a difficult album to record," admitted Kim. "We were having trouble with the mixing, as Ron St Germaine was used to working on rap records. He got very ambitious, more ambitious than us. When we got this major label deal, we were excited, thinking, 'Let's record it in a big room, live, on 48 tracks'. But it became arduous to record like that."

"Even *we* didn't know if we were going to fuck up a good thing by signing to a major label," says Lee. "*Daydream Nation* we made for $30,000, and *Goo* we probably made for $200,000. We had a chance to spend as much on a record as Aerosmith spend. I mean, they probably spent 10 times what we did, but... We could've probably put that money in our pocket, but at that point we were interested in the experiment. Was it really gonna make a better record?"

To accompany the release of *Goo*, Sonic Youth secured a budget from Geffen to shoot a promotional video for every song on the record, to be released commercially as a "video album". "It was cool for us," said Lee, of the concept. "It was one of the first things we did after signing to Geffen, bringing our whole aesthetic and the people we've worked with into play in this arena. 'Hey, we want to do all this low-budget stuff and release it on your big-time label.' It was just a natural thing on our part, but in retrospect it seems a cool thing to do."[21] The project continued Sonic Youth's practice of bringing creatives from the artistic subterranea into their realm, drawing inspiration from them and introducing their work to the group's audience, evolving an aesthetic drawn from their collaborators and their disparate approaches.

Some of these clips were triumphs of no-budget film-making, the directors using every avant technique at their disposal; installation and video artist Tony Oursler, a friend of Mike Kelley's, made the powerful short for 'Tunic', primitive video FX, early computer animation and much goofing around by the group with Oursler's proudly amateurish props helping to tell a decidedly unique interpretation of the Karen Carpenter story (footage of The Carpenters included in the clip would be excised before release, for fear of lawyerly intrusion). Close-up shots of Kim singing with a skull superimposed over her face, holding her sticks like the crossbones from a Jolly Roger, are particularly, chillingly effective.

Steve Shelley shot a promo for 'Mary Christ' that mixed footage shot on a Pixelvision camera (a toy camcorder produced by Fisher-Price that recorded in murky black-and-white onto audio cassette) of Thurston singing with effects Shelley achieved by painting directly onto celluloid, while a clip for Lee's 'Mote' – filmed by "Ray Agony", a pseudonym adopted by Sergio Huidor, who'd shot early videos for luminous Boston indie trio Galaxie 500 – incorporated Ranaldo's own Pixelvision experiments with found images and abstract video noise, to accompany the song's four-minute white-noise coda. For Lee, the Pixelvision camera's limitations – mainly its grainy, low-resolution images – were an asset. "It's the filmic equivalent of how you'd produce posters on Xerox machines: they would look all crudded-up, but there would be something so great about how they looked." Mike Watt, meanwhile, directed the clip for 'My Friend Goo', shot at Ray Pettibon's house in real time, as the track played on Watt's record player as Kim and Joe Cole played out their roles.

Geffen financed larger budgets for a couple of the videos, with an eye for promotional use. Tamra Davis, who later directed amiable weed comedy *Half Baked*, written by and starring Dave Chappelle, signed on to direct clips for 'Kool Thing' and 'Dirty Boots'. 'Dirty Boots' was, Thurston said, "An underground rock band's version of a Hallmark card", tracing a romance developed in the mosh pit of a Sonic Youth show, and consummated just before a triumphant stage dive, the female lead wearing a rock tee from Thurston's own collection, advertising an obscure Seattle rock band called Nirvana.

'Kool Thing' was the first video the group shot for Geffen, described by Thurston as "Barbarella meets Warhol", the group decked out in their most lurid thriftstore finery, jamming in a foil-clad studio, while Kim swapped between costumes and generally looked ice-cool and iconic, Chuck D guesting for his lines, delivered to camera and filmed later. "They were doing their first 'big budget' video," observed Davis, "But for me, it was a 'low-budget' video."

Upon release, MTV began showing 'Kool Thing' during *120 Minutes*, their showcase for "alternative" music. "It was kind of a 'hot' video for us," remarks Thurston, "but it didn't really go too far. I think there were a few personalities at MTV who thought that we were not 'proper' for what they wanted to promote on the station at the time. Which was unfortunate for us, and also the record company." Richard Kern's low-budget clip for 'Scooter & Jinx', a minute or so of naked girl-on-girl massage, would of course never be screened on MTV, but does in retrospect seem to anticipate the 21st-century boom in grungy burlesque, as purveyed by websites like suicidegirls.com.

The Youth also requested the services of Californian film-maker Dave Markey, for whom they'd worked on his 1986 movie *Lovedolls Superstar*. Markey had grown up in California, hungrily absorbing every word and photo the rock mags printed about the late-Seventies punk scene forming around clubs like The Masque in Hollywood, frequented by groups like X,

The Germs and The Weirdos. By the time he was 16 and old enough to go to shows, that scene had died out, replaced by hardcore. "The whole Masque scene was people in their thirties," says Markey. "It seemed so far removed. That whole scene was legendary to me as a kid, though I never saw it. It was gone by the time I got there."[22]

Markey played in his own hardcore group, Sin 34, and published a short-lived zine, *We Got Power*, which came on like *National Lampoon* meets *Maximum Rock'n'Roll*, "to poke fun at ourselves," explains Markey, "or people on the scene, people who seemed really self-important. We were trying to get people to lighten up a bit." His main focus, however, was film-making. "I'd been making films since I was a kid. My aesthetic was already in place; what 'punk' did for me was make me feel I could get my work screened outside of the neighbourhood, and maybe it gave me the confidence to do whatever I wanted with film. The DIY ethic of hardcore made me see the other side of this, where I wasn't just doing this for fun; I was doing it for larger reasons."

Markey's first film, *The Slog Movie* – a rockumentary inspired by Penelope Spheeris' influential document of the LA punk scene, *The Decline Of Western Civilisation* – was a modest work, distributed on videotape via adverts in hardcore zines by Markey himself. His next picture, 1984's *Desperate Teenage Lovedolls*, would enjoy much broader visibility, a campy tale of an all-girl rock group struggling in Hollywood, starring Dez Cadena of Black Flag, Sky Saxon of garage-rock legends The Seeds, and brothers Steven and Jeffrey McDonald, of Redd Kross. "That movie certainly did well with the critics and got a lot of notice," remembers Markey, "and really stepped up my thing. Thurston ordered a copy from me, and sent me a copy of his fanzine *Killer*. That's how I was first aware of him."

Thurston and the Youth met Markey along with the rest of the West Coast punk cognoscenti at the Gila Monster Jamboree in 1985. Along with *Desperate Teenage Lovedolls* sequel *Lovedolls Superstar*, Markey used Sonic Youth as actors in two short films, 1987's *AstroTurf* (pursued by a rabid crowd, Kim finds safety in the arms of a long-haired rocker, presenting him with a piece of AstroTurf), and 1989's *Lou Believers* (following Thurston and co around LA as they try and find out where James Woods movie *The Boost* is playing, terrorising members of the public and pretending to be Lou Reed). For *Goo*, they asked him to film clips for 'Mildred Pierce' and 'Cinderella's Big Score'. Sofia Coppola starred as Joan Crawford in 'Mildred Pierce', hamming it up *Mommie Dearest* style as Markey intercut footage of the Youth rocking out in sight of the Hollywood sign.

'Cinderella's Big Score' opened with a photograph of Kim and her brother Keller, once used as a gig flyer by the group, before following a long-haired high school student as he runs away to Hollywood and gets involved in drugs and male prostitution, before being arrested by cops, scenes Markey intercut with footage of loitering stray dogs and Thurston playing guitar on Santa Monica Pier at dusk. Kim stood on a slowly rotating playground roundabout, the boy riding directly opposite her; she delivers her vocals while staring at the camera with a calm that's almost unsettling, her words an anguished attempt to connect with the wayward boy, words aware that they're falling on deaf ears. "In the lyric, Kim was partly addressing her brother, I think," explained Lee. "You'd rather have a dollar than a hug from your sis," growls Kim, in this most haunting of songs, greatly enhanced by Markey's atmospheric film. "Don't give me yr soul, it's caught in an abyss".

"I did both videos for a thousand bucks a piece," remembers Markey. "I shot them myself, edited them myself. Super 8 equipment was getting better, and *I* was getting better, I'd warmed up and learned how to shoot stuff 'properly', yet I was really freed up to work in any way that I wanted. I didn't have any barriers around me with what I could or couldn't do."

Goo – both the album and the video collection – was the work of a group operating within a similar sphere of freedom, breaking down barriers with an album that presented their music in perhaps its most palatable form yet, while sacrificing none of their intensity, invention, perversity or artfulness. The collection of video clips asserted the group's space within the art world, acting as a conduit, at least in theory and gesture, between the more esoteric corners of culture and the mainstream. It was the work of a group who refused to conform, whose ambition spanned different media, who weren't about to take the corporate dollar without somehow infecting the hand that was feeding them with their ideas, aesthetic and approach. And yet, *Goo* was not an album of which Sonic Youth were immediately fond.

"It wasn't a perfect fit with Ron St Germain, but we got the album done," reflects Steve Shelley. "We were sort of conflicted about that record for years, it wasn't until we went back to it in 2005 and remastered it for the Deluxe Edition that we all really embraced that album. We all loved the songs, we just weren't sure about the recording of it."

"I always thought of *Dirty* as being the more accomplished record from that era," adds Thurston, referencing the Youth's subsequent 1992 album. "But *Goo*, which I had discounted before, is a much more interesting record. It's more transitional, we were moving from an exploratory period – the longer, free-form stuff we were developing during *Daydream Nation* – into more standard-yet-unorthodox rock songs. I like listening to that transitional period more than that crystallised sound of *Dirty*, where everything's been nailed down."[23]

The mainstream had invested their faith in Sonic Youth to the tune of $200,000. The underground, too, was supportive of its departing scions, save for the same lame haters who always gripe about such things. "I was happy when they signed to Geffen," remembers Martin Bisi. "I'm not much into preserving things by keeping them small, and not reaching people. Reach people, and if that in turn kills it, oh well… Someone will just have to make something new."[24]

NOTES

1 Author's interview, March 2007
2 Author's interview, March 2007
3 Author's interview, July 2002
4 Author's interview, July 2002
5 Author's interview, February 2007
6 Author's interview, March 2007
7 Interview with Mike D, http://www.leeranaldo.net/starfieldroad/pages/interviews.htm
8 Author's interview, March 2007
9 *The South Bank Show: Put Blood In The Music*, tx 1989
10 Author's interview, March 2007
11 Author's interview, March 2007
12 Author's interview, February 2007
13 Grand Royal Magazine #2, 1994
14 *Our Band Could Be Your Life*, pg 433
15 Radio interview on WPRB, August 10th, 2002
16 Author's interview, March 2004
17 The Watt From Pedro radio show, March 17 2007
18 *Spin* magazine, April 1990
19 *Reflex* magazine, 1992
20 Author's interview, March 2007
21 *Corporate Ghost* DVD commentary
22 Author's interview, May2007
23 Author's interview, March 2004
24 Author's interview, March 2007

CHAPTER NINE

The Year Punk Broke

"Our relationship with Nirvana was always very strange. They were younger than us, they came from this whole other community... They were following after Mudhoney, and Mudhoney seemed young to us. As much as I thought they were fantastic, I never thought we were similar to Nirvana to any degree. We were so New York Art-Rock No Wave. 'You guys like R.E.M. and Pixies? Are you nuts? Where are you coming from?' To us, that was ridiculous, that was laugh out loud."[1]

Thurston Moore

At the beginning of August 1990, Sonic Youth took to the road in support of *Goo*, their first such sortie since signing to Geffen. Across both legs of the American tour, and a brief European jaunt sandwiched in between, the group enjoyed the services of a larger road crew, including a much-needed guitar tech for the first time. Accompanying the group along the first stretch across America was STP, a hardcore group from Boston whose acronym spelt out Sharon Tate's Phoetus, and Bob Bert's fine noise-rock project, Bewitched. In Las Vegas on August 16, the group hooked up with their next support act, a young trio signed to Sub Pop from Aberdeen, Washington, called Nirvana.

Nirvana were fronted by Kurt Cobain, a troubled kid equally in love with The Beatles and Black Sabbath, who had formed the group with teetering fellow Aberdonian Chris Novoselic, fuelled by their shared love for (among other things) local heroes Melvins, a trio who plied inspired metallic riffage slowed down to a sludgy tempo. However, while Kurt was fascinated with rock subterranea – in thrall to punk and in love with the egalitarian, politicised punk-rock scene in Olympia – part of him also hungered for old-fashioned rock stardom. This dichotomy would, in effect, lead Nirvana to drag the underground overground, with the release of their second, breakthrough album; it would also tear Cobain apart.

The group's 1989 debut album, *Bleach*, was mostly high-grade Melvins-esque "grunge" in the Seattle style perfected by Mudhoney and others plying this acrid mess of punk attitude and metallic guitar, like Tad, a momentously heavy group fronted by man-mountain ex-butcher Tad Doyle. There were shards of pop melody shot through the blackened mass, however, such as the bruised tunefulness of opener 'Blew', or the acoustic vulnerability of 'About A Girl', where these hairy freaks sounded like blue-eyed power-poppers. New songs Cobain had since demoed were as unabashedly pop, while fusing this affection for melody with a brash sense of dynamics patterned after hardcore. He was still conflicted, however, slightly ashamed of the accessability of these new songs. "Listening to them sound-check, hearing their new songs, they would sound *dissonant*," remembers Kim. "Kurt would say afterwards, 'I really want my next album to sound like you guys.' [laughs] I'd say, no, that would be a bad idea."[2]

Having made an important bond with their mentors, Nirvana stepped off the Sonic Youth tour bus as the headliners flew across to Europe for a brief tour, playing alongside ragged Big Star-besotted Glaswegians Teenage Fanclub, Rowland S Howard's These Immortal Souls, and Minnesota's Babes In Toyland, a feral, brilliant group who casually disproved any chauvinist bullshit about women not being able to "rock", and whose second album, 1992 major-label debut *Fontanelle*, would be produced by Lee Ranaldo. As October dawned, the Youth returned to America, spending the rest of the year on the road, in the company of old friends Redd Kross, Minnesotan noise-rockers The Cows, Don Fleming's new group Gumball, grunge also-rans The Fluid, The Jesus Lizard (Steve Albini's favourite rock group, a dark and pulverising force of bad nature, signed to Touch & Go and featuring former members of Scratch Acid and Rapeman) and familiar faces Mudhoney and The Laughing Hyenas.

For Sonic Youth, the tour was something of a victory lap around a country they'd slogged across in relative poverty only a year or so before, as ever playing alongside the cream of the underground, drawing inspiration from their younger charges and bequeathing them the attention of their audience, attuned over the years to trust the Youth's intuitive choice of opening acts (which faltered with the inclusion on the bill for their Miami show of Aleka's Attic, a rock band featuring actor River Phoenix and his sister Rain, the Youth momentarily seduced by the dazzle of Hollywood royalty). The following year would bring new challenges, and a most promising opportunity that proved bittersweet in the experience.

1990 closed with a show at the Aragon Ballroom in Chicago, supporting Public Enemy, on December 29. According to attending fan Kerry Taylor, after the show audience members poured out into the wintery Chicago streets, many joining nearby activists protesting escalating tensions with Iraq, following Saddam Hussein's invasion of neighbouring Kuwait. The police struggled to contain the swelling protest, calling in swarms of backup, resulting in violent confrontations at a time when Chicago's law enforcement agency was under investigation for allegedly torturing black captives. Scenes from the group's show that night would be included on the *Goo* videocassette; footage the cameraman shot of the resulting protest riot would, however, be destroyed by members of the attending police force.[3]

> "I like Sonic Youth. They are definitely a modern rock'n'roll band in my eyes. Have you heard 'Expressway To Yr Skull'? It's unbelievably good. So beautiful! It's classic. Magnificent melody, and to hear it live, especially, it's awesome. They have several songs of that quality, they're a great band."[4]
>
> Neil Young

Taking in a circuit of sports halls and arenas across America – the "enormodomes" where most mainstream rock happened – and offering Sonic Youth at least a taste of the big time, touring alongside and at the behest of one of their all-time heroes, the Smell The Horse tour made at least as much sense as it didn't. Edgy punk groups like Sonic Youth weren't supposed to find kinship with the level of rock aristocracy to which Neil Young had been (possibly unwittingly) elevated. But then, Sonic Youth had never held truck with any punk-rock dictum demonising the Sixties, while Young had traced a truly maverick career, maintaining a sense of credibility and integrity that eluded his band-mates in super-group Crosby Stills Nash & Young.

A folk singer from Canada who drove to California in a rickety hearse to pursue a career in singing and songwriting, Young first found fame with Buffalo Springfield, songsmiths firmly fashioned in The Beatles' image, whose later music was easily as psychedelic and adventurous as the Fabs'. Splitting with co-founder Stephen Stills, Young pursued a solo career, often backed by Crazy Horse, an evergreen garage-rock group whose shambolic groove perfectly fit the unpredictable frontman. In contrast to Crazy Horse's smouldering guitar jams, Young also recorded tender acoustic ballads, country-rock albums with 40-piece orchestras, rockabilly records, even, in 1982, a vocoder-voiced electro-rock record named *Trans*, contemporaneously mocked as a baffling, self-indulgent disaster, but latterly recognised as a sincere attempt on Young's part to connect with his autistic son.

Young's career was starred with epochal albums, all of an individual flavour: 1969's *Everybody Knows This Is Nowhere*, with its long, acrid guitar solos and electrified country churn; *After The Goldrush*, his faultless, eclectic 1970 set; 1974's apocalyptic, brooding *On The Beach*; *Tonight's The Night*, his bleak and grief-stricken 1975 send-off for Crazy Horse guitarist Danny Whitten, dead of a drug overdose three years before. While most Sixties dinosaurs partied on oblivious to the punk-rock stirring beneath their Cuban heels, Young referenced it explicitly on the fiery 'Hey Hey My My (Into The Black)', saluting both the death of Elvis and the rockers who would replace him with the words, "The King is gone but he's not forgotten/This is the story of Johnny Rotten".

Like his fragile but powerful vocal, Neil Young's guitar tone was a characterful, unmistakeable, eloquent thing; for 'Hey Hey My My', Young distorted its already gravelly growl to a static-spitting bark that wouldn't have shamed a No Wave guitar-abuser. Songs like his epic, atmospheric 'Like A Hurricane', meanwhile, anticipated the kinds of potent emotion Sonic Youth would later distil from similarly abstract feedback textures.

In such a context, the Youth hooking their trailer up to Neil's luxury tour bus for a couple of months should've been a dream come true, not least with Young riding the acclaim of his recent, noisy *Freedom* album, reuniting him with Crazy Horse and wild-man producer and kindred spirit David Briggs. Young's choice of these dissonant young charges was intended as a wake-up call for his audience who, as the subsequent tour video *Weld* would depict, were mainly nostalgic baby boomers who'd deserted their hippy dreams for yuppie realities and comfortable Cosby sweaters. "I didn't want acts that people were going to say, 'Oh, I can take them or leave them'," he explained. "I wanted to get somebody that people were going to love or hate. And I think we did a good job there. Sonic Youth are way out there on the cutting edge with what they're doing, and also extremely similar to what we've been doing for a long time."[5]

The tour took in civic centres, coliseums and arenas across the country, playing the prestigious Madison Square Garden in New York. Set lists on the tour juggled Sonic favourites with tracks from *Goo*, climaxing with 'Expressway To Yr Skull', to which Young grooved in his dressing room. As Thurston noted, their contact with Neil wouldn't get much more intimate; the group met Neil exactly twice, once sharing dinner on his tour bus, and once when he forbade the group to appear on *The David Letterman Show*.

"Neil was totally aloof from his world," said Thurston. "He doesn't listen to music. He really doesn't give a shit. One thing he said that startled me was that 'real' rock'n'roll had gone totally underground."[6]

"There were a couple of problems during the Neil Young tour," says Kim. "We were told that we could have a certain amount of volume and we weren't getting it. We were gonna leave the tour and we just wanted to tell Neil why we were leaving, so we told him and he really had no idea about the volume. Our soundman had always been told that was the way Neil wanted it. We sort of had the feeling that he didn't know what was going on, and he said we should have come to him sooner. His stage manager and his production manager hated us. They thought we were just freaks, because our music was weird and we weren't all wearing tattoos, and there was a *girl* in the band. Social Distortion was on the tour too, and they were, like, dudes talking about getting chicks and getting laid. Y'know, old fashioned rock'n'roll, like Neil's crew. They just thought we were punk brats, and they kept waiting for us to show them this 'attitude' that never really came. We were always incredibly professional, except when we were on stage."[7]

Addled by bad sound, and playing to what Kim described as "real rednecks, people holding 'Fuck Iraq' banners while we were playing", Sonic Youth enjoyed responses varying from puzzled indifference to boos and bottles, and exited the tour in April, fairly disillusioned. "I really felt sorry for Joni Mitchell," continued Kim, noting the old-school chauvinism of Neil's road crew. "I mean, Neil's very sweet and everything, but he's part of that generation, and that way of thinking. It sounds like it's changed, but in rock it's there. That was when I really felt like we were confronting the mainstream; we'd signed to a major label, and I felt we were cast off in some really weird place. It wasn't the kind of tour you do to help your career, it was like old people who don't buy records, and we didn't make any money. We weren't doing it for that, we just did to play with Neil, and see what a weird guy he is."

For his part, Young remained enamoured of the Youth, and the live album he released from the tour bore their influence; while biographer Jimmy McDonough would complain that Young sweetened the tapes with studio-enhanced harmonising, *Weld* remains a document of Crazy Horse playing at their most fiery and feedback-drenched. A limited-edition bonus disc, *Arc*, contained 40 minutes of collaged drone and amp-noise, sounding like Neil's tribute to the lulling seas of noise that close out 'Expressway To Yr Skull'. "Hell, if they wanted to play, I'd be there," he said in 1995, correcting a frustratingly erroneous report that he was intending to record with Sonic

Youth. "It sounds like too much fun to pass by. Sonic Youth are great; I'd love to work with those guys if the right conditions prevailed."[8]

> "In a *Melody Maker* End Of Year poll, Thurston Moore had voted me his Most Hated Person Of The Year, because Courtney Love had been slagging me off in the fanzines, calling me sexist, as is her wont. She forgot about it the next day. Thurston said, 'I'm gonna rip Everett True's head off when I meet him,' because he felt protective of Courtney at the time. He didn't, of course; my head's still here. Although you can tell Thurston could kick someone's ass if he had to, you get the impression he's quite gentle."[9]
>
> Jerry Thackray

Sonic Youth first met Courtney Love when her group, Hole, supported them at Los Angeles' Whiskey-A-Go-Go during the fall 1990 *Goo* tour. The wildly charismatic Love had a turbulent childhood behind her, the daughter of a Grateful Dead associate who allegedly dosed her with LSD aged four years old. Growing up in hippy communes throughout Oregon, the teenaged Love found herself in juvenile hall after stealing a Kiss T-shirt, discovering British punk-rock via a kindly social worker. At 15, she flew to England, moving in with underground rock figurehead Julian Cope, before travelling the world working as a stripper. Moving back to America aged 22, Love formed Sugar Baby Doll in California with Kat Bjelland and Jennifer Finch (who would later find fame with brilliant bubble-grunge rockers L7), but was later ejected from the group. Love would also play bass with Babes In Toyland before being asked to quit by Bjelland, who would later assert that Love's Hole-era penchant for distressed thrift-store baby-dolls was patterned after her own "kinderwhore" style; passing swiftly through the ranks of San Francisco "hippy hate band" Faith No More, Love formed Hole with guitarist Eric Erlandson in 1989.

Following the Smell The Horse tour, Kim and Don Fleming accompanied Hole into the studio to record their debut album, *Pretty On The Inside*. "Courtney was amazing," laughs Fleming. "She was the most gung-ho person I've ever met. She was going to make the greatest record ever – I like that attitude in the studio. Courtney was like, 'Let's go, fuckers!', and I loved that. She gave 180 per cent on every take. I loved that incarnation of the band, they were just totally primal Hollywood freaks, the real thing."[10]

The session lasted a brief seven days, but was a dream come true for Love. "Courtney told Kim at the start," remembers Fleming, "'I have a poster of you up on my wall! For years, I've been looking at that poster saying, 'She's gonna produce my record someday!' She basically gave it all she had, because Kim was there. It wasn't like Kim really knew Courtney, or Courtney was the Courtney we all think of now. She was just this girl called Courtney."

Pretty On The Inside was very much the album you might expect from an artist with a Kim Gordon poster on her wall, a record of anguished noise, detuned riffage, brutal volume, and individual voice. For 'Teenage Whore', Gordon and Fleming perfectly framed Courtney's raging howl within the industrial clatter of her cacophonic group. The resulting din touched similar extremes of emotion as Teenage Jesus & The Jerks, albeit within a slightly more traditional rock context. Certainly, it wasn't recognisably the work of an artist with the grand ambitions Love harboured, but rather an album that would win Hole a fanbase that appreciated such sulphurous punk-rock.

"I totally respected what she was doing, and felt like, damn, she's gonna do really well with this," remembers Fleming. "She's got a few good tunes and she knows how to play 'em. When she played with us and Sonic Youth at the Whiskey in LA, she was just a phenomenal performer. I saw Hole a couple of times in the later days, and still thought she sounded good, putting on a rock show, but it seemed a little more 'Cheap Trick' to me. But I expected Courtney to go a little more 'mersh', and she did. I think that's what she wanted to do. But I like the record we made; it represents, emotionally, her reality really well. [laughs] You're there. We really broke down the wall on *that* one."

The group would liaise again with Love while touring Europe in August of 1991, another brief jaunt taking in festivals and some headlining shows, with Nirvana playing support. Every summer, rock festivals traditionally erupted in fields across Europe, boasting mud, motley line-ups and warm beer, going by names like 'Pukkelpop', 'Ein Abend In Wien' (One Evening In Vienna), and the slightly more prosaic 'Reading Festival'. Sonic Youth had been playing such gatherings since they'd started regularly touring Europe, crawling slowly up bills that swelled with their kindred. Indeed, the Youth would spend much of that month drinking beer and goofing with their contemporaries, waiting to take the stage, as Dave Markey's film of the tour would later attest.

In the 12 months that had passed since they first played with Sonic Youth, Nirvana had gone through a metamorphosis. Following the lead of their New York heroes, the group had signed with Gold Mountain management who, in turn, got them signed to DGC. The group had

"I see Free Kitten as being more experimental" – Kim Gordon, with Free Kitten band mate Julie Cafritz. **(JENS JURGENSEN/REDFERNS)**

Australian-American punk rock summit at the Big Day Out, 1993: Big Day Out, 1993. l-r: Thurston, Kim, Kim Salmon (The Scientists, Beasts of Bourbon), Nick Cave and Mark Arm (Mudhoney). **(TONY MOTT/SIN)**

Kim, 1993, switching to six string for the rest of the decade. **(STEFANO GIOVANNINI)**

Thurston shops for Carpenters vinyl during time off from the *Superstar* video shoot. **(DAVID J. MARKEY)**

Thurston with baby Coco and Siouxsie – mid-'90s. **(DAVID J. MARKEY)**

Lee on stage at Glastonbury, 1998.
(BRIAN RASIC/REX FEATURES)

Downtime at Echo Canyon, 1998. **(LFI)**

Thurston with regular collaborator, drummer William Hooker. **(JANA MUSIC PHOTOGRAPHY/SIN)**

Jim O'Rourke "Jim's an amazing musician, no 'dominating ego'. He can play all kinds of shit, guitar, powerbook, whatever. He's like grout – most people walk into the bathroom and they look at the tiles; Jim's like the grout." – Mike Watt. **(SARAH BOWLES)**

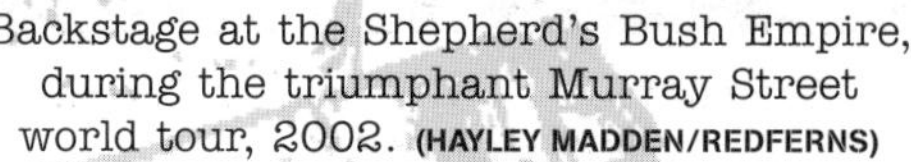

Backstage at the Shepherd's Bush Empire, during the triumphant Murray Street world tour, 2002. **(HAYLEY MADDEN/REDFERNS)**

Sonic Youth get their hands dirty, as they are honoured by the Rockwall. **(LFI)**

Kim and Thurston at the premiere of *Last Days*, Gus Van Sant's imagining of Kurt Cobain's final hours, which Kim starred in. 2005. **(LFI)**

Following Coco's birth, Kim found herself returning to painting. In recent years, she has created and collaborated on numerous artworks and installations. "Kim's a visual artist, in addition to everything else. She definitely brings that sensibility to Sonic Youth." – Don Fleming. **(STEFANO GIOVANNINI)**

Kim with Coco and Thurston in Washington DC, 2005. Coco would make her debut on a Sonic Youth disk with her vocal turn on their cover of Yoko Ono's 'Voice Piece For Soprano'. **(STEFANO GIOVANNINI)**

Lee with wife Leah Singer and daughter Sage. **(STEFANO GIOVANNINI)**

Steve Shelly, June 21, 2007, Munich.
(STEFAN M. PRAGER/REDFERNS)

Thurston. "He exuded this faith; he didn't really worry about the future. And he would sleep until two or three in the afternoon." – Kim Gordon **(SARAH BOWLES)**

Kim photographed in Berlin, 2007.
(HEIKE SCHNEIDER-MATZIGKEIT)

Lee, on stage at the Coachella festival, April 27th 2007. **(TIM MOSENFELDER/CORBIS)**

SY in the studio. **(SEBASTIAN MLYNARSKI/CONTRIBUTOR/GETTY IMAGES)**

recorded a second album – their first for Geffen – over May and June of 1991 in Los Angeles; while Geffen had suggested R.E.M. producers Scott Litt and Don Dixon or Neil Young's David Briggs, the group stuck with Butch Vig, booked to produce the album when Nirvana were still signed to Sub Pop, as they loved his work with sardonic, brilliantly heavy Wisconsin trio Killdozer. The group also bade farewell to drummer Chad Channing, subsequently replaced by Dale Crover of Melvins, Dan Peters of Mudhoney and, finally (after J Mascis ultimately turned down the offer of the Nirvana drumstool), a young drummer from Virginia, Washington named Dave Grohl, identifiable by a home-made tattoo on his wrist, self-applied when he was 12 years old, approximating three of the four bars of the Black Flag logo ("It hurt," is his explanation for the missing bar).

Like when Steve Shelley joined Sonic Youth, Grohl offered a connection to the hardcore scene that Kurt and Chris had admired from afar; Dave joined Nirvana following time playing with DC hardcore group Scream, one of a number of punk acts he'd grown up watching from the pit. "I remember seeing Naked Raygun, at a place called the Cubby Bear in Chicago in 1982," he remembers. "I loved it, the intimacy of it, that it seemed so simple and human and exciting. I talked to the singer, and I jumped on someone's head, and I felt completely at ease with the band and the audience. It was just a bunch of people having a good time. The first 'big' show I went to was the fuckin' Monsters Of Rock at a stadium in DC, and it seemed so unreal to me, it didn't make any sense. Metallica played, along with Dokken, Scorpions and Van Halen. This was after five years of going to see hardcore groups like Corrosion Of Conformity, Bad Brains, Millions of Dead Cops. Seeing this huge stadium gig, where the groups were so far away that it took four seconds for the sound of the snare drum to hit me... It made no sense at all.

"Really, my first punk-rock 'moment' was going to see *Let There Be Rock*, the AC/DC movie," Grohl continues. "It was the first time I'd felt that energy, like I just wanna fuckin' *break* something, I'm so excited that I'm losing my mind. It was dirty and sweaty, fuckin' beautiful. I had an AC/DC poster on my bedroom wall, and when I looked up at Malcolm Young, I was like, I wanna be *that* guy, fuckin' wearing jeans and a T-shirt, hasn't taken a shower all week, drunk and fuckin' just playing music for the sake of playing music. That was the kinda thing I really got into as a kid, and that just led to deeper rebellion, where I was so cynical of everything else. Because mainstream music at the time, in the early to mid-Eighties, was just so fuckin' shit. I was kinda cynical at an early age, just fuckin' wasn't buying it.

The bands I was into were either entirely focused on the music or totally anti-establishment. That was what got me off, it wasn't the flash or the image."[11]

By 1990, however, Grohl's initial enthusiasm for playing drums with his heroes had abated; that summer, Scream split after their unreliable bassist ditched them mid-tour. "We were sleeping on the floor of a beautiful house in Laurel Canyon belonging to three girls who were all mud-wrestlers at the nearby Hotel Tropicana. The Melvins were coming to town and we were friends, so I called Buzz [Osbourne, guitarist/vocalist] to tell him about Scream, and to try and get on the guest list. And he said, have you ever heard of Nirvana?" Ever since seeing Dave drum when Scream last played Seattle, Kurt and Chris wanted him for the currently vacant Nirvana drum-stool, his pulverising style the perfect backbeat to bolster Kurt's newly-written buzzsaw pop.

"Thurston was very excited about touring with Nirvana again," remembers Dave Markey. "*Everyone* was. Sonic Youth are always like that about every band that opened for them. They were a band touring their first major-label album, most bands in that situation would've been so *uptight*, competitive. 'The opening band have to have half the sound and one third of the lights we have.' Not Sonic Youth."[12]

The group contacted Markey about making the tour film days before the tour was due to begin. "There was no 'prep' time," he recalls, "barely enough time to get it together, 10 days between learning about it and going off to do it." Still, Markey's guerrilla approach delivered a fine document of this bizarre moment before this rock subculture got rudely catapulted into the mainstream, along with priceless footage of bands like Babes In Toyland, Dinosaur Jr, Gumball and Nirvana playing live, and copious moments of goofing and japery from the primary subjects and their supporting cast. "I've never seen it," claims Mark Arm. "I've heard that I'm in it, that I blow snot everywhere..."[13]

"We were playing night after night with bands that we knew," remembers Steve Shelley. "It was just a great time. In some hotel room along the way, we saw Mötley Crüe playing Wembley Stadium on MTV. I think Thurston kinda liked Mötley Crüe at the time, in an ironic way, but we weren't interested in that world too much. But they performed 'Anarchy In The UK'. And it just blew Dave Markey's mind, that this band from Sunset Strip was headlining this big stadium in the UK, and playing a Sex Pistols song. We just thought it was the funniest thing. Nobody really ever understood what we were doing, or what the indie scene was about. We still thought that it was a secret world, and it was for a long time. The funny thing is, we didn't know how twisted it was gonna get in the next six months, when *Nevermind* came out."[14]

Markey believed the spirit of punk-rock to be at a low ebb when he packed up and joined the touring Sonic entourage in Europe. "At the time in LA, all the energy of the hardcore stuff had waned and the scene had been taken over by really bad hair-metal bands, Guns'n'Roses and bands like that. It was like the whole hardcore scene had never happened; it left me in a daze, because that was my world. The Bush Sr years were dark times." The sight of cock-rock poodles Mötley Crüe ploughing through the Sex Pistols' anthem filled Markey with a bitter sense of irony, quipping to the Youth that 1991 truly was the year punk broke. He had just coined the title for his film, although he had no sense of how truthfully he was speaking.

"The title of that film has been misunderstood for so many years," he sighs. "It was tongue in cheek, an inside joke for us during the tour. It *wasn't* a reference to Nirvana and their success, which happened after the movie was shot. As far as I knew, punk was all over. Mötley Crüe covering 'Anarchy In The UK'? I don't know what else you would need for punk-rock to officially be declared dead at that point." And yet Markey's footage told a different story, from Nirvana gleefully trashing their gear before lunchtime after a set of deliciously immediate punk, to the sheer feral attack of Babes In Toyland, the frantic noise-a-delia of Gumball and, of course, the majesty of Sonic Youth, blowing minds with the closing 'Expressway To Yr Skull'. For the song's climactic explosion and droneout, Markey intercut a blizzard of strobe-lit live performance with slivers of on-the-road footage, before closing with Thurston mooning a hotel television, tuned to MTV. That he didn't then hurl said television off the balcony was just one sign of the changing times.

"Sonic Youth became a real 'festival' band for me in the early Nineties," remembers Jerry Thackray, by 1991 writing for the *Melody Maker* as Everett True, and soon to become a close confidant of Nirvana. "My eternal memory of them is standing at the side of the stage at Reading and watching Thurston Moore, the wind whipping his hair, looking every inch the rock idol, down at the front of the stage sawing his guitar in half on the monitors. They were always *so* fucking exciting, always on edge and always unpredictable; spontaneity is at the heart of all great rock music. Sonic Youth? Duh. They are the band that defines that rule."[15]

The group maintained that unpredictability offstage, as *1991: The Year Punk Broke* shows: Kim indulging her Ciccone fascination by playing out scenes from 1991's revealing tour documentary *Madonna: Truth Or Dare?* (aka *In Bed With Madonna)* with her fellow indie-rock stars, the group searching the parking lot of the Reading Festival for Iggy Pop, also playing that day, and Thurston responding to every trippy thing he encounters along the way in goofy motormouth spiel. "If you point a camera at a musician, most will run away," laughs Steve Shelley. "But I think Thurston felt he had to carry the movie, to give Dave something to play with." Bellowing sucky Beat poetry from a hotel window, asking schoolgirls if they find J Mascis sexy, and the ceremonial flushing of a freshly minted turd were just a few of the vignettes of manic Moore behaviour captured by Markey's camera.

"*Rap Damage* was kind of a dry run for what Thurston was doing in *The Year Punk Broke*," says Markey, referring to a short filmed a while earlier, featuring Thurston walking around LA and confronting strangers with foul-mouthed rap-spiel about "the hip-hop rabbit". Both *Rap Damage* and parts of *1991: The Year Punk Broke* seem to anticipate some of the TV phenomenon *Jackass*, which would surface a decade later. "It was before that, but it was in that spirit," agrees Markey. "I was just working in my own little world."

Following the One Evening In Vienna festival, which actually took place in Rotterdam, the group returned to New York while Markey flew home to LA, where he began to assemble the hours of footage he'd filmed in Europe. Nirvana, meanwhile, rested for a week in Seattle before launching on a gruelling tour in support of their second album, *Nevermind*, with a show every night and promotional duties most days. The album was released on September 24, a fortnight after lead single 'Smells Like Teen Sprit', which was accompanied by a promotional video shot by Samuel Mayer, depicting the group rocking out in a gothic high-school gymnasium.

The combination of 'Teen Spirit''s hook-laden cocktail of nagging pop melody and visceral punk-rock barbs, and Mayer's vision of twisted cheerleaders and slamming rock kids soon saw the video break out of MTV's *120 Minutes* "alternative" ghetto into "heavy rotation". As a result, sales of *Nevermind* soon passed gold status, a goal the group, their management and the suits at Geffen hadn't imagined achieving until the album had spent at least a year on the shelves. *Goo* had managed to shift 250,000 units, modest for a major-label release, but impressive for such a "boutique" signing. The success of *Nevermind*, however, would significantly raise the stakes for underground groups testing mainstream waters.

* * *

Out in LA, working on his movie, Dave Markey began to feel the after-effects of the burgeoning Nirvana phenomenon. "I remember Nirvana had just gone gold; we were, like, wow," he remembers. "And then, three weeks into working on the editing, we heard they'd sold a couple of million. 'OK, well it must be peaking now, so let's hurry up and get this film done.' And then, of course, they went on to sell mega-mega-mega-mega amounts. To Nirvana's credit, they agreed to let me do whatever I wanted with their material in this film, which was a pretty decent gesture for a band in their position."

Nevertheless, Nirvana's phenomenally swift rise and the media's resultant interest in this mysterious new band, who had toppled King Of Pop Michael Jackson's *Dangerous* album from the top of the charts as 1992 began, raised expectations considerably for Markey's low-budget Sonic Youth movie. *1991: The Year Punk Broke* – filmed only months before, when Nirvana would be the opening act on obscure festival stages, with no sense of what would come – possibly disappointed audiences newly introduced to this scene by Nirvana's crossover success. "It had a real intimate feel; *casual*," says Markey. "There was no agenda when I shot it, and that's what made it what it was. When it came out, there was suddenly this huge amount of pressure on it, mainstream audiences wanting to see at it because Nirvana was in it. A lot of critics didn't get it. 'What is this horrible piece of noise?' Same as how *Cocksucker Blues* wouldn't have clicked with the same people that loved *Woodstock*."

Markey admits that the sheer scale of Nirvana's success was near inconceivable to an artist of his generation. "I remember when my bands would press up 3,000 seven-inches and feel really great about it; that was 'success'. And then a band like Black Flag would sell 70,000 albums. The leap between that, even, seems so large. And then Nirvana comes along... I thought that Nirvana was going to have *success*, but a success that was defined in terms of a band like Sonic Youth, who sold a couple of hundred thousand records, and were 'huge'."

Struggling to get a handle on the phenomenon, one contemporaneous commentator suggested that *Nevermind* sold to the children of every divorced couple in America, which wasn't necessarily as glib as it sounded. "Kim and Thurston were sort of surrogate parents to Kurt," suggests Thackray. "They were to a lot of people, I think – the 'ultra-cool' parents these bands never had – and that's partly because they were married. All of Nirvana came from divorced families, pretty much."

"The kids chose *Nevermind*," wrote Thurston later. "Geffen had no real plans for it, hoping for modest sales. *Rolling Stone* gave it a lukewarm review. Its subsequent off-the-map success was wonderful, fantastic and completely genuine. What was disingenuous and annoyingly misrepresentative was the reaction of the corporate music industry. The alternative rock phenomenon was a youth-culture hit and it made stars out of select artists but, for the most part, it was a bunch of corn to the creative scene where Kurt came from."[16]

Sonic Youth played two more shows that year. At the Shoreline Amphitheatre, in Mountain View, California, the group appeared at the fifth annual Bridge School Benefit on November 2, a charity show headlined by Neil Young and organised by his wife Pegi, to raise funds for the Bridge School for physically and mentally handicapped children. Whatever hex (or Neil Young road crew saboteur) had cursed Sonic Youth on the ill-starred Smell The Horse tour lingered for this show, as the group struggled through acoustic versions of 'Dirty Boots' and 'Mote', beset by technical problems, before glitchy monitors scuppered 'Cinderella's Big Score', Kim smashing her guitar and shouting "Fuck!" to boos from the audience. A shambolic cover of The New York Dolls' 'Personality Crisis' later, and Sonic Youth were outta there, although Lee returned to the stage later on, joining in an all-star cover of Bob Dylan's 'Forever Young' with Nils Lofgren, Tracy Chapman, Willie Nelson and Young himself.

A month earlier, they'd played an infinitely better received set at the Ritz in New York, another benefit show, this time for listener-supported, commercial-free New Jersey radio station WFMU, beloved for its wayward and wilful broadcasting habits. Sonic Youth's headlining set was another casual triumph for a group who, bolstered now by a professional road crew, touched genius onstage with alarming regularity. It was a busy night for Thurston and Steve, who also played with their new band Dim Stars, an all-star project led by Mike Watt's punk hero, Richard Hell. Rounding out the band was Don Fleming.

"The Dim Stars project was amazing," he glows. "Richard Hell is a lot of fun to work with: he's humorous, but he's very intense. It was just a blast; it really felt great, getting him out to play, and he enjoyed it, and it was just great." It was Hell's first time in a recording studio with a rock'n'roll band since the demise of The Voidoids, who had shed all other original members save Robert Quine for their poorly received 1982 LP *Destiny Street*. In the interim, Hell had successfully battled drug addiction and focused on his writing, soon to release his searing, brilliant novel *Go Now*. Nevertheless, the Dim Stars' records rocked in a raw, lairy manner recalling The Voidoids at their most alive. "Richard was nervous about his musical skills," continues Fleming. "He doesn't think he really *has* any. He thinks he's a writer, which of course he is – but, for whatever reason, he's not as confident as he should be. It was great to give him a band with whom he felt comfortable enough to perform and be creative. We went into the studio with an idea to record an EP. Richard loved it, said, let's make an album! He got Robert Quine to come in and track some parts. He was amazing, such a fine player.

"It was a little bit of a rock'n'roll fantasy camp," he grins. "'Oh, this is when I played with Richard Hell and Robert Quine!'"[17]

For all there was to celebrate in 1991, the year ended on a senseless, brutal and tragic note. On December 19, as he returned home from a nearby video store with room-mate Henry Rollins, Black Flag roadie, LA punk "face" and sometime Sonic Youth video star Joe Cole was murdered by burglars he surprised at the house he and Rollins shared. As with D. Boon six years before, the loss of such a universally loved, charismatic and talented soul had a big impact on the punk-rock community. His closest friend, Henry dealt with the trauma through his art, publishing two books of writing, *See A Grown Man Cry* and *Now Watch Him Die* via his 2.13.61 publishing company that directly confronted his loss. In an interview shortly afterwards, Rollins said, "My friend's not coming back, he's not a ghost running around this room, he's dead." Indicating a Tupperware box in his wardrobe containing Cole's remains, scraped off the floor of their apartment, he added "That's all that's left of Joe Cole."[18]

> "By the early Nineties, we existed as a sort of big brother (and big sister) group to Kurt's generation of underground America. When Nirvana became popular, we were all called alternative rock – a less threatening term than anything with punk in the title. The original alternative rock bands – Nirvana and Sonic Youth included – never had any allegiance to alternative rock. We all had come too far and through too much for any professional advice toward stylistic adjustment."
>
> Thurston Moore

The success of *Nevermind* marked a paradigm shift in the signing policies of the major-label record industry, never ones to leave a bandwagon unjumped. The speed with which the album had sold signalled a death knell for the Sunset Strip rockers playing Sex Pistols covers with no sense of irony, and the coming of "alternative rock", the much-maligned genre invented by marketing departments to sell the wares of underground groups newly signed to the majors. Labels swollen with hair-metal signings junked their immediately obsolete rosters and began throwing money at groups who sounded, looked or smelled like Nirvana; legendary were the sums offered to groups like Helmet – led by Branca disciple and former Band of Susans guitarist Page Hamilton, and fashioning a blunt, avant riffage – by panicking A&R men hungry for the gold they imagined lurking in them thar punk-rock subcultures.

The subsequent rise of Pearl Jam only exacerbated "grunge" fever, a group formed from the ashes of Mother Love Bone, following the heroin overdose death of flamboyant frontman Andrew Wood. Pearl Jam took shape in the wake of Temple of the Dog, a project initiated by Wood's roommate and Soundgarden singer, Chris Cornell, with former Mother Love Bone and Green River musicians Jeff Ament and Stone Gossard, to record a couple of songs Cornell had written in tribute to their departed friend. Accompanying the group as second vocalist during these sessions was a surfer from San Diego named Eddie Vedder, who'd recently struck up correspondence with Gossard, and had penned lyrics for a bunch of unused Love Bone demos Gossard had sent him.

Vedder was a quiet, introverted kid, with an adolescence behind him that read like some rejected Pete Townshend rock opera, discovering that his mother's abusive husband wasn't his biological father, who had died a couple of years before of complications from multiple sclerosis, a saga he wrote into a number of songs on Pearl Jam's debut album. He was possibly the most "punk-rock" member of the newly formed group (initially named after basketball player Mookie Blaylock by sports-fan bassist Ament and, according to legend, renamed after a peyote-laced preserve produced by Vedder's native American great-grandmother Pearl), spending his teen years driving to hardcore gigs in his beaten-up pick-up truck, taping shows by his beloved Bad Religion, California hardcore mainstays blending radical polemics with lightning-quick, sugar-dipped punk.

Pearl Jam's music, by contrast, bore few traces of their punk roots; focused on the twin-guitar heroics of Gossard and Mike McCready, songs like 'Alive' were unabashedly classic-rock, down to the climactic duelling guitar showdown. Their debut album, *Ten*, encompassed the Seattle scene's love for stadium-rock flash, but without their accompanying sense of irony; Pearl Jam meant it, maaaan – brilliantly so, in places – and, accordingly, *Ten* proved to be a sales phenomenon that bettered even *Nevermind*.

Pearl Jam's success tore a fresh schism in a scene already struggling to make sense of Nirvana's bolt to fame. The groups who truly flourished during the "grunge" era were those whose music really wasn't all that far removed from the heavy rock that had long dominated MTV and the arena venues. This is no criticism of their music: Soundgarden's *Badmotorfinger* (1991) and *Superunknown* (1994) distilled the essence of heavy metal with none of the chauvinism or excess that marred the genre, while fellow

Seattlites Alice In Chains' darkly gothic metal was graced by the unearthly harmonies of frontmen Layne Staley and Jerry Cantrell (to invoke a rock crit cliché that actually holds this time around, Alice In Chains sounded like The Everly Brothers, on smack), and by Staley's chilling, autobiographical lyrics, documenting his heroin addiction.

However, very early on in the "grunge" phenomenon, it became clear that, for the *truly* "alternative" bands newly signed with The Man, the experience would prove frustrating. If the post-*Nevermind* afterglow ushered in an era of A&R whimsy on the part of the majors not seen since those halcyon early days of psychedelia Frank Zappa so fondly recalled, then the interference of the Men In Suits, expecting a return on their hasty investments, was a harsh wake-up call. Even Tad – for all their feral grace hardly the most saleable band in a market still so concerned with image – bit the major-label bait, signing with Giant, an offshoot of Warners, for 1993's *Inhaler* album, which proved every bit as abrasive a thrill as their Sub Pop releases. Unfortunately, the band swiftly found themselves perhaps the first "grunge" band to be dropped by their new corporate paymasters, following a controversial poster promoting the album depicting then-president Bill Clinton smoking a joint, a reference to his admission of youthful pot-smoking, with the unconvincing addendum that he never inhaled the drugular fumes. Tad subsequently signed to Elektra Records, but sales for their album on this label, *Infrared Riding Hood*, were poor enough to get them dropped again, and they split soon afterwards.

No, despite its subterranean roots, the public image of "grunge" was cemented by such pop-cultural confections as former *Rolling Stone* rock journalist Cameron Crowe's *Singles* – a sentimental 1992 rom-com set in Seattle and featuring Mudhoney, Pearl Jam and Paul Westerberg, formerly of The Replacements, on the soundtrack, and on-screen cameos by Vedder, Cornell and, brilliantly, Tad Doyle. There was also a hoax "lexicon of grunge" that Sub Pop staff member Maura Jasper fed a credulous journalist from the *New York Times*, concocting faux youth-speak like "lamestain", "harsh realm" and "swingin' on the flippety flop".

"I asked Jack Endino if there was ever a period when people were just asking him to make 'grunge' records," remembers Jerry Thackray, "and he said that while some bands asked to sound like Nirvana or Tad, a million more asked to sound like Alice In Chains. Because they were the *real* suburban metal, the ones that all the kids who wanted to be 'grunge' understood. They didn't understand punk."

Amidst all this macho, bombastic stadium rock, Cobain felt alienated and isolated; *Ten*'s sales eclipsing those of *Nevermind* also awakened a petty jealousy within him, and, consummate music snob that he was, he began a vocal press campaign against Pearl Jam, defaming them as "cock-rock poseurs". Kurt's disdain for the corporate rock world extended to his new-found fanbase, kids who knew nothing about his beloved Melvins, about Olympia, about punk-rock at all, for whom songs like 'Smells Like Teen Spirit' were merely a signal to go beat up some smaller kids in the mosh-pit. Kurt had been bullied by jocks his entire life, and serving as their entertainer sat ill with him.

In interviews, Kurt blasted these new jock fans, and spoke out in support of the bands *he* loved, like The Breeders, an all-girl quartet led by Kim Deal (formerly bassist with The Pixies, Boston college-rockers whose music was a premonition of Nirvana) who blended sweet pop with a most subterranean sensibility. Like Sonic Youth before him, he eloquently championed the underground bands who'd influenced him, name-checking his favourites and turning his fanbase on to unknown pleasures like British post-punks The Raincoats (who reformed at his request), Glaswegian indie group The Vaselines and, of course, Sonic Youth.

"Nirvana made a point of touring with challenging groups like Boredoms, the Butthole Surfers and the Meat Puppets and presenting them to a huge audience," asserted Thurston, "one that was largely unaware of those bands' influence. But only the Meat Puppets would click a little bit. Without MTV or radio support, no one was likely to reach Nirvana's peak."

Don Fleming had a unique perspective on the grunge gold-rush. In his dual capacity as producer for a number of these underground groups' major-label releases (Screaming Trees' *Sweet Oblivion* and The Posies' *Frosting On The Beater*, both sublime and both released in 1992, make a compelling argument for Fleming's production skills), and as frontman for Gumball, latterly signed to Columbia Records.

"The labels were afraid that the indie bands thought they wouldn't be 'cool' any more if they signed to a major," laughs Fleming. "But no indie bands really think that at all, they're all fuckin' *dying* to get signed to a major. There was no trepidation, although there should have been. You get blinded by the idea that, 'I deserve this, because we're fucking great, and if so-and-so is on a major label then *we're* gonna be on a major label'.

"Gumball were on Columbia for two records. It didn't really change much, as far as how many people were buying our records; we were selling about the same amount, which on an indie was fantastic, but on a major was *horrible*. Because I'd worked with a number of bands and already knew the pitfalls of life on a major label, we avoided most of them. I wanted what I knew we could get out of it. I was glad just to have the sort of budget I'd spent on other people's albums as a producer; we could go and make a record for six weeks in a barn in Woodstock and have a good time. Of course, I knew from the start that we'd never actually recoup any money, so I just enjoyed it. Once we'd spent the advance, we'd go on tour and make money the way we used to make money. But a lot of bands, younger bands, were like, 'We're big now, we're signed to a major'. Six months after they'd spent all their money, they'd split up."

The 1992 MTV Video Music Awards, held in September, a year after the release of 'Smells Like Teen Spirit', was like a coronation for the grunge generation, taking their rightful places as mainstream rock'n'roll icons. At the awards ceremony, Kurt and his wife, Courtney Love (they had married in February of that year) engaged in a war of words with Axl Rose, balding figurehead of the outgoing hair-metal wave, signalling a changing of the guard. When Courtney giggled as Cobain rebuffed Rose's opportunistic invitation to 'jam', Axl impotently told Kurt to "control your woman", outing himself as an archaic hangover from the Eighties in contrast to the feminised, liberal Cobain.

Kurt opened Nirvana's performance at the ceremony with the opening bars of 'Rape Me', a new song he'd wanted to play but which the producers had declared verboten; pleased with his rebellious gesture, he led the group through a coruscating 'Lithium', which climaxed messily as Kurt thrust his Fender mustang into his amplifier, and Novoselic – mildly concussed from a head-on collision with the bass guitar he hurled into the air – began calling out, "Hey, where's Axl? Hi Axl!" The evening closed with a momentary reconciliation between Cobain and Vedder; "We slow-danced under the stage when Eric Clapton was playing 'Tears In Heaven'," Vedder recalls, "as though it were a seventh grade school dance. Who led? That's a good question. That's the thing, no one led."[19]

> "*Dirty* was our most commercial record. It came out just after the big grunge explosion; I remember getting a late-night phone call from Courtney saying, 'I'm so proud of you guys, its going to be so big', so I remember thinking, maybe it will be. But, of course, it wasn't."
>
> Thurston Moore

Those underground groups already signed to major labels found that following Nirvana's success they were confronted with pressures from their corporate paymasters unimaginable when they had originally signed.

Nevermind had raised the stakes for these groups far beyond their wildest expectations only a year before.

Sonic Youth entered Manhattan recording studio Magic City in March 1992, their media visibility at an all-time high thanks to Kurt's constant and affectionate name-checking in interviews; indeed, the band had been crowned Godfathers Of Grunge, a title that would prove ultimately erroneous but nevertheless spoke of the respect this generation held for their New York elders. The Youth would employ the services of producer Butch Vig and mixer Andy Wallace for the album, repeating their roles on *Nevermind*, although this wasn't why Sonic Youth selected Vig, citing instead his work with former tour-mates Die Kreuzen.

Nevertheless, Vig and Wallace would help distil Sonic Youth's squall into something approximating radio friendliness, still broaching no compromises regarding the severity of their noise, or the themes of their songs. The album would feature more tracks than any Youth release to date: 15 songs (16 on the double vinyl). Absent were the extended epics of before; *Dirty* was concise, even as it sprawled between passages of high-impact noise and scratchy oddball vignettes. Under Vig's guidance, Lee and Thurston's guitars roared and screamed, captured in diamond-sharp fidelity, each guitarist staking out a separate stereo channel for themselves (Lee is fucking up your left speaker, Thurston rupturing your right).

The songs on *Dirty* were tight, punchy; opener '100%' burned phosphorent-bright for 149 seconds and then was suddenly gone, a corrosive blast of pop-orientated bubble-grunge, complete with brain-scrambling duo guitar break, written in tribute to Joe Cole. "I can't never forget you," whispered Thurston, as guitars chugged a T-Rex riff behind him, "It's hard to believe you took off, I always thought you'd go far."

For *Dirty*, the group played Kim to the forefront; she sings on seven songs, as many as Thurston, her songs the album's most fearless and inventive. 'Swimsuit Issue' opened with a crashing wave of white-noise guitar and tom-tom rumble, a No Wave take on Bow Wow Wow's 'C30 C60 C90 Go!' perhaps, underscoring the lyric's uncompromising stance against sexual harassment, Kim's adopted valley-girl argot yielding gloriously tart couplets like, "Dreamed of going to the Grammies/Till you poked me with your whammy". 'Drunken Butterfly' upped the ante further, a psychotic stutter-funk groupie song – the chorus ran, "I love you I love you I love you, what's your name?" – anchored to guitars that sounded like they'd been scrubbed raw with wire wool, sparking like shorting electric cables. An early demo version of the song was entitled 'Theoretical Chaos', betraying the song's debt to Theoretical Girls' 'You Got Me'.

Far from sweetening Sonic Youth's sound, Vig and Wallace captured their scree in sharp-focus, widescreen 70mm Technicolor. Recalling Paul Smith's earlier dictum that every Blast First! release should be able to stand beside a major label album on the shelves and not seem shoddy by comparison, *Dirty* amplified Sonic Youth's arty drone, honing and sharpening it until their noise could flatten every other mainstream noise-monger. The previous year's breakthrough eponymous album by thrash pioneers Metallica certainly couldn't muster anything as sonically fierce as 'Drunken Butterfly', sounding lame and tame by comparison.

Some of the album's most charming moments found the group writing their most seemingly conventional songs to date, deftly toying with the formula for maximum effect. Lee's beautiful, chilling and lovelorn stalker song, 'Wish Fulfillment', achieved its unsettling ache with a vocal from Ranaldo that recalled Bob Dylan, or maybe Neil Young; certainly its eerie balladry and epic explosions of noise echoed 'Don't Cry', from Neil Young's 1989 "comeback" album *Freedom*. The sheer pop thrill of the coiling guitar lines of 'Sugar Kane', meanwhile, played to the group's burgeoning gift for anthemicism, while a middle passage of blackened white noise reminded the listener just who was playing on their stereo.

1992 was another election year in America – one that the Democratic party, led by Bill Clinton, won, in the wake of George Bush Sr's war in the Gulf – and *Dirty* was a political album, albeit one aware that protest songs often made for poor protest and poorer song. Thankfully, Sonic Youth evaded that pitfall with an elegant sense of irony on 'Youth Against Fascism', a skull-crushing anti-Nazi stomp that also served as an attack on the protest-song format. "Yeah, the president sucks, he's a war-pig fuck" drawls Thurston, oozing cool until he catches sight of himself in the mirror, blushes at the egotism and posturing inherent in so much rock'n'roll radicalism, and sings, "It's the song I hate". That the song featured a guest appearance on guitar by Ian MacKaye, perhaps the hardcore era's sharpest and most sophisticated polemicist, only added a further complexity.

"I was in New York and eating at a restaurant called Spring Street Natural and I called Thurston just to say 'Hi'," recalls MacKaye, "and there was a message on his machine saying that they were in the studio. I was at the restaurant and I had just ordered. The studio was half a block away, so I ran down and went in and those guys were all there. My food was coming, so I had to go, but they said, 'We want you to play on something.' I don't do that kind of thing, but all those people were hanging out and saying it would be great. I'm just not a player like that; it would not occur to me to play a lick on something. The first thing I had to do was find a guitar I could play, which is of course impossible, because they're all tuned bizarrely. I picked up the only SG because I can recognise it as a guitar. I plugged it in, put on the headphones and I was really nervous. First off I don't know what to play, I don't know how to play because it was such a weird tuning, and my dinner is going to be ready in two minutes!

"So they run the tape and I'm standing in front of the speaker and I'm trying to find something, anything. So I just played some feedback. Thurston walked in and was like, 'That was great!' I said goodbye, walked out and went back to have my dinner. Six months later we're on tour in Europe, and every interviewer is asking me about my collaboration with Sonic Youth. It was one pass. I love that kind of thing, frankly."[20]

While MacKaye would prove to be the album's only celebrity guest, superstars stalked the lyric sheet. Thurston's 'Sugar Kane' alluded to the original blonde bombshell, Marilyn Monroe, while 'Swimsuit Issue' referenced various high-profile sex scandals, closing with a list of the models in that year's Swimsuit Issue of *Sports Illustrated* magazine, and Kim's deliriously sleepy-eyed 'Crème Brulee' included the couplet, "Last night I dreamt I kissed Neil Young/If I was a boy then it would've been fun." Violence surfaced again on 'Chapel Hill', with its lyrical allusions to the still-unsolved murder of Bob Sheldon, peace activist and founder of Internationalist Books, a volunteer-operated, non-profit organisation in North Carolina that supports local progressive activists.

On *Dirty*, Sonic Youth sounded like a big time rock'n'roll band – albeit one pushing any number of envelopes, and skewing the formula in every direction – bold, amplified and confident. Geffen could only be pleased with the album they had been delivered, although they baulked at the sleeve concept. They had no problem with Mike Kelley's photographs of beaten-up, spooky cuddly toys, nor Richard Kern's rear-sleeve portraits of the group. The CD tray insert made DGC's blood run cold, however; setting Kelley's photograph in a rather unpleasant context, the planned shot depicted performance artists Bob Flanagan and Sherry Rose stark naked, doing unspeakable things with stuffed animals. Included only in a limited-edition, 5,000 disc special run of the album, this shot would elude most who purchased the album. *Dirty*, indeed.

⋆ ⋆ ⋆

Sonic Youth celebrated Independence Day 1992 with a free concert in New York's Central Park, supported by Sun Ra – a fiendishly productive and creative avant-jazz figurehead who swore he was 300 years old and from the planet Saturn – playing with his Arkestra. "That was a pretty big deal for us," remembers Lee. "It was a really remarkable gig. For a time around that period, we weren't really having the best New York shows, and I don't know why. It was one of those things where we'd gotten to a certain kind of level of popularity and that's when the hometown kinda starts to go really critical on you or something like that. When we got a little famous, it was kinda harder and harder to make New York shows work, and I just remember that one being this wonderful day. I mean, Sun Ra was amazing, it was completely inspiring to play with him and meet him. We played really well that day. It was just a really remarkable, beautiful summer day."[21]

Sonic Youth spent the rest of 1992 touring the world, again selecting the most curious and wonderful support acts. Over this extended jaunt, the Youth would play with Boston's Throwing Muses, a wonderfully dark group led by Kristin Hersh; Cell, a caustic indie group featuring former Sonic Youth guitar tech Keith Nealy on drums; old hands newly signed to Warner Bros, Mudhoney; Mike Watt's mighty fIREHOSE; Chapel Hill indie-rock scrappers Superchunk; Japanese noise Dadaists Boredoms; even a bunch of Canadian rockers named after an SY song, Eric's Trip. *Dirty* sold respectably, charting at #84 in the *Billboard* top 200, bolstered by some MTV play for their videos, including a Tamra Davis-directed clip for '100%' that saw actor/skateboarder Jason Lee's first onscreen performance. While the album fell far short of the sales being enjoyed by *Nevermind*, they were solid enough to ensure Sonic Youth's continued presence on DGC while their contemporaries struggled in the majors.

The grunge era was a tumultuous time for the more extreme end of the American underground. The Butthole Surfers met the mainstream head on, hooking up with John Paul Jones, the former Led Zeppelin bassist/keyboard player with a wealth of studio experience, to deliver *Independent Worm Saloon* in 1993, an album that streamlined their freakish noise into greasy, laser-guided riffage, apeing classic metal stylings with sick flair, unafraid of unleashing the "Gibbytron" voice-modulator upon unsuspecting audiences. The album sold modestly but enough to ensure another major release, 1996's *Electriclarryland*, which harboured the group's first Top 40 hit in the very uncharacteristic 'Pepper', which presaged a later career diversion towards trance music.

Meanwhile, Oklahoma's Flaming Lips – a group indebted to Butthole Surfers for their sonic and visual lunacy – had signed to Warner Bros, and had begun a metamorphosis from drug-damaged noise terrorists to serotonin-flushed, candyfloss psychedelicists. Few underground bands have enjoyed quite so indulgent a relationship with their major label as the Lips, who exploited the corporate largesse to record *Zaireeka* in 1991, a quadruple CD set meant to be played simultaneously, the result of their "boom box" experiments, getting venues full of punters operating tape decks, or parking lots full of cars with their stereos turned way up, each playing cassettes of music that built up a wondrously cacophonic whole. Warners' faith in the Lips was repaid when their subsequent album, 1999's *The Soft Bulletin*, became a critical and commercial hit.

The Meat Puppets were plucked from obscurity while spinning their wheels in major-label limbo when Kurt Cobain invited Curt and Cris Kirkwood to "cover" three tunes from *Meat Puppets II* for Nirvana's appearance on MTV *Unplugged*. As a result, the Meat Puppets' stock rocketed, and their new major label release, 1994's *Too High To Die* (produced by Butthole Surfer Paul Leary) capitalized on this momentum, mixing their sweet country abstraction with gleaming metallic riffs. "The pierced kids who bag my groceries, if I tell 'em I was in the Meat Puppets, they say, 'No shit!'" beams Curt Kirkwood. "Whereas before, it was just 'artistes', and the people who know stuff like Graham Parker and Sonic Youth, who even knew who we were."[22]

Nevertheless, Meat Puppets' success proved short-lived; following a parting of the ways with label London Records, the group split in 1996. Cris Kirkwood struggled with drug problems and in 2003 attacked a security guard in a post office in Phoenix, getting shot in the stomach twice. "Cris just got out of jail," says Curt, who has recently reformed the group with his brother. "He's still got a .57 slug lodged next to his spine, he's lucky he can walk. We had a tough upbringing, we're creatures of the street, and we're lucky that we haven't served more time. We try to feature the, uh, *utopian* elements in our music. We don't wanna go out there and show people where you're from. When he's gotten too high, things have turned out really really bad. His wife died of a heroin overdose, one of our best friends died at the same house. Cris is a really good guy, it's just a side to him. You can take the boy out of the country, but… It's a shame."

Meanwhile, having rid himself of Lou Barlow, J Mascis pursued epic, wracked country-rock of a Crazy Horse hue throughout the Nineties, as Hüsker Dü's Bob Mould enjoyed a mid-career resurgence with his group Sugar, which alloyed his earlier group's gift for damaged melody with a full-on sonic attack derived from groups like My Bloody Valentine, British noise extremists who owed more that a little to the Youth. Pussy Galore, meanwhile, were in bad shape as the decade began, the acrid spite of their anarchic and unpleasant albums spilling over into their intra-band relationships. Julie Cafritz was jettisoned following several confrontations with Jon Spencer, while guitarist Neil Hagerty floated in and out of the group's circle.

Finally, in 1990, the group recorded their final album, *Historia De La Musica Rock*, as a trio – Bob Bert, Jon Spencer and Neil Hagerty – with a sound far removed from the alienated clatter of earlier albums, more resembling a sick blues-rock. A cover of Howlin' Wolf's blues standard 'Little Red Rooster' was played pretty straight. Remarkably for a down-home blues, this slyly erotic song had been a UK number one hit by The Rolling Stones in 1964.

After Hagerty reneged on a tour in support of the album, Pussy Galore dissolved, a last trace of ugly East Village noise. Spencer would later comment that the legacy of Pussy Galore was "losing all your friends". The group had eviscerated and assaulted rock'n'roll with an exhilaratingly bratty brutality, playing late-Eighties Reagan-hysteria nihilism for dark kicks. Spencer himself later noted that such an approach was, ultimately, "kind of a trap"[23]; whatever redemptive qualities Sonic Youth found in their harsh squall had eluded Pussy Galore. A certain twisted blues revivalism would pervade both The Jon Spencer Blues Explosion (who played The Blues as hip-hop producers heard it, all lean licks, tight riffs and insane holler) and Hagerty and partner Jennifer Herrema's Royal Trux (who played The Blues as junkies heard it, deliciously opiated and occasionally beautiful and slipping to its own inimitable groove), both of whom toured with Sonic Youth in 1992.

Closest to Sonic Youth's heart during this era, however, were Pavement, a chaotic five-piece from Stockton, California, whose literate jumble of Fall riffs and abstract indie sketchiness sometimes coalesced into precious, delectable tuneage. With scratchy lo-fi debut LP *Slanted & Enchanted* released by Matador Records in 1992, they won the hearts and minds of the underground with their resolutely non-rock moves, a refreshing contrast to the reheated stadium machismo abounding at the time. The album they would record after Sonic Youth had taken them to Europe, 1994's *Crooked Rain, Crooked Rain*, would be a lush, slanted reaction to the corporate rock they'd been exposed to, their cracked country lament 'Range Life' a paean to touring that took gleefully spiteful potshots at Smashing Pumpkins and Stone Temple Pilots, heavy-rock gatecrashers at the underground love-in.

Geffen's promotional clout scored the Youth another first in September, as they performed their first-ever network television appearance on the *Tonight With David Letterman* show. Accompanied by the in-house band, led by former *Saturday Night Live* bandleader Paul Shaffer, the group burned through a wonderfully atonal, cacophonic '100%', the studio sideman taking at least as much glee in their squalling as Lee and Thurston, the former hammering his fretboard with a baseball bat, the latter sporting a Royal Trux T-shirt and hurling his guitar in the air. Following the ad break,

Letterman engaged in some banter with Shaffer, still visibly buzzing on the Youth's anarchic performance.

"Were they actually fighting? Did tempers flare?" joshed Letterman.

"The youth of today have their 'thing', that's all I can say..." deadpanned Shaffer, shaking his head

As the audience laughed, Letterman began to shuffle his notecards, preparing to welcome his next celebrity guest, bidding fond farewell to the local noisenik heroes (who would return to his stage over subsequent years), mumbling over the studio applause, "Very popular... Sonic Youth...Very big, very popular... Sonic Youth..."

> "In the face of success, Kurt seemed to feel the need to maintain this stump position of punk-rock credibility. Save the mainstream acceptance of the relatively straight-ahead pop of R.E.M. – which Kurt loved as much as hardcore thrash – there really was no model for such success from our community. He told *Flipside*, the iconic Los Angeles punk-rock fanzine, that he hoped the next Nirvana album would vanquish their affiliation with the 'lamestream'. He recounted being taken aback by an audience member who grabbed him and advised him to, 'Just go for it, man'. I remember smiling at this, as it was how most of us felt. We didn't perceive Nirvana's status as lame. It was cool."
>
> Thurston Moore

"The weirdest and saddest thing about Nirvana," sighs Jerry Thackray, "is they signed to that management company because they trusted Sonic Youth, because they thought, if Sonic Youth think these guys are cool, then they must be. Danny Goldberg and John Silva probably *are* pretty cool, but they clearly *weren't* cool for Nirvana. That's not Sonic Youth's fault, that's not Gold Mountain's fault. Gold Mountain were used to dealing with Sonic Youth; Sonic Youth made all their decisions themselves, were very pro-active, very hands-on. Gold Mountain probably figured Nirvana were going to be like that, they thought Nirvana came from a similar kind of back-ground. But of course, they *didn't*, really. Aberdeen's not really much like New York. And Nirvana had a passive/aggressive thing going on, particu-larly Kurt; they thought it was more 'punk' not to do anything, to let every-one else handle stuff for you. And of course it's not, not really."

For Dave Grohl, Nirvana's lightspeed hurtle was disorientating, as he found himself playing the kind of show where the sound of his snare drum would take four seconds to reach kids at the back of the arena. "The thing

I started to notice was, people were starting to *pull*," he remembers. "People would pull me to an interview, or pull me to the dressing room, and people would push me onstage. And that's when I thought, OK, this is getting a little weird. There were times where I'd excuse myself from an interview to have a piss, and have an extreme anxiety attack, asking myself, why am I so stressed, so nervous? I was really happy, I didn't feel down or depressed, I felt elated. But I was pretty overwhelmed. I was only in that band for three and a half years, so everything happened over such a short period of time. A lot of it's kind of a blur."

Under this intense pressure, Nirvana began to fragment, devolving into a very public soap opera. The group had toured constantly in support of *Nevermind*, which left Cobain tired and depressed, disaffected with his fan-base, and hating the very music that had made him famous. With their success, Nirvana had swiftly become the focus of much hatred and jealousy from the punk scene; the group had "made it", and all of a sudden their years spent paying dues, and the explosive power of *Nevermind*, counted for nothing. They were declared sellouts by a nation of kids still living in their parents' basements, while ex-Dead Kennedys frontman Jello Biafra even suggested, not entirely seriously, that Nirvana were government plants, part of a top-secret FBI ruse to lure white kids away from the pernicious influence of rap.

Kurt was torn by these conflicting desires to satisfy the pop audience and to alienate them with dissonant punk noise, in the kind of self-sabotaging gesture that he believed might impress his critics. His mindset was further fractured by his heroin abuse, and by accusations in the press that his pregnant wife Courtney was also using, threatening their custody of their unborn child. Frances Bean Cobain was born days before Nirvana flew to Britain to headline the Reading Festival, at the end of the summer of 1992, a year after Dave Markey had filmed them, playing low down on the bill. Kurt dedicated a new song, the broken and beautiful 'All Apologies', to his wife and new child that night; its fragile Beatles-esque melody, sad and moving lyrics and uplifting rush of bruised noise sounded like redemption after an exhausting, damaging year. It would prove to be anything but.

* * *

As 1993 dawned, Sonic Youth found themselves back in the Antipodes as part of Big Day Out, a touring festival package styled after Lollapalooza, Perry Farrell's "touring alternative circus", a burgeoning success during the grunge era. In February, they began their return to the United States via Japan, playing with Boredoms and Japanese girl punk group Shonen Knife, favourites of Kurt Cobain's. Deep into their corporate rock "experiment", they played the most polished and accessible music of their career. However, the experience of competing in the mainstream, against the reconstituted heavy rockers of the "Alternarock" nation, left them fatigued, the sheen of their major-label material beginning to dull for the musicians playing it.

"I think that they felt they'd reached some sort of watershed," suggests Keith Cameron, "that they'd maybe gone as far in that direction as they were comfortable with, and wanted to do something else. In many ways, *Dirty* had been as challenging as many other things they've done. But it was very 'together' sounding, it was a 'big' production. I interviewed them around that time and they all seemed a little tired, a bit drained by the whole experience. Something was up with them, there was definitely something brewing. I think they felt misgivings about what was happening to Nirvana. Maybe a case of them thinking, on some level, 'Oh shit, this is all our *fault*'."[24]

In taking the underground overground, and in getting Nirvana signed to DGC, Sonic Youth's contribution to this punk colonisation of the mainstream was palpable. But the after-effects of this "revolution" would ultimately render this mainstream just as off-limits to Sonic Youth as it had been during Guns'n'Roses' reign, if not more so. Very soon, the outsiders would be made to feel their outsiderdom once more; some would draw strength from this recategorisation, others would split and be destroyed by it.

In reaction, the Youth were beginning to reaffirm their connection with the underground. Mark Sinker had left *NME* (after the paper refused to run a negative review he'd written of megastars U2's career nadir, *Rattle & Hum*) in 1988, soon relocating to *The Wire*, a magazine that chiefly covered jazz and avant-garde music; under Sinker's direction as editor in the early Nineties, however, it would widen its perspective to embrace a broad range of music, the disparate strands united and given context by the sincerity, sense and severity of argument contained within.

"I was very interested in all these different micro avant-gardes that didn't really communicate with each other," explains Sinker, "and what I was really keen on was finding crossover points where they *did*, like Sonic Youth. I wanted to start talking to the community, to these people. Sonic Youth wanted to do that as well, which was exciting. They were very generous about all the other things that were going on, they always seemed to be *interested*. That was part of why I found them very simpatico – because they were so generous, they weren't competitive with everyone else; they pointed you in different directions. They were my marker for what this future community would be."[25]

Sinker invited the group to take part in 'Invisible Jukebox', a regular "blindfold test" feature in the magazine where artists were challenged to identify unnamed pieces of music from *The Wire*'s wide spectrum of reference. Sonic Youth performed exceptionally well. "I played them something from Lou Reed's *Metal Machine Music*," remembers Sinker, referencing the Velvets frontman's perverse white-noise double set, "and they guessed the *side*. I think it was just a lucky guess, but… I played something from *Arc*, which they didn't get, and were amused by, because they said they must have heard it being played when they toured with him [Neil Young].

"They did a reverse-test for me, which I did really badly on, but what was interesting about it was the range of things that they'd picked, and sort of assumed I should know, because I was 'at' *The Wire*. Apart from being embarrassed by having done so badly, I was struck by how much they *knew*, especially Lee and Thurston. Subsequently, they cemented those links much more in terms of releases they made and shows they played."

⋆ ⋆ ⋆

As Sonic Youth prepared their dignified exit from the grunge bunfight, for a more artistically rewarding outsiderdom, the Nirvana story was going badly wrong. Mudhoney's account of touring as support to Nirvana paints a grim picture.

"It was great that Nirvana struck big," reflects Steve Turner, "because I always said, 'That guy writes such great songs; if I was running the world, they'd be huge.' And then they *got* huge. That was weird, but we felt nothing but total excitement over that fact. We just never thought that we should be there."[26]

"We had all these journalists asking us, 'What are you gonna do with your first million dollars?'" laughs Mark Arm.

Mudhoney found themselves touring with Nirvana for two weeks in 1993 in support of their recently released third album, *In Utero*. Produced by Steve Albini, the album was dogged throughout production by rumours suggesting Cobain was fashioning an unlistenable "fuck you" to his new mainstream audience; upon release, the same rumourmongers accused Geffen of hiring Scott Litt to "sweeten" Albini's takes. Whatever the truth of those allegations, *In Utero* was certainly not easy listening, an uncompromising, often brilliant and often bleak album, the work of a very tortured and unhappy man, locked in a passive/aggressive war with the very self he had invented.

"It was just fucking horrible," remembers Turner, of the tour. "Everyone was walking around on eggshells, nervous and paranoid. Once it was over, I was kind of dreading the Pearl Jam stadium tour we were booked on, a couple of weeks later. But it was like the complete opposite; the Pearl Jam guys all got on well, were friends with their road crew… It was like they'd figured out how to 'do' the stadium-rock thing, to make it work for them. And Nirvana never did."

"I hadn't really hung out with Kurt since New Year's Eve of 1992," adds Arm, "when I'd overdosed on heroin and woken up surrounded by paramedics. I'd subsequently gotten my shit together. Kurt told me that he was having the hardest time quitting drugs. I told him I'd had to separate myself from the people I was hanging around with, and that he really needed to get away from some of the people he was hanging around with.

"I should've named names, but I didn't want to get too involved in his business," sighs Arm. "The whole thing was senseless, idiotic, and I think it only happened because he was surrounded by too many people who were afraid to tell him not to do drugs. The only people making any kind of a stand at all were Chris and Dave, and they were being completely rebuffed."

Kurt's estrangement from the rest of his band, his seemingly helpless addiction to heroin, and his tangled relationship with Courtney Love came to a head as Nirvana toured Europe early in 1994. On March 4, while recovering in Rome from bouts of bronchitis and laryngitis, Cobain overdosed on "date-rape" drug Rohypnol, a failed suicide attempt that left him comatose for a day. On March 25, Love arranged an "intervention" at their house, Kurt's friends and family confronting him about his drug abuse. Reluctantly, he agreed to undergo detox at Exodus Recovery Centre in Los Angeles, where a number of other underground stars were also cleaning up; 24 hours after being admitted, he escaped the facility and flew back to Seattle, where he went on the run. Courtney hired a private eye to find her husband, while Cobain's mother filed a missing persons report with the police. On April 3, Pearl Jam played a sellout show at the Fox Theater in Atlanta, Georgia, broadcast on radio stations across the world; as introduction to the group's anti-suicide anthem, 'Go', Eddie Vedder murmured, "This one's for Kurt."[27]

Five days later, Cobain's body was discovered in the basement of the home he shared with Love and Frances Bean, dead of a self-inflicted gunshot wound to the head. He was 27 years old. An accompanying suicide note quoted from Neil Young's 'Hey Hey My My (Into The Black)', and bemoaned that he couldn't feel the joy of music any longer. "Please keep going Courtney," he wrote, "for Frances, for her life, which will be so much happier without me."

In the aftermath of his death, Kurt's mother Wendy O'Connor was quoted as saying, "I told him not to join that stupid club," referring to rockers like Jimi Hendrix, Jim Morrison, and Janis Joplin, all of whom had died in drug-related circumstances, also aged 27. But Kurt's death was not the result of rote rock'n'roll misbehaviour, nor some tragic misadventure while pursuing "high times". His suicide was motivated by a depression that had lingered within him since childhood, agitated by the pressures fame brought, and exacerbated by a heroin addiction that brought with it a sense of shame and weakness over how he'd ceded control over his life to the drug.

Heroin abuse was rife within the alternative rock scene, and many didn't survive their dalliances with the drug. Only two months after Kurt's suicide, Kristen Pfaff, who had joined Hole as bassist shortly before production began on their second album, *Live Through This* (released on April 12, 1994, four days after Kurt's body was discovered), was found dead of an apparent overdose. A year later, Shannon Hoon, lead singer with Blind Melon, Californian alterna-rockers big with the MTV crowd, lost his fight against the drug, leaving a 12-week-old daughter, Nico, behind him. Reports of Layne Staley's death, meanwhile, would often surface throughout the decade, as Alice In Chains went on hiatus following the release of their eponymous 1995 album, Staley's ill health keeping the group off the road since the previous summer. Staley collaborated with fellow addicts, Pearl Jam guitarist Mike McCready and Screaming Trees frontman Mark Lanegan, in the all-star Mad Season, releasing one album before Staley's condition worsened and he left the group. In late 1996, friends put Layne on 24-hour suicide-watch following the heroin-related death of his girlfriend, Demri Parrott; three years later, he exiled himself to a reclusive life in his Seattle apartment, succumbing to his addiction. On April 5, 2002, eight years to the day after Kurt Cobain committed suicide, Layne Staley fatally overdosed on a "speedball", a lethal cocktail of heroin and cocaine.

Lanegan was a close friend and collaborator of both Layne and Kurt's, fighting his own long battle against heroin through the Nineties. Ultimately Lanegan triumphed over his addiction, though he is keenly aware of how close he came to oblivion. "Most of my friends from the Northwest aren't around now," he says. "I really just did not want to live that way any longer. It was the end of a nightmare that had lasted for years and years. I had always hoped that I would be able to stop, but I never was able to. Eventually, I was. I was pretty stubborn, nobody likes to believe that they need anybody's help in anything, and the smarter you are (and I'm not smart) or the tougher you are (and at times I thought I was pretty tough) the more trouble you have. The smartest guys I ever met are not around any more, because they thought they could think their way out of an unthinkable situation, and the tough guys have to just be beaten up repeatedly, and some guys just never do make it out."[28]

Depression, heroin and death were not elements of Sonic Youth's rich tapestry; this dark side of the "grunge" era was like an echo of Thurston's youthful brief encounter with Sid Vicious, the heroin-stricken death-rocker reminding Moore that he played in an art-rock band, that he wasn't of this world. Older and wiser, the Youth's drug use was mostly confined to teenage experimentation. While their success and celebrity was on a much more modest scale than the outrageous fortune that had visited Nirvana, their approach to their career was crucially different and, had *Goo* or *Dirty* gone multi-platinum, would most probably have managed their fame in a manner as dignified as their contemporaries R.E.M., whose early Nineties albums *Out Of Time* and *Automatic For The People* both went quadruple platinum.

Sonic Youth lacked that certain cynicism and self-doubt that characterized Generation X and the Alternative Rock groups, the fear, suspicion and jealousy of success that ultimately scuppered grunge. But there was no doubt that Sonic Youth had loved Kurt, and Nirvana, and that brief shining moment when *Nevermind* demolished the barrier between the underground and the mainstream, and it seemed like so many outsider voices might now get a chance to be heard. More than a decade on from those dark days of April 1994, with Cobain's sad, blue-eyed gaze staring out from the T-shirts of metal kids not yet born when he died (as well as the office-wall mural of Fred Durst, frontman of jock-rockers Limp Bizkit and perhaps the antithesis of everything Kurt ever stood for), it's this memory of Nirvana that Sonic Youth recall most fondly: all that promise, and all that great music.

"You wouldn't know it now by looking at MTV, with its scorn-metal buffoons and Disney-damaged pop idols," wrote Thurston, in a *New York Times* article to mark the 10th anniversary of Cobain's death, "but the underground scene Kurt came from is more creative and exciting than it's ever been. From radical pop to sensorial noise-action to the subterranean forays in drone-folk-psyche-improv, all the music Kurt adored is very much alive and being played by amazing artists he didn't live to see, artists who recognise Kurt as a significant and honorable muse."

"Kids who dress like Kurt Cobain come up to me at these awesome weird music festivals," Thurston told Jerry Thackray in 2005, "and ask, 'Did you tour with Nirvana? Do you *like* this music?', referring to artists like Afrirampo, Joanna Newsom, Devendra Banhart.... And I say 'Yeah! *This* is what Kurt would have liked, much more than bands like Tool, whose T-shirt you're wearing right now'."

NOTES

[1] Jerry Thackray interview, July 2005
[2] Jerry Thackray interview, July 2005
[3] http://www.sonicyouth.com/mustang/cc/122990.html
[4] Guitare Et Claviers, April 1992
[5] *Melody Maker*, 1991
[6] Shakey, pg 654
[7] I Dreamed Of Noise
[8] *MOJO*, December 1995
[9] Author's interview, March 2007
[10] Author's interview, March 2007
[11] Author's interview, April 2005
[12] Author's interview, April 2007
[13] Author's interview, March 2007
[14] The Watt From Pedro radio show, March 17 2007
[15] Author's interview, April 2007
[16] *New York Times*, April 8 2004
[17] Author's interview, March 2007
[18] Q, September 1992
[19] *Rolling Stone*, June 16 2006
[20] Swingset #3
[21] Radio interview on WPRB, August 10th, 2002
[22] Author's interview, March 2007
[23] *MOJO*, December 1994
[24] Author's interview, March 2007
[25] Author's interview, March 2007
[26] Author's interview, July 2002
[27] Monkeywrench Radio Broadcast, 03/04/94
[28] Author's interview, November 2003

CHAPTER TEN
Post-'Mersh'

"We see Riot Grrrl connecting theory with action, connecting feminism with nothing less than the urge to live, which is something towards which we are impelled. The music, the literature, the hanging out – all reveal this relentless urge, the speed and seriousness of the impulsion. A call to any girl open to it."[1]

Huggy Bear

With Cobain, the scene figurehead, so suddenly and violently gone, grunge swiftly entered a terminal decline. In the immediate aftermath of Cobain's suicide, Eddie Vedder would grapple publicly with his guilt and grief, questioning the future of Pearl Jam; the group would continue but, in a bid to reclaim some control over their career and lives, they withdrew from most promotional commitments and ceased filming of videos, a decision, in the MTV age, as dramatic as The Beatles withdrawing from the road in 1966. Over the following years – and especially as they pursued a brave but doomed campaign against Ticketmaster's domination of the American touring circuit – the group earnestly attempted to put the ethics of Vedder's heroes, Fugazi, into play within the stadium-rock arena. While their music remained more classic-rock fire than hardcore fury, Pearl Jam's words and gestures proved entirely "punk".

Their contemporaries, meanwhile, would not survive the musical climate change. Indeed, as the century turned, Pearl Jam were grunge's last men standing; Alice In Chains, Soundgarden, Tad and Screaming Trees had all split. Even stalwarts Mudhoney, who had signalled the dawn of the age of grunge with the wondrous belch that was 'Touch Me I'm Sick', were on hiatus, after Gold Mountain's Danny Goldberg, during a short period as president of Warner Bros, shunned the band following their 'Into Yr Shtick', a venomous attack on a nameless scenester he perceived as a slight against his managerial client Courtney Love.

"It was weird opening for these arena bands," reflected guitarist Steve Turner, articulating a disaffection with the mainstream common among the underground musicians stranded there by the *Nevermind* phenomenon. "I liked the bands, but if I'd been a kid attending one of those shows, it would never have turned me on like the early punk shows did, where I actually thought, 'Oh God, there's a whole world out here that I never knew about'. If I'd gone to Lollapalooza as a kid, it woulda been the first and last concert I ever attended. I'd have been like, music sucks, this isn't what I'm looking for. There's nothing personal, nothing cool there. Just a big mass-marketing of 'cool', y'know? But exactly how cool can it be if everyone can have it?"[2]

Through the tumult, Sonic Youth continued onwards, plotting a course that would prove wilful, abstruse and at times puzzling, but never less than enthralling, or *enthralled*. Their resilience, their endurance, is oft remarked upon; who else from the No Wave scene continues to perform and record with such unhindered vitality as the Youth, or from the hardcore or grunge scenes, for that matter, without having spent at least a couple of years on hiatus? Chief among the reasons for the continued vividness of their music, its constant freshness, is the musicians' own undimmed passion for music, an insatiable hunger to connect with and draw inspiration from the absolute cutting edges of the musical spheres in which they operate. Were they not so gracious and generous in the transaction, you might almost describe this compulsion as vampiric; they are ardent aficionados of, and advocates for, the ever self-renewing avant underground, the source of their fountain of Sonic Youth.

"The word of Thurston was law, in the same way that, to a lesser extent, John Peel's word was law," remembers Jerry Thackray. "Thurston said Mudhoney were cool, so Mudhoney were cool. It was that simple. Courtney had been badgering Sub Pop to sign her, and they said, you've got to be kidding. And then Thurston called up and said, I think Hole are pretty cool, and the next thing you know Sub Pop's putting out their single. Thurston walked it like they talked it; there's any number of A&R men out there, but none of them are also in the coolest band on Earth. I interviewed them in 1992 for *Melody Maker*, and I started talking about Riot Grrrl, which was in vogue at the time. Sonic Youth, of course, were already aware of Riot Grrrl. I was just talking to Kim, really; Kim was getting on Thurston's ass about Riot Grrrl, which was pretty funny."[3]

Perennial early-adopters, Sonic Youth were immediately aware of Riot

Grrrl. The scene, a global movement that was progressively feminist in outlook, was in many ways the antithesis of grunge and all that followed; while its reach and visibility was dwarfed by the "alternative rock" phenomenon, Riot Grrrl's aims and methods were more "punk-rock" in essence. While this new wave of stadium-rock boys signed up with the majors, released their albums on CD and dominated the glossy mainstream press, the Riot Grrrl groups worked to a DIY ethic, starting their own labels, building an international community of their own, and pressing their songs onto seven-inch vinyl, all documented by a thriving network of xeroxed fanzines produced by audience and artists alike. Like hardcore and punk before it, Riot Grrrl's mission of empowerment sought to demolish the barrier between the groups and their fans.

The movement can trace its beginnings back to the International Pop Underground Convention, an indie music festival held in August 1991 in Olympia, organised by Calvin Johnson's K Records label. The first night of this four-day celebration of underground groups, featuring appearances from Glaswegian subterraneans The Pastels, British garage-rock eccentric Billy Childish and the Melvins, was dedicated to female artists. Included on the bill for 'Love Rock Revolution Girl Style Now' were Bratmobile, Heavens To Betsy and 7 Year Bitch, groups crucial to the Riot Grrrl movement as it developed; perhaps more important than what was happening onstage, the festival also allowed this nascent community of zine editors and pen pals to all meet face-to-face for the first time.

Also performing that night with a couple of her side-projects was Kathleen Hanna, singer with Bikini Kill who, along with the wonderful Bratmobile, comprised the vanguard of American Riot Grrrl. The group had formed the previous October, numbering Hanna, Tobi Vail and Kathi Wilcox, soon joined by Billy Karren on guitar, who knew Vail through The Go Team, a loose Olympia supergroup the latter had fronted with Calvin Johnston. Kurt Cobain had guested on one Go Team release, dating Vail while he lived in Olympia, before the success of *Nevermind*; that album's lyric sheet would be peppered with veiled references to Tobi, not least the album's debut single, which took its title from a graffito Hanna sprayed on Cobain's wall – "Kurt smells like Teen Spirit" – a reference to Vail's preference for the Teen Spirit brand of deodorant.

Taking their name from a fanzine edited by Hanna and her band-mates Tobi Vail and Kathi Wilcox, addressing sexism within the punk scene, the group released their first demo on cassette in 1991, entitled *Revolution Girl Style Now*, containing early versions of righteous rants like 'Suck My Left One' and 'Liar'. The following year, the group recorded their eponymous debut EP for Kill Rock Stars, produced by Ian MacKaye; the six-tracker closed with a song entitled 'Thurston Hearts The Who' which (like Pussy Galore's 'HC Rebellion', recorded seven years earlier) was composed of bad Bikini Kill reviews read over a caustic instrumental.

The following year, Bikini Kill decamped briefly to Britain, where they recorded a split-LP with their kindreds across the ocean, Huggy Bear. This Brighton based five-piece declared themselves "boy/girl revolutionaries", releasing seven-inch EPs spitting scratchy squall, anarchic noise and polemic lyrics via indie label Wiiija. While their righteous din was resolutely radio-unfriendly, they were no strangers to the mainstream media, making an unforgettable appearance on British youth television show *The Word* early in 1993, heckling presenter Terry Christian's laddish blether after their performance. This civil disobedience won them ejection from the studio and a cover feature in the following week's *Melody Maker*: beneath a freeze-frame of bassist/vocalist Niki, caught mid-howl, the headline read "This Is Happening Without Your Permission", a brilliantly punk-rock statement, whatever your feelings towards the movement. Debate upon the group and the larger Riot Grrrl phenomenon raged in the paper's subsequent issues, the mail-bag swollen with the conflict between blowhards who complained the groups "couldn't play" (doubtless these letter writers were fans of The Clash and The Sex Pistols who saw no irony in repeating the lame critique the prog-rock faithful had flung at those bands 15 years before), and kids who'd found themselves empowered by Riot Grrrl and its invitation to anarchic free expression.

In many ways, Riot Grrrl was a response to the conservative backlash against the gains made in racial and gender relations following feminism and the civil rights movement. Buffoonish cultural commentators, via the myth of "political correctness", sought to diminish the very real progress such groups had made towards establishing a climate of tolerance and equality. Meanwhile, right-wing politicians and fundamentalist Christian activists campaigned against the legality of abortion, prompting L7, an all-girl Californian grunge band, to form Rock For Choice in 1991, which put on a series of benefit shows in support of the pro-choice movement, featuring appearances from Pearl Jam and Nirvana. Both Cobain and Vedder were especially outspoken, feminised male rockers; ever one for the dramatic gesture, Vedder scrawled "pro-choice" on his forearm in marker pen during a 1992 MTV *Unplugged* appearance. It's a sobering thought that, if he tried that today, it's likely the footage would be considered too controversial and offensive to broadcast.

Specifically, Riot Grrrl sought to stake out a space – both actual and metaphorical – where women could feel free to make and partake of rock-'n'roll. Huggy Bear took this concept to its logical end, putting on shows where men were barred from the moshpit, or indeed the venue completely, so women in the audience could enjoy the show without being groped. Hole played one such show in London in March 1993, though Courtney later soured on the Riot Grrrl movement, writing in a *Melody Maker* editorial that she felt "sickened by the media's handling of the Riot Grrrls and their handling of the media; it's a mutually reciprocal sick relationship, and fascistic." Her comments must be read in context of her ongoing antipathy towards the Olympia punk community ('Rock Star', from Hole's 1994 album *Live Through This*, was a swipe at that scene), and her jealousy of Vail and Cobain's previous relationship. However, Love articulated a sense of displacement some older female punk musicians felt in light of this "revolution', writing, "If I'm Babes In Toyland, I'm 'pre-political'. If I'm L7, I'm assimilationist; if I'm PJ Harvey or Kim Deal, I'm inspirational but not very *now*."

"The problem now," Kim Gordon told *Rolling Stone* magazine, for a 1993 profile of Riot Grrrl, "is that if you're a woman in a band, Riot Grrrl has become a yardstick by which you're measured. I don't have anything against it. But I've been doing what I do for 10 years."[4] Still, Sonic Youth were very closely allied with Riot Grrrl; Huggy Bear had played support to the group for their December 15 show at Brixton Academy, while Kathleen Hanna was a friend. Indeed, when Courtney, in her brief honeymoon period with the scene, began distributing zines to friends and musicians she thought could aid Riot Grrrl's revolutionary mission, Kim politely told her that she and Thurston had already read them.

"Riot Grrrl was just one of those many things that Sonic Youth were supportive of," says Jerry Thackray. "Huggy Bear ripped Sonic Youth's music off something rotten, as they'd be the first to tell you. As much as Sonic Youth give to the scene that follows them, they also take from the scene, to re-energise themselves. Sonic Youth were influential on Riot Grrl in as much as showing all these bands out there that there's a way of making music, releasing records on a major and retaining your artistic integrity and still doing what you want to, and that's inspirational.

"In terms of Riot Grrrl and its feminism," Thackray continues, "Thurston, Lee and Steve were 'cool men', they weren't assholes. That's important. They actually became very influential on Riot Grrrl as soon as they started reacting to it – which was really early on, because Sonic Youth always react to things early on – with Kim Gordon moving towards the front of the group, writing and singing more songs. She even formed Free

Kitten, which was pretty much a Riot Grrrl band, and the Riot Grrrls definitely responded to that. 'Wow, Kim Gordon, she's *cool*; we thought she was cool anyway, but obviously, she's *really cool*'."

"There's one thing that really stands out about that time," remembers Frances Morgan, today a musician and editor of *Plan B* magazine, but in the early Nineties a teenage music fan. "There were lots of really cool women playing in bands, which really doesn't seem to be the case now. Kim was one of those people. When you're young, you look up to people who are cool and look like they're having fun, and are doing something you would like to do too. So Kim, and Polly Harvey, and Kim Deal, and especially Kat Bjelland and Lori Barbero, were very important to me. I was interested in Riot Grrrl, but not *musically*. Someone like Polly Harvey was my real hero. I played music pretty much all the time, I played guitar a lot, and I knew Polly was a 'good' musician, that she had 'chops', that she could play the blues; that was really cool to me. But the *spirit* of Riot Grrl, the fanzines, the DIY aesthetic, the female energy...

"In retrospect it seems simplistic, but at the time it was very necessary," Morgan continues. "It provided a lot of young women with something really special, which they don't have now. You never see anyone looking really *scruffy*, in the way that you used to. Not that scruffiness is necessarily something to aspire to, but it was very liberating for me, as a scruffy teenage girl, to see women who hadn't made a massive amount of effort over the way they looked, because what they were there for wasn't to be ornamental. If they *did* make an effort, it was often in the way that they would look *weird*. Like Kathleen Hanna or Kat Bjelland, they would have made a huge effort with the way they looked, but they would look really insane, they wouldn't look like they shopped at Top Shop, the way indie girls do now, with their polka-dot dresses and little ankle socks and shit. They would wear those things too, but with a massive tattoo running up their leg, or a big bruise on their arm, something 'wrong'.

"Kim Gordon wasn't totally like that, she was always kind of a 'lady', but she always looked iconic. I remember really wanting X-Girl clothes [laughs]... I remember her philosophy behind all that was very cool: good clothes, easy-to-wear, for young women of various different shapes and sizes. I remember reading about it and thinking it was a good thing."[5]

The Youth's friends The Beastie Boys had ridden something of a roller-coaster through the Eighties, morphing from scrappy hardcore punks to urbane, witty rappers, via a lucrative detour through beery fratboy rap (complete with a stage show featuring go-go girls in cages and a giant hydraulic inflatable penis) that the now more mature Beasties were trying to live down. Their 1989 album *Paul's Boutique*, a circuitous, utterly willful journey into sampledelia, had baffled record-buyers, killing the momentum of their 1986 debut, *License To Ill*, the first rap album to top the *Billboard* charts. But *Paul's Boutique* restored a credibility and artistic integrity their earlier shenanigans had diminished. 1992's *Check Your Head* and 1994's *Ill Communication*, mixing hardcore guitar and fecund funk with meditative hip-hop and ballistic rap, connected the Beasties to the alternative-rock audience, and in turn connected that audience to their diffuse and idiosyncratic riot of reference, a fannish mish-mash of kung-fu movies, old skool hip-hop, Adam Yauch's conversion to Buddhism, the Boys' budding politicisation, basketball, sneaker fetishisation, mysterious but still amusing in-jokes, and name-checks to their wide range of celebrity friends...

Filming the peerless video for 'Sabotage' with a then-unknown Spike Jonze and anticipating the aesthetic of Quentin Tarantino in the process, expanding their empire into their own high-quality zine, *Grand Royal*, covering their every eclectic whim (with Thurston signing on as free-jazz critic for an issue), and a clothing range, X-Large, The Beastie Boys were the epitome of twenty-something cool, an entire generation hanging on their every cultural reference and drinking deep of their various influences. The Beasties were so cool they were even clued into Riot Grrrl, Mike D rapping on 1994's 'The Scoop', "So I'll say it like the group Huggy Bear/There's a boy-girl revolution of which you should be aware". Indeed, only Sonic Youth could possibly challenge The Beastie Boys for their influence over a certain generation of music fans, so when the Beasties decided to open a women's branch of their X-Large clothing label and boutique, naturally they approached Kim.

"Daisy Von Furth and I have been friends for years," explains Kim, of her partner in X-Girl (Von Furth is the sister of Pussy Galore's Julie Cafritz). "We've always hung out and gone shopping. The Beasties wanted to design a line of girls' clothes because they saw the competition doing it. They thought that we would have good taste. Daisy is one of those people who, from the age of six or seven, has been reading fashion magazines; she knows all the editors' names, all the models' names. She's been preparing her sound bites for literally years. I love clothes, and I love anything that's visual – I'm very visually orientated – but music's really my passion. Still, I don't like to do anything badly, and I do have the drive to be involved in X-Girl.

"Basically, we make clothes that we want to wear. It comes from years of shopping, and having to deal with things like visible panty lines. I wanted to make clothes that didn't use Spandex or Lycra, that weren't body-hugging but were flattering at the same time and could maybe be worn on a wider range of figures."[6]

It seemed, just as Sonic Youth had signed to Geffen, that Kim's confidence had grown to a point where she could share the role of fronting the group with Thurston. Certainly, from *Dirty* onwards, her contributions to Sonic Youth albums were plentiful and fascinating, often the most adventurous, boldly avant tracks of the group's major-label era. She would also contribute some of their most haunting, beautiful songs, while her lyrics further explored her favoured themes: the politics and psychology of sexual attraction, female relationships, and the intricacies and scandals and hypocrisies of popular culture.

"Kim was very enamoured by the whole rise of Madonna, the power she had within the music industry," says Paul Smith. "Kim was very taken by that, by a woman doing that, and she started emulating some of that stuff."[7] But Madonna never made music as bravely uncompromising, as starkly idiosyncratic as Kim Gordon did, never screamed so skin turns to gooseflesh, nor growled with cynical venom, nor happened upon such a lazy, seductive drawl as Kim located for 'Sweet Shine', the closing (and most wonderful) track on Sonic Youth's 1994 album *Experimental Jet Set, Trash And No Star*. And she would never form a group like Free Kitten, Kim's Riot Grrrl-influenced, chaotic, squalling and beautiful collective, with Julie Cafritz and, later, Boredoms drummer Yoshimi P-We and Pavement bassist Mark Ibold, releasing their albums and singles on Riot Grrrl-affiliated labels Kill Rock Stars and Wiiija.

"I see Free Kitten as being more experimental," says Kim, "A lot of people don't take us seriously, because I'm in Sonic Youth and Julie was in Pussy Galore, so they try and call us a joke band, or a supergroup, or a side-project. In general, indie rock is not sexist and is very accepting of women, but I see the mainstream of it as being pretty conservative, like college rock or something. There's a certain competitiveness, and when people feel competitive they feel more threatened. So there are boys who say bands like Bikini Kill can't play, and the English press are always saying it about Huggy Bear, and they just don't get it. They don't understand what's really sophisticated about it, so if you're a girl band you're forced into being pop or being rock, because otherwise people won't take you seriously. It seems like there are fewer girls making experimental music for that reason."[8]

"When we were recording *Experimental Jet Set, Trash And No Star*, we wanted it to be a very simple measure. That whole *Dirty* period, touring with Nirvana and Mudhoney, we were copping real big rock moves, and only too happy to be a part of it. But out of that came a more reactive music, which was more inward and cerebral, like Lou Barlow when he left Dinosaur and started making records on his four-track, or Royal Trux with their very strange records, or Pavement decidedly bucking the hard-rock model. We responded to that, which didn't make any sense to the record company. They wanted bigger, more 'rock' records, but we didn't. We decided early on that we weren't going to follow any advice from the 'success industry'. From there we sort of spun inwards..."[9]

Thurston Moore

Even before his messy exit from Dinosaur Jr, Lou Barlow had been recording his own music using a home-studio four-track cassette recorder or, if the whim took him, other, even less "professional" recording devices. 'Poledo', the closing track from *You're Living All Over Me*, offered a glimpse into Lou's private world. "My parents had bought me one of the first cheap tape recorders," Barlow recalls, "and my cousin showed me that if you half-press the 'ffw' button at the same time as you're recording, it'll make this stretched-out groaning sound. That would crack me up; he'd keep yelling, 'We're gonna beat up Louieee!' into the microphone and play it back at me, all distorted. I started making cassettes of myself playing guitar and singing, real primitive multi-tracking between two tape recorders, when I was about 12."[10]

Such "lo-fi" experimentation would lay at the heart of Sebadoh, Sentridoh and Folk Implosion, projects Barlow would pursue emboldened by the democratising influence of cheap home-recording equipment, and a still-thriving cassette underground. "I realised I could record my own music, copy it onto cassettes and sell it through local record stores," remembers Barlow. "I did it for myself, primarily, but also with the understanding that other people would find these cassettes. The chaotic nature of it all, the swings from quiet to loud, from punk stuff to folky stuff... It immediately made sense to some people, like Eric Gaffney."

In Gaffney, Barlow had found his perfect foil. The duo recorded two tapes together as Sebadoh, 'The Freed Weed' and 'Weed Forestin'', blending scrappy punk with eerie found sounds, elliptical dope-fuelled in-jokery and brittle, bare, folk-flavoured songs that cast an unblinking eye upon Barlow's relationships and anxieties, to a brave and discomforting and insightful degree. "I felt the music of the underground had become one-dimensional, noisy," says Barlow, "and I wanted to fashion my own response to that. I knew I was on the right track when people said I was a 'pussy' for playing an acoustic guitar. I'd found my new passion: quiet was the new loud." As for Sebadoh's at times painfully honest lyrical approach, he says, "Telling it like it is is always a release. All the music I've ever loved has been like that: hardcore, Black Flag, all the Dischord bands, it was all very inward-looking, very honest. I never thought for a second of doing it any differently. The only thing I was doing that was 'new' was stripping away the noise sometimes."

Adding bassist/singer Jason Loewenstein to the line-up, Sebadoh continued to record, and even began to tour the world; performing live, the three performers/songwriters would swap instruments and take the spotlight as their whims dictated, perfectly in keeping with the group's ethos of enthusiastic, anarchic creative democracy (the antithesis of Barlow's experience in Dinosaur Jr). Sebadoh and Barlow's mess of other post-Dinosaur Jr projects were the vanguard of the "lo-fi" scene that sprang up within the underground during the Nineties, groups who sacrificed sound quality in favour of inspiration. Guided By Voices – Ohio drunkards led by a forty-something school-teacher who just happened to write perfect Sixties psyche-pop fragments as naturally as the rest of us breathe – would rise to fame within the indie scene through the decade, Robert Pollard's homely recording methods affording his songs a warm, Sixties AM radio sound. Troubled singer/songwriter Daniel Johnston, meanwhile, spent the Eighties selling his home-recorded songs about Caspar the Friendly Ghost, Captain America, and the women he could never have via cassettes he distributed to record stores around nearby Austin, Texas. There was very little about Johnston's music that would have appealed to the mainstream and yet, through the vocal support of celebrity fans (not least Kurt Cobain, who wore a T-shirt promoting Johnston's 1983 cassette *Hi How Are You?* to the 1992 MTV Video Music Awards), Johnston had his earlier work re-released by Gerard Cosloy's Homestead label, and signed to Atlantic Records for his 1994 album *Fun*.

While grunge saw many abandon their will to their new corporate paymasters, divesting their music of its radio-unfriendly facets in some doomed lunge for "alternative-rock" success, this new underground thrived with eccentrics and originals, for whom making exactly the music they wished was their definition of success. These groups exalted in their outsiderdom, exploited the freedom to experiment that the absence of commercial pressures availed them; groups like Pavement, who shambled with inspiration but, when the stars were so aligned, could equally deliver cultured and eloquent and beautiful music like Television two decades before them, or Royal Trux who, legend has it, produced records behind a veil of narcotic indulgence and, by turns, baffled, "rawked" and, on 'Back To School' (from their 1993 *Dogs Of Love* EP) happened upon the most gorgeously opiated glide since the Velvets' 'Sunday Morning'.

Set amid such a context, and with Riot Grrrl as its backdrop, *Experimental Jet Set, Trash And No Star* makes perfect sense; as the album following *Dirty*, their most considered and painstakingly crafted (not to mention radio-friendly) slab of noise yet, it was a jarring volte-face. *EJST&NS* began phase two of Sonic Youth's major-label "experiment"; having followed sage advice and honed their noise during that era when the mainstream briefly tuned its ear to the underground, they now sought to bring their most subterranean qualities to the surface, assaulting and challenging ears they'd caressed with *Dirty*'s bubble-grunge. Their Trojan horse had entered the fortress, and was now about to unveil its arms.

Some of the songs that would compose *EJST&NS* were debuted live in rough form when Thurston played support on a Japanese tour in early 1993 by Free Kitten and Steve Shelley's new band Mosquito (featuring his old Spastic Rhythm Tards guitarist Tim Foljahn and Jad Fair, formerly of Maryland underground duo Half Japanese). The Youth aired some more new songs when they headlined the Ecstatic Peace Caravan Of The Stars show at New York's Knitting Factory, which also featured a solo performance from Lee, music from avant-garde guitarist Alan Licht, and sets from Free Kitten and Mosquito. Further new material was tried out during Sonic Youth's tour of the European festivals, occupying the rest of the summer, these new tunes' misshapen, subtle and intriguing qualities standing in stark contrast to the homogenised "alternative rock" happening on most of these stages.

The group returned to Walter Sear's Sear Sound studio in October for the recording sessions, once again accompanied by Butch Vig. *Experimental Jet Set, Trash And No Star* would veer sharply from *Dirty*'s dense blast of noise, however. The album was blessed with a warm, relaxed, elemental and seductive sound better suited to its more subtle and nuanced qualities. Indeed, the album opened with an acoustic fragment that had seemingly slipped off the tracklisting of Neil Young's *After The Goldrush*. Recorded as they worked on the final mixes for the album, 'Winner's Blues' was a sad, sweet lullaby; in the immediate aftermath of Cobain's suicide, its hazy, hungover melancholy and lines like, "Burn out your eyes, burn out surprise/look out today you know it's not the same" seemed to speak of a shared disillusionment within the scene, a poignant sigh of "Toto, we're not in Kansas any more".

'Screaming Skull' attempted to make some sense of the post-*Nevermind* hubbub, inspired by a conversation Thurston shared with Dave Markey about the SST Superstore, a shop on Sunset Strip stocking SST records and T-shirts and skateboards and other wares, staffed by former Germs guitarist Pat Smear (before his stint as sideman with Nirvana for their final tours, and tenure with Dave Grohl's post-Nirvana group, Foo Fighters). "I go there," whispered multi-tracked Thurstons, with a wicked glee, "'Sister''s there", referencing the album the Youth recorded for the label; Thurston later name-checked Superchunk, a Chapel Hill indie group who were friends of Sonic Youth's, and who remained resolutely independent throughout the "grunge" era, despite being touted by *NME* as a possible "next Nirvana".

"Some younger writers call Sonic Youth cynical, which is too bad," reflected Thurston, on some critics' response to the song. "They thought I was making fun of Superchunk and SST, which I wasn't. I had been to the SST store in LA, and these ads for Superchunk flashed out at me. It was weird: here was a label and a band I'd always connected with something real, something industrious, and now they were just signs, just products in downtown LA. I think younger writers mistake our detached, sort of oblique writing for cynicism."[11]

It made sense that twitchy marijuana paean 'In The Mind Of The Bourgeois Reader' featured on the album, as *EJST&NS* was a set possessed of a stoner's restless creativity. The longest track ran five and a half minutes, many barely scraped two; the songs felt intimate, undone, endearingly half-finished and sketchy, with the unself-consciousness of a demo tape. The group hadn't sounded this loose, this raw and unmediated, since *Sister*; indeed, there is an urban myth that the group taped over the masters of *Sister* to record *EJST&NS*, and that if you turn your stereo up load enough between tracks, you can clearly hear *Sister* bleeding through the silence.

The songs were often catchy more for some weird effect or idiosyncrasy than their (still strong) melodies – lead single 'Bull In The Heather', composed its memorable hook from amelodic scrapes, growls and blasts of guitar, while 'Starfield Road' concocted a song from murderous FX pedal abuse and Thurston's sci-fi beatnik spiel. The songwriting was loose, daringly so; 'Quest For The Cup' slipped from neanderthal Bo Diddley chug to a woozy blues celebrating *Rollerderby* zine editor Lisa Carver with a trapeze artist's grace, while 'Bone' was as free-form as the group ever got, Kim's sleepy kitten-purr strum book-ended by blasts of avant jazz-flavoured Sonic squall, with a lyric inspired by Dorothy Allison's award-winning, brutal 1992 novel *Bastard Out Of Carolina*. "I've become so interested in instant songwriting," commented Thurston during the sessions. "Anybody can make noise, but can anybody do instant composition?"[12] The fresh, loose and daring sound of *EJST&NS* suggested many of its tracks bore their roots in such "instant composition".

Along with the loose, "anti-musical" approaches contained within, Thurston also explicitly referenced Riot Grrrl on 'Self-Obsessed And Sexxee', with lyrics like, "Magic marker on your belly button all right"; the tone, however, is ambivalent, Thurston murmuring, "I remember your bloody trail to the top/Took it all too far, now you just can't stop". Still, he sings, "I will build you up while they put you down". 'Androgynous Mind', meanwhile, was an anti gay-bashing polemic hidden within a terrifying, building hurricane of noise, Thurston howling, "God is gay, and you were right!" above the din.

Kim's songs were among her most intriguing yet, toying with dark carnality and playful sensuality on 'Quest For The Cup' and 'Bull In The Heather', inhabiting a suburban pill-popper's daze for 'Doctor's Orders'. Closing song 'Sweet Shine' was stunning, a warm and gentle strum opening on the same dreamy chords as Dinosaur Jr's 'Severed Lips', Kim's huskily sung words evoking the delicious confusion of adolescence, conjuring how teenaged girls explore their sexuality and desires through crush fixations on distant "heart-throbs" (the object of affection in this case being some MTV grunge-rocker with alluringly dyed hair). In some of the most gooseflesh-inducing moments ever waxed by the Youth, Kim channelled the giddy, heedless passion of her heroine Janis Joplin, whooping in a carefree and careless holler of some kind of homecoming, which, in a way, is exactly what *Experimental Jet Set, Trash And No Star* was.

Released on May 3, 1994, *Experimental Jet Set* divided critics, and wrong-footed those expecting more in the anthemic crossover vein of *Dirty* or *Goo*. *Rolling Stone* printed a mostly positive review of the album, describing it as "moody, poetic and anti-commercial", though critic Barbara O'Dair's closing grumble that "this disc sounds like a cup of mud... they've saved their integrity at the expense of quality"[13], was telling from a publication that only acknowledged Sonic Youth's existence as of *Daydream Nation*. Christgau, however, 'got' it. "After all this time, they know what they're doing when they fuck around," he wrote, in his *Consumer's Guide*, "and their long-evolving rock'n'roll groove breaks down only when they have something better to do – there's nothing aleatory, accidental, or incompetent about it."[14]

"Having Christgau defend our last album when no one else would give us the time of day was great," admitted Thurston, shortly after *Jet Set*'s release. "The album was pretty conceptual: each of us brought in an idea and we would elaborate on it. It had truncated song structures, which was inspired by bands like Guided By Voices, where it's just a great fucking chorus and a great fucking verse and that's it, what else do you want?"[15]

There was no tour to promote *Experimental Jet Set Trash And No Star*, as by the time the album was released Kim was seven months pregnant, as was apparent from the group's May 17 appearance on the *David Letterman Show*. "Folks, brace yourselves, hang on to something... Sonic Youth," announced the gap-toothed presenter, before the group tore through 'Bull In The Heather', Steve hunched over a minimal kit, playing the snare drum with a maraca as Kim, wearing an oversized New York Knicks vest as a maternity dress, growled into the mic and scraped at her bass. The Youth also filmed a promo video for the single, the only to be released from the album ('Self Obsessed And Sexxee' was mooted as a possible follow-up), directed by Kim and Tamra Davis, and featuring former exotic dancer Kathleen Hanna of Bikini Kill cutting the rug throughout, wrestling over Thurston's guitar and planting a kiss on Kim's cheek in the opening seconds.

On July 1, Kim gave birth to a healthy baby girl, resisting the temptation to name the child Lolita, opting instead for Coco Hayley Gordon Moore.

> "We let the music do the talking most of the time. There are no flashy shows or really noteworthy debacles – we're here for the music, and that's where our energy goes. Most of the rock critics would rather focus on personality than talk about music, which they are only sometimes equipped to do."[16]
>
> Thurston Moore

Sonic Youth returned to the road early in 1995, following an Aids benefit at New York's Beacon Theatre the previous December, playing on a bill that included Lou Barlow, Debbie Harry, David Johansen and porn-star and performance artist Annie Sprinkle, with film-maker John Waters acting as MC; the group gave 'Androgynous Mind' a rare live airing for the show. They played seven shows at university campuses on the East Coast in April, debuting material they'd recorded a couple of months earlier, and working through some *Experimental Jet Set* songs. Mainly, these shows served as a warm-up for their forthcoming stadium tour, playing as support to R.E.M. through the second half of May.

R.E.M.'s drummer Bill Berry had collapsed onstage following a brain aneurysm halfway through a show in Lausanne, Switzerland a couple of months earlier, postponing the tour, which was now renamed Aneurysm

95. The Athens, Georgia group were supporting their new album, *Monster*, a fiery rock record in contrast to the subdued chamber pop of their hugely successful 1992 release *Automatic For The People*. *Monster* included two songs directly addressing Kurt Cobain's suicide, 'Let Me In' and 'Star 69', the last song referencing a missed call Cobain made to his friend Stipe shortly before his disappearance. Sonic Youth toyed with changing their name to "Washing Machine" for the tour (and, indeed, for good), a reference to their newly recorded, as-yet-unreleased ninth album. Luckily, saner minds prevailed.

The group signed on to headline Perry Farrell's Lollapalooza throughout the summer; the touring alternative festival had proved something of a moneyspinner since it surfaced in 1991 as Jane's Addiction's final tour. Since then, the festival had grown, mixing alternative-rock bands with weird performance troupes like the stomach-turning grotesque of Jim Rose's Circus, turning venues into little villages peopled with kiosks hawking merchandise, food and alternative wares. Indeed, as the decade wore on, this commercialisation threatened to overshadow the music the festival was supposed to be showcasing. "At first we said no, because the music we're making now is so freaky," Thurston told *Puncture* zine, shortly before the tour. "We were going to do a tour with Pavement and Beck on our own, have fun and lose money. But this was an easy choice; everything is set up for us. I don't really want to be associated with Perry Farrell's company, but basically we just come and play. So what the fuck? I expect when we pull this free-form shit at the end of the day, people will be heading for the gates."

Nirvana had been scheduled to headline the previous year's Lollapalooza; following Kurt's death, Chicago grunge group Smashing Pumpkins stepped into the breach, frontman Billy Corgan yielding some of his stage time to allow former girlfriend Courtney Love to talk to audiences about Kurt, and about her loss. Later that summer, Hole performed at the Reading Festival, thrilling voyeurs with behaviour that betrayed her troubled state of mind.

"Courtney seemed off her head," remembers journalist Julian Marszalek of Hole's set. "The sense of belligerence from the stage was palpable. 'Yeah, let's all feel sorry for the rock star widow,' she sneered, but it was difficult not to; she was wearing a black dress, black stockings and black shoes and resembled a glam Greek widow. When she fell over and rolled around it was impossible to look away, even though you wanted to. *Live Through This* was a great album, but the Reading performance shouldn't have gone ahead; the reality of the situation veered wildly from what were undoubtedly honourable intentions. Courtney underestimated what she was taking on, and the line between performance and real life wasn't so much blurred as totally erased."[17] Love spent most of the festival hanging out with Evan Dando, heart-throb singer with indie-rockers Lemonheads, charging the stage while Sebadoh played, and punching David Gedge, frontman of British indie-rockers The Wedding Present, for the crime of having had an album produced by Steve Albini. The soap opera continued over to the summer of 1995, with Hole booked to play before the Youth at Lollapalooza.

The Lollapalooza tour would prove an experience that was, by turns, maddening, exhausting, frustrating and exultant. Whatever suspicions Sonic Youth had regarding the intransigence of mainstream audiences regarding truly alternative music was confirmed by the crowds mostly avoiding the truly uncompromising acts on the second stage in favour of the more traditional fare on the main stages, like rapper Coolio, controversial singer Sinéad O'Connor, and rock-friendly hip-hop crew Cypress Hill. Much of the audience was there for the social event, rather than the sounds exhibited, while disappointing ticket sales suggested the festival might not survive the death of "grunge".

Like the summer of 1991, the year punk broke, Lollapalooza seemed to offer a chance for the Youth to spend time with their friends and fellow performers like Pavement, The Jesus Lizard, Mike Watt and a strange elfin fellow named Beck, a prolific lo-fi artist who'd recorded dark folk albums with Calvin Johnson and had scored an MTV hit with 'Loser', his debut single for DGC, a weird but loveable blues/hip-hop hybrid with a wry take on slackerdom. However, while Thurston jumped at the chance to book underground acts like Pork Queen and Thomas Jefferson Slave Apartments, the tight schedule of this touring circus meant the Youth often missed their favourite groups' sets. Often the venues scuppered the atmosphere, placing expensive, ticketed seated areas at the front of the stage, so the kids couldn't get up close to the acts, while the Youth's end-of-the-night headline slot meant that much of the audience began their journey home before the group took to the stage.

The Youth's set list from the era mixed new, unfamiliar material with older hits, the group getting a feel for playing larger venues following the Aneurysm 95 tour. The night before the first date of the tour, at the Gorge Amphitheatre in George, Washington, the group spent six hours soundchecking, "being thrown off the stage by the local road crew at 11pm," wrote Lee, in the first of a series of online tour journals from Lollapalooza performers published regularly at the website of rock magazine *Spin*. "I guess after our last two numbers – 'World Looks Red' and a hilarious 'Confusion Is Next' – they couldn't take it any more. It was kind of Spinal Tap-like, us onstage all evening working our way through all these songs to an empty field. A fitting opening evening."[18]

However, the opening show of the festival on July 4 gave a hint to how media coverage of Lollapalooza 1995 would skew. The Youth had invited Kathleen Hanna and some friends to the show, leading to a confrontation with Courtney Love. "As we were walking to the stage, the singer from Hole was standing in our path and quipped, 'Is Kathleen joining your band now?'," wrote Thurston, who described their performance that night as "the washing machine, the cleansing music for any mind poison the audience might have been subjected to. As we returned to the trailer, I was informed that on the side of the stage while we were playing, the singer from Hole flicked her cigarette at Kathleen and then sucker-punched her in the face. Before Kathleen could respond, the Hole singer's bodyguards intervened.

"Kim suggested Kathleen should respond by challenging the offender to debate any and all feminist issues at the university of her choice," continued Thurston. "The Hole singer's retort was supposedly, 'Debate? You can't even read'. Everyone is disgusted and grossed out. Perry's bummed. Everyone's bummed. Hopefully I won't have to continue referring to this most boorish of situational tragedy."

The media focused on this high-profile catfight between the Widow Cobain and some punk-rocker none of their audience knew or cared about. San Francisco punks NOFX chimed in, recording their opportunistic and vile anti-Hanna tirade 'Kill The Rock Stars', including the lyric, "I wish I could have seen Courtney demonstrate some *real* misogyny." Tensions between Love and her tour-mates would simmer throughout the rest of Lollapalooza; Thurston recalls seeing Hole perform, and Courtney "playing the strings above the neck of her guitar, saying, 'Hey, we're Sonic Youth! Eric, you be Lee, I'll be Thurston etc etc' and then they all started bashing their instruments haphazardly and jumping around, like we supposedly do."

Still, amidst all these bummers, always keeping spirits high, was Sonic pal Mike Watt and his Crew Of The Flying Saucer band. Watt had recently recorded his first solo album for Columbia Records, a star-studded affair featuring guests spots from Eddie Vedder, Dave Grohl, Chris Novoselic, J Mascis (on a take of Funkadelic's 'Maggot Brain' that, whisper it, matches the original), Henry Rollins, Mark Lanegan, Mike D and Evan Dando, along with Thurston and Steve, spanning trucker-rock, jazz-fusion and a loving cover of the Youth's 'Tuff Gnarl'. "J Mascis was playing drums," remembers Watt, "but he said he didn't know how to play the end part, so he jumped off the drum stool and Steve Shelley stepped up. I had my head down playing my bass, and I looked up, and there was J, way across the other side of the room!"

Watt had toured earlier in the year, his band including Eddie Vedder (playing support with Hovercraft, his wife Beth Liebling's band) and Dave Grohl (touring with his newly formed group Foo Fighters) on guitars. For the current tour, Vedder and Grohl were absent, but his new band boasted two drummers and, at one show, guest vocals from Thurston. "He had forgotten the lyrics to his own song!" laughs Watt. "I've done that too, it's hard to remember everything... He was trying to make up shit on the fly, singing, "Bumble bee bumble bee bumble bee". He also said we were playing too fast to fit all the words in. It was still an honour to be on stage with him."[19] The performance would unite Thurston with Watt's guitarist Nels Cline, a highly respected avant player with whom Thurston would record several albums of inspirational, improvisational skronk.

Performing on the second stage when Lollapalooza pulled into New York's Downing Stadium on July 28 were the Patti Smith Group, playing together for the first time since Smith retired from music in the early Eighties to focus on family life with husband Fred "Sonic" Smith (who had subsequently died of a heart attack in 1994). With Sonic Youth standing in the wings, she ran through old favourites all the way back to 'Piss Factory', along with a new song, 'About A Boy', which she dedicated to "Kurt, and the boy in us all".

There were wonderful shows as well, the nights when everything gelled, when the Youth eased into their new, exploratory songs, and jammed celestially in tribute to Jerry Garcia, who passed away that summer. A highlight of these shows was 'The Diamond Sea', an open-ended, improvisational piece that shifted from a fragile, melancholy song through passages of abstract and purposeful noise, sound swelling from amps as Lee and Thurston and Kim ran through their repertoire of avant techniques, scraping guitars upon speaker stacks and wielding feedback and distortion to paint a soaring abstract symphony in drone and noise, those "castles out of vapour" Lee dreamed of when he first started playing guitar. "We ended with an extra-long 'Diamond Sea'," wrote Lee of one of these nights, at Molson Park in Ontario, "with truly wigged end sections that just went on and on from one planet to the next. Felt good and stretchy by the time it was done."

But such moments aside, Lollapalooza left Sonic Youth with the sense that their place wasn't within a rock world that lacked the patience or imagination to follow the group's new, incandescent stretches of noise, facing audiences that just wanted More Of The Same, and a media that was more interested in a young widow's very public breakdown than in the very real, very alive music happening before their very eyes. Their displacement within the new rock aristocracy was cemented at the final Lollapalooza, at Shoreline Amphitheatre, where they'd endured their nightmarish experience at the Bridge School benefit concert; pulling into the venue, the group were denied entry to the backstage parking lot, told that only members of the Hole entourage were permitted to park there. Indicating Kim behind him as "Courtney Love", Thurston was swiftly waved through, but such situations spoke the truth about the "alternative rock" myth.

The group would play Lollapalooza again the following year, but only as animated by the crew of *The Simpsons*; in a memorable episode of the show, then operating at its peak, the group accompanied Smashing Pumpkins, Cypress Hill, Seventies superstar Peter Frampton and the newest attraction of the Jim Rose Circus, Homer Simpson. *Homerpalooza*, as the episode was titled, got in plenty of jabs at Generation X and Lollapalooza's expense, while the Youth's deconstruction of Danny Elfman's *Simpsons* theme remains a thing of wonder.

"I'm thinking of all those young kids in the audience, many of whom have said this was their first concert-going experience," Lee wrote in his tour journal, "and wondering where their heads will stray from here, after witnessing Watt in full-on flannel drive, David Yow sitting two rows up from them in the seats and howling at the afternoon sun, [Stephen] Malkmus in the shadow of a plywood cactus waxing obtuse poetics and pulling off magik lead lines, Cypress [Hill] in a rain of doobies and low-end, Hole issuing tight mirror-ball bulletins, Thurston fishing for his guitar at stage-edge, Beck with that Yes-era keytar strapped on… all of it adding up to a glorious cacophony of where music as we know it has been and where it is going. The mainstream hasn't got a clue as to what all this is about, or how to handle it, and that's good: what we do is secret."

> "Al Green was amazing. He ran up to us and asked us where we were from; I said New York City, and he yelled, 'Praise Jesus, New York City is here!' Then he asked my friend, who was like, 'Uh, New Jersey' , and he yelled, 'Praise Jesus, New Jersey's here!' He did spirituals and pop tunes, Burt Bacharach, all that. At the end he collapsed and his deacons had to carry him off, like James Brown. I had some shit to say to him,

because I saw him on that show *Night Music* once, and he was making fun of Sun Ra. I remember saying, 'Fuck that guy!' So I wanted to walk into the church and say, 'You dissed Sun Ra!' But it didn't happen."

Thurston Moore visits the Reverend
Al Green's church in Memphis

"I don't know what was going on when we made the last record," Lee Ranaldo told *Musician* magazine in 1995 referring to *Experimental Jet Set*, "but there are more songs on it where we came up with one riff and made a song out of it then we've ever done. Some of them work, some of them don't." *Washing Machine*, by contrast, was an album hewn from long exploratory jams, growing from the same tentative riffs but followed through to glorious conclusions of sculpted noise. "It's sprawling in the way that *Daydream* was," Lee continued. "After that record we got more tight-fisted about recording. It was good experience, but it's great now to say, 'We don't retake each guitar part 10 times until every note is fixed.' There's bum notes all over this record, stuff that's out of tune. But it's useless to worry about that. We're going for something more immediate."

The Youth entered Easley McCain Recording, a Memphis studio famed for recording local blues musicians in the Seventies and, later, as a favoured haunt of groups like Guided By Voices, The Jon Spencer Blues Explosion and Cat Power, where Pavement cut their third album *Wowee Zowee*, and where Jeff Buckley recorded his final tracks before drowning in the Mississippi. "Making a record in New York is difficult," Lee continues, "because people always know where to find you. In Memphis we were more removed. And the town's so steeped in music; we went to this old juke joint in Mississippi, a little jumpin' shack, and it's like stepping into 1945. A group of old black guys playing the most authentic-sounding lowdown blues, people doing these suggestive dances. It's amazing that something like that still exists today." The Youth recreated that Memphis juke-joint wall as the backdrop for their Lollapalooza shows.

Assisted by John Siket, who'd engineered their last two albums, the group spent two weeks laying down songs that had grown from long rehearsal jams captured on 8-track; despite such a genesis, however, and the extended length of some tracks, there was very little self-indulgence displayed across *Washing Machine*. These tracks captured the peaks of improvisation the Youth discovered while noodling, and crafted them into songs, yielding some of their most tuneful confections yet: 'Unwind', a languid chime with Thurston's gentle vocal deftly underscored by Lee's natural tenor, and 'Little

Trouble Girl', Kim's heart-breaking lyric of a wayward daughter's guilt at her estrangement from her mother accompanied by Sixties girl-group harmonies from The Breeders' Kim Deal.

Lee contributed two songs to *Washing Machine*, the sky-gazing psychedelia of 'Saucer-Like' and 'Skip Tracer'; co-written with Ranaldo's wife Leah Singer and introduced live as a "talking blues", the song grew from observations the couple made while at a show by Riot Grrrl-affiliated indie-rock duo Mecca Normal, and referenced the Youth's crazy dalliance with Hollywood and the major labels. "L.A. is more confusing now than anywhere I've ever been to," howled Ranaldo. "I'm from New York City, breathe it out and let it in." Thurston's 'Junkie's Promise', an empathic – if not entirely sympathetic – heroin vignette, was interpreted by many as a tribute of sorts to Kurt Cobain, not least for a chorus that ran, "I heard you say, 'You know I hate myself but I love everybody else'/and did you say, 'I can't escape myself'/and then you did and now there's no one else". Commenting on such speculation via Sonic Youth's internet newsgroup alt.music.sonic-youth, Thurston responded that "'Junkie's Promise' is purely about the emotional relationship between friends, one of which is a user. Any individual involved with drug addiction will lie to his friends for the self-serving need. It's the cruelest truth of the situation. Kurt may fit this profile and he was surely in my mind as I wrote but the song is not a specific dedication to him."

Washing Machine marked the first Sonic Youth album where Kim often abandoned her bass in favour of playing third guitar, an approach that broadened the group's sonic palette, as evidenced on the album's two extended workouts. 'Washing Machine' spanned nine-and-a-half minutes with its elegant glide from scything, jerking punk-strut into blissful ambient groove, blossoming at 2:55 into a motorik chug that continues for the rest of the track, as the three guitars entwine with each other, distortion and feedback artfully manipulated until, six-and-a-half minutes in, the frazzling noise has built into an ear-piercing whiteout, elegantly dying away for the fade.

The studio take of 'The Diamond Sea' clocked in at 19-and-a-half minutes (an edit later released as a B-side would meander a further seven), its sad, wise Neil Young-esque ballad billowing into an epic noise excursion, guitars scraped and strummed and held perilously close to amplifiers to coax a roaring drone possessed of a most poignant, dramatic, emotive quality. Again, the ghost of Kurt Cobain lingers in Thurston's haunting, poetic lyric, in lines like, "Look into his eyes and you can see why all the little kids are dressed in dreams/I wonder how he's gonna make it back when he sees that you just know it's make-believe", and in the palpable sense of fragility and loss that pervades the piece. The track also echoed 'Elegy For All The Dead Rock Stars', a 20-minute instrumental closing Thurston Moore's first solo album for Geffen, 1995's *Psychic Hearts*; for that piece, Thurston chased slow, calming chords over 20 minutes, accompanied by Steve Shelley and Tim Foljahn. It was certainly one of the more profoundly challenging (not to mention rewarding) major-label releases of the era.

Referencing the more avant, out-there space-rock techniques the group explored in *Washing Machine*, Thurston told *Puncture* zine the album was "a product not so much of our influences, but of what each of us had been doing outside the group. For me it was playing with Japanese noise guitarists and listening to avant-garde stuff on underground cassette labels like Apraxia and Chocolate Monk. They're fascinating – punk is like disco to them, like bubble gum. They're into free-form jazz and German avant-garde composers. I went through a heavy period with that stuff, but there wasn't a big scene then, just No Wave really, and John Zorn. Now it's coming full force, and I'm sitting back wondering what's going to happen with it. Is it going to get big? I saw The Clash sell out the Palladium and I thought that was as big as punk would ever get. And now Green Day are selling millions of records. It's amusing to see this whole avant-garde underground growing up in reaction against punk.

"*Washing Machine* takes in some of that stuff, but it'll be weird because most people are unfamiliar with these cassette labels. They'll hear us and say, 'What the fuck is this?' The people who are familiar with it will think we're obnoxious, like we're ripping it off, making it mainstream. They'll say, 'How much did it cost to put that hiss on there?' I guess they have a point, but we're not trying to steal their underground."

Thurston had described the period following *Dirty* as a "spinning inwards", but in truth it resulted in a strengthening of the group's avant roots, an abandonment of the more traditional song-forms they'd adopted as they orbited as close as they'd get to the mainstream, in favour of following their music in whatever strange, wonderful, resolutely uncommercial directions it might take them. The major-label experiment had been a huge success, exposing them to a much wider audience, financing wonderful projects like the *Goo* video-album and, indeed, *Dirty* and *Goo*. But it seemed as if they'd taken their incursion into the malls of America as far as they could. It was time for a return to some kind of underground, dragging curious listeners they'd seduced from the mainstream with them. Sonic Youth may have helped "break" grunge, but it wasn't going to break them.

"I don't think Sonic Youth dumbed their shit down any, or co-opted, or compromised into any kind of mersh thing," says Mike Watt. "I'd never say anything those guys did was mersh; going back to my first experience with them, I just can't see them ever doing anything like that."

NOTES

[1] *Grrrls: Viva Rock Divas*, pg 150
[2] Author's interview, July 2002
[3] Author's interview, April 2007
[4] *Rolling Stone*, July 8th 1993
[5] Author's interview, May 2007
[6] *Grrrls: Viva Rock Divas*, pg 125
[7] Author's interview, April 2007
[8] *Women, Sex & Rock'n'Roll*, pg 175
[9] Author's interview, March 2004
[10] Author's interview, November 2003
[11] *Puncture* zine, 1994
[12] *Confusion Is Sex*, pg 19
[13] *Rolling Stone*, #681
[14] http://www.robertchristgau.com/get_artist.php?name=Sonic+Youth
[15] *Musician*, December 1995
[16] *The Lollapalooza '95 Tour Journals*, pg 50
[17] Author's interview, May 2007
[18] *The Lollapalooza '95 Tour Journals*, pg 4
[19] Author's interview, March 2007

CHAPTER ELEVEN

Goodbye 20th Century

"It's always been important to us to keep challenging ourselves. Every band, when they start writing new songs, shares a certain amount of suspended disbelief, where you have to feel you're starting for the first time. This record, I really felt like we were in our first rehearsal space, playing with that certain amount of freedom and lack of self-consciousness."[1]

Kim Gordon

Following the release of *Washing Machine* in September 1995, Sonic Youth spent the rest of that year, and most of the year that followed, touring the world, taking in locations both familiar and also very new, performing in Indonesia, Singapore, Thailand and the Philippines for the first time. As they neared the end of this tiring circuit, the group began to make plans that would offer them a sense of self-sufficiency and independence that endures to this day.

Late in 1996, they began work on Echo Canyon, a studio space of their own located on a floor of a multi-storey building in Murray Street, deep within New York's bustling financial area, under the shadow of the Twin Towers of the World Trade Centre. The location wasn't perfect; the other floors were used by nearby Wall Street traders who spent their downtime jamming in bad covers bands, and their lifeless versions of Pearl Jam and Red Hot Chili Peppers songs would often bleed into the studio. (Indeed, the group recorded an evening spent in pitched battle with their neighbours, trying to drown out the bad funk with distorted drone and fucked-up beatbox rhythms, and released that tape as the *Silver Session* EP in 1998, dedicated to Jason Knuth, music director for San Francisco radio station

KUSF and a keen Youth fanatic, who committed suicide that year; the release was in aid of the San Francisco Suicide Prevention Hotline.)

As Echo Canyon offered Sonic Youth the freedom to hone their new music without having to worry about studio bills or keep an eye on the clock, the group also started up their own independent label, Sonic Youth Records (aka SYR), via which they would release music that didn't really have a place on their Geffen releases. Not that the label had yet baulked at granting the Youth the creative freedom their contract protected. "After the first couple of records, the people that signed us to the label started vanishing," remembers Lee. "We tried to have a rapport with each person that tied us to the label, even though often we knew they weren't getting it really. As those people left, all of a sudden we didn't care if they got it or not."[2] However, perhaps sensing tensions in the future, as the commercial promise of "alternative rock" withered on the vine, SYR ensured the Youth would always have an avenue via which to release even their most avant waxings.

The first two releases on SYR served up shards of their intense woodshedding process, instrumental works-in-progress that jammed hard against any traditional notions of songcraft. These pieces meandered with inspiration, glancing from passages of pure noise experimentation through to exultant melodies emerging from the melee. The first SYR EP, *Anagrama*, was released via Steve's Smells Like Records mailing list in May 1997, hitting record stores a month later; its three instrumental pieces, while the most immediately accessible music that would be released on SYR, still prepared listeners for the excursions that would follow. 'Anagrama' built gradually from gentle chimes to a roaring, gloriously melodic symphony of squall before collapsing into an extended coda, echoing and refracting the original melody amidst the wreckage. 'Improvisation Ajoutée' was a brief passage of guitar noise and FX-pedal experimentation, while 'Tremens' was a three-minute vignette heavy with noir-esque menace, conjured by bleak, oily chords. 'Mieux: De Corrosion' closed out the disc with seven minutes of avant abstraction, treated and sequenced drum and cymbal tracks glitching in disharmony with roars of white-noise feedback, before a truly Neanderthal riff tore into the foreground, riding its heavy-metal thrills like some lunatic carnival ride. The track's free-form sensibility recalls the improvisational excursions of Bardo Pond, a Philadelphia space-rock group who legendarily composed their music while jamming in their rehearsal space while a block of hash cooked on a hibachi barbecue in the corner.

Where *Anagrama* titled its songs in French, the second EP, *Slaapkamers Met Slagroom*, took Dutch as its language when it surfaced in February 1997. The opening title track picked up where 'Mieux: De Corrosion' left off, the first 90 seconds a harsh, speaker-slicing mess of dissonant distortion and sibilant cymbal tone, before slipping into a dark, malevolent groove for a further six or so minutes until a series of tumbling drum rolls from Steve kicked the track into a fierce new velocity, the three Sonic guitars locked in violent conversation, emitting blasts of white noise and manipulated amp-tone until the fadeout, ten minutes later. 'Stil', meanwhile, closer resembled some jam-session by post-bop jazz cats, bells and cymbals rattling as Kim, Lee and Thurston pulled tranquil textures and tones from their interweaving noise guitars, Moore threading a sad-eyed Neil Young-esque melody through the calmed chaos. 'Herinneringen' closed the set, breaking from SYR tradition by featuring vocals, cut-up sounds and twisted words from Kim, disjointed and seemingly meaningless though they were. For all its playful toying with structure, 'Herinneringen' was the most openly pop moment the SYR series countenanced; "pop" as Kim's beloved Swiss post-punk group Liliput heard it, anyway.

The group played few shows throughout 1997, and those they did perform were composed entirely of new songs they were developing at Echo Canyon, mostly in instrumental form. In January, they backed David Bowie for a performance of his song 'I'm Afraid Of Americans' at Bowie's all-star 50th birthday party at Madison Square Garden; in March, billed as 'Male Slut' (a nom du rock Thurston's *Psychic Hearts* band used when touring his album), the group played three instrumentals at The Cooler; Thurston also accompanied jazz drummer Rashied Ali, famed for his work with John and Alice Coltrane and Pharoah Sanders, on guitar for an improvised set. In June, they played some more instrumental sets at Anchorage in Brooklyn, The Beastie Boys' all-star Tibetan Freedom Concert at Randall's Island, and a session filmed at West 54th Studio for broadcast on PBS. The group also debuted 'Hits Of Sunshine', a long, languid song featuring low-key vocals from Thurston, unspooling scattered Beat poetics. The song was written in tribute to Beat legend Allan Ginsberg, a friend and hero to the group, who passed away in April 1997.

The group played a couple of further shows that summer, debuting more new material, and including 'Sunday' in their set list (written and recorded the year before for Richard Linklater's movie adaptation of Eric Bogosian's play *subUrbia*). While Lee toured Europe with jazz drummer and composer William Hooker in October, Kim, Thurston and Steve played CBGB for the premiere party of Jim Jarmusch's documentary *Year Of The Horse*, chronicling the live adventures of Neil Young and his hardy touring band; present for the party were Jarmusch, Iggy Pop, Joey Ramone, Lenny Kaye, Little Steven of Bruce Springsteen's E Street Band, and Neil Young himself. Their final show of 1997 took place at Avery Fisher Music Hall, home of the New York Philharmonic Orchestra; for the performance, audience-members were handed a programme listing the songs in the order they would be played that night, with notations indicating that Thurston would sing vocals on 'Hits Of Sunshine' and the closing 'Sunday', and Kim for 'Heather Angel'. Tom Verlaine opened for the group.

These new songs would mostly remain in this embryonic, instrumental form until late into the production of their next Geffen-released full-length, *A Thousand Leaves*. "Because of the circumstances, the material evolved both faster and slower this time," said Steve. "Since the studio and rehearsal room were one and the same, the songs were generally caught in a very early stage of development. I think they'll change a lot when we're out on the road playing them. By December, they'll be very different and ready for our Budokan live record!"[3]

As Steve intimated, the album had a very loose and unfinished quality, different from *EJST&NS* in that those songs had fully incubated in the greenhouse of Echo Canyon and, in some cases, onstage. Rather, *A Thousand Leaves* had a ragged, sleepy-eyed ambience, evidenced by the marvellous guitar interplay that closes Lee's 'Karen Koltrane', truncated by the ill-timed end of a roll of tape, and a track sequence that was jarring (and, indeed, undecided until the very last moment). The album opened with one of Sonic Youth's most atmospheric, avant and free-form songs yet, Kim's 'Contre Le Sexisme': a vaporous cloud of amp-rumble, percussive rustle, and Kim's eerie sing-song toying with imagery from *Alice In Wonderland*, it was no '100%', capturing the group at their least instantly accessible.

There were a few tracks that resembled the rhapsodic Sonic songs of before, though they were scattered between more abstruse pieces seemingly evading any simplistic instinct to "rock", in favour of detours and meanders that yield moments of inspired improvisation, if not the glorious crescendos some may have expected. "Rather than the idea-every-minute of the last few albums," wrote Ben Ratliff in *Rolling Stone*, "the songs plod for long stretches. It really does sound like a demo, 11 songs waiting for better organisation and cliché removal."[4]

If anything, what the album lacked were the very clichés that had helped uninitiated listeners negotiate their way through Sonic Youth's dense forest of avant technique; a reworked take of 'Sunday' inched perhaps as close to conventional as the Youth were willing to go, Thurston's deadpan evocation of suburban ennui riding a sensual, motorik chug that coursed with electricity and blossomed into free squall. Elsewhere, songs hung by a thread from abstraction and chaos, the noise seeming to pull into song-shapes by whim; Kim's closing 'Heather Angel' flitted from ominous chime, to formless avant clanging, to a brutal punk strum a la 'Eliminator Jr' within six minutes, an inspired chaos but also, perhaps, an acquired taste. "This is a band, remember, that learned more than 15 years ago how to write mean song hooks," continued Ratliff, voicing the frustration of the corner of the Youth fanbase least inured to their artful skronk. "Now, however, they've ditched artifice and made their version of an Iron Butterfly record: nearly every song is a supermonolithic bummer."

Again, it was up to the group's old nemesis, Robert Christgau, to recognise *A Thousand Leaves*' true qualities. "Where a decade ago they plunged and plodded," he wrote, "drunk on the forward notion of the van they were stuck in, here they wander at will, dazzled by sunshine, greenery, hoarfrost, and machines that go squish in the night."[5] *A Thousand Leaves* was a leisurely, pastoral album, homespun and rough at the edges, happening upon an unhurried, almost rural ambience in the oxygen-starved heart of the big city. This was evidenced on Lee's elemental 'Hoarfrost' and Thurston's uplifting 'Wildflower Soul', a nine-minute epic that echoed the golden scree of *Daydream Nation*, albeit in a deftly skewed, anarchic manner, all messy and beautiful feedback roar. Kim's breathy 'French Tickler', meanwhile, offered a most seductive domestic eroticism.

The album title was a sly reference to Walt Whitman's *Leaves Of Grass*, Thurston commenting that "there's a lot of his 'New England Mysticism' that we aspire to, the way his words seem to breathe, and have colour, and shape, and texture. I'm also playing with the same type of evocation; the same way he improvised with images and words, we improvise with sounds and notes." It was an album wonderfully haunted by the spirits of Allen Ginsberg, Jerry Garcia and William S. Burroughs, all of whom had passed away in the months preceding these sessions. However, the reception the album received in some corners, and the indifference it stirred in outlets like MTV, suggested Sonic Youth were poets in a land more attuned to copywriters and jinglesmiths.

> "Sonic Youth just wanked everything I hate about them into one convenient tissue."[6]
>
> Unnamed audience member of *Goodbye 20th Century* performance

Sonic Youth spent most of 1998 touring *A Thousand Leaves* across the world, playing sets compiled almost entirely of material from the album and the SYR series. 'Shadow Of A Doubt' returned to the set list after a 12-year absence on this tour, while shows would often climax with an extended, murderous 'Death Valley '69'. Captured for posterity by television cameras, their performance at the Benicassim in Barcelona was majestic, the final tolls of 'Death Valley' giving way to a stretch of violently beautiful improvisation, Steve rattling a tambourine across his drum kit, Thurston sawing his guitar across his amplifier, Lee feeding FX pedal spray through a Moog, and Kim cooing the lyrics from 'Contre Le Sexisme' while crouched on the stage, strobes flashing and searchlights casting shadows of the guitarists many feet tall upon the backdrop. Cameras scanned the faces of the teens squashed against the barriers, rapt in awe at the noise unfurling before them.

As ever, the support acts for these shows referenced the new developments occurring within the underground, tremors sensed early by the Youth: dark Canadian avant-garde noiseniks Godspeed You! Black Emperor; Chicago post-rockers Tortoise; San Francisco improvisational noise-pop group Deerhoof; New Mexico trio The Rondelles, who spliced Riot Grrrl, twee-pop and Fifties girl-group smarts, and were signed to Steve Shelley's Smells Like Records; and San Francisco's slack-savant indie group Fuck, to name just a few. In Europe, several festival shows were rained off mid-show by severe freak storms, while in New York they wreaked tight havoc in the studios of *The David Letterman Show* with 'Sunday', released as a single and trailed by a Harmony Korine clip starring fast-maturing child actor Macaulay Culkin.

At an in-store performance at San Francisco's sprawling Amoeba record store, the Youth engaged in a 45-minute improvisation with Jim O'Rourke. A mainstay of the Chicago scene that yielded Tortoise, O'Rourke's credits as both a musician and a producer were impressive, having worked with dryly dark balladeer Smog, chaotic "Now Wave" avant-punks US Maple, James Chance-influenced maverick Bobby Conn and brilliant Dayton, Ohio electro-punks Brainiac. His work as a member of Gastr del Sol, a duo formed with David Grubbs, was legendary within all manner of underground communities, essaying post-rock, avant-electronica and sweeping chamber-pop; his solo work further pursued this eclectic vision. He'd also collaborated with Sonic Youth on the third release for their SYR label, *Invito Al Cielo* (the language this time was Esperanto, the purportedly international tongue that never quite took off anywhere in the world). The 50-minute disc excerpted highlights from an afternoon spent jamming in Echo Canyon, subject to manipulations by O'Rourke via his laptop, serving up a riot-drone of time-stretch noise and discordant horn ('Invito Al Cielo'), a luminous and hypnotic vibraphone piece digitally treated so it sounded like it was being played underwater ('Hungara Vivo'), and an extended, slow, dramatic instrumental, where the avant-guitar techniques sounded like space debris burning up on re-entry ('Radio-Amatoroj').

O'Rourke was an old friend of the group. "Thurston met Jim in a record store in England in '91," remembers Lee. "I think Jim actually came up and asked Thurston for an autograph. Jim wasn't really into the kind of music we played back then, but he recognised Thurston, and they had a conversation. Jim and I worked on a piece together in the early Nineties for some European art-music festival where I gave him a piece of me reading a text of one of my pieces and he doctored it and turned it into a musical collage based just on the vocal." O'Rourke had stayed in touch with the group throughout the decade, and for some of the American leg of the *A Thousand Leaves* tour, played support, creating music on his laptop, accompanied on occasion by drummer Marcus Pop of the experimental group Oval.

Accompanying O'Rourke and the Youth at Amoeba was William Winant, a highly respected percussionist who had worked alongside John Cage during the last 10 years of his life, also collaborating with John Zorn, new-wave group Oingo Boingo (who also featured venerated soundtrack composer Danny Elfman among their number), and Mr Bungle, the gleefully avant project of Faith No More frontman Mike Patton, who was fast earning his credentials as the post-grunge Zappa. Winant and O'Rourke would prove crucial components in the next Sonic Youth project, a brave step into the unknown that proved, decisively, that signing to a major had not curtailed the Youth's wilful ambition.

* * *

April 1999 found the four members of Sonic Youth cramped in the control room of Echo Canyon, stood before a beaten-up old upright piano, preparing to perform a piece of music scored by George Maciunas, a Lithuanian-born member of the Fluxus art movement who owned and maintained several SoHo lofts to house lowly artists. These musicians might attack a guitar with a screwdriver or a drumstick with not a second's squeamishness, or wreak wonderfully sadistic art upon innocent amplifiers; still, little could prepare people for the near-sacrilegious assault that followed, as Sonic Youth proceeded to hammer nails into the keys of the piano, as the tapes rolled. Hair cut unusually short, looking in his blazer and blue Oxford shirt like an oversized schoolboy, Thurston was first up, gingerly tapping his nail into the ivory, the vibrations from his hammer stirring a quiet moan from the piano strings. The rest of the group followed suit; minutes later, as all four crowded about the instrument, the keyboard was a mess of splintered wood and ivory, and nails, lots of them, pinning the keys down.

And so ran *Goodbye 20th Century*, the fourth release on SYR, Sonic Youth collaborating with a number of "highbrow" avant-garde musicians to present performances of works by 20th-century composers. The project was about as far removed from an album like *Dirty* as possible, and yet Sonic Youth approached this new "experiment" with the same energy, enthusiasm and focus. It was a project that risked failure on all fronts, alienating the remnants of their newly won Alternakid fanbase, and incurring accusations of dilettanteism from the "serious" music scene; it was also a project born of genuine artistic curiosity on the part of the Sonic musicians, a brave leap into the unknown for a group long fond of such a thrill. Ultimately, whatever critical brickbats it weathered and fair-weather fans it jettisoned were outbalanced by the respect *Goodbye 20th Century* won them. "We never would have dreamed of even having the 'pretension' to do something like *Goodbye 20th Century* 10 years ago," reflected Lee. "And it opened this whole other avenue of stuff we can do; we could play 20th-century music for the next five years without ever playing a rock show if we wanted, in terms of the offers we've gotten from big prestigious art venues."

William Winant selected the pieces, choosing works scored for smaller ensembles, which all the musicians could play; Lee Ranaldo was assigned the job of contacting the composers and collecting scores from the publishers. Of particular interest to him was a piece by Steve Reich, 'Pendulum Music', which recorded the sounds made by swinging microphones over prone amplifiers. "'Pendulum Music' was a piece I had long been aware of," he explained, "mainly from Reich's book *Writings About Music*, but I'd never heard it. We had to make a few attempts as swinging microphones kept slamming into the stands and interrupting the piece! The odd thing is, having known of the piece only from its written description, it sounded exactly as I pictured it would. It had always seemed an important early piece in Reich's oeuvre (in a way directly foreseeing the phase pieces which came later), and indicative of the free spirit and experimentation of the time as well. When I told Steve Reich we were planning to record it he just laughed..."[7]

One of two Cage pieces the ensemble recorded, 'Four6', had actually been written for Winant; engineer Wharton Tiers recorded several different takes of the half-hour piece with the band divided into two quartets, one numbering Winant, Thurston, Lee and violinist and composer Takehisa Kosugi, the other featuring Kim, Steve, Tiers and Jim O'Rourke. Playing two takes alongside each other, split into separate channels, the double-quartet essays an engrossing 30 minutes of squall, drone, percussive bristle, improvisational vocal play and all manner of sonic trickery, happening upon many thrilling moments in its murky meander. New York composer and accordionist Pauline Oliveros wrote a piece especially for the project, after Winant approached her about performing her 'To Valerie Solanas And Marilyn Monroe, In Recognition Of Their Suffering'; 'Six For New Time (For Sonic Youth)', performed by the core sextet, recalled the Youth's own 'Early American' with its turbulent chime.

Turntablist and visual artist Christian Marclay accompanied the group for a version of French-born experimental composer Christian Wolff's 'Burdocks', which also featured Wolff himself (Wolff also guested on his piece 'Edges', with Kim murmuring a dry retelling of *Goldilocks And The Three Bears* amid the drone). Kosugi, meanwhile, updated his graphic score for '+ –' especially for the project. The ensemble relished the open-endedness of the more conceptual pieces, like James Tenney's 'Having Never Written A Note For Percussion'. "Tenney had all these compositions for solo instruments that were musical analogs of Zen koans," explained Winant, "musical questions to ponder that would bring enlightenment."[8] A four-year-old Coco Hayley Gordon Moore also featured as vocalist, for Yoko Ono's 'Voice Piece For Soprano', performing three blood-curdling screams.

On April 1, 1999 at the Bowery Ballroom, the group headlined a bill numbering many Sonic Youth offshoots – Lee and wife Leah performing as a duo, Kim playing alongside former DNA drummer and John Zorn collaborator Ikue Mori and Brooklyn turntablist DJ Olive (the trio would record the fifth SYR release in 2000), and Thurston jamming with William Winant and Tom Surgal, a member of New York experimental duo Whiteout. Following these turns, the members of the Youth took the stage, accompanied by Winant and O'Rourke and Tiers and Takehisa Kosugi, to perform the pieces indicated upon the four-page programme handed out to the audience, including reproductions of the scores for the pieces, unconventional manuscripts like Kosugi's graphic maze of pluses and minuses, or Ono's minimal directions for 'Voice Piece For Soprano':

"Scream
1. against the wind
2. against the wall
3. against the sky"[9]

At the close of Cage's 'Four6', the musicians took their bows and left the stage; "Thank you, ladies and gentlemen, for listening" said Thurston to the audience. "Jim O'Rourke, Lee Ranaldo, William Winant, Steve Shelley, Wharton Tiers, Kim Gordon, Takehisa Kosugi... Thank you, goodnight."

The performance proved a success, and the Youth would reprise their take on Tenney's 'Having Never Written A Note For Percussion' at their next show, playing on a bill with The New York Art Quartet (legendary free-jazzers reformed for the event and accompanied by long-time collaborator, poet Amiri Baraka) as part of the annual Bell Atlantic Jazz Festival, at Seaport Atrium in New York.

The following April, the group performed another, unusual set, at Camber Sands in the UK. The holiday camp, a relic from the days before cheap airflights, when Britain's domestic tourist industry still thrived, played host to the inaugural All Tomorrow's Parties, a festival for underground and experimental rock music founded as an alternative to the increasingly corporate rock festivals that took place in the summer. Curated by Glaswegian noise-rockers Mogwai, the festival featured performances from groups like Bardo Pond, Steve Albini's Shellac, and Godspeed You! Black Emperor, the three-day bill offering fearsome and unfamiliar rock thrills. On the final night, the Youth played an adventurous set – in keeping, they thought, with the mindset of the festival – that juggled embryonic and instrumental versions of songs from their next album, and opened with a half-hour improv piece, Kim's 'J'Accuse Ted Hughes'. "Their set was a fiasco, but I rather enjoyed it," remembers music critic Steve Jelbert, reviewing the festival for *The Independent*. "My friend passed out during the first song, and was taken outside and administered smelling salts. A while later, when she was feeling better, we returned to the venue and the group was still playing the same song. The fans were standing around looking a bit disgruntled."[10]

"I kept waiting for them to play a 'song'," remembers Keith Cameron. "And it became increasingly apparent they *weren't* going to play any songs. Afterwards, they came back on and played 'Sunday'. But by then it was too late." The Youth had assumed that, as a festival for underground music, the audience at Camber Sands would appreciate the group operating at their most avant and experimental. "But the punters had had 48 hours of 'challenge'," continues Cameron. "They felt they'd done their bit for 'art' and now wanted to see Sonic Youth 'rock'. And they didn't rock. It was a bit teeth-gnashing; obviously, respect to the arts and everything, but *I'd* had enough at that stage."[11]

Thurston: "We thought it was going along very well [laughs]. But after we got offstage, we got a very cold reception from people, you know, like, 'Why did you do that?' Critically, we were just completely killed by the British newspapers."

Kim: "You're really exaggerating the whole thing..."

Thurston: "I don't think I'm exaggerating enough! The *NME* said it was 'shite'. Maybe I *am* mythologising the denigration…"[12]

But the ATP stumble didn't shake the group's resolve to explore this more avant side to their live performances, to testing the boundaries of what Sonic Youth could do or be, indeed attempting to prove that said boundaries didn't actually exist. A month later, the group played a unique set in Paris' breathtaking Pompidou Centre, the Youth collaborating with Jim O'Rourke, composer and multi-instrumentalist Areski Belkacem, and avant-garde chanteuse Brigitte Fontaine on a series of improvisational pieces, recorded and filmed for later release.

In October 2000, the Youth travelled to Ystad in Sweden for a week-long workshop conducted with a local contemporary arts museum. For the first two evenings, they played group sets followed by an ensemble improvisation, accompanied by avant musicians like saxophonist Mats Gustafsson, guitarist Loren Mazzacane Connors and percussionist Sven-Åke Johansson; during the second night, Lee's contribution to the improv consisted of clowning with a cardboard cut-out of a cello, while Kim gave Thurston a haircut. For the rest of the week, group members collaborated with other artists and musicians for a series of pieces that sometimes explored other media, each night curated by a different member of the group (Gustafsson and Connors each curated a night also), as part of the Kulturbro 2000 festival.

The following year, having completed promotional duties for their 2000 release on Geffen, *NYC Ghosts & Flowers*, the Youth took the *Goodbye 20th Century* set on tour across Europe, joined by O'Rourke and Winant and any number of European avant-garde luminaries who had befriended the group on previous sorties across the continent. In addition to the pieces performed at the Bowery Ballroom two years previously, the ensemble also added 'Burdocks', 'Treatise' and 'Six' from *Goodbye 20th Century* to their repertoire, along with Steve Reich's 'Clapping Music' and a piece by Dutch composer Konrad Boehmer composed especially for the group, 'Echelon', performed in Amsterdam with Boehmer conducting.

"The tour was a great success," says Ranaldo. "There were occasionally crowds that were a little confused, people who expected they'd hear 'Teenage Riot', and we weren't doing that stuff. So there were your handful of disgruntled fans. In London, that handful was very loud [laughs]."

"It was like a *war* in the audience," adds Thurston. "During the silent parts, like in the Cage piece, some guy in the back yelled, 'This is crap!' And then another guy in the front row yelled back, "Why don't you go home, mate?" It was nutty."

The London show took place at the Royal Festival Hall, a grand concert hall overlooking the south bank of the River Thames; Glenn Branca performed an opening set before Sonic Youth took the stage, later accompanied by Laetitia Sadler of Stereolab, and Band of Susans' Susan Stenger for 'Four6'. "The RFH show had been sold very specifically as a *Goodbye 20th Century* show," remembers Frances Morgan, in attendance that night. "It was obviously not a typical Sonic Youth gig. A lot of people didn't enjoy it – all around me people were shifting uneasily, looking bored or loudly signalling their dissatisfaction. I interviewed the band later, and Jim O'Rourke ascribed it to 'extra-musical reasons'; it wasn't really to do with the music, it was to do with expectations. They said it was only in England that they'd had that response; in Europe, and in the US, people were interested and appreciative. He implied that we have an inverse snobbery towards people who do things that are 'a bit weird'.

"And there *was* an element of that. These people were behaving like the group were *charlatans*. They'll always get that reception. They'll always sell out venues when they play such shows, and about half the people there will genuinely like it, and a few will really hate it, and think they're *really* pretentious. But they can't stop themselves buying a ticket anyway, because they know they'll get a few old songs in the encore."[13]

Whatever the reception, the music the group released on the SYR label, along with the *Goodbye 20th Century* performances, and any number of obscure side-projects, asserted Sonic Youth's ambition, their fearlessness, and their ability to adapt their aesthetic and their approach to new and diverse challenges. Their excursions in the realms of modern composition reaffirmed the respect the avant-garde community held for the Youth, while the more curious minds within their audience were exposed to a new world of music, trusting a group who'd perhaps led them towards hardcore, No Wave or any other music Sonic Youth drew upon for inspiration. These recordings and performances also opened up new horizons for a group who'd increasingly found themselves alienated from the corporate alterna-rock scene they'd helped found.

"There's all these different things opening up to do," reasons Ranaldo. "Things that incorporate what we do as Sonic Youth. And maybe our relationship to the pop world will change drastically; maybe it already has, I don't know. I can see us going on for quite a long time, especially because of the way we have lots of time to do stuff on our own individually. You never can predict how long bands are going to go on. We never would have predicted Sonic Youth lasting this long, and yet at the same time, in the early days I don't think any of us imagined it was going to be a flash thing that was going to end in a couple weeks, or in a couple years even. We always thought we had something good and it continued to be something worth doing. And I still think that."

> "Hello all, this is Lee from Sonic Youth here, we have had a fucked-up situation come down on us over this last night – a brand new Ryder truck parked at a Ramada Inn in Orange County with ALL OF OUR GEAR IN IT was STOLEN! All of our guitars, tools, amplifiers, drums, synth – EVERYTHING. We are fucked, both for the show tonight at the This Ain't No Picnic here in Orange Co., and for shows upcoming this week in Austin and Santa Fe. Our guitars are all mostly older and either very modified and/or fucked-up/beat up. They are unmistakably ours. This is really serious… all the gear we've used to write our last few LPs worth of stuff, instruments used for songs old and new which if truly lost will mean those songs will be lost forever."[14]
>
> Lee Ranaldo email, July 4 1999

The New York in which Sonic Youth recorded their 13th album was a very different city to the one in which the group had cut their eponymous debut mini-LP almost 20 years earlier. The election to office of Rudy Giuliani in 1993 yielded the city its first Republican mayor since 1965, following the troubled term of predecessor David Dinkins, just as the latter seemed to be turning the tide on high crime figures. Giuliani cracked down on petty crime and the homeless, graffiti artists and "squeegee men", in a bid to clear the streets of crime; he also threatened to cut off funding to the Brooklyn Museum for exhibiting the *Sensation* exhibit, featuring Chris Ofili's portrait of the Virgin Mary in elephant dung, closed homeless shelters, and sold public spaces and community gardens to private investors. He declared that music venues needed expensive and limited cabaret licenses if there was to be any dancing on the premises, closing a number of clubs in the process. Other music venues went the way of artist loft spaces and cheap rehearsal rooms, driven out and expunged by New York's fast-rising real estate prices.

"From the Bronx to the Lower East Side to Brooklyn, there had been a systematic ghetto-isation of these areas," says Lydia Lunch, "because ultimately, the bankers and real estate agents knew that if they broke it down to rubble, they could come back five or six years later with rents that were four or five or six times as high. Mike Davis wrote this incredible book, *Dead Cities*, about what they did to New York and the Bronx to make it what it was, so it could become what it is now, which is Disneyland."[15]

In clearing away all the vagrants and selling off the public spaces, in disinfecting its neighbourhoods of the vibrant artistic communities that gathered in its murky corners, Giuliani was killing the soul of the city, reducing it to lucrative office space. The anger this stirred in Sonic Youth, a vital part of that community, four artists drawn to live in the city by its rich cultural heritage, was channelled into *NYC Ghosts & Flowers*.

The group that recorded the album was markedly different too, not least in their artillery of instruments; on the night of July 3, while the band slept before their appearance at the next day's This Ain't No Picnic festival in Irvine, California, their Ryder truck containing their guitars, amps and other precious, irreplaceable gear was stolen. They played their set on borrowed equipment that could barely approximate the idiosyncratic voices of their modified thrift-store guitars; the reality swiftly dawned upon the group that they wouldn't be able to play a large portion of their back catalogue without the unique instruments they'd written and recorded them on, such as Thurston's "drifter" guitar, a cheap Les Paul copy with its frets ripped out, strung with bass-strings, its knobs taped over with duct tape, crucial to performances of 'Eric's Trip'.

"We bought a bunch of cheapo guitars," remembers Thurston, "and played a set of older songs. And it was really interesting doing them, because we thought, 'God, these songs are so simple'; basically we just hammered and bashed. It was really enlightening in that way. When we got back to New York, we didn't immediately replicate our set-up, we looked around the studio and picked up remnants."

"It made me appreciate vintage guitars," offers Kim. "There's definitely a difference between a new Fender and an old one. I had two Gibson SGs that I could never afford now; I bought them back when they were really cheap."

But as the group began to familiarise themselves with old instruments lurking in the deepest recesses of Echo Canyon, and set about performing fresh surgery on virgin thrift-store guitars, finding the riffs and tones hiding within them, the theft seemed something of a blessing in disguise. "It had gotten to a point where we had developed with our equipment, and were so settled in with it that we felt very confident and comfortable with what we had," says Thurston. "And all of a sudden, it was gone. When we began *NYC Ghosts & Flowers*, we felt somewhat renewed. We flirted with the idea that we're such an old band, let's be a new band."

"It was never supposed to be about relying on the equipment..." says Gordon.

"But we *did* get reliant on the equipment,"[16] nods Moore.

The songs contained on *NYC Ghosts & Flowers* had been debuted in instrumental form throughout their 1999 tours (indeed, the first two instrumentals in the set list were lost forever with the Ryder truck theft). Having recorded the bulk of the album with Wharton Tiers, the group contacted Jim O'Rourke, who came down to the studios to artfully fuck with the recordings, and cut a couple of extra tracks. "He didn't write that material with us," explains Lee, "but he mixed it and played some bass. And at that point we said, 'We're about to go out on tour, would you like to come and tour with us and be part of the band and learn some of the other songs?' He was hanging around in New York more, and he wanted to get out of Chicago, and we just started doing projects together more and more. It was very natural, it wasn't like we were looking for either a producer or a new member or anything like that, and I don't think he was looking for anything from Sonic Youth outside of friendship. It just kinda turned into something else."

In addition to playing bass on 'Free City Rhymes' and 'Small Flowers Crack Concrete', and adding electronic scree to Kim's 'Side2Side', O'Rourke's main influence on the album was to pull its more diffuse concepts into tighter focus. An earlier instrumental take of 'Free City Rhymes', available as an mp3 from the group's website, captures that song's beguiling, scattered, meditative chime; on *NYC Ghosts & Flowers,* however, O'Rourke's mix subtly shifts the foreground between the interlacing guitars, giving the track a carefree momentum that builds to a dynamic climax and eerie coda. Eschewing *A Thousand Leaves'* loose structures, its meandering pathways, the music on *NYC Ghosts & Flowers* played its avant gestures to the fore, cutting straight to its *ideas*, be it the hypnotic pulse and overlapping vocals of Kim's 'Side2Side', or the floor-shaking riot-strum of 'Renegade Princess'.

The album served as a celebration of (and memorial to) the fast-disappearing cultural subterranea of New York, the manhole-cover printed on the disc suggesting it as a conduit to this very underground. Thurston's 'Small Flowers Crack Concrete' paid tribute to anti-establishment poet d. a. levy, and rumours that his gunshot suicide covered up his murder by the authorities; the song's narrative played out scenes of cops breaking up hippy communes in cool beatnik spiel: "Narcotic squads sweep thru poet dens, Spilling coffee, grabbing 15-yr-old runaway girls… The narcs beat the bearded oracles, Replacing tantric love with complete violence". The imagery of the police swarming into the wilderness, dispersing the poets and the hippies, served as a powerful metaphor for how Giuliani was socially cleansing New York of its cultural heritage, its gnarly but potent nightlife; equally, the search "for the heart of d. a. levy, And the mind he left behind" served as evidence of the enduring, subversive power of words, even in the absence of the poet himself.

"*NYC Ghosts* definitely aimed to reference that culture in a way that was serious," confirmed Thurston, of the album's debt to the Beats. "As far as wanting to accept being part of that lineage, it is somewhat of a very fringe culture. It's recognised in rock'n'roll quite a bit, you have people like Patti Smith or Lou Reed. But there's no depiction of that lineage in our generation. Patti's generation is sort of the last of them. Moving there in the Seventies, New York has since become really familial. However, although it's always in a flux, New York has become such a different thing to what it was. It might be the end of whatever bohemian world existed there; it's being shut down. It's really scattered, and the idea of the city being in the flashpoint of cultural information has really changed. We felt like, existing in that time, it was interesting to reflect on that."

"The stuff that came after the Beats," added Kim, "the whole youth culture of the Sixties, became co-opted in the Seventies. But the literary world and art world stayed kind of as a subculture, and that's interesting."[17]

The album delivered Sonic Youth's first ever title track, an epic piece written by Lee clocking in at 7:47, an acrid talking-blues fabling the bohemia fast ebbing from New York's streets, a lament for all the city was losing. Ranaldo's lyrics spun a tale heavy with metaphor and Beat poetics, conjuring a romantic memory of what was, his blood running ice cold at the discovery of its absence, at the waste and the loss. "He's turned to dust now, one of the chosen few," he murmurs, over mordant guitar scrape. "Left out in the rain, out of town." As Ranaldo picks over the relics left of the vibrant culture that first drew him to the city, and examines a New York fast becoming as bland and surface-focused as the mainstream culture to which it was, for so long, a much-needed antidote, the guitars pull back to build a brooding, bristling and ultimately deafening wall of noise, into which Lee sings his closing words, his voice straining poignantly above the din. "I hear your voice, I speak your name," he sings, "Will we meet, to run again, through New York City Ghosts and Flowers?"

* * *

Upon the release of *NYC Ghosts & Flowers* on May 16, 2000, Pitchforkmedia.com, a fast-growing and influential music webzine covering the indie scene in depth, pulled no punches and responded with a showboating 0.0 score. "Now, finally, my generation has its *Metal Machine*

Music," frothed Brent DiCrescenzo, referencing Reed's impish 1975 double set of white noise and feedback, beloved of Lester Bangs and Sonic Youth. "At least Lou Reed had the good grace to keep his mouth shut on his grinding hallmark of pretentious ejaculation... These 40+ year olds continue to operate under the perception that they matter. However, one of the prerequisites for being 'experimental' or 'underground' is that, down the road, somebody has to be influenced by the work and appropriate elements into the common collective. The minimal noodling on *NYC Ghosts & Flowers* merely retreads the rancid corpses of beat poetry and avant-garde noise."[18]

More august organs graced the album with a kinder and, perhaps, more informed gaze, the bruised songcraft and new concision displayed on *NYC Ghosts & Flowers* bearing no resemblance in form or intention to Reed's noise pieces. "*Ghosts* is almost Luther Vandross' idea of a noise-rock album," wrote Greg Kot, in *Rolling Stone*. "Songs like the erotically charged 'Side2Side' display the band's gift for understatement and feathery feel for dissonance. The album comes as a reminder of not only how far Sonic Youth have traveled but how high they can still reach."[19] Christgau, meanwhile, awarded the group their tenth "A" grade in his *Consumer's Guide*, declaring that "heard refracting the dusk on the Taconic Parkway or spattering through the rain on Second Avenue, its refusal to distinguish between abrasive and tender or man-made and natural is a compelling argument for their continuing to do whatever they damn well feel like."

In his review, Kot observed O'Rourke's electronic manipulations and noted that he fit with the group as naturally as if he were "a long-lost fifth band member". As the group prepared to tour their new album, they invited Jim to come along, inaugurating him as their newly anointed fifth member. "We were having so much fun with Jim that we invited him to come play his parts on the road," remembers Steve. "I was always looking forward to that Eno "studio treatment" thing, and I think Jim really wanted to play in a traditional band, to play bass and guitar, and dual leads with Thurston."[20] These were the roles O'Rourke would fulfil within the band, allowing Kim to move over to guitar or, on renditions of 'Drunk Butterfly' and 'Kool Thing' from their era with Jim, ditch her instruments altogether in favour of simply singing and dancing.

"Jim's an amazing musician," says Mike Watt. "He was really important for the band, because they'd been together a long time, so it was great to bring in some fresh perspectives. Huge knowledge of films and arts. He's a great cat too, no 'dominating ego' – sort of like the traditional role of the bass player, he nurtures. But he can play all kinds of shit, guitar, PowerBook, whatever. He's like grout – most people walk into the bathroom and they look at the tiles; Jim's like the grout, in that situation. He makes music on his own too, so I guess that makes him secure enough that he doesn't have to bogart his ego. Also, he made them five, he's the tie breaker. That's the thing about trios and quintets, unlike quartets you can't have any deadlock. They can make decisions a lot quicker."[21]

NOTES

1 *We Rock So You Don't Have To*, pg 17
2 Radio interview on WPRB, August 10th, 2002
3 *A Thousand Leaves* press release, Byron Coley
4 *Rolling Stone*, May 6 1998
5 http://www.robertchristgau.com
6 http://www.subsiren.com/articles/article19.html
7 http://www.sonicyouth.com/history/misc/pendulum-lee.html
8 *Bananafish* zine #13, August 1999
9 http://www.sonicyouth.com/mustang/cc/sy040199c.jpg
10 Author's interview, May 2007
11 Author's interview, March 2007
12 *The Wire*, March 2002
13 Author's interview, April 2007
14 http://sonicyouth.com/history/misc/index.html
15 Author's interview, February 2007
16 Jerry Thackray interview, July 2005
17 *Sleazenation*, 2001
18 http://www.pitchforkmedia.com/article/record_review/21889-nyc-ghosts-flowers
19 *Rolling Stone*, June 8 2000
20 The Watt From Pedro radio show, March 17th 2007
21 Author's interview, March 2007

CHAPTER TWELVE

Radical Adults Lick Godhead Style

"When I meet people who ask me what I do, I say, 'I play in a band; they're like The Beatles, but more fucked up.'"

Kim Gordon

The April 21, 2001 issue of *NME* arrived on news-stands without the customary photograph of some young indie-rock star on the cover; instead, the paper adapted Milton Graser's iconic rebus from his 1977 advertising campaign promoting tourism in the Big Apple to declare, via slab serif typeface and pictogram, "We ♥ NY". With a tagline reading, "Bands! Tunes! Drugs! Action!", the issue offered an indie-fan's guide to New York, the city?s rock scene enjoying a resurgence of interest thanks to the media buzz surrounding local five-piece The Strokes.

The striking cover feature arrived at a point when the paper's fortunes were at a low ebb. Sales had fallen since the music press' most recent heyday, the mid-Nineties Britpop phenomenon, as the magazines scrambled, and failed, to catch the next trend in pop. Indeed, by 2001 most of *NME*'s competition had folded – the last of its weekly nemeses, *Melody Maker*, had closed its doors the year before – and later that year *NME*'s sales would be overtaken by *Kerrang!*, a weekly specialist heavy metal magazine. However, this New York issue would prove a fortuitous step for the paper, which discovered in the photogenic Strokes circulation-boosting cover stars the likes of which they'd not seen since Blur and Oasis' prime.

While the paper's excavation of NY cool dug as deep as the city's burgeoning "anti-folk" scene, in the form of crack-smokin', porn-watchin' (if their lyrics were any indication) duo Moldy Peaches, it studiously avoided the underground to which Sonic Youth had belonged. The Strokes themselves – for all the critics' claims of an earthy CBGB vibe, a Velvets-y sound – closer resembled the New Wave acts that veterans of the original punk scene recognised all too well; while Julian Casablancas conjured an impressive mush-mouthed Richard Hell slur on the group's debut EP, *The Modern Age* (2001), there was nothing challenging about their (nevertheless charming) indie-pop. Their "punk cred" was pretty low; also, the privately educated quintet included sons of AOR songsmith Albert Hammond and founder of the Elite modelling agency John Casablancas. They'd gigged around the New York circuit, played CBGB and the Bowery Ballroom and Arlene's Grocery, but they had no real connection to the still-thriving underground, or the city's rich subterranean heritage. Asked about the group, Jon Spencer coyly replied, "I think we share the same dry cleaner."

Some traces of New York's actual underground later bled into the paper's pages, hailing from the loft-party scene in nearby Brooklyn (where the starving artists and musicians had moved when gentrification saw Manhattan rents skyrocket) founded by psychedelic experimentalists Oneida, and including such adventurous groups as TV On The Radio, Yeah Yeah Yeahs and Liars, all of whom were intimately familiar with the city's tradition of artful noise. Initially, however, *NME*'s coverage was surface-deep, buying into the hype hard enough to blithely publish *Vice Magazine* editor Gavin MacInnes' '50 Things I Hate About New York' list, in which he included "Puerto Ricans" with no editorial censure. Certainly, Sonic Youth remained conspicuous by their absence from the New York issue.

NME wasn't the only organ to be "sleeping on" the Youth in 2001; challenging albums like *A Thousand Leaves* and *NYC Ghosts & Flowers* had earned the group an awkward status in the rock press, both respected and vilified for the chances they took, taken for granted by their supporters, and subject to showboat drubbings from every hip young critic on the block, sharpening their knives in a bid to Kill Their Idols. The group had gamely wandered out into the artistic hinterlands, the critics thought, and long may they idle there.

Sonic Youth's next album, however, would remind everyone just how vital a force they remained, 20 years into their career.

* * *

When the first hijacked airliner struck the World Trade Center at 8.46 on the morning of Tuesday September 11, 2001, Jim O'Rourke was asleep at Sonic Youth's Echo Canyon studio. He'd been working late the night before on pre-production on Sonic Youth's next album. The catastrophic sounds outside woke him instantly, however. "The studio was just two short blocks away from the World Trade Center," he remembered. "A jet engine fell from the sky and landed on Murray Street, within eyeshot of the studio's front window."[1]

The tragedy and its aftermath impacted on subsequent sessions for the album (which would take its title from Echo Canyon's location, *Murray Street*), as the group struggled to gain access to their studio, caught in the eye of Ground Zero. "After September 11 we couldn't get back into our studio for two and a half months," remembers Lee, "and then it was a matter of getting past National Guardsmen on every corner. We had to show paperwork and prove we worked in the building. Then we had a bunch of electrical problems with our gear, so we didn't start tracking *Murray Street* until the first week of January 2002."

"We worked all through the winter," says Thurston. "It became pretty annoying, constantly surrounded by all these 'disaster groupies', come from all over the world to gawp at the wreckage."[2]

"It was strange to go down there to work and be huddled in that studio, and there was nothing, just these empty buildings all around,"[3] adds Kim. She and Thurston no longer lived in New York, having moved with Coco to a house in western Massachusetts in 1999, while still maintaining their apartment in the city. At the same time as recording *Murray Street*, the group was working on the soundtrack for a movie by French film-maker Olivier Assayas, *Demonlover*. The director had requested the score contain a riot of sound and noise to accompany his narrative. "Concurrent with us making this record," recalls Thurston, "they would dig up the street, then they would patch it. Then they would dig it up again and they would patch it; they kept changing and rearranging conduits of water and electricity. To me, it was like they were working on their own record. So we got this idea of putting microphones out of the window, over the street. When you see *Demonlover*, you're going to literally hear Murray Street. That's real rock musique concrete. It had a lot of resonance for us, working creatively in an environment that had been destroyed."

"September 11 changed things," observes Lee, "But New York is this place that's ever-changing, and yet ever the same. Even something as major as *that*... It's still New York, if you know what I mean. Obviously people were shaken up by it. But New York moves onwards, like a roller coaster."

Five of the songs that ended up comprising *Murray Street* began life as idle strums by Thurston, following a visit from his brother. "He'd retuned my acoustic guitar to some weird tuning, not too far from the tunings we use," remembers Thurston. "I immediately wrote four or five songs. I felt really inspired by it. I planned on doing a solo album with these songs, I felt they were kind of unfinished somehow, and I knew if I gave them to the band they would transform them to a unified band composition."[4]

The music that grew from these early acoustic strums took on a more grandiose, anthemic character than any Youth tuneage since *Daydream Nation*, mixing the sonic subversion of recent releases with some of those unabashed rock moves they'd ditched in the aftermath of *Dirty*. Where *A Thousand Leaves* seemed deliriously diffuse, and *NYC Ghosts & Flowers* darkly avant, there was a focus to *Murray Street*, a simplicity, an unforced joy, that made it so easy to love.

Hassles regarding access to the studio aside, the sessions were relaxed. An Electronic Press Kit filmed to promote the album offers a glimpse into the *Murray Street* sessions: Jim rewiring effects pedals so they emit "sounds they're not supposed to make"; Lee clowning around with Sonic Youth voodoo dolls handed to the group by a fan after a show; and Thurston instructing Jim to play "Townshend windmills" during one passage ("It starts with the feet slightly wider apart than the shoulders, arm fully extended," jokes Lee), swinging his own arm across his guitar by example.

"We joked that it was our attempt at a 'classic rock' record,"[5] says Steve; certainly, with its four guitar players (Jim switching between bass and lead), the newly O'Rourke-augmented Youth could muster an impressive guitarkestra at will, these new songs catching those instruments deep in wonderful conversation with each other. On 'Rain In Tin', they conjured a symphonic effect sounding not unlike Glenn Branca jamming with the Dead, guitars chasing their own circuitous riffs and figures, meeting for crescendos where the interlocking strum rose up with dramatic power, before falling back away to their melodic interplay.

But, more so than any Sonic Youth album since *Washing Machine*, these were *songs*, their avant explosion set pieces expertly placed between verses and choruses; the sense of structure in particular recalled *Daydream Nation*, the songs having multiple sections and exploring the possibilities of the riffs and guitar-soundings at length, but with a discipline that benefited the listener. *Murray Street* found Sonic at their most lucid and most eloquent, deftly balancing their exploratory impulses with an ever-present sense of clarity.

Thematically, the album skipped between blind optimism in the potential of the underground ('The Empty Page'), to articulating a potent sense of disaffection with the mainstream ('Disconnection Notice'), to a taut epic lasting under five minutes that sang in tribute to an older generation of pop-cultural figures whose power hadn't diminished in the passing of the years. "It's not that solid a theory," explained Thurston, "but in the late Sixties and early Seventies you really had this dividing line in the culture where youth was radical and adults were square. But now there are radical adults, from Neil Young to Yoko Ono. That's what 'Radical Adults Lick Godhead Style' is about. I mean, radical youth culture is *huge,* but completely hidden from the mainstream. There is another demographic that is an alternate to MTV, which is totally corny and square. And it's really exciting to me, because I love all these great new bands like Lightning Bolt, Black Dice, Erase Errata and Quixotic. I still feed off that energy."

'Radical Adults Lick Godhead Style' closed with an apocalyptic noise-jam, facilitated by Jim Sauter and Don Dietrich of Borbetomagus, fleeting visitors to Echo Canyon. "Thurston got in touch via email and asked if we wanted to be a part of the record," remembers Dietrich. "It might have been Jim O'Rourke's idea, that what this one song needed was the Borbeto horn section, and so we thought, sure, why not, Sunday afternoon we're available. So we did it. We asked them, what do you want? We could do two tenor bells together... We tried to keep it as close to the tone of the song as best as we could. I guess they liked it, as it's on the record. My opinion is that it seemed a very small amount of music from what was a whole afternoon, though we spent the rest of the time jamming with Thurston and Lee and Jim."[6]

The blister of Borbeto blare in the closing grooves of 'Radical Adults' was only one of *Murray Street*'s avant flourishes; Lee's 'Karen Revisited' (later renamed 'Karenology' for live performances) bled from bruised psychedelic churn to an extended eight-minute coda of screaming amp-tone, meditative guitar meander and drone, a resonant soundscape of swelling ambience and abstract invention, part of which was taped at the song's debut in New York at the Bowery Ballroom on October 7, 2001. The show had been a hastily arranged benefit in aid of the World Trade Center tragedy, the group supported by Cat Power (wayward, haunting singer/songwriter Chan Marshall, whose early records had been released on Steve's Smells Like Records), improvisational duo Chris Corsano, and Tom Verlaine, while Kim played an opening slot accompanied by O'Rourke, DJ Olive and radical gay poet Eileen Myles.

The album closed with a pair of Kim-fronted songs; the climactic 'Sympathy For The Strawberry' distilled the gentle, eerie charms of the opening moments of *Daydream Nation* over nine minutes, as double-tracked Kims sang in conversation with each other and sketched hazy harmonies over a hypnotic chug that built imperceptibly until, in the dying seconds, the quaking strum blots out Steve Shelley's drums. By contrast, 'Plastic Sun' was a tense two-minute blast of concentrated squall, Shelley's impatient hi-hat rasp propelling Kim's cold-eyed growl, couched in skronky guitar shrapnel.

The track had been released the year before, on a free CD attached to the May 2001 issue of excellent young women's magazine *Jane*, an earlier take with a lyric that made a sly reference to Britney Spears (which would be replaced for the album release). The lyric, written by Thurston, railed at the plasticity of mainstream culture, suggesting a growing enmity (or at least ambivalence) towards the manufactured pop world that had fascinated them during the early years of Madonna's reign. Their young daughter, however, kept them connected to what was going on in the world of MTV. "Coco's not terribly influenced by her age group," Thurston explained. "She's not heavily into Britney Spears or anything. She knows that stuff exists, but I don't think she really gets off on it. Kim told her, 'All this music is written by old men'. That kind of changed her perception somewhat."

"I told all her school friends too," laughs Kim. "Things are worse than ever. But I think, at the same time, the underground's very strong. There's a lot of great music being made; they'll never squelch that."

> "They've touched a lot of people, and it continues. They're stewards of this ship that has all these facets to it, and I think they enjoy it. They're very serious about it. When you think of all the connections they've made throughout their career, connections they continue to make with new artists coming through, its almost like 'Six Degrees Of Sonic Youth'. That should be the title of your book..."[7]
>
> Don Fleming

"What do you do when your favourite band starts sucking?" asked Amy Phillips of the *Village Voice*, in her review of *Murray Street*. "Stop buying their albums. But what if you can't, because you're so into them that you just have to know every note they record, even if it's unlistenable crap?" Addressing the band, she continued, "You've been around as long as I've been on this earth. You have summer houses in western Massachusetts. You opened for Pearl Jam. You're on a rotting, almost nonexistent major label. For a group that has always relied so heavily on the currency of cool, these aren't very encouraging signs. Sonic Youth, please break up."[8]

It wasn't so much the vehemency of Phillips' vitriol that made her review – headlined "Sonic Euthanasia" – quite so controversial. It was more that her criticisms ran so completely counter to the general critical and fan response to *Murray Street*, an album greeted as a return to form by listeners turned off by the more experimental excursions of recent years. Her barbs seemed ill-chosen: attacking the Youth for being old, for having trundled on for two decades, would only have made sense if the group had gotten bored, lazy or uninterested over the years. Their restless, endless fascination with the possibilities of their music spoke otherwise; Sonic Youth were true Radical Adults. Similarly, the jibe about the summer house in western Massachusetts (which was actually their main residence; the group spent most of their summers on the road) seemed foolish. "Whose idea was it to price out the artist bohemia of NYC?" replied Thurston, when asked whose idea it was to move to the sticks. "We pay less and live larger here."[9]

The reality of Sonic Youth's esteem within the new generation of underground rock also made a lie of Brett DiCrescenzo's absurd drubbing of *NYC Ghosts & Flowers* on the Pitchfork website, when he claimed, "These 40+ year olds continue to operate under the perception that they matter"[10]. In the two years that had passed since that review, the underground scene was again in blossom, many of the groups clearly indebted to the sound, style and fearlessness of the Youth. And, in their grand tradition, Sonic Youth invited groups like ENON (formed by Brainiac's John Schmersal, following the tragic death of that band's frontman Timmy Taylor in 1997), Erase Errata (electrifying post-punks of a Riot Grrrl hue, who formed a side-project with Kim called Anxious Rats that played support on a couple of shows), Michigan noise mavericks Wolf Eyes, and Brooklynites Yeah Yeah Yeahs and Liars, to accompany them as they toured *Murray Street* across the world.

The impression Sonic Youth's legacy had left on these artists was no more clearly noticeable than in Liars' second album, *We Were Wrong So They Drowned*. Recorded in 2003 with TV On The Radio's Dave Sitek, out in the wilds of New Jersey, the album revisited the traumatic, discordant industrial trauma of *Bad Moon Rising* to unspool a creeped-out tale of witchcraft and intolerance. These were groups who'd grown up on the Sonic Youth back catalogue, for whom they'd always been unimpeachable icons, leading these young musicians-to-be on a trip through the avant-garde that left them forever changed.

"I was 15 when I first saw Sonic Youth," remembers Nick Zinner, guitarist with Yeah Yeah Yeahs. "I hadn't really heard their music before, but was making a transition of my musical interests and my identity, from metal to punk, and my friend Jim was super into them. It was a small club, it was loud as fuck, and I remember Thurston was wearing a racing driver's jacket. I was completely blown away, and the next day scrounged up every tool in my mom's house and got to work making noise with my guitar on my 4-track. Suddenly, noise wasn't just noise, but the start of an entirely new vocabulary: soft noise, beautiful noise, drone-y noise, melodic noise, noise-y noise... They had flipped the notions of 'what is music?', 'what is guitar playing?', and 'what is a song?' for me, completely.

"Before I moved to New York, my friends who lived there would tell me about Sonic Youth sightings there, like, 'I saw Thurston in the Other Music record store!' Well, what records did he buy?! 'I saw Lee coming out of a hardware store!' What crazy tool of sonic destruction did he get?! They were heroes, yet totally accessible, and normal. They continue to have a strong presence in every artistic area: art shows, improvisational collaborations at small clubs, DJ nights, and obscure film-house benefits, while still playing amazing shows, making great records, and being more clued in to new experimental music than any critic or magazine could hope to be."[11]

An indication of just how influential Sonic Youth remained upon the underground came when they were invited to curate the very first All Tomorrow's Parties in America, originally booked for the weekend of October 19–21, 2001 but postponed after 9/11 until March 14–17 the following year. "It's kind of funny that we were invited to curate this festival," says Thurston, "because we weren't exactly the most popular act at the ATP we played." But the Youth proved expert at the task, building an eclectic roster for the weekend's performances at UCLA, spanning revivified power-pop legends Big Star, poetically psychedelic NYC rap duo Cannibal Ox, SST survivors Saccharine Trust, Jeff Tweedy's Americana travellers Wilco, electronic avant-gardist Aphex Twin, free-jazz pioneer Cecil Taylor, Bay Area rapper/producer Madlib (hip-hop's Lee Perry), Warhol-era poet Gerard Malanga, and avant-garde composer Tony Conrad, along with a clutch of Sonic friends, including Lydia Lunch, Smog, Cat Power, Television, Bardo Pond, Deerhoof and Boredoms.

Sonic Youth themselves closed the festival on Sunday night, various members of the group performing on the other days with side-projects and new collaborators: Kim, Jim, Ikue Mori and DJ Olive played a set on the Friday, while Saturday saw a set by Lee, accompanied by his wife Leah and Chicago-based electronic improviser Kevin Drumm, and a collaboration between Thurston, Nels Cline, Mats Gustafsson and William Winant, musicians with whom he'd recorded a number of improvisational albums.

An unlikely guest at All Tomorrow's Parties LA was Pearl Jam frontman Eddie Vedder. The Youth had toured as support to Pearl Jam in August 2000, won over by Vedder's sincerity and activism (he played a number of benefits for 2000 Green Party Presidential Candidate Ralph Nader that year).

"None of us were Pearl Jam enthusiasts, but we've known Eddie for years, through mutual friends," remembers Thurston. The tour offered Sonic Youth another chance to play the kind of stadium venue Pearl Jam took in their stride, and if Pearl Jam's fans mostly greeted the Sonics' set with the same indifference as Neil Young's audience a decade before, Vedder did his best to win them over to Sonic Youth's side. "Sometimes he would go out before us," says Thurston, "and play a solo acoustic set of two or three songs that he'd been working on. And they were startlingly good."[12]

Headlining Friday night at the Ackerman Ballroom was a supergroup by the name of Asheton/Mascis/Watt, uniting J Mascis and Mike Watt with The Stooges' Asheton Brothers. Since his *Ball-Hog Or Tug Boat?* LP, Watt had signed on with Perry Farrell's post-Jane's Addiction project, Porno For Pyros, recording and touring their second album. When Thurston was approached by friend and film director Todd Haynes to record tracks for the soundtrack to his 1998 movie *Velvet Goldmine* (a gaudy fantasy set during the glam-rock era), he enlisted Watt, Steve Shelley, Don Fleming, Mark Arm and Ron Asheton to form The Wylde Rattz.

Like The Dim Stars project, The Wylde Rattz offered Thurston a chance to live out some rock'n'roll dreams. "Everyone knows The Stooges' songs, but not how Ron plays 'em," explains Thurston. "That to me was the most enlightening thing, sitting across from Ron Asheton, showing me the chords that I knew, but showing me how *he* played them, and there was this real subtle swing, and it was real distinct, real genuine to him. All of a sudden, I was privy to 'the blueprint' and that was completely amazing to me. Ron realised we were all there as students and aficionados, we weren't just session musicians working on a movie soundtrack. Me and Fleming were high-fiving each other when he did his take. I think Ron got interested in the fact that there were people like us who were really into the virtue of Stooges music."[13]

"We recorded a whole album, which still hasn't come out," remembers Don Fleming. "There were some Stooges songs, and we also come up with some originals, and some songs Ron had written with his partner Niagara." Thurston and Fleming also played in the 'Backbeat' band, with Dave Pirner from Soul Asylum, Afghan Whigs' Greg Dulli, R.E.M.'s Mike Mills, and Dave Grohl, covering songs that The Beatles performed on stage during their early years in Hamburg for the soundtrack to the 1994 movie dramatising that period of their career.

Watt had been laid low with an infection of the perineum in 2000, which left him sick and swollen and bedbound for nine weeks. Recovery was slow but steady, thanks to The Stooges. "I just wanted to get strong," remembers

Watt. "I had tubes in me from the surgery and shit, I couldn't play. It was the first time I'd had to stop since I was 13. I formed a couple of Stooges cover bands, one on the West Coast with the Porno For Pyros guys, and one out on the East Coast, with J and Murph. Their songs had a lot of feel and not a lot of chord changes, so they were good to play."

As his two Stooges covers bands began to play shows, Watt slowly got his strength back, and accepted an offer to play bass in Mascis' post-Dinosaur Jr group, The Fog. J hadn't toned down his volume in the intervening years. "I remember playing with The Fog and thinking, Jesus Christ, I can't hear a single fucking *thing* I'm playing!," laughs Watt. "And I play a little loud too. J said it was hard for him to sing every song every night, and suggested I sing some Stooges songs. When The Fog came through Ann Arbor, J asked me to call Ron Asheton. We got him in to play some gigs with The Fog, where the closing songs would all be Stooges songs. Then Thurston curated All Tomorrow's Parties in 2002, and he asked for us to play a Stooges set, with Scotty Asheton on drums. Scotty was living in a truck, he didn't even own a set of drums any more. So we rented him a drum set, and we played, the Asheton brothers, me and J. We did some tours in Europe like this, and Iggy got wind of it and asked Ron and Scotty to play on his *Skull Ring* album. And that led to the fucking Stooges reunion that I play bass in today!"

The unlikely and circuitous story of The Stooges' unexpected reunion in 2005, and his crucial part in it, still leaves Watt awed. "When I called Ronny up and had him come down to the Blind Pig in Ann Arbor to play with The Fog," Watt laughs, "J said to me, first you rip off a guy by learning from his records, and then you get to *play* with him. J owed a big debt to Ron Asheton, he said, in learning to play the guitar off *Fun House*. But The Stooges might never have reformed if it wasn't for J Mascis and Thurston Moore."[14]

⋆ ⋆ ⋆

Over the first weekend of April in 2004, Sonic Youth found themselves once again ensconced at the charmingly anachronistic Camber Sands Holiday Centre in East Sussex, curators of another All Tomorrow's Parties festival. The first of several such gatherings to be held at the camp that year, the line-ups for each day had been chosen by Pavement's Stephen Malkmus, appearing with his new group The Jicks, ATP organisers and bookers Foundation, led by Barry Hogan, and Sonic Youth. For the entire weekend, Kim and Thurston's modest chalet paid host to a never-ending stream of friends and fellow musicians, owners of obscure record labels laden with bags full of vinyl for the band, and journalists come to interview the group about their forthcoming 15th album, *Sonic Nurse*.

The group had found a comfortable groove on *Murray Street*, and the new album, their second with Jim O'Rourke as floating fifth member, thickening their sound and facilitating yet more florid, muscular guitar interplay, was very much in the same vein; having contributed only two songs for the previous album, however, Kim stepped back into the spotlight with *Sonic Nurse*.

'Mariah Carey And The Arthur Doyle Hand-Cream' was the first track on the album to surface, released as one side of a split seven inch with Erase Errata, released on New York underground label Narnack in 2003 (the track was retitled 'Kim Gordon And The Arthur Doyle Hand Cream' for *Sonic Nurse*, perhaps to avoid unnecessary controversy). A raucous clatter blending delirious, detuned pop with neon harmelodic squall, the song further signalled Sonic Youth's unease with modern pop culture, swiftly devolving to a trash state with few redeeming camp qualities. Kim's target wasn't the glamorous multi-octave songstress, however, but rather the way the industry treated Carey, following her turbulent exit from both Columbia Records, and her marriage to Tommy Mottola. Carey signed to Virgin records for a reported $80 million in 2001, but her first release for the label, the soundtrack to her big-budget Hollywood flop *Glitter*, tanked; following rumours of an emotional breakdown and a suicide attempt, and a bizarre appearance on MTV's *Total Request Live* where she handed ice lollies to members of the studio audience before beginning a haphazard on-camera striptease, Carey checked into hospital and took a break from her exhausting promotional duties.

"Mariah is the epitomy of a certain kind of diva," explained Kim, "competitiveness embedded in her, desperate to sell records. That's her imperative: no one's telling her to behave the way she does to get media attention." The song conjured up Carey's tabloid exploits, including a humiliating stage-managed "relationship" with rapper Eminem while he worked on her post-*Glitter* comeback album, and the broken-glass suicide attempt. It was, in a sense, revisiting themes of sexism and pop culture that had studded Kim's earlier work, although, unlike Karen Carpenter in 'Tunic' or the sexually-harassed secretary in 'Swimsuit Issue', Kim chooses not to give Carey a voice in the song, singing instead a Greek chorus watching her escapades with sympathetic sorrow. In Kim's lyric, Carey is a helpless victim of her own candyfloss sex appeal, her self-identification as a product, "Like Miss Monroe your head don't know exactly what your body's doing".

"She gets criticised a lot," Kim continues, "as if it's her fault someone was willing to pay her $80 million to make music for them. It's like those voyeuristic reality TV shows, where everything's about confrontation and melodrama; this fascination, left over from the Witch Trials, for humiliation… I just don't understand how people can *watch* them."[15]

Building on the previous album's successful fusion of graceful classic-rock moves and fissures of overloaded avant din, *Sonic Nurse* caught the Youth at their most accessible and obtuse, sometimes in the same song. Opener 'Pattern Recognition' was a thrilling blast of chaotic noise-rock, bristling with chance melodies and Kim's caustic slide guitar, and a sly reference to the group's role as "cool hunters"; the track climaxed in an extended coda of feedback and drone, a glorious release of tension.

'Unmade Bed', meanwhile, revisited the sombre tenderness of 'The Diamond Sea', Thurston narrating a tale of a girl's helpless love for a man who's no good for her, with the sad empathy you might expect from the father of a young daughter. Recalling the poignant burnt-ember vocals and glowing, emotive guitar interplay of some wracked Neil Young & Crazy Horse ballad, 'Unmade Bed' was Sonic Youth at their most mature, potent and polished. The album as a whole was a jubilant riot of musical invention, honed squall and fractured beauty, furthering the vividness and vivacity of *Murray Street* with songs that chimed and conversed with confidence and eloquence. The autumnal evening glow of the choppy 'New Hampshire' happened upon the kind of coiling, psychedelic excursions the Youth had pioneered on *Daydream Nation*, Lee's 'Paper Cut Exit' similarly throbbing with an eerie, paranoid clip. Kim's 'Dude Ranch Nurse' and 'I Love You Golden Blue', meanwhile, were vulnerable, hypnotic and, in the latter case, utterly seductive.

Sonic Youth's performance at All Tomorrow's Parties that year was sublime, entirely erasing any lingering memories of their 2000 appearance. The low-ceilinged main auditorium swarmed with bodies, as seemingly every denizen of Camber Sands crammed in the room to catch this group, so emblematic of all that All Tomorrow's Parties stood for. As a heat-haze infested the room, hulking black speakers shuddered and oozed warm, colourful, bruised noise. I remember a group of boys near me stripping their shirts off; the ambience was that of a rave, a combustible sense of excitement and glee, a thrilling chaos. As the dying screes of an encore of 'Kim Gordon And The Arthur Doyle Hand Cream' bled out across the room, Lee Ranaldo took the microphone and invited the audience to stick around.

At that exact moment, having set up their equipment on the beer-stained carpet at the back of the room, actually within the audience, the highly portable hurricane of improv-noise that was Providence, Rhode Island's

Lightning Bolt began their pulverising set, causing giddy anarchy among the crowd. The duo – whose deranged music pitted FX-screwed bass against hyperactive drums in avant-thrash death matches at psychedelic velocity – took pride in playing in unusual surroundings, and this show was one of several impromptu performances they put on across the festival site, culminating with a brief set at 11 in the morning, setting up on the grass outside the chalet of BBC DJ John Peel. This segue between Sonic Youth's noise and the fiery battle-rattle of Lightning Bolt was their most audacious appearance at All Tomorrow's Parties, however.

It almost seemed like a metaphor for Sonic Youth passing the baton of experimental rock'n'roll invention to the next generation; as *Murray Street* and *Sonic Nurse* had proved, however, Sonic Youth had no intention of relinquishing their thrones as benevolent monarchs of noise.

* * *

Sonic Nurse closed with Moore's meditative, delicate 'Peace Attack', a hymn for cessation of war, a brutal show of gentility, powered by interlacing, chiming guitars, chasing a loose but heart-swelling melody. It was as explicit an act of civil disobedience as planting a flower in the barrel of a cop's gun, another potent statement from Sonic Youth in an American election year, directed at "religious zealot war pigs Cheney, Rumsfeld, Bush and Ashcroft".[16]

With a savage logic that later proved unsound, President George W. Bush answered the terrorist attacks of September 11 by declaring war on Iraq (despite the lack of evidence linking the country to the terrorist action), unseating President Saddam Hussein and plunging the country into what the Bush administration reluctantly acknowledged as a bloody civil war. Bush had only just won the presidential election in 2000, losing the popular vote to Democrat contender, outgoing Vice President Al Gore, but winning the electoral vote under a hail of allegations of voter fraud. Bush's actions following September 11 had won him his highest voter-approval ratings, incumbent presidential candidates traditionally retaining power during wartime; however, Iraq was fast becoming a quagmire, and popular opinion was beginning to turn against Bush.

'Peace Attack' had sprung from a book project Thurston had been involved in during February 2003. "I wrote a poem every day of that month," he remembers. "It just so happened to be at the same time that the US administration was enforcing a war. The song is dealing with this reality of the USA commodifying peace, calling it 'The Peace', y'know? 'We're going into Iraq to establish The Peace', this McDonald's-isation of the word 'peace'... The fact that they were using language as a way of deceiving the public and turning things around...

"In a way, I don't wanna give what they do any value whatsoever, by putting any reactionary anger towards it in anything I do musically," he sighs. "I will gladly stand up against it publicly, but as far as artistically, I don't want to be part of it. Or I don't want it to be part of me. Maybe it's sort of disingenuous of me, because there's a certain privilege you have if people are listening to your music; maybe you're obliged to get your message out there..."[17]

In March 2003, in collaboration with designer/film-maker and Sonic friend Chris Habib, Thurston launched www.protest-records.com, a "virtual" record label dedicated to uploading free mp3 files of songs running counter to the blood lust of the times. The 70 tracks numbered contributions from the likes of Cat Power, Mudhoney, Brazilian composer and Tropicalia pioneer Tom Ze, the Beastie Boys, Christian Marclay, The Evens (a duo featuring Ian MacKaye and his partner Amy Farina), and a recording of Allen Ginsberg's piece, 'End Vietnam War', recorded in 1976. Sonic Youth offered up their 'Youth Against Fascism', while Thurston collaborated with Mike Watt for 'Fourth Day Of July', written and originally recorded by Tom Rapp's Sixties psych-folk collective Pearls Before Swine.

"WWW.PROTEST-RECORDS.COM exists for musicians, poets and artists to express LOVE + LIBERTY in the face of greed, sexism, racism, hate-crime and war," read the website's mission statement; Habib's polemical stencils made their point with imagery, be it a burning flag or a Bush'n'crossbones. Media artist Matt Rogalsky's contribution was particularly intriguing, editing George Bush's March 13 2003 address to the world – "a 13-minute speech in which he gave Saddam Hussein 48 hours to get out of town", explained Rogalsky – down to just the pauses and dead air between his words. "The thumping sounds you hear," he continued, "which a number of people have taken to be a reference to the 'drums of war', are simply the reverberations of Bush's voice inside the White House."[18]

"One of the reasons I started the website was to give voice to all these people who really *do* have the resentment, the anger, to write songs or poems or whatever, in opposition to it," says Thurston. "It was just a gesture anyway. I want to expand it, to get some visual artists involved. I tried to think, who on the internet deals with the most money? And *the* multi-million dollar industry on the internet is these fucked-up porn sites. So I thought, maybe I should approach some of these porn sites, to see if they would be willing to offer any of their, uh, *materials* in opposition, free, the way musicians have offered their music for free. I mean, what kind of people are involved in the porn industry? What are their politics? Obviously, they're super-capitalists. And I'm, uh, 'interested' in capitalism, set apart from the model that's affiliated with Bush and Cheney. I haven't done it yet [laughs]. I kinda don't wanna go *near* it, in a way, but it'd be funny. I wanna do something that will freak people out."

Under a cloud of allegations of voter suppression and malfunctioning vote machines, and to the dismay of those who wanted an end to the war in Iraq, George W. Bush was re-elected to office in the 2004 election. His inauguration was held the following year, on January 20, at the United States Capitol in Washington DC. That night, The Black Cat, a local music venue, hosted Noise Against Fascism, a show in protest of Bush's re-election, featuring a mess of noise acts, including Mirror/Dash, Kim and Thurston's intermittent side-project, as which they'd released a couple of obscure seven inches on labels like Byron Coley's Forced Exposure.

Headlining the bill were To Live And Shave In LA, an ongoing free-form avant-garde noise project of floating membership; that night, the line-up included founder member and underground music legend Tom Smith, along with a number of longtime collaborators, plus Don Fleming and Thurston. "There were about six or seven of us playing that night," remembers Fleming. "Andrew WK was on drums; Rat Bastard, who was an original member of the band, played electronics. Ed Walcott played an oscillator. It was a very bizarre night. Most people had just left town, because they were scared to be on the street. In DC, they were telling people, don't go out tonight. They were having all these official inauguration parties all over town, and they shut down a bunch of the streets, so that the people going back and forth to all these parties wouldn't have to go through any traffic. It was hard to get around, because you couldn't get very far without running into one of these roadblocks.

"It was a very charged night. To Live And Shave In LA is a full-frontal attack unit, especially in those conditions," continues Fleming. It was a blast of raw energy for pretty much the whole set. Tom Smith is the singer, it's sort of a Captain Beefheart thing – we take all our cues from him, he kinda conducts us. He has the songs in his head, he knows what song he's playing, and we go with the flow of it.

"Everyone felt like, *this* is an artistic statement, to say that what's happening is wrong, and fucked up. That was the mood of the night, that was the conversation that was being had. It was very political. It was cathartic – you feel like you're doing something, you're not just sat at home, staring at the television, being pissed off about it. You're out, communicating with other people about it. It wasn't like a protest concert, like we were going to march on the White House. It was more a community of people who were here to say 'fuck this'. It had meaning, to play the show in DC, because it was gonna be the most fucked-up time to do it."

> "A lot of bands are very formulaic, they only have one idea. I guess that's why they get shitty. I think most bands burn out because they're young and their relationships are immature. It's hard to stay together, but we broke through to the other side. Indeed, the other side is why we're here."
>
> Thurston Moore

Twenty-five years or so into their career, and a decade and change into their major-label "experiment", Sonic Youth operate on terms that suit them. As 2005's promotional commitments proved, taking in trips to Japan and Europe, as well as shows around the US, the group had managed to balance family life and road life, touring during school holidays and bringing Coco on the road with them.

"She's always excited about going on the big bus and all that," said Kim, in a 2001 interview she shared with Suzanne Vega, another mother who rocks. "She's the only one who actually sleeps on the bus [laughs] – because she's done it as a baby – while everyone else is totally exhausted. But there's some venues where you just don't want your kids hanging around. Because maybe the building's falling down, or there's electrical wiring hanging out of the walls, or there's weird graffiti or penises drawn all over. Whatever. Aside from having a huge crush on Eddie Vedder – to the point where she asks me questions like, 'Well, if you didn't meet Daddy, could you have married Eddie?' – she's got a pretty normal life."[19]

They tour with friends, fans and followers, still using their supernatural A&R talents when selecting support acts, and playing at festivals across the world, celebrating the still-vibrant underground that formed them, fed them, and followed in their wake. In the aftermath of Kurt's death and the disillusionment of the "alternative rock" era, it had seemed like Sonic Youth might have crept back to the subterranea that spawned them and accept an honorary cultdom; instead, "spinning inwards", as Thurston described their progress, has only served to nurture their myth, to strengthen their music, and to create an example generations of experimental musicians would love to emulate. "Sonic Youth didn't really make sense in terms of 'grunge'," says Jerry Thackray, "because grunge, for better or for worse, was mostly metal, and Sonic Youth have never played metal. They obviously fit in a lot better with the scenes that have sprung up among their 'godchildren', like All

Tomorrow's Parties, or Weird Americana. Those are probably the first scenes that have surrounded them since No Wave, because they didn't exactly fit in with the SST movement either."[20]

"They're advocates of causes," adds Don Fleming, "especially cultural causes. It plays out in the way that they put on shows, and curate festivals. They're in a unique position to do it now, because they've done it a lot, and more people want them to do it because they're very skilled now at knowing how to get a project off the ground and done. They've risen to that challenge, and continued to push the limits, to find the right things to get behind. There's always a lot of passion when Thurston puts things out on his label, and when Steve does. They see the big picture, that so many of the arts are inter-related."

"Something Sonic Youth have played upon, as they've gotten older, is this role as 'curators', organisers," adds Frances Morgan. "It's really important to them, that through their influence they can bring things to people's attention, other art forms, film, fashion, whatever – they have that influence. I don't think it always works – I don't like Thurston's writing, I think it's awful. But at the same time, I appreciate the value in Thurston Moore saying, in his hepcat beatnik way, 'Hey, this band's cool, check it out'. And people *will*, and if it's a band like Lightning Bolt, then fucking *great*."

Sonic Youth have outlived every scene they've been attached to, and certainly most of their contemporaries within those scenes. Of their kindred, some split for good, but most reform a few years later when their audiences have begun to miss them, with sometimes impressive but mostly diminished returns. But Sonic Youth's lifeline remains pristine, unbroken; they continue, not with a dogged cockroach's invincibility, like The Ramones as they toured endlessly for decades, scraping some sort of a living from fans who wanted the same three chords every night. No, Sonic Youth have thrived, grown, changed through every one of those years. Their back catalogue isn't the sound of one idea flayed into the dust, but a timeline charting the development and refinement of their original ideas, branching out as inspiration takes them; it's evidence of their endless fascination with both the noises they make, and *could* make, and the noises made by others.

They share a healthy relationship with each other, not tantrum-tossed by the storms of immaturity or drug-madness, not subject to the scandal and trauma of, say, Fleetwood Mac. "I've tried not to make it like we're a 'couple' within the band," Kim told *Spin* magazine in 1990. "That's one of the reasons why the band has lasted however long. I mean, that could be so annoying for the other members of the band. Maybe it is. When Thurston and I are alone, we don't really talk about the band business unless we absolutely have to. Otherwise you don't have any sort of separate life, and it becomes a 24-hour nightmare. But really we were together when the band started, so it's hard to say whatever kind of effect it's had, because we don't really know anything different."[21]

Crucial to their stability is the porous nature of the group, tolerating (indeed, encouraging and enabling) a dizzying wealth of extra-curricular activity on the part of these musicians, a most convenient open marriage. Indeed, were this book to attempt to chronicle all of the various recordings the Youth members have released under a variety of guises over the years, it would be twice the length it is now (as it is, I have noted the most pertinent tip of an iceberg you are recommended to explore at your leisure). They don't limit themselves to music, either; whether it's their poetry readings, their visual-art shows (Kim has been especially active in the art world, creating a number of installation pieces across the globe and returning to painting shortly after Coco's birth), their film projects, their magazine articles or Thurston's crazy plan to end the Iraq war with internet porn, the members of Sonic Youth remain engaged in a constant blur of creative activity. From the outside, to the curious fan, this is incredibly seductive.

"Kim's an artist in a band, a visual artist," says Fleming. "That's what's amazing about all of them, that they're multi-talented, but she especially brings that to the plate. I saw an installation piece she did recently with Tony Oursler, and I just felt like, wow, wouldn't it be amazing if Sonic Youth was more like this, with the screens in front of you, all these great films running? I think that she's like the 'artist' of the band; that's why the band has that cultural importance. They all bring something to it, which makes it a whole that none of them could do alone. It's like any great band, take them apart and it's oh, Jesus… Well no, I wouldn't *really* say that – they all do great solo stuff. But Sonic Youth is more than the sum of its parts. And they don't think it's 'done' yet, I never get that impression from any of them; there's always something else important to do, to deal with."

Nirvana may have been the first underground group to truly breach the mainstream, but Sonic Youth, through their creative consistency and their continued advocacy of the underground, have set an example that suggests that a group with a desire to create art, to push boundaries, to stir controversy and to challenge their audience can exist and thrive within the major-label world. Pessimists might suggest, however, that success stories like Sonic Youth and The Flaming Lips are only exceptions to the rule that such acts will perish within the corporate realm. Indeed, at the time of writing, Sonic Youth themselves are unsigned, their Geffen deal having ended in 2006. Perhaps they will re-sign with the label, which, in addition to releasing their albums since 1991, has begun to remaster and repackage elements of the group's catalogue in expanded and deluxe formats. "The Universal reissue people are separate to the rest of the label, totally different people," says Kim. "They're excited to have that catalogue."

"When we reissued *Dirty* a couple of years ago, it was exciting," adds Thurston. "They asked to do a series – *Dirty*, *Goo*, *Daydream Nation* – as part of their collection of 'classic masters', along with people like Bob Marley. They asked us to be part of the 'Universal family'. I remember the guy at the record company who runs Geffen now saying *Dirty* was a really significant record for him, and that if he was there when it came out it would have been a huge record. So I said, 'By the way it's being reissued'. 'Oh, is it?' 'Yeah, if you go down two floors they'll tell you this'. That's how ridiculous it is for us. So I said, 'Now's your chance!'"

"He's someone who says words like 'I guaran-fucking-tee it',"[22] laughs Kim.

With business partner Andrew Kesin, Moore has recently engaged in a distribution deal with Universal, where they will release albums on Ecstatic Peace that might benefit from major-label support. The revivified label has enjoyed a busy 2007, releasing acclaimed albums by improv masters Sunburned Hand Of The Man, minimalist stoner-metal group Awesome Color, twisted blues excursionists MV& EE With The Bummer Road, and glorious, destructive noisers Magik Markers, among many others. The oft-postponed Thurston Moore solo album is also due in 2007, via Universal, suggesting a continued Sonic relationship with the corporate behemoth.

But maybe they will sign to another major, or one of the larger indie labels, like Matador or Sub Pop, whose business model is better suited to make a profit from Sonic Youth's (relatively) low-budget, high-profile and steady-selling records. Certainly, their final album for Geffen, 2006's *Rather Ripped*, stirred much speculation and anticipation before release. Would it reflect the more "out" music being performed by the group's recent touring partners, like the wonderfully unhinged skronk-rock of California's Comets On Fire, or the delicately dippy psych-folk of Devendra Banhart (discovered by and recording on the label of Sonic friend Michael Gira)? Would it be the unlistenable anti-commercial "fuck you" that Universal might have been fearing all these years?

Rather Ripped proved to be the most accessible, relaxed, pop-orientated release of Sonic Youth's career, distilling the adventurous psychedelia of their recent albums into elegantly crafted, seductive and addictive songs. The group had parted ways with Jim O'Rourke shortly before writing the album, their fifth member exiting to pursue ambitions in film-making, and to live in

Japan. Pared down to a quartet once again, Sonic Youth embraced a new-found concision; where *Murray Street* and *Sonic Nurse* had gloried in their fearsome guitarkestra and the colossal riffs and pools of noise they could unleash, *Rather Ripped* honed the florid din down to tightly coiled melodies.

Again, the genesis of these new songs lay in a possible solo project of Thurston's. "I got a gig last year writing some TV commercial cues for HSBC bank," he told the official Sonic Youth website. "I think they used one or two. So I have this whole grab bag of Sonic riffs and I did these miniature jams, really concise. For the TV commercials, they said, 'We want something that's like 'Kool Thing'.' I could write 'Kool Thing' all day and every day, but I choose not to [laughs]. I really liked making all these miniatures; I thought maybe we should make a whole record of these 10-second songs. I would bring them into rehearsal and the band would develop them into songs."[23]

The melodic, pop nature of this glorious Sonic song style took many by surprise, even Coco Hayley Gordon Moore, who said that the chiming squall of 'What A Waste' reminded her of the theme tune to US sitcom monolith *Friends*; she has a point, though perhaps turnaround is fair play, as that show had incorporated riffs originated by Pavement and The Replacements' Paul Westerberg into their incidental music. On *Rather Ripped*, guitars mostly *sounded* like guitars, playing sans effects, lost in Thurston's nagging cobweb riffs and melodies; a working title for opening track 'Reena' was 'Stonesy', while elsewhere the group's rhapsodic guitar interplay begs comparison with the 12-string fluency of The Byrds, or the electrified, articulate conversations of Television.

There was a certain life-affirming spirit to the album that delighted, in songs like Thurston's 'Incinerate', with its vulnerable and utterly addictive hook, or the revving chug of 'Sleeping Around'. Still, within the relative normalcy of these songs the group was unafraid of unleashing some psychotronic noise-outs, but these were mostly tightly restricted, unleashed sparingly for maximum impact. The dreamy, just-woken splendour of the elemental 'Do You Believe In Rapture?', and Thurston's hypnotic lyrics for the deliciously spaced-out 'Or', seemingly stolen from idle after-gig backstage chatter and dull interview questions, proved the group had refined their ability to fuse adventurousness with accessibility to a high art.

Soon after the album's release, on June 13, 2006, the Youth returned to the road to tour the new material. They were boasting new blood too, ex-Pavement bassist Mark Ibold stepping up to fill Jim O'Rourke's shoes; "I saw that cat play at the last All Tomorrow's Parties," says Mike Watt, fervent fan of Kim's bass-playing. "He was cool, though Kim got to play bass too. Thurston even played bass at one point."

"To keep things fresh and interesting for yourself is mighty admirable. There's something about the template Sonic Youth have made which allows for that, to keep moving and reinventing themselves, so they didn't end up becoming a cartoon of themselves, or working to a formula. It's about them keeping their minds open and trying to get beyond it. John Coltrane said something about how he believed all musicians were searching for a sort of truth. And I think that fits Sonic Youth."

Mike Watt

Though the members of Sonic Youth are now in their forties and fifties, whatever hardships their Savage Blunders entailed have treated them well: Thurston remains the towering eternal teenager, wind whipping through his stupid mop, while Ranaldo only looks more dashing as his salt'n'pepper locks turn further grey, Kim retains her deathless sense of cool and style, and Steve still looks like the fresh-faced, innocent "new guy", 20 years after he joined the band. They still resemble the young musicians who arrived in New York so many years ago, in love with the romance of low-rent Manhattan and the viral, feral, free music being made in its basements and lofts.

In many ways, Sonic Youth have left more of an impression on rock'n'roll than rock'n'roll has left on them. When the group formed, for all Thurston's teenage fixations on megastars like David Bowie and Alice Cooper, they never nurtured dreams of such outrageous fortunes, not even secretly and shamefully like Kurt did. They knew it was so unlikely as to be not worth striving for, and so instead pursued their music and worked and strived to make Sonic Youth financially viable, creating a new paradigm for rock'n'roll success: creative freedom and modest financial stability. A group like The Velvet Underground starved and were considered failures by the old system; building their way from the underground, and connecting with the mainstream on *their* terms, Sonic Youth established a model that supports longevity for artists who would struggle to succeed on the mainstream's terms. It's an example that's proven highly influential on the generations that followed. "The price of creative freedom is you don't get to live in some coked-out, stripper-laden Dave Lee Roth fantasy," says TV On The Radio's Dave Sitek, "but since when had that been the goal of genuinely creative people anyway?"[24]

"The worst thing about being fifty is that you're inching towards the great unknown,"[25] Kim has said, and much of the New York they were first seduced by has since fallen by the wayside, even the iconic CBGB, which closed in October 2006, four months after Sonic Youth played their final show there. Still, while the musicians are only mortal, they show no sign of quitting, still pursuing new ideas and songs hiding within their weird, homely gear, still getting a buzz off of all those infinite possibilities. Their name, Sonic Youth, still fits their electric, ever-hungry art, as enamoured with sound itself as ever, and still retaining the fearlessness and curiosity of their earliest days.

Where they go next is anybody's guess, which is, of course, part of the thrill. Perhaps their decision to spend the summer of 2007 touring the *Daydream Nation* album in its entirety, in advance of its 20th Anniversary Deluxe Edition remaster, will lead them to once again move away from the lucid accessibility of their recent material, to take another brave and blind leap into the dark. Perhaps, with typical perversity, they'll return with an album so "pop" as to make *Rather Ripped* resemble *Bad Moon Rising*. Ultimately, though, you know you can trust Sonic Youth. They're the Radical Adults, who truly Lick Godhead Style.

NOTES

1 *Guitar Player*, November 2002
2 Author's interview, June 2002
3 *Interview* magazine, 2002
4 *Murray Street* EPK
5 *Pulse* magazine, 2002
6 Author's interview, March 2007
7 Author's interview, March 2007
8 *The Village Voice*, July 10-16 2002
9 Jane, May 2001
10 http://pitchforkmedia.com/article/record_review/21889-nyc-ghosts-flowers
11 Author's interview, May 2005
12 *The Wire*, March 2002
13 The Watt From Pedro radio show, February 14 2007
14 Author's interview, May 2007
15 Author's interview, April 2004
16 *Sonic Nurse* press release
17 Author's interview, April 2004
18 http://www.protest-records.com/mp3/rogalskynote.html
19 www.heroinemagazine.com, found at http://saucerlike.com/articles.php?x=display&id=1
20 Author's interview, April 2007
21 *Spin* magazine, April 1990
22 Jerry Thackray interview, July 2005
23 http://www.sonicyouth.com/mustang/sy/song.html
24 Author's interview, May 2004
25 *Observer*, June 6 2004

Sonic Youth Selected Discography

Note: An exhaustive discography of the group's releases, including countless singles, EPs, limited releases and bootlegs is available at their official website, www.sonicyouth.com. Another site, http://saucerlike.com/discography.php, offers something approaching a comprehensive list of the members' various solo project releases.

Albums

Sonic Youth
(Neutral, 1982)
The Burning Spear / I Dreamed I Dream / She Is Not Alone / I Don't Want To Push It / The Good And The Bad
(Geffen, March 2006; Expanded reissue)
Bonus Tracks: Hard Work (Live) / Where The Red Fern Grows (Live) / The Burning Spear (Live) / Cosmopolitan Girl (Live) / Loud And Soft (Live) / Destroyer (Live) / She Is Not Alone (Live) / Where The Red Fern Grows (Demo)

Confusion Is Sex
(Neutral, 1984)
(She's In A) Bad Mood / Protect Me You / Freezer Burn-I Wanna Be Your Dog / Shaking Hell / Inhuman / The World Looks Red / Confusion Is Next / Making The Nature Scene / Lee Is Free
(Geffen, 1995; reissue, includes Kill Yr Idols EP)
Bonus Tracks: Kill Yr Idols / Brother James / Early American / Shaking Hell (Live)

Sonic Death: Early Sonic 1981–1983
(Ecstatic Peace, 1984)
Sonic Death

Bad Moon Rising
(Blast First! / Homestead, 1985)
Intro / Brave Men Run / Society Is A Hole / I Love Her All The Time / Ghost Bitch / I'm Insane / Justice Is Might / Death Valley '69
(Geffen, 1995; reissue)
Bonus Tracks: Satan Is Boring / Hallowe'en / Flower / Echo Canyon

EVOL
(Blast First! / SST, 1986)
Tom Violence / Shadow Of A Doubt / Star Power / In The Kingdom #19 / Green Light / Death To Our Friends / Secret Girls / Marilyn Moore / Expressway To Yr Skull / Bubblegum (CD only)

Sister
(Blast First! / SST, 1987)
Schizophrenia / Catholic Block / Beauty Lies In The Eye / Stereo Sanctity / Pipeline/Kill Time / Tuff Gnarl / Pacific Coast Highway / Hot Wire My Heart / Kotton Krown / White Cross / Master-Dik (CD Only)

Daydream Nation
(Blast First! / Enigma, 1988)
Teenage Riot / Silver Rocket / The Sprawl / 'Cross The Breeze / Eric's Trip / Total Trash / Hey Joni / Providence / Candle / Rain King / Kissability / Trilogy (The Wonder, Hyperstation, Eliminator Jr)
(Geffen, June 2007; Deluxe Edition)
Bonus Tracks: Eric's Trip (Home Demo) / The Sprawl (Live) / 'Cross The Breeze (Live) / Hey Joni (Live) / Silver Rocket (Live) / Kissability (Live) / Eric's Trip (Live) / Candle (Live) / The Wonder (Live) / Hyperstation (Live) / Eliminator Jr (Live) / Providence (Live) / Teenage Riot (Live) / Rain King (Live) / Totally Trashed (Live) / Total Trash (Live) / Within You, Without You / Touch Me I'm Sick / Computer Age / Electricity

The Whitey Album (credited to Ciccone Youth)
(Blast First! / Capitol, 1989)
Needle Gun / (Silence) / G-Force / Platoon II / Macbeth / Me And Jill/Hendrix Crosby / Burnin' Up / Hi! Everybody! / Children Of Satan/Third Fig / Two Cool Rock Chicks Listening To Neu / Addicted To Love / Moby Dik / March Of The Ciccone Robots / Making The Nature Scene / Tuff Titty Rap / Into The Groove y
(Geffen, 2006; remaster)
Bonus Track: Macbeth (remix)

Goo
(DGC, June 1990)
Dirty Boots / Tunic (Song For Karen) / Mary-Christ / Kool Thing / Mote / My

Friend Goo / Disappearer / Mildred Pierce / Cinderella's Big Score / Scooter + Jinx / Titanium Exposé
(Geffen, September 2005; Deluxe Edition)
Bonus Tracks: Lee #2 / That's All I Know Right Now / The Bedroom / Dr Benway's House / Tuff Boyz / Tunic / Number One (Disappearer) / Titanium Exposé / Dirty Boots / Corky (Cinderella's Big Score) / My Friend Goo / Bookstore (Mote) / Animals (Mary-Christ) / DV2 (Kool Thing) / Blowjob (Mildred Pierce) / Lee #2 / I Know There's An Answer / Can Song / Isaac / Goo Interview Flexi

Dirty
(DGC, July 1992)
100% / Swimsuit Issue / Theresa's Sound World / Drunken Butterfly / Shoot / Wish Fulfillment / Sugar Kane / Orange Rolls, Angel's Spit / Youth Against Fascism / Nic Fit / On The Strip / Chapel Hill / JC / Purr / Créme Brûlèe
(Geffen, March 2003; Deluxe Edition)
Bonus Tracks: Stalker / Genetic / Hendrix Necro / The Destroyed Rom / Is It My Body? / Personality Crisis / The End Of The Ugly / Tamra / Little Jammy Thing / Lite Damage / Dreamfinger / Barracuda / New White Cross / Guido / Stalker / Moon Face / Poet In The Pit / Theoretical Chaos / Youth Against Fascism / Wish Fulfillment

Experimental, Jet Set, Trash And No Star
(DGC, May 1994)
Winner's Blues / Bull In The Heather / Starfield Road / Skink / Screaming Skull / Self-Obsessed And Sexxee / Bone / Androgynous Mind / Quest For The Cup / Waist / Doctor's Orders / Tokyo Eye / In The Mind Of The Bourgeois Reader / Sweet Shine

Washing Machine
(DGC, October 1995)
Becuz / Junkie's Promise / Saucer-Like / Washing Machine / Unwind / Little Trouble Girl / No Queen Blues / Panty Lies / Untitled [Becuz Coda] / Skip Tracer / The Diamond Sea

A Thousand Leaves
(DGC, May 1998)
Contre Le Sexisme / Sunday / Female Mechanic Now On Duty / Wild Flower Soul / Hoarfrost / French Tickler / Hits Of Sunshine (For Allen Ginsberg) / Karen Koltrane / The Ineffable Me / Snare, Girl / Heather Angel

SYR4: Goodbye 20th Century
(SYR, November 1999)
Edges / Six (Third Take) / Six For New Time / + - / Voice Piece For Soprano / Pendulum Music / Having Never Written A Note For Percussion / Six (Fourth

Take) / Burdocks / Four6 / Piano Piece #13 (Carpenter's Piece) [For Nam June Paik] / Piece Enfantine / Treatise

NYC Ghosts & Flowers
(Geffen, May 2000)
Free City Rhymes / Renegade Princess / Nevermind (What Was It Anyway) / Small Flowers Crack Concrete / Side2Side / Streamxsonik Subway / NYC Ghosts & Flowers / Lightnin'

Murray Street
(Geffen, June 2002)
Empty Page / Disconnection Notice / Rain On Tin / Karen Revisited / Radical Adults Lick Godhead Style / Plastic Sun / Sympathy For The Strawberry

Sonic Nurse
(Geffen, June 2004)
Pattern Recognition / Unmade Bed / Dripping Dream / Kim Gordon And The Arthur Doyle Hand Cream / Stones / Dude Ranch Nurse / New Hampshire / Paper Cut Exit / I Love You Golden Blue / Peace Attack

Rather Ripped
(Geffen, June 2006)
Reena / Incinerate / Do You Believe In Rapture? / Sleepin' Around / What A Waste / Jams Run Free / Rats / Turquoise Boy / Lights Out / The Neutral / Pink Steam / Or / Helen Lundeberg

The Destroyed Room: B-Sides And Rarities
(Geffen, December 2006)
Fire Engine Dream / Fauxhemians / Razor Blade / Blink / Campfire / Loop Cat / Kim's Chords / Beautiful Plateau / Three-Part Sectional Love Seat / Queen Anne Chair / The Diamond Sea (alt. ending)

Bibliography

Books

Alabama Wildman, Thurston Moore, Water Row Press, 2000

Jrnls80s, Lee Ranaldo, Soft Skull Press, 1998

Online Diaries: The Lollapalooza '95 Tour Diaries, Various, Soft Skull Press, 1996

Please Kill Me, Legs McNeil and Gillian McCain, Grove Press 1996

The Real Frank Zappa Book, Frank Zappa and Peter Occhiogrosso, Picador, 1989

Psychotic Reactions And Carburettor Dung, Lester Bangs (ed. Greil Marcus), Serpent's Tail, 1996

Women, Sex And Rock'n'Roll: In Their Own Words, Liz Evans, Pandora, 1994

Grrrls: Viva Rock Divas, Amy Raphael, St Martin's Griffin, 1995

Confusion Is Next: The Sonic Youth Story, Alec Foege, Quartet, 1995

Our Band Could Be Your Life, Michael Azerrad, Little, Brown, 2001

Bring The Noise, Simon Reynolds, Faber, 2007

Noise: The Political Economy Of Music, Jacques Attali, University Of Minnesota, 1985

We Rock So You Don't Have To, ed. Scott Becker, Incommunicado Press, 1998

Nirvana: The True Story, Everett True, Omnibus, 2006

Shakey: Neil Young's Biography, Jimmy McDonough, Vintage, 2003

Periodicals

(where not cited here, please see endnotes for individual issue # references)

MOJO, *Sounds*, *Rolling Stone* , *NME*, *Melody Maker*, *New York Times*, *The Village Voice*, *Spin*, *Bomb*, Winter 1996, *Swingset*, #3 2003, *Cosloy Youth*, #1 January 1988, *Vice* magazine, February 2007, *The Catalogue*, October 1988, *The Observer*, June 6 2004, *The Guardian*, Sept 30th 2005, *Grand Royal*, #2 1994, *The Village Voice Rock'n'Roll Quarterly*, 1988, *Guitare Et Claviers*, April 1992, Q, September 1992, *Puncture*, 1994, *Bananafish*, #13, *The Wire*, March 2002, *Guitar Player*, November 2002, *Pulse*, 2002, *Jane*, May 2001, *Sleazenation*, 2001

Online Media

Ink19 interview, *http://www.ink19.com/issues/january2003/interviews/alanVegaPartI.html*

Lee Ranaldo interview *http://www.sonicyouth.com/dotsonics/lee/ints/corregie.html*
Lee on Rhys Chatham's Meltdown *http://www.sonicyouth.com/dotsonics/lee/index.html*
Rhys Chatham essay *http://perso.orange.fr/rhys.chatham/Essay_1970-90.html*
New York Foundation For The Arts interactive, *http://www.nyfa.org/level3.asp?id=303&fid=6&sid=17*
Kim Gordon on Janis Joplin *http://legacyrecordings.com/janisjoplin/apprec.html*
Glenn Branca interview, *http://media.hyperreal.org/zines/est/intervs/branca.html*
Robert Christgau interview, *http://archive.salon.com/ent/music/int/2001/05/09/xgau/index.html*
Index Kim & Thurston interview, *http://www.indexmagazine.com/interviews/kim_gordon_thurston_moore.shtml*
Christgau on SY, *http://www.robertchristgau.com/get_artist2.php?id=1280*
Interview with Mike D, *http://www.leeranaldo.net/starfieldroad/pages/interviews.htm*
http://www.pitchforkmedia.com/article/record_review/21889-nyc-ghosts-flowers

Radio Shows, Podcasts

Mobilization Audio Histories Project, *http://www.mobilization.com/artists/sonicyouth/index.html*
The Watt From Pedro Show, *http://twfps.com/*
NPR *All Things Considered*, broadcast June 12 2006
Interview with Lee Ranaldo, WPRB, broadcast August 10th 2002

Video

Gila Monster Jamboree, 1985 (dir: unknown)
Put Blood In The Music, 1989 (dir: Charles Atlas)
1991: The Year Punk Broke, 1992 (dir: Dave Markey)
End Of The Century: The Story Of The Ramones, 2003 (dir: Jim Fields, Michael Gramaglia)
Corporate Ghost: The Videos 1990 – 2002, 2006 DVD of SY promo videos
Cut Shorts, 2006 DVD of Dave Markey's short films

Sleevenotes

Raincoats, *Odyshape* reissue 1993 (DGC)
Glenn Branca, *The Ascension* reissue 2003 (Acute)
Glenn Branca, *Lesson No 1* reissue 2004 (Acute)
Sonic Youth, *Confusion Is Sex/Kill Yr Idols*, reissue 1995 (Universal)
Sonic Youth, *Dirty* Deluxe Edition 2003 (Universal)
Sonic Youth, *Goo* Deluxe Edition 2005 (Universal)
Sonic Youth, *Sonic Youth* reissue 2006 (Universal)

Acknowledgements

Apologies if I forget anything; I forget things...

Thanks, first and foremost, to Jerry Thackray, and his notorious alter ego Everett True. You've always been a ladder in a world full of snakes, and without your encouragement and friendship and the opportunities and challenges you keep throwing my way, I probably wouldn't be writing at all, and I certainly wouldn't have written this book. Consider yourself well and truly forgiven for the "chilli-oil spaghetti" incident. Thanks also to Chris Charlesworth, my editor, whose support and guidance made up the difference when my confidence ebbed. I hope I haven't let you down.

Thanks to my friends and family, especially Mum, Nan, David, Jeremy, Lauren and Steve, for helping to preserve my sanity. You will be seeing a lot more of me again, now. Thanks also to Mr Chang, the world's greatest cat, for the tranquil purring that accompanied my typing way into the wee smalls.

To my proofreaders: Kara Cooper, John Doran, Alex Hannaford, Sophie Harris, Alex Milas, Manish Agarwal and Steve Jelbert: thank you for your advice and insight on the text, and for making writing this book a slightly less lonely experience.

I owe a huge debt to all of my interviewees, who were endlessly generous with their time and their memories and their opinions, and were an inspiration: Mike Watt, Paul Smith, Bob Bert, Jim Sclavunos, Lydia Lunch, Curt Kirkwood, Dave Markey, Don Fleming, Don Dietrich, Mark Arm, Stuart Braithwaite, Tim Kerr, John Robb, Keith Cameron, Mark Sinker, Frances Morgan, Mark Coleman, Steve Jelbert, Julian Marszalek, Martin

Bisi, and Nicholas Sansano. Getting to wander about the corridors of your minds was a pleasure in itself.

Thanks to the press agents and managers who got me in touch with many of my interviewees, not least Sarah Lowe, Zoe Miller and Nita Patel. Extra thanks to Nita, who has proven a more able archivist of my writing than I am myself.

Thanks to Angus Batey, John Robb, Martin James, Ben Myers, Bill Brewster and Phil Sutcliffe for encouragement and advice right at the very outset of this project. And thank to the NBT hivemind, for salty input when invited.

I believe that children are the future; Isaac Thackray, Fred and Harper Keeler, Hamish Stanley Cameron, Madeleine "Ramblin" Rose Jelbert and Lida: rock on.

Thanks to the webmasters of Sonic Youth's enthralling and exhaustive website, www.sonicyouth.com, a vast and priceless archive of tour dates, set lists and information, which I spent most of my first years on the internet poring over. Now I can pretend that I was "researching", as opposed to killing time in a most entertaining fashion.

★ ★ ★

And thanks, of course, to Sonic Youth, for all of the music they've made, the music they've turned me on to, and for an example that couldn't help but inspire. I hope I've done your vast achievements justice.

★ ★ ★

This book is dedicated to my dad, Terry Chick, a wonderful man who indoctrinated me with a passion for ugly noise and rock'n'roll destruction when he showed me The Who's *The Kids Are Alright* at a far-too-tender age. I don't remember you as much of a Sonic Youth fan, but I like to think you'd have enjoyed the book. With love and thanks and everything else that's good.

SC x x